SENTIMENT & CELEBRITY

A middle-aged, bearded, and apparently hale N. P. Willis strikes a dramatic pose in this 1850s-era photographic portrait taken in Matthew Brady's studio. Photographic print from glass negative, Brady studios, ca. mid 1850s. The Library of Congress, Prints and Photographs Divisions, LC-BH82-5206.

SENTIMENT & CELEBRITY

· · ·

Nathaniel Parker Willis and the Trials of Literary Fame

THOMAS N. BAKER

New York   Oxford

OXFORD UNIVERSITY PRESS

1999

Oxford University Press

Oxford   New York
Athens   Auckland   Bangkok   Bogotá   Buenos Aires   Calcutta
Cape Town   Chennai   Dar es Salaam   Delhi   Florence   Hong Kong   Istanbul
Karachi   Kuala Lumpur   Madrid   Melbourne   Mexico City   Mumbai
Nairobi   Paris   São Paulo   Singapore   Taipei   Tokyo   Toronto   Warsaw

and associated companies in
Berlin   Ibadan

Copyright © 1999 by Oxford University Press, Inc.

Published by Oxford University Press, Inc.
198 Madison Avenue, New York, New York 10016

Oxford is a registered trademark of Oxford University Press.

Library of Congress Cataloging-in-Publication Data
Baker, Thomas Nelson.
Sentiment and celebrity : Nathaniel Parker Willis and the trials
of literary fame / Thomas N. Baker.
p.   cm.
Includes bibliographical references (p.) and index.
ISBN 0-19-512073-6
1. Willis, Nathaniel Parker, 1806–1867.   2. Authors,
American—19th century—Biography.   3. Celebrities—United States—
Biography.   4. Authorship—History—19th century.
5. Sentimentalism in literature.   I. Title.
PS3326.B35   1998
818' .309—dc21   98-5728
[B]

1 3 5 7 9 8 6 4 2

Printed in the United States of America
on acid-free paper

ACKNOWLEDGMENTS

Every scholar incurs debts in pursuing a long-term project. These are mine.

For permission to quote from materials in their collections I would like to thank the following repositories: the Archives of American Art, Smithsonian Institution; Beinecke Rare Book and Manuscript Library, Yale University; Burton Historical Collection, Detroit Public Library; Columbia University, Rare Book and Manuscript Library, Butler Library; Historical Society of Pennsylvania; Houghton Library, Harvard University; the Joint Free Public Library of Morristown and Morris Township (whose archivists were particularly helpful in supplying me considerable numbers of photocopied letters); Joseph Regenstein Library, University of Chicago; Manuscript Division, Rare Books and Special Collections, Princeton University Libraries; Massachusetts Historical Society; New-York Historical Society; New York Public Library, Manuscript and Archives Division, and the Henry W. and Albert A. Berg Collection; New York State Library, Manuscripts and Special Collections; Rare Book and Manuscript Library, Columbia University; Sophia Smith Collection, Smith College; Tioga County Historical Society; University of Virginia, Alderman Library, Special Collections Department. Indeed, I owe a general debt of gratitude to the staffs at all the archives I consulted for their prompt and helpful service.

A portion of this book, later considerably reworked, appeared as "Congregational Orthodoxy and Literary Gentility in the 1820s: The Case of Nathaniel Parker Willis," *Retrospection* 4 (1991), 73–81. Thanks go to the Department of History at the University of New Hampshire for permission to reprint portions of this article contained herein. For permission to publish quotations from the papers of Nathaniel Parker Willis, I wish to thank one of his descendents, Hannah Locke Carter, a person who has aided my research on a number of occasions. My appreciation also goes out to Sandra Tomc, a compatriot in "Willis" studies, who graciously allowed me to examine her then-unpublished article on Willis and dandyism. No less important to the completion of this project was the sterling work done by the staff of the University of North Carolina at Chapel Hill Libraries, particularly Becky

Breazeale and her crew at the Interlibrary Borrowing Department. I could not have done it without you.

My thanks also go out to those mentors and peers in Chapel Hill whose cogent and sympathetic criticism contributed immeasurably to the betterment of this manuscript. These people include Charles Capper, Everett Emerson, Philip Gura, Tracy K'Meyer, Lloyd Kramer, Kathy Nasstrom, Barb Ryan, Lisa Tolbert, and Adam Tuchinsky. My advisor John Kasson, in particular, read through many drafts, encouraging and challenging me at just the right moments; I hope that you see your influence in these pages. To Peter Walker I also extend thanks, especially for awakening the writer in me; your careful criticism has improved my literary and historical skills immeasurably.

Lastly, the personal thanks—to my sister, Cathy Baker, a scholar and a doer of the first degree; to Kate Parrent, for love and affection; and, finally, to my father, Bill Baker, for sparking my love of history these many years ago. I dedicate this book to you and to the memory of my mother, Barbara Baker, whose good humor and good sense will sustain me always.

CONTENTS

Chronology   ix

ONE • Celebrity Comes of Age   3

TWO • Beauty's Apostle   13

THREE • American Pelham   39

FOUR • The Spy Who Came to Dinner   61

FIVE • The Coming Aristocracy   86

SIX • Affairs of Honor   115

SEVEN • Trials of Celebrity   134

EIGHT • Outrageous Fictions   158

NINE • Echoes   187

Notes   193

Sources and Bibliography   227

Index   243

Plates follow page 114

CHRONOLOGY

1806 Nathaniel Parker Willis born 20 January at Portland, in the District of Maine.

1812 The Willis family moves to Boston, Massachusetts.

1816 Willis's father establishes the *Boston Recorder*, an evangelical Congregationalist weekly newspaper.

1821–23 Willis attends Phillips Academy, Andover, Massachusetts, then known as a bastion of Trinitarian Congregationalism. Experiences religious conversion.

1823 First poem published in his father's *Recorder*. Enters Yale College in September.

1827 Serves his class as valedictory poet and is graduated from Yale in September. *Sketches*, a debut volume of poems, published in Boston.

1828 Engaged by Samuel Goodrich to edit *The Legendary*, one of the new genre of gift-books.

1829 Edits *The Token*, another of Goodrich's gift-books. Theatrical attendance and other evidence of backsliding lead Park Street Church brethren to excommunicate young Willis. In April, at the age of 23, he begins editing his own periodical, the *American Monthly Magazine*. Publishes *Fugitive Poetry*, his second volume of poems, in September.

1831 *American Monthly Magazine* ceases publication in July. Willis leaves Boston and joins the staff of George Pope Morris's well-established *New York Mirror*. Sails for Europe as its traveling correspondent in October. Lands at Le Havre on 3 November.

1832–34 Travels in France, Italy, and the eastern Mediterranean, eventually returning through Italy to Great Britain, for Willis the scene of great social and commercial success.

1835 Publishes *Melanie, and Other Poems* in the spring. Marries Mary Leighton Stace, daughter of the Royal Ordinance keeper at Woolwich, on 1 October.

Publishes *Pencillings by the Way*, a compendium of his travel writing, in November.

1836   Abortive duel in February with Frederick Marryat, the author of sea stories, over remarks connected with *Pencillings*. *Inklings of Adventure*, a compilation of magazine fiction, published shortly afterward. Willis and his new wife return to the United States in May.

1837   Willis's first play, a tragedy, *Bianca Visconti*, produced at the Park Theatre in August. Willis buys Glenmary, a country cottage at Owego, New York, on the upper Susquehanna River.

1839   After breaking with Morris at the *Mirror*, Willis establishes the *Corsair* with Dr. T. O. Porter. Sails for England on 20 May. *A l'Abri* (later retitled *Letters from under a Bridge*) published. *Tortesa the Usurer*, another tragedy, produced in New York.

1840   *Loiterings of Travel*, a collection of short fiction, published. The *Corsair* fails in March. A month later Willis returns to the United States. He then associates himself for a year or so with the *Brother Jonathan* and the *Dollar Magazine*.

1841   Willis begins selling tales and poems to *Graham's* and *Godey's*.

1842   A daughter, Imogen, is born. Financial setbacks force Glenmary's sale. Willis reestablishes his family in New York City.

1843   Rejoins G. P. Morris, now at the *New Mirror*.

1844   In June, delivers "Lecture on Fashion" at the Broadway Tabernacle. Postal rate hikes prompt Morris and Willis to convert the *Mirror* to a daily newspaper, the *Evening Mirror*. Edgar Allan Poe hired for a time as a sub-editor.

1845   Publishes *Dashes at Life with a Free Pencil*, a compendium of periodical work, and *Poems, Sacred, Passionate, and Humorous*. Mary Willis dies in childbirth. Her distraught husband sails for Europe, accompanied by Imogen and her nurse, the escaped slave Harriet Jacobs. For much of the visit he is ill with "brain fever."

1846   Returns from Europe and establishes the *Home Journal* with Morris. On 1 October marries Cornelia Grinnell, with whom he would have four children. J. S. Redfield publishes *The Complete Works of Nathaniel Parker Willis*.

1848   Ill with "rheumatic pleurisy."

1849   Defends Poe's memory in the *Home Journal*.

1850   Willis named in Forrest divorce suit. Physically assaulted by Edwin Forrest in Washington Square. Charles Scribner begins issuing his uniform series of Willis's prose works.

1851–52   Willis is deeply involved in the sensational divorce imbroglio of the Forrests. Following the trial, he sails to the West Indies on a long-overdue health cruise. For the next decade he suffers periodic bouts of illness—probably consumption complicated by epilepsy.

1853   Willis retires to Idlewild, a house near Cornwall-on-Hudson built with money from his second wife's dowery.

1854   Publishes *Out-doors at Idlewild*, a collection of his rural correspondence. Figures in the roman à clef *Ruth Hall*, written by his sister Sara Payson Willis ("Fanny Fern").

1856   *Paul Fane*, his only full-length novel, published in November.

1859   Publishes *The Convalescent*, a compendium of *Home Journal* columns.

1860   Travels through the Midwest with his father-in-law.

1861   Leaves Idlewild for Washington, D.C. Befriends Mary Todd Lincoln.

1864   Longtime partner G. P. Morris dies.

1865–66   In failing health.

1867   Dies at Idlewild on the afternoon of his sixty-first birthday.

SENTIMENT &
CELEBRITY

Celebrity Comes of Age

Go-eethee. No, sir, I haven't heard of Go-eethee, but I suppose he's
the N. P. Willis of Germany.

> punchline to a popular nineteenth-
> century joke circulated by
> Thomas W. Higginson

In the 1810s, the printer's art still entailed inking the era's hand-operated presses
with lye-soaked sheepskin balls "knocked up" with wool, a tedious and unpleasant
task that left an indelible impression on many a shop apprentice. It most certainly
did with Nathaniel Parker Willis (1806–67), though not perhaps in the usual manner. When this onetime printer's devil recalled laboring at his father's side in the
intervals of his schooling, it was "*balling* an edition of *Watts's Psalms and Hymns,*"
lines of which he claimed to that day rang to "the tune we played with the ink-
balls, while conning them over."[1]

Doubtless this kind of nostalgia came easier to those like Willis who escaped the
workaday confines of their ink-stained youth, for his fortunes—like those of his
father and American society generally—ultimately had less to do with the prospects
of this essentially eighteenth-century artisanal trade than with the golden horizons
of an expansive, steam-driven culture of popular letters poised to flourish in coming
decades. Having been awakened to an evangelical faith shortly after his first son's
birth, Nathaniel Willis the elder was to dedicate his editorial skills and newfound
zeal to spreading God's word among the young nation's swelling corps of readers.
Years conducting the Congregationalist *Boston Recorder* and, subsequently, a children's religious weekly called the *Youth's Companion* would endear the name of
Deacon Willis to many a pious New Englander. (Isaac Watts's *Psalms and Hymns*
was thus not mere window dressing.) His son Nat (or N. P., as contemporaries
would know him) was destined for even wider fame as one of antebellum America's
best paid and most prolific poets, editors, and "magazinists"—a mechanic of the

pen rather than ink and type. Indeed, so adept was Willis at stealing the literary limelight that for a time he was said to be the "most-talked-about author" in the United States.[2]

By contrast, when N. P. Willis is mentioned today it is generally as a footnote to someone else's story. Edgar Allan Poe's enthusiasts have long cherished his one-time boss as a steadfast champion of their hero, an apologist for his problems with drink, and a comforter of his bereaved mother-in-law. Yet it was not until Ann Douglas's *The Feminization of American Culture* (1977) reintroduced Willis (some-what uncharitably, but not wholly undeservedly) as one of Victorian America's so-called vampires of sensibility—the "male sentimentalist"—that he piqued any con-siderable interest among modern-day students of American letters. Since then, Willis's currency has depended (as it did to a significant extent in his own day) largely on his acquaintances. His longtime domestic servant, it turns out, was Har-riet Jacobs, now celebrated as the courageous author of *Incidents in the Life of a Slave Girl* (1861). In the latest edition of this veiled autobiography, Willis appears marginally as the unattractive, Southern-sympathizing "Mr. Bruce"—a curious re-versal of fortune for the humble servant and her once-famous employer. Then there is Willis's sister, "Fanny Fern" (Sara Willis Parton), whose newspaper columns and literary works are now receiving a second look by scholars interested in gender relations and the culture of print. In Fern's most interesting book, *Ruth Hall* (1854), her eldest brother figures as the outrageous "Hyacinth Ellet," a character who ob-structs Ruth's progress toward independence at every turn; Willis is, as well, a malefactor in Joyce Warren's recent biography of Fern. Yet these are only narrow windows into what was a complex and multifaceted life, one marked by victimi-zation as well as villainy. My own interest in Willis centers on a subject scarcely addressed by existing scholarship: his pivotal role in promoting the formative stages of what has been called the modern *culture of celebrity*—that self-sustaining con-juncture of social, commercial, and emotional impulses and interests that since Willis's day has increasingly directed our attention toward a kaleidoscopic spectacle of storied personality. It is here, I believe, that we can begin most fruitfully to rescue him from the footnotes.

I have opted throughout to consider the historical problems suggested by Willis's experience within a loose biographical framework. His story is well suited to this broad-ranging yet potentially dynamic approach. For one, our present understand-ing of Willis's place within American culture hinges far too much on the testimony of a few interested contemporaries; fair judgment requires a more balanced and comprehensive treatment of his life and times. While my study is by no means exhaustive (I have, for instance, merely gestured to his extensive role in promoting convalescence as a lifestyle during the 1850s), nonetheless, I intend it to serve as a modern biography of sorts, given that no full treatment of Willis's life has appeared since Henry Beers's biography in 1885, and that without benefit of a century's worth of rediscovered correspondence and subsequent scholarship. More than this, Willis's experience was—as I hope readers will agree—fascinating, even fantastic, in its own right; its complex dimensions richly deserve the extended treatment best delivered by narrative.

Yet these advantages would still cheat my intentions if a semibiographical method did not also help to illuminate the broader historical meaning discernible in his experience. Perhaps more than any other nineteenth-century American literary personality, Willis lived a life that cast him as a perennial player in the grand theater of public life. His progress in the world's eye, moreover, took him through several distinct phases, each illustrative of its own peculiar set of cultural questions and tensions. Organizing my inquiry around these defining episodes in Willis's public career has allowed me to trace the broad course of the transatlantic culture of celebrity that he did so much to quicken, amplify, and shape, even as it freed me to probe more deeply into the contested dynamics of that culture. Honoring Peter Briggs's insight that celebrity has always been essentially "a collaborative social form and process" that derives its meaning from the oppositions it entails as well as the consensus it enacts, I think it illuminating to explore the ways Willis negotiated the demands and opportunities of his groundbreaking status, and how his contemporaries judged the spectacle of his life and the codes of behavior he championed. In other words, it is my contention that Willis's significance, for both his generation and our own, is best understood if we consider his life as another (and potentially revealing) instance in the long and varied history of the cultural politics of self-dramatization.[3]

To help frame this story, it will be useful to bear in mind several broad historical trends. The first of these is partly technological and partly commercial in nature, and it concerns the growing capacity of late-eighteenth-and early-nineteenth-century entrepreneurs of print to capitalize on psychic bonds and links of desire forged between the reading public and the objects of its fascination. Along with the concurrent rise of commercially viable popular musical and theatrical amusements, this development was among the most crucial factors in promoting the personality-saturated ethos that prevailed in the United States by the time of Willis's death in 1867. A look at the world of print that preceded it will suggest why.

For all its connections to the nascent international republic of letters, the gentry-dominated society of colonial British America had remained largely a close-knit culture of face-to-face relations dedicated to agricultural and mercantile pursuits. Here on the imperial margins, the commerce of day-to-day life proceeded as much through the familiar exchanges of patronage, deference, and drawing-room sociability as it did through the impersonal channels of the market. The colonial culture of print reflected the modalities and priorities of this provincial world. Newspapers of the day still dealt primarily in mercantile and imperial news, reports of wondrous events, and, with the coming of the revolution, political polemics. One result of this situation was that, beyond the local scene, insight into what we would call the "private lives" of public characters remained limited indeed. Because the publishing industry was still in its infancy and amateur dabblers in belles-lettres generally circulated their manuscripts among a familiar audience of club members and *salonnières*, moreover, the public presence and commercial wherewithal of colonial-era authors was also sharply circumscribed. The eighteenth-century practice of masking identities behind cognomens only furthered the effacement of public authorial personality. Yet signs occasionally pointed to the commercial dimensions of the world to come. In 1762, for instance, the Philadelphia booksellers Rivington and Brown were savvy enough in their grasp of the nascent market for metropolitan gossip to advertise Tobias Smollett's *Peregrine Pickle* as a volume

> in which are given the Characters of many Considerable Persons, now existing in 'Europe,' and amongst others, that of the celebrated 'Lady Vane,' from Materials wrote by herself, and dressed up in a pretty Novel, by the Ingenious Doctor 'Smollett,' in which is exhibited a View of that Lady's Intrigues, Gallantries, Elopements from her Lord, &c. the like not to be equaled in any other real History of the present Age.

It was in large part upon a growing hunger for just such inside information, along with a complementary appetite for communion with genius and fame, that Willis made his way in the world.[4]

In certain respects, this situation reflected nothing so much as good timing, for Willis came of age at precisely the time in Western history when the commercial potential of a culture of celebrity was reaching significant proportions. Already in mid-eighteenth-century Europe, a mushrooming proliferation of scandal sheets, published collections of private correspondence, and biographical anecdote registered the potential for packaging access to the inner life of metropolitan society and the world of arts and letters. An actor like London's David Garrick, for instance, rates notice for more than his gentlemanly friendships among the nobility, groundbreaking though they were for raising the status of his profession. His ubiquitous presence on—and off—the stage also called forth showers of commentary on the content and style of his character, some captious examples of which (anticipating modern methods of publicity) Garrick himself wrote to stir up talk. And it was the promise of revelation on which such gossip and criticism traded, as much as the sway of Garrick's naturalistic theatrical style, that served to dramatize what was becoming an eighteenth-century preoccupation: plumbing the tension between what theater historian Thomas Postlewait has called the "artifice of social manners and the integrity of personal sentiment."[5]

In the hands of a figure like Jean-Jacques Rousseau, whose famous autobiographical *Confessions* (first published in 1781) served as an alluring model of the new Romantic impulse to bare all, this tension (henceforth a leitmotif of celebrity) was not so much resolved as creatively represented in a commercially sellable form. The confessional autobiography, like the era's novels and memoirs, spoke to a widespread and socially diverse audience of readers simultaneously eager to confirm themselves in their heroes' image and anxious lest postures of sincerity be revealed as hollow and contrived. These people, as Leo Braudy observes in his monumental history of fame *The Frenzy of Renown*, were in effect becoming the *fans* whose desire for a "new quality of psychic connection" with the objects of their fascination was driving the emerging culture of celebrity. Although it was then still in its formative stage, celebrity's commercial and emotional dimensions were such by the 1790s that a talented lionizer like James Boswell could parlay his intimacy with the great Dr. Johnson into a scarcely less bright glory and not feel the need to apologize for his impertinence. Why should I repress my delight at achieving such satellite fame, Boswell mused in the preface to the second edition of his wildly popular *Life of*

Johnson. "I have *Johnsonized* the land; and I trust they will not only *talk*, but *think* Johnson."[6]

Pin-pointing the precise moment when such thinking and talking coalesced into a self-sustaining culture of celebrity is impossible. Yet we can say, with some certainty, that between 1790 and 1830 the market for access to renown, in both the Old and New Worlds, assumed an enhanced scope and intensity that laid the groundwork for our modern condition, in which fame is both a durable commodity and inseparable from public attention to personality. Consider the history of the autograph. Once an idiosyncratic fancy, autograph collecting—a kind of virtual possession of fame—became all the rage from London to Cincinnati during these days. Prized as talismans of genius and emblems of status, signatures of celebrated individuals were purchased in Pall Mall shops, begged from harried correspondents, even purloined, then treated with characteristic Victorian excess to luxurious volumes of morocco gilt interleaved with hagiographic commentary. Further technological advancements—most notably, the collodion process that paved the way for the popularization of inexpensive carte de visite photographs in the 1860s—only fed this already considerable obsession.[7]

A range of developments fed this flowering of desire. Most significant were a host of social and technological innovations surrounding the medium of print. This was true especially in the United States, where literacy was widespread and the federal postal system reflected a republican commitment to the free circulation of information. The proliferation of subscription libraries in the new republic, along with significant developments in paper-making and printing technology (including stereotyping and steam-driven presses), new techniques in engraving and lithography, refinements in the structure of publishing, and advances in the organization and scale of distribution all meant that by the 1830s print could be produced and vended both attractively and cheaply enough to reach a wide range of readers spanning every social class. Information once thought a luxury, fit only for the gentry, now seemed increasingly a modern cultural necessity; it was in these days, for instance, that the nation's first generation of professional authors, such as Washington Irving, James Fenimore Cooper, and Catherine Sedgwick, became the object of wide public attention. At the same time, America's booming cities were also becoming veritable entrêpots of commercial amusement, dispensing musical and theatrical entertainment on a scale that dwarfed that of the previous century and providing bases from which the era's "star" attractions—internationally known actors, musicians, and dancers such as Edwin Forrest, the Norwegian Ole Bull, and "Jim Crow" Rice—crisscrossed the land on tour. In the hands of Yankee impresarios like Phineas T. Barnum, moreover, refinements in the art of publicity provided the leverage to fan adulation into frenzy. Encouraged by Barnum's genius at ballyhoo, New Yorkers in 1850 welcomed Jenny Lind, the "Swedish Nightingale" (as they had welcomed author Charles Dickens and dancer Fanny Ellsler several years before her), with all the fanfare once reserved for royalty—which, in a sense, Lind and her kind were becoming in this new age of democratic culture.

Contemporary observers were quick to recognize the emergence of this new brand of cultural elite, at once elevated above the people yet beholden to their adulation—which is at least partly why they were moved to invent a term to designate the phenomenon. Long used to signify a quality or condition of renown (as in a "celebrated" person), the word "celebrity" itself entered the Anglo-American vernacular in these days as shorthand for fame embodied. So far as I have been able to determine, Lady Sydney Morgan, the Irish feminist and gadabout, was among the first to record the new usage in print, though the term "celebrity," as she used it in 1829 to convey the peculiar status of famous British personalities, had undoubtedly already achieved a certain oral currency among her confrères. From the start, this neologism reflected both the promise and misgivings that sparked its coinage. Especially in the United States, where the new celebrities were often more or less talented men and women from the middle to lower classes whose status devolved less from established institutions (the church or landed gentry) than from a mercurial cultural marketplace, there was always the fear of ill-deserved and capricious popularity. That the "people" were sovereign was certainly a nineteenth-century republican commonplace, but they also frequently fell prey to puffery and manufactured sensation—that much a range of social critics knew—hence the era's abiding concern to sort out enduring fame from mere fleeting celebrity. As years passed, this somewhat quixotic pursuit played out against the backdrop of a rising din of publicity, for by the 1850s, talk of celebrities—manufactured or otherwise—echoed on both sides of the Atlantic, firing ambitions, inspiring emulation, fueling speculation, and marking a central preoccupation of Victorian life. So it was that the twentieth century's great dream factories—Hollywood and network television—did not invent our modern fascination with celebrity *ab nihilo*, but instead built on decades of interest and industry.[8]

Though he is now all but forgotten, N. P. Willis was among the first Americans to grasp the enormous commercial and social potential that Hollywood and its publicists would later realize so spectacularly. Already acclaimed, as he was, for his precocious religious poetry and fashionable magazine *jeux d'esprit*, this ambitious son of an evangelical deacon became inextricably linked with the pursuit and publicity of renowned personality and exclusive society when his gossipy travel book *Pencillings by the Way* exploded on the Anglo-American literary scene in 1835. Henceforth, the hunt after celebrity—with its implicit claim of public sovereignty over the domestic affairs and feelings of the rich and famous—found in Willis a tireless proponent and practitioner. (He was also probably the first American to use the new term, celebrity, in print.) Precisely because of his enthusiasm for turning so-called private experience to public account, he came to enjoy considerable international popularity and garner remarkable financial rewards in the thirty years preceding the American Civil War. This was no mean achievement in the days when the profession of letters was only beginning to pay, and it suggests one potentially lucrative path of advancement available to that era's new entrepreneurs of print. Having made himself into both a literary "lion" and "lion-hunter," however, Willis simultaneously had to justify and to suffer the predatory journalistic practices that underwrote much of his career. For precisely this reason, a study of his life is especially revealing for those wishing to explore the burdens and promise of fame in a world fast being transformed by print.[9]

Of course, America's "penciller by the way" was not the only entrepreneur of his day to trade on the voyeuristic luxury entailed in opening views into private lives. In many respects, such speculative pursuits were, even then, among the nation's defining obsessions. Searching the annals of the nineteenth-century press will uncover, for instance, the crusading widow Anne Royall, an outspoken itinerant whose scandalous pen portraits of American personalities infuriated those who met with her ill-treatment, and who, at the behest of her evangelical enemies, once faced conviction as a common scold. We might also recall antebellum penny journalists such as James Gordon Bennett of the *New York Herald* and Gothic novelists such as George Lippard, both of whom played, in new and compelling ways, to public appetites for inside information. Yet, in a fundamental sense, Royall, Bennett, and Lippard were working beyond the proper middle-class consensus that was coming to govern much of American experience, gadflies bent on exposing polite society's foibles as they exploited their commercial potential. Willis, on the other hand, sought forthrightly to authorize his breach of domestic security under the seal of gentility, in effect annexing the pursuit of celebrity to the province of good taste— and with remarkable results. Buoyed by a self-assured sense of style and uncommon access to privileged social circles, he eventually established himself as among the nation's foremost arbiters of fashion, manners, and taste. By posing as a kind of antebellum "Mister Manners" for a generation of middle-class consumers as yet ill at ease in their gentility, Willis contributed substantially to the ongoing process of social articulation and stratification that the historian Richard Bushman has called "The Refinement of America."[10]

All of this brings us to a second—and related—historical development that helps to frame Willis's significance: the rise in Western culture of what I call the *sentimental persuasion.* By this term I mean to encompass a whole constellation of values extending from faith in the moral superiority of private society to the celebration of domestic affections, refined aesthetic sensibilities, and Romantic intuition, all of which served to align a growing body of adherents behind the philosophical premise that a refined, even exquisite, emotional susceptibility led naturally to a virtuous and benevolent disposition. As scholars have noted, this structure of feeling drew on several long-standing cultural traditions, including Enlightenment universalism, evangelical religiosity, and the eighteenth-century "cult of sensibility." But in the United States at least, it approached its zenith beginning only in the early nineteenth century, with the spread of a female-centered domestic ideology and a commercially viable market for popular letters especially among the middle class. One upshot of this new emotional condition was the rise of benevolence as a social value; another was the diffusion of Romantic ideals of friendship among both men and women. And yet, given the day's reigning psychological precepts, which construed womankind as the special repository of heart-centered sensibilities, it is not surprising that women (and those who identified with a feminine point of view) became the most enthusiastic admirers—and the greatest consumers—of the flowering of sentiment produced in these years.[11]

A few examples alone will suffice to establish the fact that the fruits of this flowering were capable of moving people in remarkable ways. The unprecedented volume of sales generated by Harriet Beecher Stowe's stirring abolitionist novel *Uncle Tom's Cabin* (1852), for instance, neatly demonstrates how sentimental appeals could sustain the most ambitious of benevolent causes; it is now an academic commonplace to observe how this zealous polemicist concluded her exposé of human bondage by entreating readers to *do* right by first *feeling right* about the problem of slavery. More often than not, however, such impulses accrued to less radical— and more therapeutic—ends. Especially among genteel American women, for example, the language of beauty and holy affections customarily associated with sentimental literary expression frequently seems to have been used to convey, among other things, intense longings for communion with kindred spirits. In this regard, mere men of "affairs"—businessmen, laborers, and the like—would rarely do as the object of a sentimentalist's ardor. Thus, several scholars have suggested that the noticeable upsurge of women seeking literary lives in the antebellum era probably reflected not only economic necessity, but the yearnings of wives and mothers for a purer and more meaningful variety of friendship, one often realized in (or at least imagined as) a kind of erotically sublimated "sisterhood of sensibility."[12]

Interestingly, the dream-work of celebrity seems to have worked in a similar fashion, though without the bar of sex-exclusivity. Consider the titanic emotions conjured in a letter by one American fan of the violinist Ole Bull: the New York poetess and *salonnière* Anne Lynch. "I have never found one to love with my whole soul," she confessed to her new idol in 1845,

> and perhaps it is well, for I should die and be consumed with the intensity of that passion, but friendship is as beautiful as love and that I cannot live without, though even here I have never been satisfied. I have never met a nature who could return to me the half of what I could give, and so my life has been one long famine and my heart the cannibal of itself. If I seem to you too enthusiastic in my expressions of friendship for you, remember that my heart has been frozen for a whole lifetime and it must naturally overflow on meeting one so large and so noble as your own. Ah, Ole Bull! if I could tell you the history of my life, so cold, so barren without and so volcanic within!

A brush with celebrity, it seems, was an opportunity to share a depth and variety of feeling exhibited only to a special few.[13]

It is probably not mere coincidence that a woman of Lynch's disposition should also have sought out Willis's friendship and patronage, for he was unsurpassed among literary men of his day at ministering to such volcanoes of sentimental desire. Much of this had to do with the way he positioned himself, both personally and commercially, as a connoisseur of feeling and beauty. While he was still a student at Yale, Willis's precocious religious verse had tested the American market for a new brand of gorgeous piety that married Romantic sensibilities to Christian belief. Then, even as this Wordsworthian disciple fell away from the strict propriety of his adolescent faith, sentiments of beauty and the beauty of sentiment continued to animate his lifelong pursuit of a republican aesthetic life, one in which refined women figured centrally as both ornaments and boon companions. Interestingly, market incentives appear to have enhanced rather than diminished this engagement as his literary fame grew. In modeling the progress of his personal sensibilities for a large and appreciative readership centered on the nation's genteel domestic circles, Willis was able to compound the rewards he was already reaping from his trade in celebrity with the equally lucrative wages of sentiment.

Yet it would be a mistake to suppose that Willis's remarkable commercial success and claims to popular affection in the antebellum era went fundamentally unchallenged. On the contrary (and for reasons that often had everything to do with his contemporaries' misgivings about the commercial and cultural sway of sentiment and celebrity), few public figures of his day aroused more conflicting emotions or provoked more contention than he did. As *Arthur's Home Magazine* put it in 1854, "No man has lived more constantly in the public eye for the last twenty years than Willis, and there is no American writer who has received more applause from his friends or more censure from his enemies." While some observers declared him to be the best hope of American poetry, an ambassador of refined living, even a model gentleman, others (both sentiment's hardheaded detractors and true believers alarmed at its perversion) judged his poetry to be cloying and enervating, his taste ornamental and empty, and his lifestyle rococo and dissolute. Critics as diverse as the proslavery Democrat James Gordon Bennett, liberal Congregationalist Horace Bushnell, and radical feminist Elizabeth Cady Stanton regularly denounced "Namby-Pamby" Willis as a kind of genteel confidence man of letters who was leading the republic—especially its daughters and mothers—down the proverbial (perfumed) garden path. Precisely where he and his considerable legion of fans were headed—to fashionable idleness, simpering sentimentality, or worse— depended on the particular fears and anxieties of the critics. Willis himself contributed greatly to the shape of this controversial estate. Rarely one to censor his opinions, he made a profession of holding forth on the state of society generally and on gender relations in particular, often in ways calculated to stir emotions all around. Equally important, over the years commercial impulses and his own demons led him into a series of very public and very equivocal scandals and breaches of etiquette, all of which served to test his fans' constancy and his critics' patience. One of antebellum America's best-loved personalities, Willis also ranked among its most vexing.[14]

This condition was never so apparent as when, beginning in the mid-1840s, he sought to establish the nation's celebrities as a kind of new aristocracy of fashion. In Willis's own mind, this plan was a most republican solution to the problem of exercising a salutary authority in his generation's increasingly commercialized and urbanized social environment, for who was better equipped to reform and refine presumptuous vulgarity—in both high and low quarters—than those men and women whom nature had marked by talent and beauty as of finer clay? Rather than clinching the case, however, Willis's commercial and social initiative merely set the stage for a decade in which he was to figure repeatedly at the center of a divisive struggle in the press and in society over the very meaning of middle-class gentility and sentimental culture. It is a measure of the complexity of his personality, and the manner in which it was contested in the reading public, that he appeared in this debate alternately—and sometimes simultaneously—as the savior of refined womanhood and its betrayer; a paragon of manly honor and an effeminate rogue; a villain and a victim.

To probe the alternate versions of Willis, both the confidence man and the sentimental hero, is to plumb the social frictions, cultural anxieties, and commercial interests that drove his generation to their uneasy accommodation with the forces then remaking their world. Once, fame had meant pursuing honor by performing for royalty, but with the advent of Willis's brand of sentimental celebrity it now meant negotiating the straits of notoriety and renown by performing symbolically before a wider and more socially diverse audience, many of whom longed to achieve a sense of wholeness through emotional identification with their parlor idols. That this therapeutic congress was inherently problematic followed not only from the guilty pleasures entailed in trespassing precisely those boundaries of "privacy" and propriety that sentimental culture was explicitly pledged to safeguard. Troubles stemmed as well from the fact that such putatively "authentic" experiences realized their meaning primarily within a dynamic commercial economy whose value hard-core sentimentalists tended to discount, even as they tapped its resources. While antebellum Americans sought consciously to fortify the domestic sphere against invasion, they were equally likely—in the service of commerce, moral instruction, and the pleasures of communion with kindred spirits—to authorize certain poten-tially disruptive views into their newly privatized lives. It was precisely because Willis embodied these and so many other of his generation's contradictory impulses—the simultaneous pursuit of business and sentiment; authenticity and theatricality; equality and status—that he seems to have preoccupied his contemporaries.[15]

In a society flooded with print, moreover, Willis's presence probably seemed well-nigh inescapable, so that the thorny questions of power and culture posed by his highly publicized successes and trespasses were difficult ones to ignore. What class of men and women would exercise sovereignty in the commercialized and democratized world of the mid–nineteenth century? And through what cultural forms, and with what social consequences, would that authority operate? These were, of course, questions of concern for the new celebrities themselves as well as for their fans and the critical community at large. And they remain so today, despite the interval of years.

If only because he served so often as a kind of critical lightning rod illuminating the modern ethos of sentiment and personality then being ushered in N. P. Willis is worthy of renewed attention.

Beauty's Apostle

... poetry has a charm, and a strong one, but it is because we see
the man through it, that we keep it freshly on our lips, and use it as
the voice of our own affections.

N. P. Willis, "The Editor's Table,"
American Monthly Magazine (December
1829)

Shortly into the New Year's season of 1828, Connecticut's once-ballyhooed bard
James Gates Percival spied yet another fair-haired boy on America's poetic firmament. "You have a new star in your horizon, N. P. Willis, Esq.," he ribbed a friend
back in Boston, "and I presume your wise men of the East have gone to worship
him."[1]

Jest or no, this observation was apt. Since its publication the previous October,
Sketches, a thin volume of the twenty-two-year-old poet's Romantic verse, had sold
well, generating considerable enthusiasm around New England and as far south as
Athens, Georgia. Fans particularly esteemed the volume's lyrical revisions of biblical
episodes (written over the signature "Roy"), several of which had already won monetary prizes for their affecting imagery and refined religious sentiments. Chiefly on
the merits of these "Scriptural Sketches," Henry Ware Jr. of the Unitarian *Christian
Examiner* now pronounced "Roy," though still a learner, a "poet, one who thinks,
feels, and writes for himself, with a quiet and delicate beauty, and occasional touches
of deep pathos which give most encouraging promises of future eminence." So
respected was Ware's judgment around New England that soon Willis was, to his
own happy amazement, "deluged with notifications to be present at new places"
and "treated with attention by the Governor, Solicitor-General, Attorney General
+ 500 others." Privately, critics worried that the precocious poet wrote too easily—
"Wordsworth and Mrs. Hemans lackadaisified," as Percival sniffed. Yet the young
man's more extravagant admirers were not to be swayed from their devotion, and

they hailed his coming as a wondrous prospect for American letters. Anointment thus came early to Deacon Willis's clever boy.[2]

In part this situation reflected poetry's unprecedented visibility, both at home and overseas in Britain. Long regarded as the queen of the arts, verse had assumed a striking new commercial and cultural clout with the advent of Walter Scott's best-selling *Lay of the Last Minstrel* in 1805. For the next twenty years, poetry experienced a never-to-be-repeated golden age of popularity, sustained by the likes of Scott, Byron, and a multitude of lesser lights. Of these, Byron most spectacularly embodied the potential for celebrity entailed in a poet's mantle. In 1812 the first and second cantos of *Childe Harold* sold forty-five hundred copies over six months in Great Britain alone and made their author wildly popular. So frenzied had public appetites become by the appearance of *The Corsair* in 1814 that an entire run of 10,000 copies sold out on the day of publication. "You have no notion of the sensation," Byron's flabbergasted publisher gushed in the wake of this dramatic turn of events. "You cannot meet a man on the street who has not read or heard read *The Corsair*."[3]

Though not strictly accurate, this last contention did contain the germ of an important truth. By the late 1810s, low-priced octavo editions of the modern British poets aimed at the middle classes were selling in the tens of thousands; because each book commonly passed through several hands, it could be said that a remarkable portion of the mushrooming reading public was thus queuing up for its dose of poetic culture. Nor was the appetite for verse restricted to Great Britain. Like many readers in the cultural orbit of London and Edinburgh, Americans also cottoned to these literary developments, buying and reading volume upon volume of imported and pirated editions as a general rage for poetic sensibilities ensued. By the end of the decade, British and American youth were regularly assuming the open collar and melancholy mien of the Byronic hero, eager to signal attitudes of social and cultural rebellion. As important, sensitive souls were taking up poetry with an eye toward establishing claims to fame, even fortune. But the golden age could not last.

In Britain the crisis came with the economic jolts of 1825 and, a year later, the spectacular failures of several leading publishing houses. Gone almost overnight were the unprecedented payments that had subsidized the British poetry boom. Also gone, for the most part, were the literary giants who commanded such commercial rewards. In the United States matters did not resolve so starkly, perhaps because its market for poetry had never boasted much in the way of wages. In the days of Willis's coming-of-age it was thus still possible to dream of national destiny embodied in a rising star like his. And with the verses of the young nation's bards copied freely from "poetry corners" in the weekly press and read eagerly in circulating libraries, schoolrooms, and parlors, so, too, could this promise still be conjured from slender means: one thin volume, for instance, the compendium of several years' newspaper work.

As befitting a people steeped in ideals of progress and piety, Americans in these days seemed particularly eager to celebrate poets who—like Willis—struck a note of aestheticized religiosity in their biblically inspired verse. Part of the broad transformation of eighteenth-century American Protestantism into its Romantically inflected antebellum character, this inclination to indulge in what Lawrence Buell has called "Literary Scripturism" drew vitality from the prevailing belief (articulated by

Scottish Common Sense philosophers) that taste was a God-given faculty of the mind whose proper cultivation produced a range of pleasurable emotions awakened by nearer commerce with the divine. It followed, then, that the pursuit of beauty, correctly construed as a spur to religious affections, was a noble calling. For Willis— as for many sensitive and ambitious men and women of his generation—this dispensation opened a world of social and aesthetic opportunities. In the short term, the mantle of a Romantic poet of nature's god equipped him with a serviceable cultural style that went a long way toward crafting a provisional answer to the problem of finding a place for himself in the dawning Jacksonian social order, where the pressure to achieve status was often as great as the opportunities that fueled ambition. Precocious literary triumphs also inaugurated a lifetime love affair with the aesthetics of sentiment, a perennial romance that would eventually help to establish the youth as arguably his generation's most popular apostle of beauty— this in an era when appreciation for that particular quality of excellence was assuming a significant role in American aspirations for the self and the nation.[4]

But Willis did not assume this consequential station without confronting certain personal and professional dilemmas and difficulties, some of which were evident even this early in his career. These troubles can reveal as much about the tangled sources of his literary and social progress, and the impulses that drove the new culture of celebrity, as can the acclaim that had paved his way.

In His Father's House

At first blush, the household headed by Nathaniel Willis, the poet's father, might seem one peculiarly unfit to produce an American apostle of beauty. Standard Unitarian accounts of the period characterize the rock-ribbed Trinitarian parishioners of the Willises' so-called Brimstone Corner Church at Park Street as appreciating neither aesthetic prompting nor faith's sunny side; rather, their religious connoisseurship was said to run to doomsaying and, worse still, infant damnation. Of course this portrayal is mostly caricature, even if it neatly encapsulates the era's charged sectarian rivalries. In these days, when New England's Congregational meetinghouses rang with the clash of liberal Christians battling their more doctrinally conservative orthodox brethren for control of the Puritan inheritance, many among the region's mostly Federalist Unitarian-leaning social and intellectual elite liked nothing better than to preen themselves on their superior aesthetic and moral sensibilities. With these, they justified both their distaste for stern and sober latter-day Calvinists and their dreams of establishing a socially powerful class of right-thinking gentlemen-scholars to police, as one Harvard Phi Beta Kappa orator put it, the world's "follies and extravagances" by directing "the taste and intelligence of [the] people on all subjects." Thus the common put-down of ill-bred orthodoxy.[5]

Nonetheless, refined literary expression, if voiced properly and addressed to appropriate themes, could be as alluring to socially conservative revivalists like those at Park Street as it was to New England's liberal Christians. Yale College's future president Timothy Dwight (later dubbed the "Pope of Connecticut" by his sectarian foes) had intimated as much, when in his 1772 college commencement oration he praised the Scripture's "eloquent and poetic beauties." Fifty years later, young N. P. Willis's vogue attested to the increasingly ecumenical relish for such tastes, even if New England's denominational antagonists tended to approach their aesthetic sensibilities along different paths. Such divergences were to shape the social and psychological estate of Park Street's budding poet in several ways: first priming him for a celebrity among evangelicals and nonevangelicals alike; then leading him to wander from the precincts of his first fame. In doing so, he would test the boundaries of American taste in ways that underscored its considerable fluidity as well as its fundamental disjunctures.[6]

Like much in postrevolutionary America, the impetus behind the exacting evangelical discipline destined to dominate Willis's childhood had its origin in the era's social and political upheavals. It had been a call from prominent Maine politicos to edit the Jeffersonian *Eastern Argus* that initially led the journeyman printer Nathaniel Willis, his father, to convey his bride, the former Hannah Parker of Holliston, Massachusetts, to the bustling seaport of Portland in 1803. Here the young couple began raising a family, while the husband settled in to decry the "aristocratic" policies of Downeast Federalists. A year after his first son's birth in January 1806, partisan excitement over issues of land speculation and separation from Massachusetts had escalated to such a pitch that the elder Willis was jailed on a conviction for libel, having printed an article that called a political antagonist, among other things, a "SWINDLER and DISSEMBLER." Although the "Old Trojan" declared his release after three months' incarceration a triumph for Republicanism and free speech, prison and partisan invective evidently weakened his stomach for the acid world of political hackwork. Within eighteen months he had sold his share in the *Argus* to concentrate on more transcendent matters.[7]

Hannah Willis had already begun attending prayer meetings with the town's charismatic young Congregationalist preacher Edward Payson when her husband's religious conscience began to stir in the stormy winter of 1807–08. Soon, Payson's devotional prayer and strict sabbatarian exhortations were working a change of heart in the husband, as they had in the wife. Doubtless the sober prospect of looming economic collapse helped to underscore the presumptive stability of the rock of ages. Seemingly overnight, Jefferson's embargo had wrecked Portland's once-brisk trade, driving the city's banks to ruin, its sailors to idleness, and its citizens to despair. "The poorhouse is already full," the newly returned Payson lamented in December 1807. "All confidence is lost; no man will trust his neighbor; but every one takes even his brother *by the throat, saying, Pay me what thou owest.*" With business thus waylaid, religion alone flourished, offering comfort and guidance in a time of afflictions. This it most certainly did for Nathaniel Willis, who reportedly marked his conversion to evangelical Christianity in the spring of 1808 by forgoing a ball to attend a prayer meeting. Henceforth, the former party polemicist and his wife devoted themselves to God's service in the Congregational Church.[8]

This devotion guided the young family through good times and bad. It was, for instance, probably not simply hard times but Nathaniel Willis's temperance-inspired refusal to sell liquor that sunk the grocery he established after selling off the *Argus.* Then in 1812, when prospects appeared inauspicious for setting up in Portland as a printer of religious tracts and pamphlets, Willis took his family to Boston, eventually settling at 31 Atkinson (later Congress) Street in what Dr. Oliver Wendell Holmes recalled as a "large, square painted brick house." From the start, the Willises were welcomed by the zealous evangelicals of the city's Park Street Church, where Nathaniel promptly became a church publicist and, eventually, a deacon. His stature among the movers and shakers of Trinitarian Congregationalism climbed considerably in January 1816, when he helped to establish the *Boston Recorder*. The elder Willis's role as proprietor, printer, and titular editor of this self-proclaimed "first denominational newspaper in America" was destined to last until 1844, furnishing both a springboard for his son's literary career and inspiration for the *Youth's Companion*, an innovative, evangelically oriented juvenile newspaper spun off from the *Recorder*'s children's department in 1827. Here, along with the usual accounts of exemplary conversions and deaths, Yankee children were instructed through homilies, domestic tales, and juvenile poetry to love God and obey His commandments. Like his eldest son, Nathaniel Willis thus helped to spread evangelical attitudes as well as transform them.[9]

Not surprisingly, Nathaniel's domestic government reflected his godly commitments generally. Park Street's brand of neo–Edwardsean Congregationalism was, if nothing else, a patriarchal faith that honored the prepotency of God as Father—when, to cite one telling example, the denomination's ministers were faced with the unsettling "new measures" of their Finneyite Presbyterian revivalist allies, they all resisted the innovation of allowing women to pray and exhort in "mixed society." So it was that the future deacon naturally expected his growing family—there would be nine children in all—to obey both God's word and his own. In particular, this meant disciplining the self to avoid worldly snares. Dancing was thus strictly prohibited in the Willis home, as it was in many households that abjured easy roads to heaven. So, too, was attendance at the theater, as well as, on the Sabbath, all games, toys, secular reading, and picture books other than John Foxe's anti-Catholic *Book of Martyrs* (more properly, *Actes and Monuments of the Church*), a volume whose gruesome copper-plate illustrations of death and dismemberment were perennial favorites in Puritan and post-Puritan households. These prohibitions did not necessarily signal a barren relationship. Much like Harriet Beecher Stowe's famous father Lyman Beecher, another early nineteenth-century orthodox patriarch who presided imperiously if devotedly over an energetic and conflicted household, Nathaniel Willis presumably disciplined his children because he loved them. For such a man (reportedly possessed of a dry wit and an eye for female beauty but content, as one parishioner remembered it, to "expound without ideas"), concern for his children's salvation was the ultimate test of fatherly devotion. Add to this the parade of ministerial emissaries who often repaid the hospitality of the family's so-called Prophet's Chamber by engaging in religious conversation with the children, and it is clear that Nat and his siblings grew up in an atmosphere heavy with spiritual obligations and expectations. None were to escape its effects, N. P. Willis least of all.[10]

If the Willis children later recalled a sunnier outlook, it was apt to be in connection with their mother. By all accounts, Hannah Parker Willis eschewed the forbidding sternness of her husband's orthodoxy, inclining instead toward a devotional religion of inspiration and beauty. We might expect as much from her special relationship with the family of her Portland pastor. For all his latter-day Calvinist moralism (and periodic bouts of melancholy, which he kept mostly to himself), Payson was at least as notable for practicing a style of extemporaneous public prayer ("devout poetry," he called it) that aimed to wash away the "rubbish of worldly cares" with a stream of holy affections. He also seems to have been a man capable, in his personal relations, of considerable tenderness, especially toward children of the faithful, whom he regarded as his blessed lambs. Perhaps it should not surprise us, then, that Payson was often startled out of his spiritual doldrums by a ravishing vision of Christ, who figured in his pious imagination as the inspiration for a seraphic love. Like many New England women, Hannah seems to have taken whole-heartedly to this hopeful, if still spiritually demanding, brand of devotional piety, as she most certainly did to her pastor and his family. For years, the Paysons had a home away from home in Boston—as did the Willis brood in Portland, and among the Willises' many ministerial visitors it was Payson alone (with his "low and musical voice" and "soft and liquid" eyes) whom the children later remembered as the bearer of sunshine. Their mother apparently radiated a similar—and equally welcome—spirit of sweetness and light, so much so that her special love and understanding figured in family lore as a cherished antidote to the father's stern visage and periodic headaches. That, according to her daughter Sara, Hannah Willis reportedly "talked poetry unconsciously" while performing her household duties must also have contributed markedly to the literary sensibility that ultimately predominated among the children.[11]

This situation was especially crucial to the emotional development of young Nat, who, it might be said, always fundamentally remained his mother's son. Satisfying the demands of orthodox evangelical discipline must not have been easy for a child of his expansive temperament. And if Hannah, good Christian wife that she was, doubtless concurred in the necessity of binding her eldest son's boyish fancies, in contrast to her husband, she apparently did so with a sympathetic regard that fostered a deep and lasting bond of affection. All evidence suggests that the future poet cherished his "friend-mother" (a term of endearment coined in the author's semi-autobiographical novel *Paul Fane*) as a special confidante, one who happily learned "by heart each leaf of her boy's mind as it was written and turned over." Indeed, this relationship was so central to N. P.'s sense of self that, along with inspiring a lifelong reverence for her brand of womanly virtues, Hannah's maternal attention served, in effect, to confirm his identity: "My veins are teeming with the quick-silver spirit which my mother gave me," he once asserted. "What-ever I accomplish must be gained by ardor, and not by patience." That this inheritance evidently fell short of satisfying his hunger for love and regard (and indeed may even have en-couraged its unhealthy excesses by posing an unrealistic model) is suggested by N. P.'s restless ambition for notice, both public and personal.[12]

Predictably, as the Willis children grew older, their parents grew increasingly anxious over their spiritual welfare. Unlike the family's Puritan forebears, who counted precocious conversion unusual if not unheard of, early-nineteenth-century evangelicals like the Willises were coming to expect a quickening of the conscience by the middle years of adolescence, so that spiritual regeneration became a rite of passage. As the teenage years approached in such households, search for signs of salvation intensified, with parents and clergymen prompting children to probe their feelings for evidence of guilt and despair that must perforce precede "hope" of sanctification. In this hothouse atmosphere, it is no wonder that concerns for the soul regularly reached crisis proportions, often with profound personal and psychological consequences. That, at least, was the case with young Nat Willis.[13]

In accounting for the future poet's religious and aesthetic sense, we should not neglect the impact of education; the Willises most certainly did not. Keenly aware of the advantages proper schooling might hold for a child's spiritual and worldly prospects, Nathaniel especially insisted that his children, sons and daughters alike, receive a thorough, biblically based education to fit them for their station in godly society. For his eldest son, this insistence meant early schooling with a Reverend Dr. McFarland in Concord, New Hampshire, followed by a year at the Boston Latin School and then two years' boarding at Phillips Academy in Andover, Massachusetts. This last choice in particular reflected the father's religious requisites. Boston Latin, while convenient to the family house on Atkinson Street, was too closely tied to Unitarian-dominated Harvard College for the future deacon's comfort; Andover's Phillips Academy, by contrast, was a bastion of evangelicalism run by the redoubtable "*revival* man" and disciplinarian John Adams, and situated within the bosom of the new Calvinist orthodoxy at nearby Andover Theological Seminary. Founded in 1808 to oppose the takeover of Harvard by liberal Christians, the seminary supplied many of the ministers and missionaries who were then transforming American Protestantism into a dynamic international force for social and religious reform. Closer to home, many ardent seminarians tried out their convictions next door by helping Adams minister to his students. One young man who did so was Louis Dwight, the future prison reformer from Stockbridge, Massachusetts, and soon-to-be husband of N. P. Willis's younger sister Louisa. As a friend and mentor, Dwight was to be instrumental in turning the teenage academy student from irresolution to Christian profession.[14]

The particular occasion of this momentous change was a series of revivals that swept Phillips Academy and other New England Trinitarian institutions in the winter of 1822–23. The previous November, a minister visiting the Willis household in Boston had entreated sixteen-year-old Louisa with the seriousness of her spiritual estate; prompted by repeated letters pressing the matter, she "obtained a hope" at Thanksgiving time. Soon afterward, three of the other Willis girls (the youngest, nine years of age) were, with the help of Nat's visiting friend Louis Dwight, similarly "affected." "Our house," as their father put it proudly, "was indeed a house of prayers and tears." Meanwhile, young Nat had returned to Andover unaffected; when his sisters sent word of their "happy change," the boy's reply was, as his father phrased it, "full of rebellion against God and hatred of the truth." This reaction seems consistent with N. P.'s previous outlook: at age fifteen, he delayed admission to the church because of sinking doubts, worries that a year later led him to lament to his parents that "as to being a Christian, it is morally *beyond my power*." By his own account, such regrets often led to tears and restored resolve, but soon he was again lost in what he called "mazes of pleasure and folly." Now, however, religious excitements were to banish all such irresolution, at least for a time. After Christmas, the revivals at Phillips Academy began again in earnest;

then, like many students there, young Willis harkened anxiously to the ministering of the masters and seminarians. In response, the boy's father journeyed to Andover to strengthen his son's resolve, sending up a "Testament" soon afterwards. This suffocating solicitude (eminently characteristic of a certain brand of antebellum evangelical parenting) and the prevailing excitements seem to have turned the tide. In a day or two, the boys were conducting prayer meetings of their own, with seminarians (Dwight conspicuous among them) looking on; as young Nat put it, "we prayed and sung, *prayed and sung,* till it seemed a little heaven on earth." A few days later the victory was won. "My heart is so overflowing with joy and gratitude and happiness," the dutiful son then wrote his father with evident relief, "that I could not rest till I had sat down and told you *all.*" With a "Mr. Styles" talking so volubly that the boy "could almost see a halo round his head," the meeting rooms at Andover had been filled with agitated and exultant students sobbing their repentance to one another. Filled with the Lord's spirit, Willis in particular felt "proud as Lucifer" that his words seemed to strengthen others searching out signs of hope. His self-doubt melted away; he believed himself saved; he prayed only for humility. "It is and must be," he explained to his father, "the burden of my supplications." So it was that N. P. Willis entered Yale College in September 1823 a professing Christian.[15]

Most likely, Nathaniel Willis enrolled his first-born son at Yale to save him from Harvard. The jewel in the crown of Unitarian New England, this almost 200-year-old college across the Charles River in Cambridge had by this time a well-deserved reputation for producing elegantly turned out and clannish liberal Christians. Yale, on the other hand, having been "saved" from all manner of infidelities by the attentions of President Timothy Dwight some twenty years earlier, might have been expected to abjure the worldly heresies entertained nearer to home. As Nathaniel apparently intended his son for the ministry, it was doubly necessary that the boy be instructed by divines of impeccable orthodox credentials. A proper Calvinist education was also calculated to reinforce the salutary influence of a Christian upbringing and might well expand the social opportunities of the son of a man who, though destined to be a deacon, had begun life as a printer and Jeffersonian polemicist. For all these reasons, Yale seemed the place for N. P.[16]

Once he arrived in New Haven, however, ministerial preparation claimed less of Nat's creative energies than did the pursuit of poetry. Already at Andover he had begun to array his thoughts and feelings in verse; at college (where he was never much of a scholar) he admitted proudly, if a bit guiltily, to having "poetized to a considerable extent." Characteristically, Willis addressed his first published poem (printed in the *Recorder* shortly after his conversion) to "My Mother." Here he conceded, by way of his new promise to walk in Christ:

> I've been a wild and wayward boy,
> Since first claim'd I a parent's care—
> And oft have dashed the cup of joy,
> That crown'd my mother's anxious prayer.

Doubtless this turnabout was a balm to Hannah Willis's heart, as were the poems of contrition that periodically followed. But her husband, the church activist and publicist, must also have been proud—and probably relieved as well—when his son turned to praising God and godly ways in verse; he was prouder still when other pious Christians began to notice the talent blossoming in their midst. For "Roy," as the Yale student called himself, was soon recognized as a rising star.[17]

It should be noted that N. P. Willis's swift ascension to the position of the *Boston Recorder*'s favorite poet marked not only a significant passage in his own aesthetic education but in that of American evangelicalism as a whole. It did so most importantly because it traced the trajectory of a growing segment of New England society that yearned to see its Messiah lauded in refined language, its sovereign deity praised by the genteel. A reflection of a general reorientation in self-fashioning toward a more genteel ideal, this desire cut across denominational lines and reached deep into even otherwise socially conservative Congregationalist circles, if not necessarily into the ranks of the new unlettered "sects" of the day—Baptists, Methodists, Disciples of Christ, and their like. Consider the example of Joel Hawes, the future Hartford divine and author of the influential orthodox evangelical cautionary tract *Lectures to Young Men* (1828). As a seminarian at Andover in the mid-1810s, a concern for life's minor morals led him to confide in his fiancée that he was "afraid of the kitchen" for the personal qualities it seemed to threaten: "refinement of taste, delicacy of feeling, and elegance of manners." These genteel traits the young Hawes "delight[ed] to see in others," but as he thought they could be acquired only in conversation with what he called "elegant authors and people of cultured minds," he hoped his betrothed would be liberated from domesticity's more onerous tasks. So, too, was the great evangelical moralist Lyman Beecher, for all his rugged zeal, keen to recapture the "cultivated in intellect and refined in taste" from their Unitarian proclivities. Here is a case in point: when the ultraorthodox Zilpah Grant declined an offer to assume the assistant principal's position at his eldest daughter Catharine's Hartford Female Seminary (itself an important institutional expression of the new refined evangelical piety), the elder Beecher wrote to counter objections that the school was too worldly in its practice. "Hitherto religion had been associated with poverty and ignorance, or, at best, with solid, strange, coarse, unpolished orthodoxy," he lectured Grant. "I do not expect that taste and refinement will convert the soul, but who can tell how many have been repelled from religion by a want of them[?]" To such men, orthodox in spirit yet innovative in method, piety properly seasoned with taste and refinement seemed an indispensable recipe for recouping the souls lost to Unitarians and other liberal Christians.[18]

For a time, it seemed as if N. P. Willis might be the answer to orthodoxy's prayers in this regard. For even as he addressed himself to pious themes, the young poet's fertile imagination and rare sense of beauty set him apart from the run of the mill. At least, that was the opinion of the evangelical worthies gathered around the *Boston Recorder*. In 1825, the paper announced the establishment of an annual poetry contest designed to improve its readers' appreciation of Christian virtues and encourage the spread of refined sensibilities. Its inaugural winner was "Roy's" mildly Byronic "Misanthropic Hours," a three-part meditation that called to task the trifling pride of women before the higher beauty of God's love ("Without that meeker grace, she'll be / A lighter thing than vanity"). We cannot know precisely why the three-man panel of orthodox clergy and educators honored young Willis's verse with their prize, yet we can conclude one thing: though one judge blanched at "Roy's" fashionable misanthropy and voted instead for "Eliza's" safely devout poem "The Monthly Concert of Prayer," pious sentiments alone were deemed insufficient to carry off the prize. Afforded the opportunity, the *Recorder* chose elegant faith over rough piety.[19]

The announcement of the following year's prizes underscored this preference. In the category of poetry, the honor and ten-dollar premium went again to "Roy." This time he won with two lyrical blank-verse reworkings of biblical tales, "The Sacrifice of Abraham" and "Jepthah's Daughter," both of which employed a sentimental lyricist's touch to embellish the old stories of faith tested. Granted, this year's judges did not think "Roy" perfect (for one, they may have been taken aback by his portrayal of Jepthah's daughter as a kind of Hebrew parlor belle sporting "beautiful, dark Jewish eyes" and a "shape Praxiteles might worship"), but he had, as one referee phrased it, "decidedly the most poetry." Equally important, his "poetical excellence" neatly complemented the object the committee wished to encourage with its other prize—this one for the best account of a religious revival. It was intended to "induce an improvement in the *style* of such narratives; to divest it of cant phrases and vain repetitions, and commend the intelligence of itself, by the dress that it wears, to persons of cultivated taste." Here was a de facto manifesto of genteel orthodoxy addressed, like young Willis's poems, to a literate and cosmopolitan class ("persons of cultivated taste") rather than to country Calvinists, whose unsophisticated piety introduced "cant phrases and vain repetitions" (that is, traditional revival tropes) into what might otherwise be convincing evocations of evangelical fervor. This concern for style probably reflected orthodox worries that rustic revival reports fueled Unitarian propaganda, insofar as formulaic claims of evangelical success now often met with skepticism, even derision, in socially sophisticated quarters; ridicule like the Reverend Orville Dewey's that Calvinist "judges of religious purity and decorum seem not to have learnt the morality of washing their faces" doubtless struck home. Also at stake was the efficacy of a new conversion modality, one that relied less on meetinghouse enthusiasm than parlor-centered literary habit, and one on which, not coincidentally, denominational newspapers like the *Recorder* staked their future.[20]

Some latter-day Calvinists clearly chafed at such innovation. In conservative evangelical circles, flirting with style had traditionally been tantamount to entertaining the devil. This was so because directing Christians to concern themselves with externalities—manners, dress, and literary style—risked suggesting that piety might be judged by appearance alone. That, indeed, was the crux of evangelical objections to the Unitarian heresy, which, under the guise of a refining disposition, was said to reduce religiosity to a cipher for worldly desire. For much the same reasons, certain orthodox observers now questioned the *Recorder*'s rush to legitimize a pleasing form and sweet address. "Is the assassin the less murderous, because of the *splendid* dress which he may happen to wear?" asked one conservative critic regarding the current rage among evangelicals for imaginative works on religious themes. So, too, queried another, might it not be "unwise" to resort to religious fictions "while we have so rich a store of facts?" Fiction, this wary critic suggested, was by nature overdrawn, producing false sentimental excitements calculated to counterfeit "that hallowed ecstasy which the faith of the gospel can alone afford." Even the *Recorder*'s editors had to acknowledge the power of such arguments. As one of Nathaniel Willis's coadjutors, Calvin Stowe, Harriet Beecher's future husband, reminded the newspaper's patrons in 1830, "the Christian, by his necessary connection with physical objects is always exposed to the danger of deadening the vividness of his faith in things unseen, of losing his spiritual mindedness (as it is most appropriately termed by the early Puritan writers), and of coming under the influence of worldly opinions and feelings."[21]

Nonetheless, Stowe and like-minded evangelical activists shrank from wholesale condemnation of belles lettres. In the face of disestablishment and rationalist defections, revivals promised to retrieve some lost souls, but their tendency to degenerate into unrestrained emotionalism threatened to alienate many others, especially those raised to appreciate the finer passions. Such individuals would require an altogether more measured appeal calibrated to their cultural expectations. "Will you not learn to distinguish between the means and the ends?" one "Philagathos" asked naysayers of orthodox fiction in 1826. "In the beautiful poetical fictions which have appeared in our religious newspapers within one or two years, is there nothing to be approved or admired, but everything to be condemned?" To such minds, it was merely a matter of using instruments adapted to the modern world.[22]

In defending "poetical fictions," the *Recorder* joined a swelling chorus of observers who, like the Romantic nature poet William Cullen Bryant, were arguing in the mid-1820s that "by leading the mind to dwell upon *Scriptural figures* more intently" poetic treatment of biblical personages would "naturally deepen and confirm" the power of religion. And it is surely not mere coincidence that the very poet who occasioned Bryant's observation served as a significant model for Willis's style. While he was a student of President Dwight's at Yale, James Hillhouse had delivered a celebrated commencement oration on "The Utility of the Imagination," in which he argued that the powers of this faculty helped the mind to conceive the sublime idea of God and it was thus crucial for realizing what the Bible recommends: "fervency in piety." Though he ultimately established himself in New York City as a somewhat dandified hardware merchant, Hillhouse nonetheless rose to his own exhortations: his picturesque, biblically inspired blank-verse Phi Beta Kappa oration published as *The Judgment* (1821) was followed in due time by *Hadad* (1825), a well-received dramatic poem that revolved around Absalom's rebellion against David. This last effort had particular impact on the budding muse of the young Willis. Years later he recalled how *Hadad*'s "bright, clear, harmonious language" was to him the "opening of a new heaven of imagination." More than this, Hillhouse himself seemed to the college-age Willis (who knew him slightly) a poet "whose mind was well imagined in his person"—elegant and dignified, with a "sweet voice" and a pleasing taste in dress. Judging by the blank-verse experiments in the *Recorder*, this recall did not lie: the impress of Hillhouse's example is readily apparent in both the florid style and biblical subject matter of Willis's "Scriptural Sketches." So, too, was Hillhouse's elegant bearing to resonate in Willis's personal outlook, a matter which shall be considered in greater depth later in this text. For now it is sufficient to link Yale's poetic aspirant and his appreciative fans to the quickening impulse among evangelicals and liberal Christians alike to revel in pious feelings stirred by imaginative evocations of God and the religious in nature, an inclination for which Willis's highly wrought "Scriptural Sketches" were both a significant aesthetic expression and an influential catalyst.[23]

For many observers all this was well and good. But a glance at the spell cast by another of Willis's early poetic exemplars—Great Britain's William Wordsworth—will serve to suggest toward what more dodgy company such aesthetic innovation might lead an ambitious young man of fine sensibility. Long spurned by American critical authorities and common readers as a crypto-pantheist and "bib-cloth sentimentalist," and known stateside primarily by reprints of the *Lyrical Ballads* (1802), this great Romantic poet was only just beginning to receive a measure of his due in America during Willis's teenage years. The Boston publication of Wordsworth's four-volume *Poetical Works* in 1824, for instance, moved the weighty Unitarian *North American Review* to bemoan the poet's mysticism, but also to regret the prevailing neglect of the "man who has done more than any one living to restore to poetry the language of feeling." Similar sentiments echoed in the young Waldo Emerson's comment that "I should not worry myself with abusing Mr. Wordsworth, not even for his severe egotism, . . . but that he has occasionally written lines which I think truly noble." In Willis's case, reading Wordsworth and other English Romantics in the Brothers Society's Library at Yale seems to have confirmed his budding appreciation for religion's fundamental aesthetic cast—an insight that, not incidentally, licensed poets, as much as ministers of the gospel, to amplify and distill the essence of God's nature. Like Richard Henry Dana Sr., a onetime *North American Review* contributor, author of *The Idle Man*, and perhaps Boston's most discerning early admirer of Wordsworth's poetics, young Willis would ultimately come to believe that "here the love of beauty is made religion; and what we had falsely esteemed the indulgence of idle imaginations, is found to have higher and more serious purposes, than the staid affairs of life. . . . In the luxury of this higher existence, we find a moral strength, and from the riot of imagination comes our holiest calm." Plagued by melancholy following his wife's death, Dana—Trinitarian Congregationalists would be happy to learn—eventually recoiled from this High Romanticism into the comparative certainties of orthodox faith; he was one of the most conspicuous old-family liberal Christian converts of the season of revivals inaugurated in 1826 by the indefatigable evangelical warrior Lyman Beecher. To the delight of some and to the dismay of others, N. P. Willis was destined to realize *his* Wordsworthian inheritance in a radically different fashion.[24]

Boy Wonder of the Bagatelle

Throughout his college days, Willis's reputation as a sincere and pious "Scriptural Poet" grew steadily. Only "Misanthropic Hours" seems to have muddied this progress, leading otherwise appreciative fans such as the young Quaker poet John Greenleaf Whittier to lament that

> Thy lyre
> Which could so feelingly portray

> The anguish of the royal sire,
> And conquering Jepthah's deep dismay— . . .
> So soon would leave its lofty tone— . . .
> And voice of charity disown.

Though Whittier could hardly have known it, this regrettable declension was only the tip of the iceberg. At Yale, the "mazes of pleasure and folly" were already tempting Deacon Willis's son from the sterling public character he projected as "Roy." In time, vocational considerations would also complicate matters—but only after Willis's white-hot revival faith had cooled precipitously, leaving him once again spiritually despondent and increasingly impatient with what he would later call the "bare and unqualified denunciations" of the New England clergy. Instead, as we have already glimpsed, the young collegian warmed perceptively to new aesthetic pursuits. This tendency served to open new doors for Willis, even as it complicated his situation, both at home and in the world of print. Such were the rewards and burdens of a life coming to be lived in the public eye.[25]

These complications surfaced soon enough in family correspondence. As early as his freshman year in New Haven, for instance, a homesick Nat was informing his father of a social recoil that smacked for all the world of backsliding. "I find but few among the students whom I should choose as companions," the son admitted sadly; most of his fellows he condemned as "profane and dissipated" boys whose "highest ambition seems to be to show off as a high fellow, and see who can overreach the government and laugh at its offices." But he also shrank from those whom Deacon Willis probably saw as his son's natural constituency. "The pious students in my class are mostly *men*," the freshman complained peevishly, "without any refinement either of manners or feeling—fresh from the country,—whose piety renders them respectable, and who without it would be but boors." Boston-bred Nat Willis could not abide such country cousins. Instead, he claimed to entertain the society of only those "few students who have both piety and refinement" and some, he confessed daringly, "who, though not professors of religion, respect it, and who are moral in their outward conduct, whatever be the state of their hearts."[26]

Such talk was already to sidle toward Unitarianism. Though the Willises may have drawn solace from news of their boy's membership in Yale's temperance and Bible societies, they soon heard further evidence of his spiritual woes. Writing in the wake of one of the college's periodic revivals, for instance, he lamented to an anxious father that doubts now made him "very much alive to the frequent fallacy of the hopes which are experienced in revivals." My "feelings are most peculiar and most trying," the young man admitted ruefully only a year after his heady conversion. "I am under one ceaseless and enduring conviction of sin, one wearing anxiety about my soul, without making any visible progress"—hard news, certainly, for a family that prided itself on devotion to God and godly ways. As if this situation was not bad enough, signs of what Nathaniel had once called a "hatred of God" again appeared in his son's correspondence. "I know what you will write about it," Nat closed his letter testily. "I could anticipate every word you can say upon the point. But so it is, and I have done with *all* discussion of it."[27]

In light of such disavowals, it is tempting to see the "Scriptural Sketches" as young Willis's perhaps unwitting attempt to reconcile his own budding aesthetic and religious sensibilities with the expectations of his family. Of course, ascribing psychological motives is always a dicey business, perhaps never amounting to more than informed speculation. Yet it does seem likely that poetry—especially that composed on biblical themes—served a crucial function for N. P. in mediating his parents' presumable dismay at the turn of events, even as it also provided a covert means to voice the anxieties incumbent on his familial position. For all their flirtation with refined religious sensibilities, antebellum New England's Trinitarian Congregationalists explored the world of nature's beauty on a short leash. And it is probably a sign of the psychological chafing that often ensued that several of the boy's early Scriptural prize poems (viz, "The Sacrifice of Abraham" and "Jepthah's Daughter") treated the plight of beautiful, nature-loving children destined for sacrifice by their fathers to satisfy the dictates of an inscrutable God. By the young man's own admission, verse also served to soothe his occasional slides into melancholy and homesickness, for as he told his father, when *"all"* are "out of the way, and I am in need of something to brighten my feelings, I can find in the flow of fancy a forgetfulness of the darker side. I have written a great deal in this way since my college life commenced, and my writing will *always* depend on the thermometer of my feelings."[28]

One hint at where this mercurial temperament was taking Willis appears in a college-era letter to his book-loving sister Julia, recounting an episode later reworked into a well-known magazine tale entitled "The Lunatic's Skate." Lured abroad by a summer moon following a Friday evening prayer meeting, the young poet appears to have experienced, on this night at least, a preternatural Romantic epiphany worthy of "Young Werther" himself—or so he cast it to his favorite sister. "I really think we had better lay it down as a rule," he confided to her conspiratorially, "never to go to sleep while the moon is shining. In fact, Julia, I suspect (for I find no one who sympathizes with me in this feeling) that I am something of a lunatic,— affected by the rays of that beautiful planet with a kind of happiness which is the result of a heated imagination, and which is not felt by the generality of the common-sense people of the world." With the mood of enchantment set, so it went: a midnight stroll along a windless bay of "liquid silver," followed by a naked swim in the "cool, refreshing waters, with sensations which must be felt to be understood." Setting aside, for the moment, the obvious erotic overtones of this account, we are left with an incident highly evocative of the kind of aesthetic and moral migration undertaken by so many young Americans in Willis's day: conventional religious impulses and moral verities overcome by a Romantically inspired poetry of feelings steeped in an imaginative appreciation of nature's beauty.[29]

Yet more than nature lured Willis from his appointed course: schoolboy roughhouse and worldly fashion drew him on as well. In those days, Yale boasted a faculty of five professors, seconded by eight poorly paid tutors. Generally future ministerial candidates, these young men performed the unenviable task of both drilling and policing what one tutor called their "lawless" students. And there *was* much need for discipline. When not pondering Livy or playing football on the green, the school's 350 predominantly teenage students indulged in all manner of adolescent hijinks: "hissing" and "scraping" the tutors, "smoking" and "squirting" freshmen, and window-breaking, on up to participating in full-scale student revolts such as the so-called Conic Sections Rebellion, for which most members of the sophomore class (Willis included) were temporarily suspended. (One wonders precisely which of these outbreaks led to one tutor's grim comment that "I have learned a good deal of human nature and human depravity, lately, and hope to improve by the lesson.") But for Willis it was not all beer and brawling. Given his literary tastes and social ambition, he was also careful to patronize New Haven's small-but-select fashionable circles, which revolved around the likes of Mrs. De Forest, the rich and elegant widow of the U.S. consul to Argentina, and Mrs. Apthorp, who ran a famous female seminary in town. It was here, on Sabbath evening calls and at fashionable parties, that young Nat first apprenticed himself to the arts of mixed society—refined small talk, flattery, easy deportment, and elegant dress—that would later redound to both his personal and professional advantage.[30]

The attentions of well-heeled college chums and their families only furthered this rarefied social education. In his days at Yale, young Willis encountered boys of various backgrounds: rustics such as the future Congregational publicist and re-former Horace Bushnell; backcountry "aristos" such as his close friend and longtime correspondent George James Pumpelly, the son of an Upper Susquehanna Valley landowner (and later the model for Willis's "Job Clark" and "Bosh Blivens"); Southern planters' sons given to brawling and duels; and, perhaps most important for Willis's future, self-confident scions of the early republic's mercantile and professional elite. It was young men from this last group who introduced him to the social opportunities of a glittering world far removed from his father's strict evangelical set. Consider one winter vacation spent among the haut ton of New York City. Here the budding poet arrived, courtesy of a schoolfriend's family, to a "splendid levee" hosted by the city's outgoing mayor, received an invitation to dine on New Year's Day with the parents of an admiring belle, and spent the following evening ensconced at a "genuine *soirée*" given at the "great Dr. [David] Hosack's," where, in addition to marveling at the surrounding luxury, Willis met "all the literary characters of the day . . . [Fitz-Greene] Halleck, the poet (a 'most glorious fellow'), among them." Everything glittered before admiring eyes. "You could not lay your hand on the wall for costly paintings," the wonder-struck undergraduate gushed appreciatively to his family back home, "and the furniture exceeds everything I have seen." The next day, there were New Year's calls to be made up and down the streets, then a glorious dinner at a posh house on St. John's Park. "They live in the French style," Willis enthused of his hosts, "and the last course was sugar-plums!"[31]

This eye-opening progress occurred in the winter of Willis's senior year at Yale; the following summer, before commencement, he embarked on what amounted to America's grand tour, traveling for six weeks across New York State along the new Erie Canal to Niagara, then up into Canada before returning home. New experiences and social opportunities abounded along the way. On this trip, Willis reacquainted himself with the great summer resort at Saratoga, whose exclusive society was to figure conspicuously in his early prose writings. Along the way at Albany, he also probably first met John Bleecker Van Schaick, in many ways his beau ideal of a gentleman. A bachelor lawyer with a literary bent, Van Schaick had visited London and Paris, and he wore his travels well. Willis later remembered his elegant and obliging friend as "unequalled" in "wit and brilliancy of conversation . . . the best balanced and most highly gifted character we have ever intimately known." Even more profoundly than did James Hillhouse, Van Schaick served Willis as an alluring model of deportment and sensibility worlds away from strict orthodox divinity. So, too, did Willis's first "man-friend" (as he later called him) provide a sounding board for his admirer's dreams; much of our knowledge of Willis's mind and activities at this time comes from letters addressed to Van Schaick and to the young man's "best and most valued" college friend, George Pumpelly.[32]

Among the most important lessons Willis learned in these days was that a poetic reputation and style had a way of opening doors. In New York City, for instance, though only a young man of twenty years, Willis was, according to his own lights, "much flattered . . . by the attentions of literary men and women; the latter more particularly," he noted appreciatively in a letter home, "who seem to consider it quite the thing to find a poet who was not a bear, and who would stoop so much from the *excelsa* of his profession as to dress fashionably and pay compliments like a lawyer." More than this, celebrity's brand of erotic dreamwork was apparently already beginning to perform its beguiling magic. "La, how I should love to see Mr. Willis!" the Yale poet reported hearing a "very *blue* young lady" quoted. "I am sure I should fall in love with a man who writes such sweet poetry." This was probably neither the first instance, nor would it be the last, in which fans would confound literary character with dreams of its author's charms. Nor was this a lesson in the erotics of representation whose value—either cultural or commercial—Willis would soon forget.[33]

As the pride of Park Street drifted from his evangelical moorings, he was thus already beginning to realize some of celebrity's most valuable perquisites—its social and amorous rewards foremost among them. Soon, he was to learn how a poetic reputation might also solve, at least temporarily, an impending vocational crisis like that faced by many young men of his day. However gratifying the honor voted Willis by his senior classmates of delivering their class day poem, it presumably did little to settle the question that must have nagged at his conscience: how to wrest a serviceable income from a talent for verse and a studied disinterest in other avenues of advancement. In the mid-1820s, vocational prospects for poetic souls remained inauspicious; Philip Freneau's famous lament that America's tinkers were more solvent that its versifiers (because a "tinker has something that people will buy") still generally held true. To complicate matters, counting on paternal largesse, as did some of Willis's well-heeled classmates, was out of the question—Yale's tuition had been strain enough on his father's modest income. So it must have been with some relief that Willis received news soon after taking his degree that Samuel Goodrich, the publisher, wished to bring out a volume of his poetry and engage his services as editor of a new kind of periodical.

This overture was a godsend. If nothing else, the new graduate could now see hope of retiring the debts he had been piling up in past months. More important, Goodrich's offer opened the door to a new world of commercial potential entailed in the growing demand for print, especially among American women, a class of readers whose tastes were coming increasingly to dictate publishing policy. Goodrich himself was instrumental in effecting this transformation. At age eighteen, this sixth son of a Connecticut minister had been apprenticed to the dry goods trade before moving to Boston and establishing himself in what would prove to be a long, prosperous, and influential publishing career. Willis's *Sketches* (1827) was one of Goodrich's first ventures, but certainly not his last. Writing as "Peter Parley," for example, the onetime dry goods merchant quickly became a household name as the author of a new brand of didactic, sentimental children's literature. Equally important, along with several other American publishers, he helped pioneer a thriving trade in so-called annuals, as the new holiday gift-books of the period were commonly known. Designed after financially successful British and German models, these richly appointed anthologies of prose, poetry, and engravings quickly assumed a commanding position in the growing literary market by stealing alike, as one observer put it, "into the palace and the cottage, the library, the parlor, and the boudoir."[34]

Like the refined poetry generally featured therein, the gift-books that Goodrich set his new apprentice to editing were designed to appeal to self-consciously refined souls eager to buy into a rarefied atmosphere of elevated sentiment and feeling. As presents destined for a daughter's boudoir or a parlor's center table, these costly but usually diminutive volumes were expected to carry a surplus of emotion, the token of a loving regard. No characteristic was more essential to this effect than the books' sumptuous physical presentation. A tribute to advances in the printer's art, the elaborate, gilt-embossed bindings of the annuals were often matched within by high-quality steel engravings, gold-edged pages, clear typography, and bleach-white paper. Gift-books were thus meant to be seen and handled, as well as read. As if to underscore this physicality, editors occasionally commissioned authors to accompany their elegant engravings with verse-on-demand; Willis himself wrote several such poems to this sort of enforced inspiration.[35]

Though high-brow critics blanched at the result, branding such books sentimental trash, fans of the annuals applauded nonetheless: by the 1830s, gift-books had assumed the status of requisite accessories to gentility. As such, they heralded the growing commercialization of sentiment that underwrote the dynamic new literary culture of the period. In this respect, the vast flotilla of annuals that issued from publishing houses in the antebellum years traded most profitably on the notion that tokens of friendship and remembrance were best purchased ready-made. Educated chiefly by the self-conscious literary language of belles lettres to regard untutored expression as a sign of vulgarity and a refined tenor as evidence of elevated sensibilities, the purchasers of volumes with names like *The Keepsake, The Token, The Souvenir,* and *Remember Me* banked on the prospect that gift-book recipients welcomed luxurious presentation and a kind of greeting-card eloquence as the fittest memento of longing and affection. Much to publishers' delight and profit, the annuals proved to be a gift that kept on giving, like the era's social visits, initiating recurrent rituals of mutual obligation that reflected and reinforced the putative gentility of both giver and receiver. With the presentation of an annual, friends enjoined friends to recall old times and revisit old feelings, associating the pages of beauty with the beauty of sentimental friendship. Thus, aesthetic sensibilities, class aspirations, and depth of feeling came to be bound up in the luxurious keepsake volumes exchanged among genteel friends. By the mid-1840s, American publishers alone were issuing almost sixty gift-books yearly on a tide of sentimental longing.

For writers like Willis, who faced the prospect of fashioning a vocation from a literary bent, the fact that friendship and nostalgia were becoming big business proved a welcome development. Apart from the annual prizes now offered by various literary journals, financial recompense for prose and poetry remained uncertain and usually inconsequential. Gift-books were among the first periodicals to pay contributors and editors with any regularity. As a result, they soon became favored retail outlets for Americans seeking to vend literary wares; Nathaniel Hawthorne, for one, got his start supplying the annuals. And if the bargain entailed sometimes meant tailoring work to suit gift-book expectations, so be it; most would-be authors jumped at the chance to profit as well as publish, though some clearly blanched at the genre's commercial impositions.

This was not so of Willis, who apparently was put off more by impositions upon his time than by restraints upon his muse. This blithe confidence was clear from the facility with which he switched genres. The Yale graduate's first undertaking for Goodrich was *The Legendary*, projected to be a biannual collection of prose and poetry dedicated to illustrating American scenery, manners, and history. Shortly thereafter, Willis also agreed to edit *The Token*, his employer's flagship annual. In each case, the novice editor mixed conventional gift-book fare (prose, lyric poetry, and engravings) with his own flair for the dramatic. Particularly noteworthy in this regard was the addition of short fiction to his repertoire. This is a genre that Willis would later work up into a signature mode. Here, however, the mildly humorous and extravagant prose stylings of his commercial maturity were still relatively restrained and focused chiefly on his limited social experience among the belles and beaux at Saratoga or traveling along the Erie Canal. To sketches such as "Leaves from a Colleger's Album" (inspired by his vacation encounters), Willis also added several quasi-mystical Wordsworthian meditations on nature's redemptive power, all of which served to flesh out a public character at once more worldly and more Romantically contemplative than "Roy's" evangelical admirers might have expected.[36]

Still, the most emphatic punctuation to Willis's social evolution in these postcollege days was his coincident assumption of yet another poetic alter ego. Money, it seems, was again at the root of matters, for welcome though it was, Goodrich's salary fell short of satisfying the recent graduate's financial wants. To satisfy his creditors Willis therefore signed on, alongside several other "callow bards," with the Democratic polemicist Nathaniel Greene to furnish weekly doggerel for the *Statesman* over the signature "Cassius." Greene's primary objective in this enterprise was to show up a rival political newspaper. For this purpose, he was willing to pay what others would not: five dollars a verse, with the sole stipulation, as his hired-poet later remembered, that the "strain should be humorous and the topics local and modern." This request Willis was happy to fulfill; over the next several years, "Cassius's" throw-away rhymes ("not one of them takes me over fifteen minutes," he admitted to George Pumpelly) satirized local personalities and celebrated New England ladies with equal facility. While he continued to supply the literary wants of refined ladies, the heretofore pious poet was thus also drifting toward the sort of Grub Street shenanigans that bordered on disrepute. The new pseudonym may then have been in part to deflect potential offense; certainly, Willis was candid enough to inform Pumpelly that he had adopted "Cassius" as cover, "so that if my muse does not hire out well nobody will know it."[37]

Happily for Willis, Cassius was a hit, particularly with the new set of literary sophisticates he had taken to patronizing back in Boston. At their most solid, these included Willis's friends in the artistic circle gathered around Washington Allston, America's great biblical painter, a friend to Samuel Taylor Coleridge, and, by most accounts, an urbane and congenial, if somewhat retiring, companion. Like Van Schaick and Hillhouse, the cigar-smoking Allston, then at the height of his social and cultural influence if not his artistic or commercial powers, offered Willis a model of gentlemanly deportment that blended a sophisticated, slightly bohemian elegance with considerable cultural attainment. So, too, did Allston's associates—the onetime backwoodsman, now celebrated Boston portrait painter Chester Harding, for instance—comport with the cosmopolitan personal style the young poet was rapidly assuming. This self-conscious sophistication took many forms, but it was realized perhaps most characteristically in a monthly supper club that brought Willis together with rising men such as the future educational reformer Horace Mann, the poet Rufus Dawes, Charles Sumner, and even the famous politician Daniel Webster, in addition to Willis's boon companion Harding. Here, urbanity found its mates in the gentlemanly conviviality of good food, beguiling conversation, and a round of drinks.

Not all of Willis's new acquaintances and admirers radiated such respectability. Doubtless to Nathaniel Willis's dismay, his eldest son spent a good deal of time directly after college indulging in a dizzying succession of social amusements: visiting, dancing, and attending Boston's forbidden theaters. Much of this activity took place among well-heeled companions of Willis's own age; thus his letters reveal him, by turns, practicing the "Spanish Dance" at "Blake's," running his horse along the shoreline to the seaside resort at Nahant, and flirting with this week's belle. Nathaniel Greene's "callow bard" also moved among a slightly older crowd, becoming, for instance, quite a favorite with the self-styled queen of Boston's fashionable Unitarian elite, the widowed and worldly Mrs. Harrison Gray Otis. Her favor—and the social éclat it implied—registered how far Willis had come from his strict evangelical roots. As he himself would write, "The pale of Unitarianism is the limit of gentility."[38]

As they had in orthodox circles, the young man's poetic talents shone in such gay company, though the stakes had changed since "Roy's" initial appearance in the *Boston Recorder*. Now an elegant address was less likely to elicit devout reflection than the potential for an advantageous social introduction or diverting coquetry. Willis, who certainly knew how to work a good thing, was keenly aware of this situation. Even at college he had professed to a classmate, only half jokingly, that he could "do anything with *any body who respects me.*" He attributed this manipulative facility to a sympathetic magic, one destined to sustain him throughout his career: "*words*—my dear fellow—the alchemy of combination is the great secret—and that secret I understand and can pour it in a woman's ear till she thinks my pug nose Hyperion's, and my butcher face a model for an Apollo." And pour he did, till many a young lady's ear ached with delight. Curly-headed, naturally handsome, and dressed to the nines, Willis cut a striking figure in Boston's Unitarian-dominated high society, and if too flashy by a yard for some people, he charmed many all the same. In this respect, the poetry of deportment and the poetry of print apparently contributed equal measure. It was, for instance, probably not merely idle boasting when Willis reported to Van Schaick of having been buttonholed at a fancy ball by a flirt with an "unaccountable 'taking' for our friend Cassius." To Boston's boy wonder of the bagatelle, such dalliance waxed routine.[39]

The rewards of these free-and-easy pursuits were many: social advancement, flattering attentions, diverting amusement, and, increasingly as time went on, sexual experience. We know of this situation because town gossip and Willis's surviving letters to male friends teem with testimony regarding the erotic swath he was apparently cutting through Boston. For all Willis's adolescent hand-wringing, there is little evidence to suggest that he ever shrank from sex. Instead, he seems to have rushed to embrace its pleasures with a wanton exuberance that often belied better judgment and that in all likelihood reflected a voracious desire for affirmation. At the age of nineteen, for instance, the college junior was boasting to his pal George Pumpelly that he stood in danger of being seduced by a neighbor's nursery maid who had seen him walking naked in his room as he tried to cool himself on a sultry night. She had, he reported with salty glee, been reading the famous pornographic volume *Fanny Hill* (as John Cleland's *Memoirs of a Lady of Pleasure* was commonly known), and though the pictures were beautiful, the girl had had "no one to practice with her." "Phew! She is young and handsome," Willis exclaimed, "and, I presume, carried away with that rascally book . . . and it is hardly to be surprised that with such objects of contemplation before her, to wit, my naked person, and the corresponding pictures and inculcations of Fanny Hill, she should have done otherwise."[40]

Whether anything came of this particular opportunity is impossible to say. Young men have long liked to brag of sexual conquest, often to lay claim to status as "men of the world." And if Boston's resident sentimental moralists-in-training were likely to bristle at bawdy tales of wild-oat sowing (as did Willis's supper club acquaintance Horace Mann apparently later on), there certainly *were* Corinthian elements within Willis's circle who could be expected to warm to the telling. Perhaps a desire to curry their favor while indulging an exhibitionist's egoism begins to explain the tendency in Willis's letters for his sexual adventures to assume the air of a French farce. Thus, a delicious affair with the newly seduced mistress of "young Gen'l Winthrop" is said to fizzle only when the poor girl's fear that the "Gen'l" would shoot the two conspirators d'amour overcame her thrill in juggling lovers, while, on another occasion, an overzealous town watchman who evidently caught Boston's young Lothario and that particular evening's belle trying to sneak back into her house is flogged until he reluctantly agrees to let the lovers go. So it went until, by his own count, Willis seemingly stood in danger of running out of women to pursue. Evidently, more transpired in the stereotypically prim and proper city of Beecher and Channing than common account would have us believe.[41]

But then so was more going on in Willis's mind and heart than we might be tempted to conclude from this casual sexual athleticism. For one, given the right outlet, the surplus of his emotions was fully capable of overflowing in an extravagant flood of tender feelings, as it did when, not long after leaving college, Willis confided to Pumpelly, after much "speculation" on the "singular nature" of their attachment, that he loved him with an almost sisterly affection. Other men, Willis here claimed (in a statement that suggests much about both his predilection for womanly society and his tendency to invest close friends with immoderate regard), invariably "disgust[ed]" him after a time, and he eventually wearied of their company, but not so with "Pump." Whether it was his compatriot's "freedom from vice" or "personal beauty" that contributed to this peculiar "dash of romance" he felt for this "manliest" of his acquaintances, Willis could not say for certain. Still, he "half believe[d]" he could pass his life at his friend's side—"and if *mio idalo* could be forgotten, love [him] like a woman."[42]

For all this letter's homoerotic overtones, it is probably wise, in the absence of corroborating evidence, to resist the urge to pronounce it proof of Willis's closeted gay identity, and not only because such extravagant declarations of affection between men (and between women) were the lingua franca of antebellum sentimental culture. There is also the matter of *mio idalo*. The sister or cousin of a college friend, this particular "Miss Woolsey" figured in the poet's overwrought imagination and letters as a "noble" woman of unsurpassed charm. (It was she who, in September 1827, apparently inspired the sonnet "I have been gazing on thee, Genevieve," meant to accompany a portrait by Francis Alexander, a poem that Willis immodestly called the "most perfect piece of composition I ever wrote.") Sadly, however, it seems that neither Miss Woolsey nor her father was especially impressed with the ardent suitor's prospects and middling background, and so Willis was put off, ostensibly until having attained a manly station. This repulse only set the deacon's son to trying harder, yet not without forcing him to confront some of the essential tensions of his precarious foothold in society.[43]

Though all confidence and charm on the surface, Willis appears to have churned emotionally with the contrary demands of his station, the prompting of his heart, and the stirrings of ambition. We know of this conflicted condition chiefly through a revealing letter written several months after his return from Yale to Boston. Charged by Pumpelly with having "changed" in the months since leaving New Haven, Willis herein denied the imputation, except insofar as his ambition had turned "loftier" and his determination to pursue it "firmer." If the prickliness of this response suggests a sore conscience, what followed was further evidence of emotional distress. "I was speaking of *ambition*," Willis then remarked seriously. "I have lately thought much of *this*. Don't think I overvalue myself—but listen. I am 21 years old. I feel within me the *power* to be a man, and a distinguish'd one, if I can have time + opportunity to unfold and cultivate it." So far, so good, but then came the disturbing paradox, one faced by many young men in antebellum America's volatile labor market, yet not so often with such acute distress. "I *love*, as you know," Miss Woolsey's overwrought admirer continued fretfully,

+ the price of purchase is, (I have reduced it to fact) the sacrifice of my fame + my powers forever. Shall I prove it to you? If I enter into business as an Editor, which is my only way of getting a living for a family, I must give up my whole energy to it, and ruin my style, + fritter away my mind in newspaper paragraphs. I must do this, or give up Miss Woolsey!—how, may God help me, for I am distracted between them. I *do* feel capable of working out a *name* + I do idolize—Heaven only knows how much + how sinfully, that noble creature!—I cannot give her up—and yet to relinquish my ambition will break me down, and make me a dog—unworthy of her, + unworthy of my own self, which I cannot bear. I have written nothing yet which I value a straw, but there is in my mind matter just waking into life which if I can once express, will make my name live after me. I want 4 or 5 years for a poem on an entirely new subject and plan, which I seldom think over without tears, + how can I relinquish it? It makes me miserable.[44]

No doubt this was an extravagant recital of woes, but one neither wholly unwarranted nor entirely self-serving. If nothing else, Willis's complaint underscores the fact that even as his prospects were looking up, certain difficulties—personal, vocational, and religious—loomed unresolved. So, too, did the consequences of those difficulties. In love, they soon proved devastating: after a time, Miss Woolsey snubbed her suitor for good, leaving him dismayed and emotionally numb. "Since my cut by Miss W. I have not known what affection was," Willis commented sadly to Pumpelly in the summer of 1829. "I fear it is dead with me." In its place stepped an apparently empty passion, judging by the merry-go-round sexual odyssey "Pump's" friend was driven to pursue. In the larger world of literary reputation, matters resolved themselves neither so swiftly nor so tragically. Yet the developments that Willis's personal and professional volition had helped conjure into being were steadily moving him toward a kind of reckoning.[45]

Reckonings and Accommodations

By the fall of 1828, together "Roy" and "Cassius" had been spreading N. P. Willis's fame throughout the parlors, ballrooms, and boudoirs of the young nation for over a year. But the task of reconciling such incongruous characters in the face of mettlesome parlor suppositions and newspaper speculation was proving more troublesome by the day. In this respect, Willis was learning what all celebrities of print must eventually acknowledge: the fact that, especially under the new conditions of modern American literary life, assuming an authorial persona was no guarantor of critical immunity. As the Boston poet would himself soon observe:

The truth is, that we know no such thing as an abstract impression of the works of any living author. The moment a man comes before the public in these days of universal curiosity, a thousand circumstances of his personal character and habits transpire. He is known and criticized in connection with his books, or even separately, and the reader sits down to his perusal with prejudices and partialities which affect very essentially the aspect and tone of his productions.

As if to demonstrate the truth of this axiom, after the New York *Enquirer* summarily unmasked the *Statesman*'s hired pen in the spring of 1828, several newspaper editors reprimanded Willis for advertising his romantic conquests, charges of dissipation that the poet's friends protested rather ineffectually. The poet himself complained peevishly of having "no liberty" while his name was public and resolved to change his signature to "Epicurus"—"to disguise, if possible," as he put it, "the nonsense of a five dollar inspiration."[46]

At home in Boston, "Roy's" orthodox brethren also began to fret. With Lyman Beecher's installation at the newly consecrated Hanover Street Church in the spring of 1826 and the settlement of Beecher's Yale-trained son (and Willis's onetime tutor) Edward at Park Street Church six months later, the city's long-smoldering doctrinal antagonisms had flared again. Lyman Beecher especially was nothing if not confrontational, and he meant, plainly enough, to reassert biblical purity in this town seemingly given over to soirees, dancing assemblies, and the theater. After a season of revivals swelled Calvinist ranks, Boston's wary liberal Christians (who in 1825 had, along with like-minded compatriots, finally come out and established their own American Unitarian Association) barred their women and children from attending orthodox prayer meetings and rejoined the polemic assault against what they saw as a crabbed and dangerous faith. Thus under attack and chastened to a reawakened sense of crisis, Boston's Trinitarian divines were not likely to ignore creeping apostasies in their midst. One sign that they did not ignore them was that disciplinary actions at Park Street soared to an all-time high during Edward Beecher's brief ministerial tenure, after which time the younger Beecher himself was ousted as too woolly a thinker for his hard-line parishioners. In this tense social and religious climate, it would have been surprising had young Willis's fashionable antics not also raised eyebrows and opposition.[47]

Eventually, such orthodox misgivings would drive him toward a confrontation with his father's faith. In the meantime, however, it still seemed possible for Nat to imagine a serviceable accommodation between the evangelical professions of his youth and the beguiling charms of worldly fashion. By his own lights, a rare spirit might hope to bridge these seemingly irreconcilable realms. Getting the rest of the world to believe it was the trick. In some respects, this task was destined to be a lifelong—and, in many ways, defining—burden of Willis's personal and professional career. Many times in the future his situation would require negotiating poles of expectation bound respectively by piety and worldliness. But the youth's unsettled prospects now made this situation seem particularly onerous. Unremitting spiritual interrogation and fame's easy blandishments had, from an early age, saddled Deacon Willis's eldest son with a hair-trigger sensitivity to admonishment, one that he did not soon outgrow. So, too, in the place of college indulgence did parental pressures to quash appetites for pleasure in favor of sober money-getting lead, not surprisingly, to what Willis would later call feelings of being "crowded." No document reveals this condition more plainly than "Unwritten Poetry," the young editor's chief contribution to *The Legendary*'s inaugural volume.[48]

Though professedly a meditation on religio-aesthetic consolation, "Unwritten Poetry" reads more like an anxious apologia, so much does the tale's protagonist, Paul Lorraine, echo his delineator's own uneasy social and psychological estate. This insight is no less compelling because the story's plot is banal. An uncommon soul much petted by worldly society though loath to engage in its money-getting, young

Lorraine idolizes the angelic Marion Graham but finds his devotion troubled by rumor, misguided prejudice, and his own peccadilloes. To his credit, Willis seems to have acknowledged at least some of his own shortcomings when portraying himself under fiction's cover. We are told, for instance, that Paul had "been caressed more than was good for his character" and had "dipped deeper into pleasure than his better angel whispered him was innocent." Repeatedly, too, a wayward "susceptibility" to feminine charms had beguiled him into passing fancies. Yet if the flesh is admittedly weak, Willis evidently wanted his readers to believe that the heart beats constant: in the dreamworld of fiction, at least, Paul's inner soul remains true to Marion's fine nature. Indeed, such inner nobility obtains generally: though Paul Lorraine is said to mingle with the world, he nonetheless keeps "the poetry of his feelings apart from their profanation." In this regard, his "worldly accomplishments" are said to be merely the "dress of the masquerader," and his dissipation but a half-life cloaking the "fine impulses of his boyhood."[49]

Here, as Willis saw it, was the crux of many misunderstandings. Paul is not like other men; he has what his author calls (following the lead of Wordsworth's "Tinturn Abbey") the poet's "peculiar gift of vision"—a "delicate perception" that Willis claimed to allow "one man to detect harmony, and know the forms of beauty better than another." This uncommon sensibility is both Lorraine's burden and salvation, as Willis surely believed it to have been his own. In his boyhood, it made Lorraine unaccountable to the mass of his fellows; during his adolescence, its outer manifestations were also sadly "misunderstood" and "misrepresented" as degrading dissipation. Nonetheless, in the end, it is precisely this special consolation of the poet that rescues Willis's alter ego from abject despair, for when Marion Graham's consumptive death threatens to crush his spirit, the sublime beauty of Trenton Falls ultimately reclaims him. After months of dejection, Paul weeps freely and painlessly in its shadow, redeemed by his love of beauty, the sign and source of his better nature.[50]

On one hand, "Unwritten Poetry" was clearly a sophomoric and self-absorbed plea for understanding, probably intended specifically for Miss Woolsey's eyes. It was also a measure of the hold Romantic religious and aesthetic sensibilities had assumed over its author's fertile imagination. True, at this awkward juncture in his life Wordsworth's overwrought disciple still shrank from an unequivocal embrace of the pantheistic implications of his Romantic avowals, at least in public. Even while daring in "Unwritten Poetry" to herald nature's prepotent moral sway, for example, he had backpedaled precipitously when this stance threatened to undercut his father's brand of religious faith. "My object," the younger Willis explained to his readers in a bizarre footnote that excepted religion ("the purest of all principles") from his general premise, "is to illustrate the effect of nature on rare and imaginative minds, and not to state a theory of any general bearing whatever." Yet, in confidence, orthodoxy's wayward youth was capable of voicing the most extravagant of fancies, even though they assumed a characteristically therapeutic form. "The cares of the world can*not* cloud the eye of him who keeps it open to the clear sky + the beautiful things in nature, wherever he can find them," Willis confessed to his friend Van Schaick in a moment of bracing reverie. "Growing old is a term for artisans

+ slaves—a material + base propensity—the *spirit* does *not* grow old—and a single look at its nature will tell you it gains glory as it advances."[51]

His college and postcollege reading had, in fact, transformed the Yale poet into quite the closet idealist, and it is startling indeed to see where Romantic cultural currents were leading him. "I wish to heaven you read German [which Willis apparently did not, though by this time he had read—and treasured—Pumpelly's gift of Goethe's *Memoirs* in translation], or knew their sublime philosophy," he descanted wistfully in the "gains glory" letter,

> the only one which is worthy of the dignity of immortal reasoning—They [*sic*] look at life as an ante-room to a magnificent temple—and do not waste their worship before they get to the altar. It is damn'd beautiful to think of men who consider the whole range of existence as passages to one great godlike nature, and do not look aside or loiter with their very wings folded behind for the wretched perishing ambitions of money-getting and sense.

Of course, such High Romantic sentiments were heresy when breathed among the brethren, and (as Ralph Waldo Emerson would soon demonstrate by the divinity school address) among mainstream Unitarians, for that matter. Yet Willis trusted Van Schaick as he did no other male companion but Pumpelly, and, having warmed to his subject, he was not to be restrained. "Oh my glorious friend," he continued on feverishly,

> I could tell you a sometime dream of mine that would make you stir in every pulse as if you were shaking off the chrysalis of a life—I *do* believe we are to be noble and more magnificent beings than we are—and by the Gods, when I suffer myself to dream of what it is—it makes me sick of myself + like Caesar, "weary of the world."

The dreamer himself recognized this outburst as a bit excessive: "You are laughing at this, *sans doute*," he concluded this stirring passage. "You may!—I do not often expose myself so—but when I do, I am perfectly in earnest, and I feel elevation enough to care little what is thought of it."[52]

Doubtless such reveries acted to sooth an anxious and self-involved soul. Still, mundane cares persisted in staking their claim to Willis's attention—as he well knew. "There is no man under Heaven who makes life more a matter of common sense than I," he assured Van Schaick, whom he was dosing with his fanciful visions, "I, who make my own bread + butter, + have at my heels, day after day, duns and deacons, the one trying to cure the repletion of my purse, the other the diarrhea of my morals." Characteristically, a habit of avowing mastery led the aspiring sophisticate to downplay his predicament, but he was less in charge than he might have supposed. Indeed, only weeks passed before the Park Street brethren began oiling the machinery of church discipline with an eye toward his correction. Then even Willis admitted that the circumstances made for "bloody bad business at home." But no matter, he commented airily. Having already petitioned his former tutor Edward Beecher for dismissal to St. Paul's Church (which "patronizes worldly amusements + only asks morality"), the young man hoped soon to be settled more comfortably in his religious professions; the harshest penalty on the horizon—

excommunication—seemed too fantastic an eventuality for serious concern. Time would belie this confidence, however. The crisis came on 29 April 1829, when the Park Street elders expelled their once-favored son from church fellowship, citing the twin sins of ducking communion and patronizing the theater.[53]

In the polarized social and religious climate of late 1820s New England, this kind of disciplinary action was serious business, aimed plainly to police the bounds of propriety and piety in a world overrun by blasphemy and heresy. Inspired by biblical injunction and a sense of moral decline, evangelical ministers sought time and again to bind their congregations to a rigorous code of Christian behavior; only by satisfying God's dictates, said church leaders, were His people fit to claim religion's earthly and otherworldly rewards. Thus chastened to their duty, God's people searched, in turn, both for the strength to live out their convictions and the words to express the progress of their faith. The rise of the popular religious press meant that this delicate negotiation proceeded more than ever through the offices of print, which now began to preempt the clergy's influence in local religious affairs.[54]

This situation is precisely why we ought to note "Roy's" abiding appeal among pious readers. The poet himself was long destined to remain a stranger to organized Christian worship, but for several years after his excommunication, he continued churning out his trademark "Scriptural Sketches" and related religious verse, much to the delight of a wide range of fans. Even many orthodox Congregationalists— including the editors of the *Boston Recorder*—refused to be put off by the transgressions of one who had so eloquently expressed their often-inchoate desires for a more aesthetically satisfying faith. As the *Recorder*'s editor Calvin Stowe argued, when introducing Willis's "The Leper," "The stories of the Bible all contain the soul of poetry; and he who has a heart to feel, and power of language to express, the simple emotions of nature's own children, can gather the richest harvest from the glens of Mount Lebanon and the plains of the Jordan." Though they might proscribe the man, many devout souls, it seems, could condemn neither the sentiment nor the style of Willis's poetical effusions without questioning the flowering of their own Romantic religious affections.[55]

As the popular success of Congregational reformer Horace Bushnell would soon demonstrate, this situation helped create a world in which poets increasingly served as the ministers of vernacular religion and ministers increasingly had to be poets. Such an outcome was a lucky one for Park Street's prodigal son; in the future, he would need the reservoir of goodwill generated in these early days to forgive him a host of trespasses. At this point, however, he was too absorbed in new aesthetic and commercial plans to give these matters much thought. It is to these concerns, and their cultural ramifications, that we now turn.

American Pelham

A judicious and limited voluptuousness is necessary to the cultivation of the mind, to the polishing of the manners, to the refining of
the sentiment, and to the development of the understanding.

> Willis's favorite quotation from William
> Godwin

Even as the process of excommunication proceeded apace, Park Street's errant son had been exploring the practicality of realizing his most fervent ambition: to experience Europe's romance firsthand. "You can't imagine what a mystery there is to me in every thing which I have not positively handled," the twenty-two-year-old N. P. Willis admitted late in September 1828. "It is all beautiful, and man as I am & ought to be, I cannot get over the delusion. I won't wish to, till I have been abroad."[1]

Setting aside the more speculative psychological inferences suggested by this positive need to "handle," we are left with at least one certainty: like many an ambitious American, Willis thought that Europe alone could cap his cultural education. After all, the Old World whispered of moss-covered antiquity and the atmosphere of genius—just the sort of romantic qualities workaday Boston conspired to quash. And so, in the midst of his dissipation, he clung to one dream as an article of faith: the future lay across the sea.

But fancy—as is often the case—stumbled on the problem of finance. "I don't know how I am to get the money in advance to travel with," the spendthrift poet moaned in a particularly low moment. "I can secure it afterwards, but $2000 is not found in the street." Worse still, such inauspicious prospects apparently could make him feel "like a poor miserable devil," despite the tonic of what he called his "naturally extravagant animal spirits." Not all was black, however. Samuel Goodrich himself had assured his protégé that literary talent would pay his way abroad. But months of humdrum editorial apprenticeship had brought the would-be traveler neither suitable offers nor financial independence, only the chance to indulge theatrical protestations of "dissatisf[action] and miser[y]." So, reluctantly, he began to convince himself that he must postpone his fondest ambition and become, as he told his father, "a man of grave reputation." In autumn 1828, with his "old gentleman's" blessing and material support—secured by a promise to renounce "all journeys, horses, and amusements"—Willis thus turned from gay society and Goodrich's annuals to prepare his very own literary journal, presumably consoled by the expectation that its success would do more than any other enterprise to buoy his traveling prospects.[2]

At this stage in his life, Willis plainly itched to hatch a scheme to make his romantic impulses pay, if only because out-and-out commercial success alone probably had the power to establish him as his own man. Yet while he was negotiating the expectations of his father's world, the son also clearly hoped to overtop them. This he aimed to do by demonstrating the viability of a fresh cultural style associated less with New England's traditional centers of power in the academic and clerical establishment than with the fashionable impulses of a dynamic female-oriented market for popular letters. Since the turn of the century, Boston's literary axis had been dominated by a close-knit circle of self-styled Federalist scholar-gentlemen—first, with the Anthology Society and its organ, the *Monthly Anthology and Boston Review* (1803–11); then, at the *North American Review* (established 1815). Together with the region's newer Unitarian theological reviews and women's magazines, these periodicals aimed to express, police, and propagate the dominant moral sentiments of the community. (The prospectus for Sarah Josepha Hale's *Ladies' Magazine*, for instance, promised her magazine would do nothing to weaken parental authority.) Willis did not share this intent. Now that Park Street's writing was on the wall, he became ever more enamored of playing out the stylistic and commercial potential of a variety of voluptuary pursuits that were at once lighthearted, aesthetically oriented, and self-consciously sophisticated. His success at conjuring this alternative to Boston's didactic tradition may be gauged by the speed with which his *American Monthly Magazine*'s medley of romantic verse, parlor fiction, and foppish affectation established its editor as New England's most conspicuous oracle of literary fashion, even as it also helped to transform him into a disturbing symbol of that fashion's excesses. Willis's debut as a "magazinist" thus rehearsed several themes destined to prove central to the coming culture of celebrity, from its preoccupation with style to its concern for safeguarding female sensibilities.[3]

Voluptuary Pursuits

From the moment the prospectus of what quickly became known as "Willis's Magazine" announced its editor's intention to emulate one of London's most successful magazines, Yankee readers were primed to expect a product beyond the ordinary. Familiar to New Englanders from the stateside reprints of Nathan Hale Sr. and compendiums such as the *Athenaeum, or Spirit of the English Magazines*, the "scientific and elegant *New Monthly*" (as one American reviewer called this popular periodical) eschewed the sometimes plodding seriousness of the heavyweight British reviews, models for such solid Federalist journals as New England's own *North American Review*. Instead, it banked on the appeal of an eclectic magazine format that played deliberately to a Romantic interest in the range and play of human character. It was, in this respect, no accident that William Hazlitt's now-famous "Table-talk" series appeared alongside the contemplative essays, spicy humor, and light fiction of the *New Monthly*. By following this periodical's plan, Willis thus aligned himself with some of the transatlantic literary currents that were most responsible for defining both metropolitan modernity and celebrity's modern incarnation.[4]

This course reflected more than a little bravado. Having excited expectations with his sacred poems and prompted misgivings with his parlor doggerel, Deacon Willis's son knew all too well that literary New England doubted his talent. Granted his poetic vogue, he was, after all, essentially green as an editor. He was also young and impecunious. Furthermore, no journal of the kind he proposed had yet to survive the American literary marketplace more than a year or two. All the same, Boston's would-be editorial phenomenon had been boasting around town of his surefire prospects. So it was particularly important for Willis that his *American Monthly* commence auspiciously.

No doubt he meant his lead article, "Unwritten Music" (another in the signature series of "Unwritten" meditations begun in *The Legendary*), to promote precisely that aim. Yet if this curious confection of Romantic religiosity, fashionable presumption, and Calvinistic dread was intended to signal Willis's best intentions, it did so in a remarkably conflicted fashion, one that managed to underscore both the incongruities and the scope of its author's ambitions. Beginning confidently enough, the new editor offered readers the Romantic Christian truism that nature teemed with beautiful "unwritten music" echoing God's love for His world. (For all intents and purposes, this religio-aesthetic creed was merely a restatement of what he had already said in "Unwritten Philosophy": that "there was in the varieties of natural beauty, a hidden meaning, and a delightful purpose of good; and, if I am not deceived, it is a new and beautiful evidence of the proportion and extent of God's benevolence.") A Highland custom of comforting the dying with the "perfect harmony of the voices of nature" then led the philosophical essayist to muse that even death was not dreary—though he would later equivocate on this point. For the moment, he was happy to conclude that, whatever the charms of nature's sonorities, God's most glorious instrument remained the human voice. It was at this point that the good intentions of "Unwritten Music" began to unravel.[5]

Human voices, it turned out, were not so transparent after all. Though Willis sought to identify an agreeable address with "noble qualities" (male voices of pleasing tone, he asserted, generally belonged to gentlemen), his own social experience led him to concede that sonority sometimes masked an adventurer's designs. This situation held true even for women: a lady's sweet voice was surely a "glorious gift" of power, though of a "childlike" innocence or "practiced witchery" he could not say. Perceptive readers could only wonder if God's sweet voice in nature might be susceptible to similar equivocation. Far from demonstrating that "unwritten music" rang in the world's essential goodness, Willis thus only confused the issue, under-cutting his ostensibly innocent assertion that "there is nothing like a sweet voice to win upon the confidence."[6]

Perhaps this confusion merely reflected literary ineptitude. More likely it regis-tered the conflicting tug of Romantic sensibilities, commercial expedience, and residual religious conscience. Prudence alone suggested that Willis recall his early pieties as a hedge against readers' defections. Yet the desire to adopt a more worldly posture loomed large indeed in "Unwritten Music," even if it revealed itself in fits and starts and in ways that were sometimes unintentionally comic. Consider this passage: no sooner had the ticking of a clock at a dying friend's bedside moved the essayist to drop to his knees in classic Calvinist style, guilty at playing the profligate with time, than church bells were rousing him with thoughts of the lyric poet Thomas Moore ("whose mere sense of beauty is making him religious"). Just as quickly, the city's tolling Sabbath bells reminded Park Street's heir that "the fear of God is brooding like a great shadow," except that the same chimes heard in the country inspired him to declare a "Sabbath in nature"—an entirely sunnier prop-osition. We can almost see Deacon Willis and the poet Wordsworth batting their boy's aesthetic and religious impulses between them.[7]

For his part, young Willis himself could hardly have been blind to the potential social and commercial costs entailed in letting either side win too easily in this shuttlecock exchange. Sectarian combat, it should be remembered, still raged in New England, and religious partisans were primed to pounce on the impolitic. So it was that, along with aggressively worldly essays plumbing the "Philosophy of a Cigar" and thinly veiled tales recounting the editor's adventures, the *American Monthly* also featured pocket biographies of some of Boston's celebrity divines. While such pious excursions—like the sacred poems à la Roy that still occasionally issued from Willis's pen—might be construed as sops to convention and certainly were at times moral poses (see, in this regard, Willis's "Hymn" for the Wareham Temperance Society, composed when his magazine was singing the praises of its editor's "long-necked Rudesheimer"), it is not necessary to convict the *American Monthly*'s editor of utter hypocrisy to fathom his chameleon stance. As many a Romantic Christian knew, the scale of nature's divine beauty ran from the sacred to the profane, and it was an article of faith for a voluptuary like Willis that the aesthete's discriminating ear might comprehend the whole.[8]

Nonetheless, it *was* the ephemeral charms of modern literary artistry that ulti-mately held sway at the *American Monthly*, especially after Willis introduced his outrageous dandy-editor persona in the magazine's fifth issue. At his most contem-plative, he could, in this guise, resemble nothing so much as an American "Elia": dreamy, digressive, and apt to invest trifles with great significance. This emphasis on the charms of idle fancy is not surprising, considering that Washington Allston's London friend Charles Lamb ("Elia's" creator) was a particular idol of the young editor, as Lamb was for a number of Romantically inclined New Englanders in these days. Yet, there were also echoes of the famous "Noctes Ambrosianae" in Willis's presentation. Written collectively by the Scottish Tories of *Blackwood's Ed-inburgh Magazine*, this boisterous literary roundtable featured "Christopher North," the "Ettrick Shepherd," the "Tickler," and sundry compatriots holding forth on all manner of things and people, from the notorious "Chaldee Manuscript" to the milk-and-water verse of the "Cockney Poets." Like many in the English reading world, Willis grew up on the "Noctes." At college he turned his own experience at a "forbidden oyster house" into a Yale version of the series, but he had evidently burned the whole when the hangover lifted. In his *American Monthly*, Willis now moved "Maga's" familiar banter to more elegant quarters, smoothed the rough edges (losing much of the original's earthy humor), and invited his readers to sip Johannisberg Riesling rather than quaff Newcastle Ale.[9]

If the "Noctes" was a compound of talk, Willis's "Editor's Table" was a compound of affectations. Chief among these was the dandy-editor himself. Month after month, Willis's self-absorbed editorial alter ego prattled on about Percy Bysshe Shelley's poems (then all but unfamiliar to Americans), the latest French novel, his own feelings (intensified by sickness), and his fictive cousins Sybil and Florence, the beneficiaries of choice tidbits from his readings. Subscribers also heard about the editor's studio garret, which reeked of small luxuries and conceits—the props of a rare connoisseur. His chair, for instance, reportedly came roundabout from Versailles, auctioned in a lot of cast-off furniture, while the drawers of his ancient mahogany desk (bought while its owner was a college freshman) overflowed with scrapbooks. Among the leather-bound editions of Robert Southey's "Thalaba" and Lamb's "Elia" lay, by turns, a japonica; a vase of rosemary-scented Hungary water; an ivory-handled olive fork kept to cool the editor's palms; and lolling nearby, a pair of pet spaniels, "Ugolino" and "L. E. L.," fed absentmindedly with sweetmeats and such. The whole was, in short, a scene to scandalize proper Bostonians—which was, of course, precisely Willis's point.[10]

A further desire to proclaim the distinctive quality of his taste probably also underwrote Willis's conspicuous affection for certain antique English authors— Thomas Browne, Jeremy Taylor, Richard Burton, to name a few. Recently rediscovered by the likes of *Blackwood's* and the *London Magazine*, these so-called Puritan or Pre-Restoration writers offered Britons and Americans alike a welcome antidote to a creeping dissatisfaction with arid neoclassic formalism. Searching for a more engaging voice, future "Young Americans" such as Evert Duyckinck and Cornelius Mathews would also come to champion the quaint expressiveness of their distant literary forebears. But Willis was unusually precocious in his eagerness to proclaim of the charms of the antique, perhaps because (reflecting his reading of "Elia") such a stance seemed ideally calculated to distinguish his outlook from the run-of-the-mill. "I love to select single thoughts from these old writers," the young literary antiquary confided to readers in one of his many "scrap-book" articles of such extracts. "There is a gem-like distinctiveness about them which relishes."[11]

If the elements of this literary bijouterie suggest that some intellectual discipline undergirded the young editor's ease, it was, nonetheless, one strikingly at odds with his country's most cherished myths. Whether gauged by his literary stance or actual lifestyle, Willis was certainly no self-restricting Ben Franklin ("a heartless old *slate and pencil*," the young man called him elsewhere) advocating moderation as a tonic for a shopkeeper's propriety. The *North American Review* and, more recently, Mrs. Hale's *Ladies' Magazine* had already staked out that territory. Instead, the *American Monthly's* editor pleased himself to observe (with the impudence of an Epicurean provocateur) that "the appetites must be managed or they lose their fine edge, and it is true of conversation and reading, as of eating and living luxuriously." Willis was also not above still further thumbing his nose at New England's moralists of desire, whose understanding of the art of living extended only to the cultivation of sentiments proper to Christian perfectionism. "I have an extravagant friend," he once whispered to his readers, "who, at certain seasons of the year, becomes economical for the sake of a new sensation. He says the contrast is quite exciting."[12]

Precisely what Willis hoped to accomplish by assuming this foppish (and perhaps somewhat self-parodic) posture is difficult to pinpoint. It seems likely that the spectacle drew at least some impetus from a lingering need for attention. Hannah Willis's nurturing of her firstborn son's sense of his own delicate sensibilities was clearly insufficient to satisfy his emotional needs. And winning a way into a more congenial social atmosphere than that of orthodox divinity had often meant, for Willis, posing beyond his station, and in ways that contemporaries were apt to think led him over the top. Sixty years hence, one Boston blueblood distinctly remembered how the upstart editor had once arrived so late to a commencement ceremony at Cambridge that his gig ended up closing out the governor's procession. This result did not seem to bother the elegantly attired young gentleman, who calmly picked up his "broad-brimmed Leghorn hat" and, with an air of "supreme nonchalance," tossed the reins of his horse to a waiting hostler before sauntering casually up the "broad aisle" of the old parish meetinghouse in the wake of the procession. "If he did not ascend the stage, and seat himself among the dignitaries," Willis's memorialist chuckled, "it must have been because there was no room."[13]

Such grandstanding was doubtless amusing enough to an exquisite on the make. In this particular case, however, there was also the mundane need to sell magazine subscriptions; presumably Willis believed that playacting the dandified confectioner of taste would help to drum up sales. In this respect, he found welcome corroboration in Lady Sydney Morgan's *Book of the Boudoir* (1827) and the literary style he described as the sort of "rambling, familiar gossip" ("the undress of the mind") that approached his beau ideal of magazine prose. The Irish-born Morgan pleased her American admirer most of all by seeming to dissolve the distance between reader and author into an uncommon intimacy—precisely what Willis himself aimed to do in his groundbreaking "Editor's Table." By here addressing readers tête-à-tête, he also strove to foster a sense of familiar community, asking only that his subscribers ante up for the pleasure of his company. In return, Willis promised—as he would throughout his literary career—to unmask convention and explore the esoteric. "We will let you into a thousand little secrets that can only be told in an under tone," the future celebrity journalist vowed saucily at one point in his prattling, "and tell you who pulls the wire to all the literary puppets, and everything that is interesting about those two great divisions of this wicked world—people and things."[14]

Early on, Willis thus recognized a central feature of the emerging culture of celebrity: that its traffic in style and secrets was also a trade in personality, a commercial enterprise dedicated to packaging inner experience and private relations for broad public consumption. Faced with a world whose progress seemed to be spiraling increasingly toward dispersion and atomization, antebellum Americans were inclined to freight this market for intimacy with mounting value, even as they worried about publicity's impact on the familiar relations of home and family. Willis apparently understood as well as anyone gossip's potential to play havoc with social and domestic peace. As if to anticipate exceptions, he was quick to caution would-be critics that a familiar style did not befit all: few "possess the art of graceful trifling," he remarked in reviewing Morgan, and they by temperament—not study. Yet even in this early stage of his career, Boston's go-ahead editor was not content to see the broader world excluded wholesale from the pleasures of such rare alchemy. "There are evils in the train of such writing, no doubt," he counseled readers in his best serious tone, "but they fall upon the writer only. Weaknesses are exposed, the dignity of authorship is invaded, the liberties which are allowed only in the intimate scenes described, are claimed by the world—but this interferes with nothing of which the reader is at liberty to be jealous." Editorial mediation thus seemed to promise the general mass of readers immunity from an eavesdropper's disrepute.[15]

By drawing criticism upon himself and like-minded writers, the young N. P. Willis plainly sought to absolve readers of complicity in his disclosure of intimate thoughts and conversations, encouraging them to justify their interest in "people and things" as harmless and free of sin. In doing so, he—like other early merchandisers of so-called private experience—inevitably walked a fine line between arousing interest and provoking scandal. If Willis the "magazinist" now mixed his messages, one moment extolling the poetry of religion, the next a pretty woman's charms—all the while whispering that beauty deceives—his readers were left to place their confidence in the quality of his sensibilities.

Lewd Natty

Some fans appeared to be eager to do just that. So it was that not long after launching the *American Monthly* in April 1829 that its editor could sigh with relief that his bragging seemed not to have been in vain: his magazine debut was causing no small "sensation." At least that is how a reviewer for the *Bower of Taste* characterized public response. She herself demurred from all the hoopla: "The whole appears to us, like an entertainment at a fashionable rout, made up of *trifles, jumbles,* poetic sugar plums, *frost work,* and *kisses.*" Still, by June subscriptions approached a respectable six or seven hundred, and promised to rise further. Deacon Willis was reportedly "thunderstruck" at this result; very few American magazines had so quickly approached such heights. While not yet the equal of an established purveyor of belles lettres like the *New York Mirror* (with its circulation of five thousand subscribers), the *American Monthly* was nonetheless making remarkable headway in New England's expanding market for popular letters. Its editor could thus be satisfied with his deferment of European travel.[16]

Precisely who comprised the *American Monthly*'s subscribers—and thus what class of readers hearkened most eagerly to Willis's message and style—is impossible to say, as no subscription lists remain. Still, we can get some inkling of their character and interests from the sort of contributor Willis attracted. They were not well-established figures of New England's Federalist literary elite, mature poets such as

William Sprague or the Reverend John Pierpont (though Willis knew both men), or even "Wild Man" John Neal, a popular and controversial contemporary from Portland whom Willis offended by snubbing his assistance. He did not aim low, however. A surviving letter shows that Willis hoped Richard Henry Dana Sr. would pen a critique of Coleridge, Wordsworth, and Shelley for his first issue, though nothing seems to have come of the request. Neither did the several members of the supper club who pledged their services (including Horace Mann, Daniel Webster, and Edward Everett) probably ever deliver their promised contributions. Instead, Willis drew mainly from up-and-coming writers, some of whom were destined to rank as the next generation's most important literary movers and shakers. Chief among these were a number of Everett's students at Harvard; several of Willis's literary-lawyer friends from Albany; the *Knickerbocker*'s future editor, Willis Gaylord Clark (who swiftly came to think Willis's magazine the "stalest thing that I ever saw"); and a half-dozen or so aspiring New England poets, including the "Sweet Singer of Hartford," Lydia Sigourney. Even young Edgar Allan Poe may have sent Willis a poem for publication, though his unsolicited contribution ("Fairy Land") seems to have been rudely rejected. As the *American Monthly* could pay little if anything for their articles, what united such contributors (apart from, in certain cases, personal friendship with the editor) was most likely a desire to appear in a periodical with what T. G. Appleton later called "the true magazine flavor."[17]

Given the remarkable proliferation of reading rooms and circulation libraries since the 1790s, the audience for such a "magazine" might be expected to hail from a variety of social circumstances and backgrounds, though subscribers would have been apt to share sufficient educational advantages and cosmopolitan tastes to appreciate the modern English format and style Willis adopted. Most likely, this meant young readers educated to at least a modicum of cultural literacy and social sophistication, such as those of the liberal Unitarian circle gathered around the teenage Margaret Fuller. She, at least, was flattered when a friend showed her fictionalized letters to "Lord Nat" (as she called Willis in her letters) and he pronounced them "capital." And though serious pietists were undoubtedly scandalized by offerings such as "Unwritten Music," preferring instead plain Puritan tradition, many of America's more romantic souls thought Willis's productions "monstrous fine." It is a sign of the scope and dynamism of antebellum literary culture that some of these fans came from as far away as Ohio and Kentucky. To suggest further the impact and reach of such enthusiasm, we need only note that when the New York *Tribune*'s earnest editor, Horace Greeley, later urged Willis to publish a volume of selections from his lifelong writings, he made a point of remarking, "I want such a one for my boy, so that, should I live to see him sixteen, I may try 'Unwritten Music' on him and see if it impresses him as it did me at about that age, when it appeared."[18]

Of course, there *were* those in the literary establishment (as noted) who worried that Willis was going too far in playing to this younger, increasingly feminine crowd. Even one of Samuel Goodrich's authors recognized the dangers in recent developments when he counseled Willis to write for "masculine intellect" instead of the circle of youth and fashion. As Samuel Kettell argued in his *Specimens of American Poetry* (1829), literary reputation depended on the opinions of "men of sense and education"; he who sought to "control public opinion" and thus "establish a lasting reputation" would have to address himself to such arbiters. "They will examine his merits and determine his character," this early New England anthologist advised Willis helpfully. Kettell did not see any "escape" from this trial of reputation, either:

> Character, good or bad, established on any other basis, passes away like leaves on a stream; but once settled in the minds of intelligent men, it is soon communicated to others, and diffused over the community. If unfavorable, it is as a millstone about the neck of the possessor; if favorable, it is an instrument by which the laudable ends of ambition, and the pure purposes of philanthropy may be easily secured.[19]

There was considerable insight in this analysis, particularly regarding the propensity of literary reputation and social leverage to boil down to an issue of character. Yet this trickle-down model was probably too hopeful for the dawning age of mass literature. Here, "intelligent men," arrayed as critics in the traditional neoclassical/ Federalist mode (viz, "the reviewer as executioner"), might still hope to sway public tastes in certain instances, yet the broadening class and gender composition of the literary public meant that, in the future, the calculus of "character" would hinge as much on womanly impulse and commercial puffery as it would on the self-styled reasoned judgment of masculine intellect. Kettell, whose poetry anthology was positioned to profit from the new, more female-oriented marketplace, might have guessed as much. That he continued to speak the language of salutary masculine control suggests the cross-purposes that regularly plagued his—and Willis's—generation, one which hoped to sustain exacting aesthetic criteria and standing social and gender hierarchies while extending the benefits of culture through the marketplace.[20]

In warning away his boss's protégé from the ephemeral world of parlor fashions, Kettell presumably meant well. Yet by interrogating the serviceability of a foppish posture, Goodrich's anthologist reiterated at least some of the elements of attacks already being directed at Willis's innovations. In reviewing *The Legendary*'s "Mere Accident" in the *New England Weekly Review*, the young George Prentice had taken it upon himself to ask "Cassius" precisely what he was doing with that maiden in the "shady nook deep in the greenwood." Prentice then reprinted the offending passage for his readers' consideration. "I pressed her fingers half unconsciously / And fell in love—but was that *all*?" "Probably *not*," Prentice surmised for the benefit of those enraptured by Willis's appeal. "But what *was* all?" he asked. Most certainly not "marriage," as one imaginative defender of the sly poet suggested. Instead, this particular self-appointed censor felt sure that Willis's verse was of such a character as to make it unfit for the eyes of the young women likely to be its primary consumers. He therefore took pleasure in proclaiming that his moral tocsin had barred *The Legendary* from many a parlor "to which, but for exposure of its indelicacies, the popularity of Mr. Willis might have introduced it."[21]

As this rebuke suggests, Willis's literary work seems to have fed a host of anxieties, much of which were spawned by the phenomenal growth in women's readership since 1800. In complaining, for instance, of the injurious effects wrought by the proliferation of novels, critics of the day often cited the specter of impressionable female minds seduced from salutary pursuits into a kind of morally enervating sensual indulgence. Later, when women like Susan Warner and Harriet Beecher Stowe were dominating the market, this masculinist critique would expand to encompass the dereliction of the entire literary enterprise entailed in the predominance of a "scribbler's" readership. Willis, like some latter-day Lovelace, suggested further that the intimacy of print that infused his voluptuary prose and poetry was even more explicitly a seduction, an immoral education of the senses, leading from the merchandising of gossip and secrets to the corruption of female desire. In this regard, social anxieties surrounding the state of sexual propriety fed directly into worries over the propriety of innovations in the literary marketplace.[22]

Following the *American Monthly*'s launch, and particularly after the introduction of its dandy-editor, such anxieties multiplied. By July 1829, matters had evolved to the point that the *Salem Gazette* was noting disapprovingly that "criticism [of Willis], the most carping and trifling ridicule and abuse, even *personal*, have [*sic*] been unceasingly discharged from certain presses." The *New England Galaxy* only chided its competitor for slapdash trifling, but the *New England Weekly Review* spoke more bluntly. Resurrecting the now-familiar charge of womanizing, its editor suggested that if Willis were a philosopher, he would define man as a "kissing animal." In the same vein, Sarah Hale likened the *American Monthly*'s Romeo to "the keeper of a Harem, who itches to be kissing all the pretty girls he sees, and who courts all that consent to flirt with him among his passionate admirers." A correspondent of the *Hartford Review* delivered a jibe in verse that further underscored the dangerous ambiguity of Willis's courtship of female readers.

> Not quite a woman, by no means a man,
> Escaped from school the puny stripling ran.
> In tuneful mood, with sordid rhymes to greet,
> The ear of every girl that walk'd the street:
> Rhymes that his pitying friends essay to hush,
> Rhymes that no woman reads without a blush;—
> Black, white, or yellow, no one comes amiss;
> "Give me," lewd Natty cries, "a melting kiss."[23]

As this slur suggests, all restraints eventually fell away in the rush to pillory "Lewd Natty." For having taken his literary voluptuousness to extremes, Willis now was paid back in kind. Donning the robes of the "guardian of public morals," the *Galaxy*'s Frederic Hill even went so far as to accuse the *American Monthly*'s dandy-editor of advocating pederasty. The "filthy paragraph" under consideration was one in which Willis promised to reacquaint his audience with what he called "some of the finest of the fine old stories of the ancients, illustrating human passions in their boldest forms." Smirking all the while, Willis claimed to be mystified by the allusion. "We fear we shall die in ignorance," he reported facetiously. "We certainly shall unless Mr. H., or some other person equally skilled in the 'dark sciences,' enlightens us." Piqued at this impertinence, Hill retorted that

> though Mr. Willis has been a naughty boy—a very naughty boy, in his day,—yet it
> is impossible he ever could have had the slightest knowledge of any earthly passion

whatever, except for his spaniel bitch 'L. E. L.,' his bottle of hartshorn and water (he is subject to periodical qualms)[,] his *vinaigrette*, and the hem of his cousin Florence's petticoat.[24]

Such sexually charged digs at the young editor's "pet slut" L. E. L. occurred so frequently in these days as to constitute a leitmotif in Willis-bashing. Letitia E. Landon herself, the era's most conspicuous voice of lovesick ladies (and the spaniel's infamous namesake), figured high upon moral blacklists for having reputedly risen in British literary circles through an affair with William Jerdan, the editor of the London *Literary Gazette*. Willis's joke in naming his lapdog after this romantic but scandal-tinged queen of the annuals had thus partaken of a certain saucy impudence. Yet for those inured to this whimsy, he more aptly deserved his spaniel's company because he had also made himself a "puppy" of sorts, as a favorite nineteenth-century put-down of dandified youth termed it. And it was clear that many New Englanders thought such impudent curs—self-important and sniffing after their daughters—deserved summary whippings. "O, if Mr. Willis would but kick the brute down stairs," one Bostonian reportedly remarked upon encountering the canine L. E. L. in the *American Monthly*, "there would be some hope of him."[25]

The fact that critics hoping to purify public tastes themselves sometimes abandoned high-minded restraint and descended into brawling does not seem to have caused excessive hand-wringing around New England. Some observers certainly decried the precedent, but since the dawn of the early republic the prevalence of so-called tomahawk criticism had time and again corroborated Samuel Johnson's quip, "Authors are like privateers, always fair game for one another." In this spirit, probably the most consequential blast against Willis's reputation came in William Snelling's mildly sensational *Truth; a New Year's Gift for Scribblers* (1830), a latter-day dunciad dedicated to curing the system of the newspaper puffs and parlor celebrity that fostered gift-book trifling. Clearly Snelling also hoped to ride the horse he wished to bring down by playing off the popularity of the present stable of American poets. This he did by subjecting each versifier to ridicule in turn. Though granting "Childe Willis" literary promise, for instance, he portrayed him as vain and snooty, turning up his nose at passersby as he walked the streets in "band-box trim." Now almost de rigueur, as well, was the practice of running down Willis's enterprise by questioning his manliness. So Snelling also joked that

> When W-ll-s saw the light, 't is said his sex
> Did for a month the neighborhood perplex.
> ('T is doubtful now.)

One might perhaps expect such sexual indeterminacy to dissipate anxieties. Yet by abandoning male terrain for whispered secrets and promises of sensual indulgence, Willis had seemed to gain disturbing access to the world of women. So it was important for Snelling to close with a stanza aimed at undercutting this advantage:

> Natty filled the *Statesman*'s ribald page,
> With the rank breathings of his prurient age;
> And told the world how many a half-bred miss,
> Like Shakespeare's fairy, gave an ass a kiss.[26]

Whether such summary treatment of New England's poets worked any reform is an open question, though the book did sell well enough to reach a second edition. In Willis's case, it probably also confirmed a determination to give as good as he got. Perhaps under the assumption that the best defense against critical aspersion was the moral high ground, he had inaugurated his *American Monthly* by promising never to "descend, either to the ungentlemanly seasoning of personal abuse, or allusions to private differences." This resolve lasted all of four months. Then, to satisfy a tangle of desires, Willis sparred repeatedly with several prominent New England editors, along the way ribbing Lydia Maria Child for using the colloquial "nice" to describe "hard gingerbread" in her thrifty and decidedly antivoluptuary advice book *The Frugal Housewife*. In a particularly juvenile moment, he even stooped to tar *Truth*'s author with the unfortunate nickname "Smelling."[27]

Before long Willis had thus leaped, spurs and all, into the literary cockpit. On one hand, this decision was probably good business: public quarreling rarely fails to draw interest and the deacon's boy *was* capable of witty repartee. Yet the choice also underscored another of celebrity's predicaments: in a world of segmented literary markets, a rise in one circle—the world of fashion and society—might mean a fall in another, the circuit, in this case, of masculine endeavor. At this point in his life, this predicament and its seesaw cycle of overpraise and vilification clearly left Willis anxious, as much about his sense of self as about his precarious social perch.

One early indication of this situation is the *Legendary*'s story about Paul Lorraine; another is a review of *The Literary Remains of the Late Henry Neele* prepared for the *American Monthly*'s maiden issue. Here, in what Willis called a "valuable" article whose composition had "exhausted him," he appears to have voiced anxieties usually masked by bravado. After ascribing Neele's poetic sense (like Willis's own) to a rare affinity for the "loveliness of outward things, and the fine creations of other and loftier spirits than his own," the young litterateur lamented that his fellow poet's "disappointed ambition" would not allow him to bear this gift easily. Ultimately, it led him to suicide, the "victim" (his biographer had concluded) "of an over-wrought imagination." And to what did Willis ascribe the pain that drove this act of self-annihilation? Nothing less, he charged, than the poisoned pens of heedless critics, for poetry was not, in this reviewer's opinion, a "mere intellectual product," but a man's "*own* feeling, and his *own* character." Now he asked,

> Imagine your best and most sensitive feelings subjected for one moment to the rude handling of men who are bound by no law and less principle to respect them, and to whom ridicule in its most unfeeling guise is a professional indulgence! . . . [The critic] can affect materially the public opinion—not of the author's writings merely—but of his heart and character. He can give to the eyes that pass him in his walks a look of ridicule. He may associate him in the minds of those whose respect is the life of his heart with ludicrous images—nay—he may destroy his own self-confidence—and what is far more, his own self-respect.[28]

If the attraction of striking a voluptuary pose was thus plain enough in Willis's early magazine work, there was also this insistent demand to be taken seriously—a hunger to be credited with sincerity in a medium notoriously prey to calculated design. That is, as print increasingly provided antebellum Americans a cultural space in which to work out a variety of commercially and psychologically rewarding identities, it also held out (however tenuously) the promise of fostering an economy of feelings capable of producing genuine sympathy between reader and author. In the coming years, the ongoing tension between these at least partly inimical tendencies would continue to haunt Willis and the culture of celebrity he promoted, even as it laid the groundwork for his appeal.

The Trouble with Silver Forks

Overtures to the female market were not Willis's only innovations to disturb his contemporaries; many observers were equally put off or unnerved by the allure of his arch-sophisticate posture. By assuming the role of a merchandiser of literary sensibility and an emissary of fashion, the *American Monthly*'s editor threatened to turn former virtues into a grab bag of styles consumers might indulge at their whim. Many critics therefore found it easy to cast him as herald of a disturbing social trend that celebrated style over sincerity, appearance over substance, and cosmopolitan tastes over homespun virtues. This inclination becomes all the more understandable when we survey the cultural situation that helped to give meaning to Willis's journalistic enterprise, for in the 1820s he was hardly alone in promoting his fashion-conscious sensibilities.

Critics worried most that Willis—and those like him—set a bad example by snapping refinement from its moorings in good sense, moral sincerity, and sensual restraint. On the whole, proper Americans wanted to believe, as did the day's leading aesthetician, Hugh Blair, that "improvement of the taste seems to be more or less connected with every good and virtuous disposition." To dispute this proposition was to undermine one of polite society's central means of establishing identity and social preeminence. Yet many of these same Americans were also deeply suspicious of the forms a refining disposition might assume. In particular, they worried that self-conscious polish cloaked a naked contest of social climbing and sexual intrigue. Willis had implied as much in his paean to "Unwritten Music," when the prompting of experience led him to cite the deceptions of voice. But if so-called polite society was at bottom a game of theatrical imposture, and character merely a pose (as the *American Monthly* suggested), then perhaps refinement—and the status it sustained—rang morally hollow after all. Insisting that "true" taste was self-evident did not contain this anxiety, especially when the antics of poseurs like Willis seemed to be carrying the day.[29]

It should be noted that distrust of Willis's sort of self-fashioning had a long history in Anglo-American experience, stretching back at least to Puritan critiques of theatricality. Nonetheless, several significant cultural innovations conspired to deepen such misgivings just as Willis arrived on the scene, so much so that, to many contemporary observers, America seemed fairly awash with marketplace ambitions and status-chasing. To begin with, modern refinements in public accommodations and amusements refueled the ever-popular notion that "good society" was turning its back on republican virtues. The opening of the Tremont Hotel in October 1829, for instance, ushered in a new era of public luxury in Boston. Its impressive block-long facade, marble mosaic floors, newfangled water closets, and gaslit public corridors placed the city's newest commercial wonder on par with Europe's grand hotels, a far cry from the simple inns heretofore available to American travelers. Willis himself (who roomed there after college) had heard the Tremont faulted only for lacking mirrors in its parlors. And if the two-dollar-a-day rate meant that wealthy patrons alone enjoyed the hotel's private rooms and free soap, its luxurious lobby and barroom beckoned nonetheless to a broader public who came to lounge and mingle in what one English visitor would presently call "a life of idleness and vacuity of outward pretence, but of no good feeling." In this regard, society at the Tremont reproduced the kind of promiscuous posturing that pious New Englanders had long associated with the morally degraded precincts of the theater.[30]

This was particularly true given that actors and their fans undoubtedly wandered over from the new Tremont Theatre located across the street. Long proscribed by Puritan conscience and later by a republican prejudice against foreign luxuries, theaters in Boston had existed since the mid-1790s, appealing to a motley crowd of visiting merchants, Unitarian bluebloods, shop-boys, and prostitutes. The Tremont's launch late in 1827 upped the ante considerably. In an effort to attract a more seemly clientele and thus head off criticism, its manager resolved to bill his theater as a "reformed house" suitable for refined and elegant patrons. But even before the cornerstone was laid, local evangelicals and other conservative social critics began howling at this presumption. Alongside news that Madame Hutin, a French opera dancer, had introduced New York City to the "public exposure of a naked female," Nathaniel Willis's *Recorder* inveighed against the "Rapid Progress of Sin" entailed in Boston's newest venture in popular entertainment. Eventually, charges that the new theater (like its Unitarian patrons) hid moral deformity under a veil of refinement—or, as the *Courier* put it, dressed "impiety" in "delicate clothes"—forced the Tremont's proprietors to appoint a committee to investigate charges of drunkenness and prostitution. Then, when their report whitewashed certain criticisms, at least one commissioner felt compelled to register his dissent, noting particularly that inmates at the House of Refuge freely admitted to having stolen regularly from their masters to fund their theatrical habit. This contest was not entirely one-sided, however. In the heat of controversy, defenders of the so-called reformed drama suggested that its hyperpious critics look to their own quarters before defaming the Tremont's reputation. "Who has not heard of the bonnet and shawl left in the pulpit" in the Hollis Street Church or the seductions in the singing gallery ("2nd row") of the Essex Street Church, the *Boston Statesman* asked pointedly. Charges of hypocrisy and sexual impropriety, it seems, cut several ways in these controversial times.[31]

With the introduction of masquerade balls in the late 1820s, it must have appeared to some that seduction and theatrical imposture were poised to overrun society. As with the drama, many citizens worried lest the assumption of costumes and masks overturn habitual restraints thought to check licentious inclinations, especially among the young. "We dare say this is *gentility*," one Providence, Rhode Island, paper sniffed at this newly fashionable pursuit, but it is of a most corrupting tendency. The excitements of balls and splendid assemblages (all proper, and even refining when not engaged in to excess) are abundantly sufficient to carry individuals out of themselves, so as sometimes to forget the true dignity of personal character,—but when under an assumed character,—a complete disguise,—all the personal responsibility is laid aside, not only extravagance but even viciousness of conduct, is to be seriously apprehended.[32]

There was some truth in this charge, especially with masqueraders whirling away the night intoxicated by the Spanish Dance, as the newfangled waltz was known around Boston. Significantly, this controversial pastime (an "indecorous exhibition," one weighty New England Federalist called it) paired partners in relatively close embrace for the first time in the history of social dance, doubtless heightening sexual excitement. Willis certainly thought so. As he told a college friend of this "wicked" pleasure, any glance but heavenward "sinks your eye to the sweet depths of . . . hem' excuse me George." Whether such amusements were actually leading to ethical anarchy, as many moralists claimed, is debatable. Yet such social developments certainly primed critics for reports that indecency boiled beneath the surface. In late 1828, for instance, New York City's Common Council moved decisively to ban masquerades in an effort to stem moral decay, but not before news reached Boston (just as Willis was launching his magazine) that Gotham's watch had raided a den of iniquity in the rough Five Points area and caught "black and white, harlots and clerk boys" reveling in a "subterranean fancy ball." Here, it seemed, was false refinement's bitter harvest embodied: racial promiscuity and youth-led-astray ensconced in an underworld of wanton passion.[33]

As if to throw such unrestrained revelry into stark relief, hard times around New England underscored the disturbing contrast between idle workers and idle fashion. With shipping declining steadily through the 1820s, Boston in particular had already seen itself falling behind New York City when financial panic in 1825 and recession in 1828 further darkened New England's economic outlook. In the midst of these troubles, Boston's population had skyrocketed (up 40 percent in the 1820s), as foreign immigrants and country youths looked to the city for opportunity. Though Willis himself claimed to be weathering the storm better than most, many young men arrived in New England's metropolis to find that jobs were scarce. Prospects had soured so by 1830 that the *Boston Courier* wondered whether parents should continue to educate their sons for "exalted spheres" if all this training accomplished was to unfit them to cope with the troubles they would encounter. In such tight economic straits, youth's prodigal tastes appeared to pose a fundamental danger to social order. As the *Providence Daily Journal* saw it, the rich might have the financial wherewithal to "put on their backs silks enough to load a camel," but when poorer citizens imitated their well-heeled neighbors, problems ensued. In this regard, the *Journal* had seen even "*ladies of color* as well and as costly apparelled as their mistresses. . . . How can they afford it?" the paper asked. Better that the "extravagant" curb themselves "for fear of example."[34]

No wonder critics of the prevailing social and cultural drift also rose to decry one of the decade's most influential new literary currents: the "Silver Fork" or "fashionable" genre of British novels, which booksellers and publishers began introducing to American readers in the mid-1820s. Issued in great numbers from the likes of Henry Colburn's London publishing house (an enterprising "trade" firm despised by Britain's "gentlemen publishers" for its lack of taste and deference to station), these novels reveled in the hyperaristocratic world of Regency and post-Regency England, where style and fashion, in the person of Beau Brummel, could snub a king. By retailing gossip and gazetting prominent personalities under cover of fiction, "Silver Fork" authors figured to cash in on the notoriety of these exclusive circles as they also satirized manners. To this recipe, Colburn, the "prince of puffers," added his own special fillip: published "keys" to identify the aristocratic celebrities portrayed. This scheme worked wondrously. In addition to making the commercial fortunes of several important early Victorian authors, the send-up of high society in books such as Benjamin Disraeli's *Vivian Grey* (1826–27) and Thomas Henry Lister's *Granby* (1826) established Brummel as an international icon of style and made London's Almack's—the hangout of haut ton—a byword for exclusiveness and a popular tourist attraction.[35]

Edward Bulwer's *Pelham* (1828) was among the most successful and aesthetically significant of these fashionable imports, as well as the "Silver Fork" most directly implicated in Willis's social and commercial fortunes. Written while its socially ambitious author was still in his early twenties, Bulwer's extravagantly clever second novel followed the progress of its eponymous hero from the exclusive world of soirees and spas, down into the darkest gambling "hells," and back again to the highest political circles of the land. Popular acclaim for this and subsequent novels (*The Disowned, Deveraux, Paul Clifford,* and *Eugene Aram,* to mention only a few) propelled Bulwer to preeminence in Anglo-American literary circles, where for years he rivaled the commercial draw of Walter Scott and Charles Dickens. Social and political power followed swiftly on this commercial success. Authorial visibility soon enabled the future peer to set up as a parliamentary advocate of Radical Utilitarian reform, while his wryly impudent literary efforts spread a new gospel of style. Widely adopted as a chapbook for dandies, *Pelham* almost single-handedly changed the fashion in men's coats from many-hued to black, thus introducing a sartorial style that would come to define (strangely enough) that most antidandaical of nineteenth-century creatures: the colorless bourgeoisie. Bulwer's novel also helped to dispel the prevailing vogue for Byronic misanthropy and Werthian ennui—or so its author claimed. If postrevolutionary dreamers idolized Goethe's Werther and Byron's Corsair (Romantics deranged by passions), after 1828, admirers on both sides of the Atlantic found Henry Pelham (an intellectual dandy who mastered his passions) at least as compelling.[36]

Bulwer's *Pelham* struck a chord with its fans partly because it modeled an alluring, if controversial, code of conduct for would-be men of the world. Throughout the novel, its author reversed the popular put-down of dandies as sartorial slaves by suggesting that Henry Pelham was a dandy by choice, not nature, and by insisting that this choice made him a powerful social actor, not a weak-kneed, conceited fool. Read sympathetically, *Pelham* is, in this sense, an extended essay in the dandy's refusal to be marginalized, even an assertion of that character's preeminent claim to the helm of society. Henry Pelham, for instance, initially assumes the character of an "egregious coxcomb" because observation assures him that success depends upon being "distinguished from the ordinary herd." By curling his hair, affecting an "air of exceeding languor," and dressing in an unassuming style (a "low person," Pelham observes, would have done the contrary), the ambitious social climber is noticed, and thus enters the circle he intends to conquer. In all this, Pelham's affectations are genuine enough—he carries wrinkle water to keep his face smooth—but they never cloud his judgment. His dandified posture is instead a calculated manipulation that embodies Bulwer's favorite adage: "He who esteems trifles for themselves is a trifler—he who esteems them for the conclusions to be drawn from them, or the advantage to which they can be put, is a philosopher."[37]

Not surprisingly, *Pelham*'s wit, philosophy, and social program were a revelation for Willis, as they were for many culturally ambitious and self-consciously sophisticated young Americans (including such disparate spirits as Margaret Fuller and Edward Everett Hale). Even as critics disparaged the novel as "kitchen maid's literature," its remarkable popularity also prompted stateside publishers to pirate it at least eight times in the next decade. In Willis's case, the hullabaloo surrounding *Pelham* assumed special meaning, for it was only after people around Boston began calling him after Bulwer's hero that the young sophisticate read the novel. A short time thereafter, he appears to have embraced wholeheartedly the identity of an "American Pelham," spicing his conversation and private correspondence with the novel's lingo, excusing his etiquette as *Pelham*'s product, and repeatedly comparing his friends to its characters. The novel's dandified aesthetic also clearly influenced his "Editor's Table," though to what extent it is impossible to say. If nothing else, it seems likely that *Pelham* confirmed Willis's feelings that a man of acute sensibility must manage life to wring the most from it. Perhaps the novel also corroborated his experience that "reading" society, as Henry Pelham did, was the surest road to advancement.[38]

Like Willis's *American Monthly*, however, *Pelham* was as notorious as it was famous, and for similar reasons. The self-same wit, social satire, and inspired foppery that moved Willis to call the novel "a great thing" led more serious souls to condemn Bulwer's tour de force as profoundly immoral and socially dangerous. They did so in great part because Bulwer refused to distinguish satire from celebration. Instead, in anticipation of Thackeray's satirical realism, he claimed to portray the world as it was, not as some wished it to be. "Nothing," the young novelist observed in defense of his method, "is without its use; every word in the great thoroughfares of life, has a story which observation can easily extract." As Bulwer saw it, fiction might therefore claim the whole of experience as its province, entering into both debased and exclusive society without corruption, portraying vice without didacticism, and justifying as its hero a "mixed character" of both weak and noble qualities. In doing so, Bulwer's *Pelham* described a society Americans increasingly recognized as their own. In particular, the novel's virtuoso verisimilitude reproduced the radical exteriority of a world in which heroes appeared to have no hearts, only gestures and masks. In several senses, Bulwer's reliance on habits, features, and habiliment— rather than on internal dialogue or omnipotent narration to suggest interests and motives—placed readers in the position of those confronting the new urban and print worlds. Here, appearance and rhetoric were often all one had to determine character. And as attitude and visage constantly shifted in a confidence game of character manipulation, success appeared to accrue not to the virtuous, pious, or moral, but to the consummate student of surfaces. Bulwer had the audacity to suggest that such a man—that is, Henry Pelham—was a modern hero.[39]

What ennobled Pelham, Bulwer argued on several occasions, was that rather than repudiating worldly desires entirely, he triumphed by subordinating them to a heroic moral and intellectual code. Pelham's example was thus intended to preach a parable of how a man, "even a gentleman," might be both a "votary of Pleasure" and a "disciple of Wisdom." That a great many New Englanders chose to accept neither Bulwer's moral premise nor his claim that a dandy could be wise (or that they even failed to grasp his point), stemmed less from the English author's weaknesses as a writer than from common disbelief that fashionable society might be anything but immoral. The roots of such a view lay deep within the Puritan conscience. Even as Christian nurturing began to replace will-breaking as the preferred child-rearing technique and the concept of childhood innocence opened up a beachhead of sinlessness in a world of sinners, many pious souls continued to believe that worldly commerce remained mined all around with temptation. In this respect, no "man of the world" could ever be just a man *in* the world. Nor could dandies be expected to transcend their affectations. Bulwer's notion that "characters" were masks to be manipulated by a masterful self—a position embraced in practice by Willis in his "Editor's Table"—thus succeeded only in convincing many that society teemed with deceivers and that Bulwer and his kind were fooling themselves and, what is more, fooling others.[40]

It was the others who worried critics most. Even at this late date, post-Puritan moralists commonly invoked a psychology of reading that claimed fiction lulled readers, especially ostensibly impressionable females, into a critical torpor that left them prey to immoral designs. Ethical ambiguity, as many American critics of fashionable novels were quick to proclaim, was then de facto vice, and *Pelham*, in particular, a modern *immorality* play. "The professed moral," the *Christian Examiner* remarked on Bulwer's vogue, "by which is meant the direct truth or instruction the writer aims to impress, is not the important thing." Instead, what mattered was fiction's perilous sway. In this regard, writers like Bulwer—and Willis, for that matter—had a responsibility to structure their work to avoid ethical ambiguity. The fact that "mixed characters" existed or that belles really did use their conversational powers for social advantage was not reason enough to depict such things. Doing so would only encourage moral weakness.[41]

That Bulwer and Willis chose to mix their messages, infusing virtuous impulses with sensual indulgence and portraying Jehovah cheek by jowl with Thomas Moore, was often the crux of criticism. Beneath the witty banter, ringlets, and macassar oil of modern literary culture, many sensed a danger more treacherous than even that posed by the arch-villain of evangelical demonology himself. Lord Byron had at least worn his vice on his sleeve. But in reassuring a Mrs. Tuthill that her son would outgrow his "Pelham" phase, an earnest young John Greenleaf Whittier noted that "the same Pelham novels, are in my opinion, far more dangerous than the open licentiousness of Byron, or Sterne." As Whittier saw it, disgust arising from "direct outrages on the moral sense of the reader" acted as an "unfailing antidote of the poison." This was not so when beauty and vice were confounded:

When a writer possessing the power of charming the minds of his readers to every subject which he touches, endeavors to break down the pure and beautiful action of delicacy in the human beauty—tells the young and the lovely who [pour] over his pages, that the passionate impulses of nature must be obeyed; and seeks to confound sensual indulgency with the nicety and holiness of love,—then, is there danger, especially when a veil of glowing language and beautiful sentiment is thrown over the moral deformity.

Vice was never so seductive as when arrayed in the trappings of beauty.[42]

Whittier was seconded by the highest authorities in the land on this view. Again commenting on fashionable novels, the Unitarian *Christian Examiner*, for instance, warned its readers that "the manners of the present day are beginning to exhibit sundry affectations, the tendency of which is, to sap the foundations of social virtue." First, New England had endured the rage for Byron, with its melancholy poses and profligate pursuits. "Then came Mr[.] Pelham," the *Christian Examiner* moaned, "with his nonchalant style of manners, his beautiful curls, and the gentlemanly 'scorn which sits so beautiful upon the lip'—and the mania seized a large class of young men, whom an evil star had cursed with leisure." Things had progressed so far that it even seemed impossible to "enter a drawing-room without encountering some youthful fop, possessed of the Pelham spirit, and striving most vehemently to enact an imitation of the copy drawn from a most despicable original." This development was no laughing matter. "The moment our young men assume the ridiculous and effeminate manners, which come to us adorned by the charms of perverted genius, heightened by the beauties of imagery and the fascinations of style, and above all rendered seductive by a vitiating *sentiment* which makes them tenfold more dangerous by making them less revolting," then, the *Christian Examiner* concluded woefully, "we may bid farewell to the moral purity, the hitherto unstained sanctity, of our beloved New England homes."[43]

The trouble was that one look at the world seemed to confirm the ascendancy of Bulwer's adherents. Booksellers, as the *Bower of Taste* complained in 1830, pandered to the wishes of "club-loungers, non-descripts, and boudoir princesses," who directed "the taste of the town." And Europeanized fashion, in the person of an upstart like Willis, had usurped the rightful sway of sober critics and common sense. "Does a noted tailor," the *Bower* asked despairingly,

> or dress-maker open a magazine of wares in our metropolis?—out pounces a volume panegyrical [*sic*] of fop life, in which descriptions of attire are canvassed and culled from the pages of Ackerman's Repository, or the Parisian *Journal des Modes*: or is a new club-house opened?—out springs before the public a concoction wherein the whole true and particular account of hell-life is noted down for the benefit of the uninitiated and future blacklegs; or does an *Artiste Cuisinier* gain celebrity by the impertinence of his personal deportment, or the apt exercise of his metier, or *his profession*, as he euphemistically terms it?—forth issues a *novel* of extravagant length, in which the hero is eternally dealing in stale jokes, stolen from the really witty books our gallican neighbors have been pleased to give on the importance of the kitchen.

Modern literature thus seemed to have seduced its readers into a tawdry affair with luxury, fashion, and effeminate elegance. For this offense, its hometown heralds—

Willis chief among them—were to be scourged and hounded till they mended their foppish ways.[44]

The Mines of Golconda

Clearly, assuming the character of an "American Pelham" was dicey business. And though Willis may have been best suited among his contemporaries to carry off the pose, even as his future looked brightest trouble was brewing. This predicament was not wholly a matter of the rising critical din, though it was related to that development. As the *American Monthly* moved into its second year, New England's prevailing economic doldrums had also been steadily undermining Willis's once-rosy commercial prospects. More troubling still, compulsive philandering threatened to torpedo some of the more promising means of escape from these worsening financial straits. In the end, the combined effect of personal attacks, financial hardship, and Europe's allure proved too much for the fledgling magazinist; in late summer of 1831 he all but fled Boston in disgrace. Willis's tenure as Edward Bulwer's most conspicuous American avatar thus closed on a sour note, leaving both him and his native city glowering across an uneasy divide. Four years later Willis could still write his mother venomously, "they have denied me patronage, abused me, misrepresented me, refused me both character and genius, and I feel I owe them nothing. . . . The mines of Golconda would not tempt me to return and live in Boston." By this time, of course, he no longer felt he needed New England's approval. How this situation transpired is a long and complicated story, richly evocative of the evolving state of celebrity, but one that we can here only preface in concluding affairs in Boston.[45]

As with so many aspiring authors of his generation, money or—more accurately—the lack of money lay at the root of Willis's problem; that is indeed why he had initially put off Europe to found his magazine. Even then he was already living on credit, owing one friend for a substantial loan, with three or four hundred dollars more payable to "one tailor or another." And though the new publishing firm of Pierce and Williams had extended liberal terms to gain a contract in hard times, their young editor had still signed over his first year's profits in the bargain. It was to be some time before he saw any returns from his literary venture. In the meantime, Boston's "Pelham" often went light in the pocket from supporting what he rightly called "the style of a gentleman on the income of a shop-boy." By summer of 1829, in fact, Willis was so "poverty-stricken" that he begged Van Schaick to buy from him two small pictures; they had cost thirty dollars, but he would take what his friend offered. In October, Willis again hit up his New York friend, this time for a five-hundred-dollar loan (at 1 or 2 percent better than Albany rates) to hire writers.

But even with the hundred-dollar payment from Pierce and Williams's publication of his second volume of verse (*Fugitive Poetry*), the new year saw Willis "barely able to make expenses"; to satisfy his creditors, he had to sign on (sub rosa, of course) as a proofreader. To limit his magazine's production costs, he would eventually assume full responsibility for its printing arrangements. Yet, even amidst

such financial straits, Willis could not forgo extravagances, especially those calculated to enhance the figure he cut in Boston. In May 1830, for instance, Willis
reported to George Pumpelly of owning a new square-topped gig ("built after my
own taste") that "all the town abuses or admires"—depending on their opinion of
its owner. "Come on and ride with me," Willis begged his college chum, "before
the 'sheriff's sale' puts it out of your power. God only knows how my debts are to
be paid."[46]

God may neither have known nor cared, but Boston's most conspicuous magazinist was being at least somewhat disingenuous in professing to entertain no
schemes of deliverance. Indeed, for quite a period of time, money troubles and
onerous editorial duties had him testing the only solution he could imagine: contracting a financially advantageous marriage. After only a year of magazine labor,
in fact, he was declaring privately that he was fully prepared to "burn the Editor's
Table + sink the quill incontinently" if a "moneybag" would "make love" to him.
Yet such matches did not come easily, despite Willis's way with women. Following
his graduation from Yale, he had pursued several matrimonial prospects; each of
the young women's fathers refused his suit as a risk. By October 1830, however,
Willis thought he had found a woman to answer his prayers, if not all his dreams.
She was Mary Benjamin, the sister of his present literary compatriot and future
enemy Park Benjamin. Though neither "handsome" nor "come out" (and thus,
Willis observed, by common measure "not fashionable"), the Benjamin girl was,
her suitor noted, "just seventeen," "worth some 50,000 in hand, and twenty in
expectation," of noble character, with a "heart crowded with affection," a "mind
as vigorous as I wish it," and, better yet, fond of Willis to "idolatry." Not that
affections lay at the heart of the matter: "I wish I could love her only one half as
well," the worldly poet admitted sadly to Pumpelly, but the truth was that the
experience with Miss Woolsey had "shocked" his heart till it was "numb." Still,
Willis was fond enough (and covetous enough) of his Mary to bristle inordinately
when her guardian, James Savage, rudely rebuffed his proposal.[47]

Granted his literary notoriety and shaky finances, the crux of the problem, Willis
admitted privately, was his "side-scene amours," which had lately threatened to get
out of hand. For a while, he had taken to meeting the widow Otis ("Cleopatra
Redidivus!") for love on the sly. This liaison was scandalous enough, what with
"Cleopatra's" habit of receiving her admirer in dishabille while the Otis children
played in the parlor. But Willis's propensity to get too "white" ("I always overdo
a love matter," he once confessed to Van Schaick) seems routinely to have led him
to run risks of making a spectacle of himself. Once while pursuing a tryst, he even
claimed to have landed half-dressed in a frigidly cold street after jumping from a
second-story window, intent on escaping a man returned unexpectedly to visit the
"kept" mistress, who, in turn, "kept" Willis on the side. "Blast his genitals . . . for
interrupting earnest men in their amusement" was all the midnight prowler could
say about that unwelcome development. Presumably, salacious whispers of such
incidents fueled the personal character of critical assaults. They also plainly served
to chill any ambition Willis may have had of contracting an advantageous match
in Boston. After the Benjamin incident—which evidently included a blowup with
Mary's brother Park, as well as the "dragon" guarding Willis's "fruit"—the design-

ing suitor understood his predicament. Rather than gamely pursuing another match following Savage's rebuff, Willis resolved instead to flee to Italy and await his mistress's majority.[48]

Given his precarious finances, the only way to accomplish this end was to sell the *American Monthly*. This the overworked editor would have done tout de suite had he not worried that his enterprise might sink before proving a success. "That thing is my pique," he observed in October 1830. "I would not be the slave I am to business for ten times the profit it brings, had I not been taunted with rashness and folly in establishing it." Early the following year, in fact, Willis claimed to have entertained several offers for his "Maga," but the "devil" of it was, he sniffed, "they are from men whom my subscribers would desert at once, + I should have the double mortification of selling them an empty nut, + seeing it *go down*—which is too much for my pride after all my boasting of its success." Happily, however, patience eventually paid off. In August 1831, Willis officially joined the *American Monthly* to George Pope Morris's commercially successful Knickerbocker weekly the *New York Mirror* and soon saw his name added to that periodical's masthead as an assistant editor. A month later, he was gallivanting up and down the eastern seaboard on assignment.[49]

But to what end was all of this? Having mortgaged himself to found the *American Monthly*, then jeopardized his investment by a risky play for high cultural stakes, Willis certainly learned that a controversial pose might enliven a modern magazine. But this insight was gained only at the cost of arduous work and an equivocal notoriety that paid in galling social slights and critical deprecation as well as in hard-won dollars. It probably *was* presumptuous, even a bit perverse, to expect Boston's tight-knit and moralistic literary establishment to readily welcome a lapsed Scriptural poet turned Pelham. Yet it was the peculiar virulence of the city's scorn and its eagerness to run him down that left the bitterest taste. Still, Willis did not turn his back on his native city without some measure of satisfaction. For one, his new magazine's extensive circulation promised to expand his readership without the strain of sole editorial responsibility. New York, his future base of operations, was also an up-and-coming city, vibrant, bustling, and aggressively cosmopolitan, arguably antebellum America's fittest home to ambition. Finally—and best yet—Morris pledged to send his new assistant to Europe as a roving correspondent. There, Willis could fulfill his long-held dream of travel, lick his wounds, and await Mary Benjamin's coming-of-age. He still had his literary talents and the lessons of a stormy editorial debut to sustain him; he left behind in Boston a pack of critics and a three-thousand-dollar debt.

• F O U R •

The Spy Who Came to Dinner

A chield's amang you takin notes,
  And faith he'll prent it.
                    Robert Burns, "On the Late Captain
                    Groses's Peregrinations Thro' Scotland"
                                        (1793)

The first days of June 1834 found Willis once again confirming the maxim that charm will pay. Three years earlier, a hostile Boston had seen him off to Europe with little but a fund of resentments and his literary and social talents. Now he stood poised at the door of perhaps the most brilliant society in all of Great Britain. What lay within was destined to make his career.

Settling himself into Lady Marguerite Blessington's glittering salon, the American traveler might have fancied that he had stumbled on a "Silver Fork" novel: from London's prince of dandies, Count Alfred D'Orsay, to the renowned Pelham himself, Edward Bulwer, no more celebrated assemblage of upstart genius, flashy elegance, and aristocratic liberalism could be found than the one at Seamore Place. "Radical Jack" Durham, leader of the Whig reformers, had made Blessington's dinners his prime resort. And the host herself was celebrated on both sides of the Atlantic for her recently published *Conversations with Lord Byron* (1834). Admission to such exalted society was thus quite a plum for a young American. Better yet, eager bonhomie apparently proved an endearing quality: after a time, the assembled lions seemed as taken with their guest as he clearly was with them. Retiring later to conjure the evening's spirit for his readers back home, Willis therefore had ample reason to rejoice: nothing in his extended travels could match such a moment— not bad for the wayward son of a brimstone deacon.

The heady weeks that followed more than realized the promise of this auspicious debut. "What a star is mine!" the exultant traveler crowed to his favorite sister back home in Boston only days after his initial triumph.

61

All the best society of London exclusives is now open to me—*me*! a sometime apprentice at setting types—*me*! without a sou in the world beyond what my pen brings
me, and with not only no influence from friends at home, but a world of envy and
slander at my back. Thank heaven, there is not a countryman of mine, except Washington Irving, who has even the standing in England which I have got in *three days*
only.

This was only slight exaggeration. Countess Blessington's introduction opened a
world of opportunities to Geoffrey Crayon's would-be successor. Within the week,
he was gallivanting about London like a peer's son on a spree. Life sparkled with
daily favors: glittering soirees at the Hertford Street home of the Bulwers; breakfast
with the famous poet "Barry Cornwall" (Bryan Waller Proctor); and a much coveted
interview with the aging Charles Lamb. (Willis would write publicly about the latter
event, "Wreck as he certainly is, and must be, however, of what he was, I would
rather have seen him for that single hour, then the hundred and one sights of
London put together.") For Willis, there was also admission to the exclusive Alfred
and Travellers' Clubs; budding friendship with Mary Russell Mitford, the beloved
author of *Our Village*; and, of course, those memorable evenings among the celebrities and men of the world at Seamore Place. It was a brilliant time for a starstruck
Boston boy.[1]

Happily, good fortune only ushered in more of the same, as Britain's bon ton
rushed to accept the American traveler as one of their own. Mitford spoke for many
when she informed a friend, "I liked much Mr. Willis. . . . He is a very elegant
young man, and more like one of the best of our peers' sons than a rough republican." So he must have seemed in his modish bell-crown hat ("very large at the
top"), George Stultz coat, and Paris boots, dandling a malacca stick—the very pink
of fashion, and not at all what Mrs. Trollope had warned cultured Britons to expect
of Yankees. In early September, at the invitation of the aged Earl of Dalhousie and
his invalid wife (whom Willis had met while traveling through Italy), Mitford's
uncommon republican arrived in Scotland, fatigued from a bout with bilious fever
but eager to employ the sheaf of introductions carried in his bags. While in the
north, he visited with John Wilson ("Christopher North" of "Noctes" fame) and
Lord Francis Jeffrey (the celebrated former editor of the *Edinburgh Review*), took
in a ball at the Scottish capital, and spent ten glorious days billeted among Tory
nobility at the Duke of Gordon's country estate. The only disappointment came
on the return to London, when recurrent scrofula kept the young American from
passing an intended week with Miss Mitford at Reading and calling upon William
Wordsworth and Robert Southey with his introductions. Still, no experience could
have been finer. "I get on everywhere [even] better than in your presence," the
wonder-struck sojourner confessed to Lady Blessington—now his confidante and
greatest benefactor—after one particularly memorable evening. "I only fear I talk
too much; but all the world is particularly civil to me, and among a score of people,
no one of whom I had ever seen yesterday, I find myself quite at home today—
Grace a Dieu!"[2]

Indeed, there seemed no end to Willis's blessings; that winter he fairly reveled
in his fortunate estate. Between nights at the opera and days at his club, romance
followed romance. "I am up to my eyes as usual in a desperate *affaire*," the dashing

Yankee traveler wrote to Van Schaick in January 1835, "and it is not the first in England. I think, by the way[,] that this is the most libidinous country I ever was in. I find my old amatory poetry of days gone by does me a world of time and trouble." Two months later the young Lothario was bragging of living "on nothing now-a-days," for he had "two lady friends" who sent him carriages, gave him presents of clothes, provided tickets for the opera, and committed "adultery" with him whenever he was "in the mood." Yet amidst such dalliances there was time for enduring friendships as well. The spinster novelist Jane Porter—"a still handsome and noble wreck of beauty," Willis once called her—quickly proved a steadfast literary ally and solicitous, even motherly, friend; the two would correspond regularly until her death in 1850. At several country homes Willis was welcomed regularly as a son. "I had a letter the other day from Honourable Mrs. Shaw," he wrote his mother in the summer of 1835, speaking of one of his most generous benefactors, "who fancied I looked low-spirited at the opera. *Young men have but two causes of unhappiness,* she says, *love* and *money.* If it is *money,* Mrs. Shaw writes to say, you shall have as much as you want; if it is *love,* tell us the lady, and perhaps we can help you. Where could be kinder friends?" he asked appreciatively. Indeed, when his brother-in-law came to pester him about returning home to America, Willis positively squirmed. "Really I am so gloriously treated here," he protested, "that I hang back terribly from the idea."[3]

The concurrent ascent of the young man's professional star undoubtedly increased this reluctance. Already, the engaging letters of several years' travel on the Continent and in the Levant had gained him an enviable celebrity among his countrymen across the sea; in a fit of bravado, Willis's stateside partner, Morris, once bragged gleefully that some five hundred papers had annexed the correspondence to their columns. Hyperbole notwithstanding, such talk was ample testament to the American hunger for exotic and cosmopolitan intelligence that Willis both shared and fed in these years. Now fortune promised him even brighter prospects. Almost immediately upon his arrival in London, several popular British magazines had inquired after Lady Blessington's newest protégé; with this introduction, Willis's prose and poetry was soon gracing their pages regularly, acquainting a whole new audience with his literary talents. The so-called Slingsby Papers written for Henry Colburn's *New Monthly* proved a particular favorite and ultimately made their engaging author something of a minor lion. To capitalize on the interest, Saunders and Otley planned to bring out a new edition of Willis's verse for British readers. In March 1835, *Melanie and Other Poems,* with a preface by "Barry Cornwall," greeted the world.[4]

In other words, though not yet thirty years old, the *Mirror*'s peripatetic correspondent could once again congratulate himself on a spectacular—and for an American, almost unprecedented—social and professional coup. If Willis's "Scriptural Sketches" had secured him a pious favor, and his *American Monthly* a regional vogue, Blessington's imprimatur was now fast making the "sometime printer's apprentice" a transatlantic phenomenon. Having been fairly chased from Boston, it was surely sweet satisfaction to confound his detractors with such a flourish. Yet as it turned out, the sources of this extraordinary good fortune were ultimately to discomfit Willis: six months hence, his private Elysium was threatening to crash precipitously around him. When the crisis came, he and his many readers would get a signal lesson in the perils and rewards of the new literary celebrity, as well as a foreshadowing of the rapidly changing character of the Anglo-American world of print.

Storming Society

Willis's impending troubles stemmed most directly from the intrusive journalistic innovations that had from the start underwritten his extended European peregrinations. In this regard, his experience comprises a significant chapter in the culture of celebrity's ongoing opening of private life to public scrutiny. Before exploring such matters, however, we ought to consider just how Willis managed his dizzying ascent into British high society, if only because the prevailing mechanics of travel that sustained his remarkable progress had at least as much to do with his checkered fortunes as did his celebrated pen.

As we saw earlier, Europe meant many things to the deacon's dreamy son. Though he would admit it only years later, chief among these was the chance to test his social ambitions. In this respect, the young journalist was like many an aspiring Yankee, only more so. Saddled with a deep-seated insecurity, and still smarting from the failure of his magazine and the refusal of Mary Benjamin's hand, he nursed a rankling conviction that Boston had pursued an ill-natured vendetta against him—hectoring him unmercifully, hounding him from society, sabotaging his literary projects, and eventually expelling him altogether. Travel seemed to promise vindication: prove himself in Europe, and he might yet return to face down this legacy of embarrassment, exclusion, and debt. And so, armed only with a thirst for adventure, a winning manner, several letters of introduction, and his five-hundred-dollar advance from Morris, the *Mirror*'s junior editor had set out across the sea to cultivate uncommon acquaintance and experience wherever he might find it.

Little in Willis's advent suggested his future fortunes. Presumably, none but Le Havre's customs men paid any mind to the young American who debarked from the merchant-brig *Pacific* in early November 1831 before setting off for Paris with his school-boy French and being very much alone. Judging by his initial letters to the *Mirror*, Willis spent many of these early days strolling anonymously through the French capital. Doubtless he enjoyed these rambles: stumbling upon the brutal spectacle of a staged dogfight or discovering the fraud of a beggar-woman whose pathetic child was made of wax. Yet soon he must have yearned for the society of his countrymen. Like many a traveler, he then turned to previous acquaintance and letters of introduction to secure company in a foreign land.[5]

There was nothing extraordinary in this strategy. By the 1830s, any American privileged enough to visit Europe in a character above a deckhand's could expect at least a smattering of introductions to ease entry into foreign society. With regular transatlantic steamship runs still five years away, communication between the Old and New Worlds remained fitful; correspondents measured replies in weeks or months. As they had for generations, letters of introduction cheated this remove—

and many others—by making acquaintances of strangers. In this regard, they functioned as portable reputations, shorthand characters for a culture perennially on the move. With recommendations in hand, bearers came guaranteed by the commender's good name. Custom dictated at least a perfunctory interview; friendship often obliged more familiar welcomes. So it was that the amenities of private society were extended overseas, at least for those who could afford the travel.[6]

Young though he was, Willis's literary and social connections meant that he could expect an unusually high caliber of recommendations; he even carried one introduction from then–Vice President Martin Van Buren. But less exalted acquaintance ultimately better served the young traveler. A year earlier, he had opened a fruitful correspondence with the convalescing Yankee art student Henry Greenough, recently arrived in Florence to study alongside his elder brother Horatio, the up-and-coming sculptor. Though the two Bostonians scarcely knew each other, Henry (with the blessing of stateside family members and at Willis's prompting) was soon sending back extended descriptions of Florentine society that quickly found their way into the *American Monthly*. Then, when Willis abandoned Boston for Europe, he came laden with family letters for the expatriate Greenoughs. Arriving in Paris and unexpectedly finding Horatio waiting to execute a bust of Lafayette, the *Mirror*'s traveler thus fell gracefully into a particularly well-connected circle.[7]

Horatio Greenough was the special favorite of James Fenimore Cooper, who, since publication of his *Leatherstocking Tales*, had become one of America's most celebrated authors. In the early 1830s, Cooper was also widely acknowledged to head the American expatriate community gathered in Paris around the venerable Lafayette. Greenough himself would soon return to Florence (where he was to do his brother's correspondent further service), but first, in his company, Willis remade the acquaintance of Samuel F. B. Morse, the painter, future inventor of the telegraph, and another of Cooper's protégés. Morse, in turn, introduced his new associate to Cooper, Lafayette, and other republican luminaries, including the noted British linguist and editor of the Benthamite *Westminster Review*, Dr. John Bowring. Though Cooper and Lafayette seem to have been too preoccupied with Polish politics to pay Willis more than passing courtesy, the voluble Bowring was especially attentive to his new acquaintance: after only one meeting, he proffered several valuable introductions to friends in Italy. Throughout the young American's stay in the French capital, Bowring presented him to interesting persons. A chance meeting with Willis's one-time supper club companion, Samuel Gridley Howe, also proved socially and journalistically advantageous. Then attending Parisian hospitals on a mission for the Massachusetts Institute for the Blind, Howe shared lodgings with Willis until called away on an ill-fated errand to deliver funds to Polish refugees. Although deeply involved in both his medical observations and—like Cooper, Morse, and Lafayette—the Polish-American Committee, Howe always found time for his friend: escorting Willis to Versailles and the Italian opera; introducing him to the ragged but romantic Polish revolutionaries who thronged the city; procuring him an invitation to the monthly banquet of the liberal *Revue Encyclopédique*; and generally including Willis in his peripatetic activities. After only several weeks abroad, the *Mirror*'s young editor could thus tell his readers of mixing with the creme of Paris's republican elite.[8]

Of course, these advantages might have amounted to little had Willis not proven an agreeable companion, but surviving evidence suggests that everyone—or at least those who moved in the small world of Parisian expatriates—seemed thoroughly charmed and extraordinarily eager to be of service. William Cabell Rives, the American minister at Paris, for instance, obligingly secured Willis an audience at court. Though the young traveler groused at the requisite knee breeches and tailcoat, the standing invitation to royal balls entailed in the honor was surely a feather in his cap. Even more remarkable, a vacationing American consul by the name of Carr (described by another American traveler as a "tall gaunt Randolph looking figure, full of strange oaths which he utters lolling upon two or three chairs") was so taken with Willis that he lavished presents on his new friend, paid his expenses, and proposed to take him to Tangier as his official secretary. Though tempted, Willis ultimately refused this offer. Instead, he moved directly to Italy in the spring of 1832. When he did, Rives—not to be outdone by his prodigal colleague—graciously attached Willis to the American legation. This invaluable courtesy promised to short-circuit the frequent customs delays otherwise inevitable when touring the Italian states. Coupled with the many introductions furnished by those such as Dr. Bowring, it also promised to open doors of the choicest society to one who months before had been wandering Parisian streets debunking charlatans. As an attaché, Willis was welcome at all courts recognizing the American republic. In his diplomatic uniform, moreover, he might expect to pass muster before all but Italy's most exclusive aristocrats.[9]

So far, no special expedient had been necessary to turn this trick; even the post of traveling attaché was common enough, at least in American diplomatic circles. But already Willis had proved how far luck, an engaging personality, and a few well-placed introductions might take a man. His ensuing fortunes would reveal, as well, just how vulnerable private society had become to designing ambition. Part of this situation owed to circumstance, for perhaps more than any other situation, society on the road realized the fluid potential of nineteenth-century Western culture. Here, the pleasures of wayfaring routinely attenuated habitual reserve (and sometimes even class exclusivity), often promoting remarkable familiarity among perfect strangers. More particularly, the tourist trail rewarded the very qualities Willis possessed in abundance: an eager and ingratiating exuberance, a polished manner, a pleasing mien. Though embarked upon a shoestring, he did not have to seem so: life in foreign climes could be remarkably cheap, and cultivated bearing went a long way toward suggesting a gentleman's station. Then, too, the picturesque air of a poet's mantle added immeasurably to the young traveler's charm. Best of all, cut loose from Boston's choking propriety, Willis could slough off past histories, becoming in practice what he seemed. For one who had long ago staked his soul on the world's good opinion, these were tremendous social and psychological advantages. Soon, they would prove instrumental in enabling Willis to seize the considerable opportunities presented by the new and exciting scenes steadily unfolding before him.[10]

And seize them he did. For the next several years, Boston's Pelham played the rambling tourist to perfection: tracking repeatedly across the Italian peninsula with newfound friends; wintering in Florence with Horatio Greenough (where Willis briefly fancied himself an artist); even hitching a six-month cruise through the eastern Mediterranean, courtesy of the officers of the frigate *United States*. And whether tramping in Childe Harold's footsteps, sojourning among artists and expatriates, or exploring Istanbul's exotic bazaars, Willis was tempted to declare this life nonpareil. Wealth, he happily told his readers, made "less distinction" here than anywhere in the world. Better yet, no Calvinists questioned him; no critics scolded him; no creditors hounded him; no detractors disparaged him—at least not on his side of the Atlantic. The roving attaché could not have been more pleased. "You can exist elsewhere," he once told his readers with evident relish, "but oh! you *live* in Italy."[11]

This remarkable progress owed much to the leverage of introductions. Count Porro, for instance, who knew Willis only through his letter from Dr. Bowring, had sent off his new acquaintance from Marseilles with what Willis gleefully called introductions to "half the rank of Italy." These included one to the Marquis Borromeo, whom Porro predicted cavalierly would grant the young American use of one of his palazzos, "as he has five or six and is happy when people he knows occupy his servants." This casual prodigality was not singular: wherever Willis went, such chains of hospitality worked their magic; even brief acquaintance often produced a fistful of introductions to friends farther up the line. It is, in fact, hard to avoid the conclusion that such recommendations had become a kind of inflated currency, opening doors almost willy-nilly into even the most exalted society.[12]

They certainly did in Willis's case, for just such a transaction was instrumental in spurring his subsequent British success. While sojourning in Florence, he had evidently availed himself of Horatio Greenough's introduction to visit the renowned British poet Walter Savage Landor at his villa in the hills of nearby Fiesole. The two men apparently hit it off—not long after Willis's final departure from Italy, Landor was to assure his young friend by post, "I know not any man in whose fame and fortune I feel a deeper interest than in yours." Willis, for his part, was characteristically winsome. As he paused in Florence before heading off for England in the late spring of 1834, for instance, he had grandiosely offered to have Landor's *Imaginary Conversations* (minus the "political" dialogues) reprinted in America; they were, he reportedly assured his urbane and reputedly imperious host, among the "most *thumbed* books on his table." Astoundingly, Landor warmed to the scheme and entrusted his guest with the only copy of the multivolume work in his possession, corrected in his own hand and comprising an additional sixth unpublished volume still in manuscript. This was not the only indication of an uncommon rapport. Willis left Fiesole bound for England almost overloaded with tokens of his host's esteem—apart from the *Imaginary Conversations*, carrying off a picture by Aelbert Cuyp and a manuscript of Landor's *Citation and Examination of William Shakespeare*, the latter to be presented to Lady Marguerite Blessington, who would supervise its publication in London. Landor in turn made sure that his young acquaintance was well received by his longtime friend and literary ally, the countess. Sparing no praise, he announced Willis as "the best poet the New World has produced in any part of it," and a diplomatic attaché, to boot. This seems to have done the trick. "I received your MS," Blessington wrote Landor not long after his courier's appearance at Seamore Place, "and am delighted with it. Mr. Willis delivered it to me with your letter, and I endeavored to shew [*sic*] him all the civility in my power, in honor of his recommendation."[13]

Thus it was that the "sometime printer's apprentice" had burst so auspiciously upon the scene at Seamore Place—a spectacular exemplar of the social leverage of charm, literary repute, diplomatic custom, and, most significant, prodigal recommendations. It is indeed hard to underestimate the advantages conferred on Willis by such embarrassingly glowing reports as Landor's or the trail of introductions that preceded it. At the very least, without them there could have been no interview with Charles Lamb (a second recommendation from Landor to his friend Henry Crabb Robinson having been instrumental in the arrangements) or, for that matter, with Blessington herself. Hence, there would have been no shortcut to society and literary fame. Originally, Willis's stay in Britain was to have lasted only several weeks. As we have seen, sustained by Landor's extravagant kindness, the dashing attaché moved quickly to establish himself among friends and admirers whose company must have seemed the stuff of dreams.

For Willis there was only one problem, but it was enormous. In this exalted social circle (if not at home in America), he had yet to reconcile the gentlemanly character he so gracefully assumed with that of the roving journalist which had for many months sustained it. When the truth eventually came out, the ensuing storm of outrage was to top all such previous outbursts against him.

Silly and Ill-Starred Letters

Though one might not guess it from Willis's experience, letters of introduction were meant to safeguard as well as extend familiar society. Like many forms of social currency, they implied a mutual promise: at most, that traveler and host share a sympathetic kinship; at the very least, that each act with courtesy and tact. The snag was that the custom of extending introductions had always assumed the essential integrity and security of private society; by the 1830s, these safeguards were fast being breached by the offices of print, as well as by the casual issue of recommendations. Willis's example in particular would suggest just how profoundly journalistic innovation was eroding domestic safeguards, especially among the class of literary celebrities whose company figured so prominently in the young American's foreign correspondence.[14]

As is often the case, money lay at the root of this situation. When it came to his shoestring grand tour, a lack of funds had always required that Willis maintain an eye for finances. Park Street's prodigal son was, after all, blessed with neither patrimonial allowance nor munificent patronage. Having barely escaped his creditors in Boston, neither was he in any position to fund his own travel. It thus fell to his new partner at the *Mirror* to bankroll the trip. The deal struck with George Morris—ten dollars' payment for each of fifty letters, the entire sum to be advanced to cover forthcoming expenses—obliged Willis to coin his passage from the shifting canvas of daily experience; in short, he had to travel to write and write to travel. Even as it was making his name, however, this journalistic enterprise would eventually lead him into trouble.

The format of the proposed letters to Morris would also cause a problem. They were meant to be, quite literally (as their initial title suggested), the "first impressions" of a young man encountering foreign scenes and society. Such fleeting observations were, Willis once commented, "worth all the tame after-philosophy of the best observers." Having read enough European travel accounts to know that customary reports of comparative statistics and public monuments no longer satisfied, Willis hankered after an excuse to provide better fare. He was to find his nearest model in Edward Holmes's *A Ramble among Musicians in Germany,* a volume its American admirer had once called full of "delightful wayward thoughts, which make the author and the reader so intimate, and within a narrative compass comprises a wonderful amount of interest." In some sense, this was little more than Willis's magazine philosophy packed for the road. Abroad, however, such familiarity assumed a special mimetic significance. As the young Romantic had once suggested,

> the pleasure of reading travels is not to store up a mass of foreign localities and dimensions . . . ; but it is to be so carried into the country discussed, by the author's vividness of description, and power of familiarizing it to our imagination, that we conceive ourselves there, and experience all the natural sensations of surprise and strangeness.

The plan was thus: what Willis felt, so would his readers; his eyes would be theirs, as would his revelations and sensations. One might say that, in effect, he proposed to extend them their own letters of introduction.[15]

Having granted free rein to his first impressions as a matter of philosophy and style, Willis pursued his scheme with singular determination. A Romantic's disposition to "see almost any sight *once*" led him, moreover, into many strange and wonderful circumstances: in Paris alone, he underwent a claustrophobic sitting for a plaster cast with Dr. Johann Spurzheim, the renowned phrenologist; attended a macabre masqued ball at the height of the cholera epidemic (a possible source for Poe's "The Masque of the Red Death"); and returned shaken but uninfected from a hellish descent into the plague house at the Hôtel Dieu. His reports of such episodes did not spare the squeamish. In this last instance, Willis regaled the *Mirror*'s readers with a gruesome parade of gothic horrors: once-beautiful women writhing before him, mouths foaming, eyes staring from their sockets, faces a "frightful, livid purple"; untended corpses scattered among the dying; "carousing" patients dosed with alcoholic punch, sitting bolt upright with "pallid faces and blue lips." The suffering, he admitted, had "almost smothered him," but not enough to dissuade him from his stated creed, nor to spoil the prodigious effect. Though certain decorous journalists forbore from the "general pillage" of his letters (New York's *Spirit of the Times,* for one, found the Hôtel Dieu sketch "too sombre" for reprinting), Willis was generally rewarded for his "first impressions" with a rapt American audience eager for vicarious thrills and wonder and, in the case of the cholera, not a little anxious at its impending spread.[16]

For the most part, this achievement was accomplished without crossing the pale of propriety. The Hôtel Dieu scene, for instance, may have been gruesome, but it was nothing not already served up by garden-variety gothic novels. The sketches of British society Willis dispatched to the States, on the other hand, posed some troubling ethical problems. These difficulties stemmed chiefly from his ambiguous status as both a private guest and a public journalist. After all, here more than ever he had been freely invited into drawing rooms and breakfast chambers, and he now proposed to retail his familiar experience with customary candor and latitude. So it was that in his inaugural communication Willis begged indulgence for the propriety of his forthcoming correspondence. "There is one remark I may as well make with regard to the personal descriptions and anecdotes with which my letters from England will of course be filled," he informed his readers matter-of-factly.

> It is quite a different thing from publishing such letters in London. America is much farther off from England than England from America. You in New York read the periodicals of this country, and know everything that is done or written here, as if you lived within the sound of Bow-bell [that is, within the sound of the bells of the Church of Mary-le-Bow, in Cheapside, London]. The English, however, just know of our existence, and if they get a general idea twice a year of our progress in politics, they are comparatively well informed. Our periodical literature is never even heard of. Of course there can be no offense to the individuals themselves in anything which a visitor could write, calculated to convey an idea of the person or manners of distinguished people to the American public. I mention it lest, at first thought, I might seem to have abused the hospitality or frankness of those whom letters of introduction have given me claims for civility.[17]

If this sounds like an opportunist's special pleading, in a sense it was. The intoxication of social triumph was heady stuff; with all his resentments, Willis was not about to miss the chance to advertise his rising star. Then again, he *had* long ago pledged himself to deliver first impressions to his readers, and these *were*, after all, "distinguished people" he proposed to write up. To renounce his plan now would be to fly in the face of proven practice and to forgo his greatest social opportunity yet. Distance would thus have to excuse what proximity had long condemned, and with remarkable results. At least in part because of this latitude, Willis's highly colored sketches of British literary society, especially in the storied precincts of Seamore Place, managed to achieve a sense of immediacy unsurpassed among his contemporaries—just the sort of thing to delight the literary dreamers back home.

Having disposed of the thorny problem of propriety early on, Willis seems to have dispatched his subsequent foreign correspondence without an anxious conscience. As late as February 1835 he still maintained, with apparent conviction, that their fame must be restricted to America. Declining a flattering proposal by the ever-solicitous Mary Mitford to write up England, he explained that, having been "overwhelmed by kindness," he could scarcely compose such a book (and here he resorted to his own flattery) without recourse to the sort of superlatives for which his countrymen would "tear [him] to pieces." Moreover, as so much of his "magnificent" experience owed to "private" hospitality, neither could he "make a book interesting without trenching on what is sacred." Fatefully for Willis, this pious circumspection rested on a monumental miscalculation.[18]

Fifteen years earlier, an American traveler might have pursued his scheme with relative impunity. Historically, British readers had little use for the newspaper work of their former colonists, even less for their belles lettres. American literature's earnest provinciality often seemed pale by comparison to the sophisticated British literary tradition. The high cost of print in the mother country (because of taxes, often five times that in the United States) also tended to dissuade London publishing houses from gambling on even the most promising of foreign imprints. Yet by the time Willis set off for Europe, circumstances had begun to change. The breakthrough successes of Irving and Cooper in the preceding decade were advance notice of a growing British interest in American literature; by the mid-1830s, both Catharine Maria Sedgwick's novels and William Cullen Bryant's poems had begun to gain an audience and commercial advocates overseas; William Ellery Channing's Unitarian essays had their enthusiasts as well.[19]

Willis himself was an early beneficiary of this awakening. Back in 1831, Alaric A. Watts, the doyen of English gift-book editors, had reprinted Willis's "I'm twenty-two—I'm twenty-two" in the *London Literary Souvenir*; one year earlier, Mary Mitford had tapped his "Unwritten Philosophy" and "Unwritten Poetry" for her *Stories of American Life by American Authors*. Willis was, in fact, noticed rather often in Britain for an American poet. In addition to the publications already noted, the *Literary Gazette, Fraser's*, and the *Eclectic Review* all spent at least several pages on his volumes in the period between 1828 and 1833. The *Edinburgh Literary Review* also republished several of his poems. And to put the lie to Willis's own calculations, the London *Morning Herald* apparently had known enough of the *Mirror*'s star correspondent as early as 1833 to send to Smyrna to offer him a thousand dollars a year for political articles—a proposal he wisely refused, given the nature of his journalistic talents.[20]

Clearly, American periodical work could, on occasion, be "heard of" in Britain, although its audience must have remained relatively select. In fact, through the 1830s, British editors were beginning to review—and praise—the best known of American periodicals with increasing frequency. One editor who did so most single-mindedly was Robert Shelton Mackenzie of the *Liverpool Journal*. With an eye for a developing market and an unusual penchant for Yankee literature, this young entrepreneur of print had signed on with New York City's *Evening Star* in December 1834 to report British literary gossip. (This was just after Willis had begun sending his British letters to Morris.) At home in Liverpool, Mackenzie also spread news of American literary affairs, including, of course, the phenomenal success of Willis's letters. Indeed, so highly did he profess to regard their descriptions ("the best sketches I had any where seen of London literati and their modes of living and talking" was his subsequent claim) that he began reprinting them for his home audience soon after they first appeared in the *Mirror*. So it was that at the very moment Willis counted on Britain's long-standing blind spot toward American letters to secure the propriety of his reports, that tradition was on the wane.[21]

The waning was not immediately apparent, however. From the moment of his arrival in Britain, to the point when he discontinued his public letters on his return to London in November 1834, Willis had assiduously recounted his remarkable progress for readers back home. Owing to a backlog of correspondence, however, George Pope Morris did not announce their imminent publication until three months later. Then, in late February, when the first of his associate's British letters appeared in the *Mirror*, even Willis's best intentions could not stem the ensuing outcry.[22]

Problems surfaced first in America, where a spate of extravagant puffery provoked a howling controversy. For all their pretensions to middle-class respectability, the *Mirror* and its journalistic allies were not above indulging in the shameless self-promotion and inflated praise that marked antebellum literary culture. Not surprisingly, Willis—the darling of so many hearts—came in for his share of such treatment; indeed, for months on end the *Mirror* had been crowing unabashedly over the descriptive power, stylistic grace, and unflagging interest of his travel letters. Circulation of the new series from Britain only redoubled the braggadocio. Not long after the commencement of Willis's "Pencillings by the Way" (as his letters were now titled), one partisan proclaimed their author to be "the most elegant delineator of society and manners, the most captivating traveller that ever left the new world to record his opinions of the old," adding, for good measure, a station among the first poets of the age.[23]

This was too much for Colonel James Watson Webb. This testy New York editor had never liked Willis's style; neither could he abide the *Mirror*'s recent drift into ostentatious Anglophilia. Just weeks beforehand, Webb's *Courier and New York Enquirer*—a Whig commercial daily traditionally aligned with the high-toned *Mirror*—had been hard upon its usual course, puffing its fellow paper as "always clever and entertaining." But that was before Willis's "tittle-tattle of European and English coteries" and the installation of an émigré Englishman as literary editor had begun turning the *Mirror* into what Webb would later call "an American periodical in name only." Now the colonel seized on Willis's British correspondence to open a cut-and-thrust paper war that was destined to last nearly a year and have profound consequences for the absentee subject of the quarrel.[24]

Most important, Webb broached several questions of propriety that would haunt Willis for years to come. First, there were the claims of civility and hospitality. In his latest communication from Blessington's salon, Willis had repeated some unguarded dinner-table conversation—in this case, Thomas Moore's denunciation of Daniel O'Connell for letting down the tone of Irish nationalism by refusing to duel those he would verbally abuse. This was just the sort of journalistic freedom calculated to play havoc with Willis's wishful defense of his letters. "Anacreon" Moore was a renowned lyric poet who had once resided in the United States; O'Connell, the "Great Agitator," was the champion of radical Gaelic nationalism. Together, these two were perhaps the most notable Irishmen of their day. To retail their differences in the British press would clearly have been to ask for trouble; in New York it was still to tempt fate. For Webb, this indiscretion was much more, for it suggested to him that the *Mirror*'s pet correspondent lacked the essential tact that alone safeguarded private society and public morals. Any true gentleman, the colonel instructed his readers loftily, would shrink instinctively from such breaches of confidence.[25]

As if this was not enough, there was also the cloud of ill repute that hung over Willis's new favorites. Many Americans adored Marguerite Blessington and her gossipy *Conversations with Lord Byron*; several exuberant partisans had even recently seen fit to cap a literary celebration at New York's Canandaigua Falls by engraving her ladyship's name on a convenient boulder. Yet for all her charms, rumor had it that Willis's beloved countess was something less than the paragon of moral loveliness he had propounded in his letters. Webb (who was happy to play the game of gossip when it suited his purposes) now jumped at the chance to press her example to the task of checking foreign fashion's sway. As he told his readers, "women of reputation" had long snubbed the widow Blessington for reportedly consorting with her stepdaughter's estranged husband, the "French adventurer." Alfred D'Orsay. This illicit connection would explain why men alone frequented the countess's salon. As for these men—Willis's flashy chums Bulwer and Benjamin Disraeli the younger chief among them—the *Courier and Enquirer*'s head summarily dismissed them as second-rate scribblers. All of this brought him to this conclusion: if Willis thought to play upon his compatriots' credulity by advertising his fashionable friends' so-called genius (thus puffing himself up into a greater fame by his acquaintance), Webb would not allow the ruse. Recording the "wise opinions," "witty remarks," and "original thoughts of great men" was one thing, he reasoned, but the *Mirror*'s "captivating traveller" had only shown himself to be a purveyor of "mere *verbiage* and small-talk" calculated to "pander to the low tastes and worse feelings of mankind."[26]

Publication of this tremendous outburst once again thrust Willis's character into controversy's cockpit. Though several writers stateside rushed to his defense (except Morris, who refused on principle to answer personal attacks), Webb clearly struck a chord: U.S. editorial opinion ran sharply against the young American's "leaky pen" and toadying Anglophilia. And because the "Silver Fork" morals of Blessington's coterie were already commonly blamed for encouraging some of the nation's most disturbing social trends—including the much bemoaned spread of worldly cynicism, slavish adherence to European fashions (both sartorial and literary), and unhealthy adulation of celebrity—Willis's panegyrics from Seamore Place thrust him nearly overnight into the post of four-square America's most conspicuous whipping boy. Indeed, no less a satirist than the *Southern Literary Messenger*'s Edgar Allan Poe was soon to skewer the *Mirror*'s correspondent for his tuft-hunting ways in a tale called "Lionizing." New York's James Kirke Paulding thought this "quiz . . . not only capital," but "understood by all." While this observation was not strictly accurate (at least one Virginian could find neither "wit nor humor" in Poe's squib), it was nonetheless true that, with Webb's help, Willis had once again writ himself into the equivocal character of America's foremost Pelham, only this time on a transatlantic stage and in the company of the genuine article.[27]

Meanwhile, developments overseas were further testing Willis's hopeful calculation of the previous year. In several sketches of the London literati, Blessington's American pet had indulged in the customary frankness, as well as the ebullient adulation that marked his letters. He described the celebrated and much romanticized Edward Bulwer, for instance, as "short, very much bent in the back, slightly knock-kneed, and . . . as ill-dressed a man for a gentleman as you will find in London" but fascinating all the same. Now—probably via Mackenzie's *Liverpool Journal*—the substance of these accounts resurfaced across the Atlantic.[28]

For Willis, the catastrophe had transpired. In late April 1835, thoroughly mortified, he evidently tried to head off a scene with a quick round of apologies tendered through Lady Blessington. But the *Examiner*'s political correspondent, Albany Fonblanque—whom the glib traveler had described uncharitably as "sallow, seamed and hollow, his teeth irregular, his skin livid, his straight black hair uncombed and straggling over his forehead," with a "hollow, croaking voice" and a "smile like a skeleton's"—fumed at the ill-treatment and spurned Willis's regrets. Bulwer was more temperate but no less severe in his rejoinder. While admitting to Willis that he himself was "too long inured to publicity to feel annoyed at personal reflections," *Pelham*'s famous author could, nonetheless, hardly countenance the disturbing precedent against domestic immunities set by the American's candid letters. "As a public man," he reasoned,

> I should consider myself a fair subject for public exhibition, however unfavorably minute, except, indeed, from such persons as I have received as a guest. . . . Such invasions of the inviolable decorums of society impair the confidence which is not more its charm than its foundation. I think you have done great disservice to your countrymen in this visit to England, and that in future we shall shrink from many claimants on our hospitality, lest they should become the infringers of its rights.

In this regard, Bulwer was apparently good as his word: only a month later, the American poet Henry Wadsworth Longfellow complained of a cold reception accorded him by the genuine Pelham.[29]

What Bulwer suggested in his letter regarding the claims of civility also threatened to blast the sort of celebrity journalism on which Willis had lately embarked. If nothing else, acceptance into the private society of even "public men" implied for Bulwer—as it had for Webb and other "gentlemanly" men—certain social responsibilities. These included the doctrine that familiar company and its banter must remain off-limits to report—even though an ocean intervened between readers and subject. Britain's Captain Basil Hall had certainly understood this proscription when he resolved to avoid mentioning private friends in his recent book of travels, though, as with Frances Trollope's *Domestic Manners of the Americans* (1832), his strictures on American democracy had nonetheless drawn howls of indignation throughout the United States. Perhaps too late, Willis now began to realize the consequences of his wishful calculations. Though complaining of Fonblanque's rude reply, he admitted to Lady Blessington that he had never read a more gentlemanly note than Bulwer's: "He gives me no quarter; but I like him the better for having written it, and he makes me tenfold more ashamed of those silly and ill-starred letters." This private apology evidently satisfied Blessington, who, despite her annoyance at the turn of events, clearly regarded Willis with great affection. After some coolness, she took up again with her American favorite; through it all, her salon remained open to her young admirer.[30]

Matters might have rested here had not national and personal antipathies intervened. Sometime in the mid-summer of 1835, the Scotsman John Lockhart, longtime editor of London's *Quarterly Review*, obtained a broken series of Willis's correspondence: all told, some fifty-odd of the almost one hundred forty letters eventually published in the *Mirror*. Today, their provenance remains a matter of conjecture. But we do know that by this time, talk of the "Pencillings" was current in several British circles: Mackenzie had undoubtedly begun his reprints in the *Liverpool Journal*—Mrs. Hewitt, the poetess, having written to express her admiration of them; several other papers evidently followed Mackenzie's lead; and Longfellow certainly discussed his compatriot's letters on a visit to Thomas Carlyle and Leigh Hunt in early June. Lockhart apparently knew enough of the "Pencillings" to gather as many as he could. Whether these letters were culled from the back files of a club reading room or sent onward from the United States by some obliging antagonist of Willis's is, in one sense, immaterial. Once in Lockhart's hands, they were fully sufficient to the task he had in mind.[31]

Like Bulwer—and Webb before him—Lockhart deplored the erosion of domestic immunities wrought in the wake of a quarter century or so of invasive travel reports. In fact, several years later he was to express the decided opinion that "all persons who kept journals" should be summarily excluded from society. But he was also a rock-ribbed Tory who knew what to do with Yankee indiscretion, especially such as would discomfit advocates of democratic reform such as the much despised Dan O'Connell, and even Bulwer himself, whom Lockhart once called a "Norfolk squire, and horrid puppy." As editor of the *Quarterly*, Lockhart had launched salvo after salvo against popular pretense, never losing a chance to contrast the salutary order of the traditional landed estates with the deplorable convulsions of placeless democracy. For the past decade, too, every book of travels crossing his reviewer's desk had been sent off with a barbed notice on this perennial theme. Americans, who were especially sensitive to slights upon their national pretensions, thus had come to regard Lockhart as a chief antagonist in the hot war of words long joined between Britain and the United States. Willis had said as much in a letter to the *Mirror*, when he called the Scottish reviewer "the most unfair and unprincipled critick of the day." Goaded at least in part by this uncharitable aspersion, Lockhart was now to prove why he was also one of its most effective.[32]

The particular occasion for this was a contemptuous notice of the fugitive "Pencillings" in September's *Quarterly Review*, a review that was to change Willis's life. When Lockhart was through with his so-called greenhorn sonneteer of "ultra-sentimental delicacy," he had, with stunning rhetorical efficiency, reduced the American traveler to the status of an "animal": that is, a *domestic spy* who, like the proverbial tale-telling servant, was fit only for contempt. Payback aside, this cut and thrust appealed most directly to class solidarity and a conservative political order, for having clinched his case against Willis by once again rehearsing Moore's compromising table talk, Lockhart could scarcely hope to forestall such confidential gossip's further circulation. Yet he could hope to galvanize the "better sorts" on both sides of the Atlantic to make an example of the loose-lipped traveling attaché, thus closing the ranks of society (and celebrity, for that matter) against the putative depredations of democracy and the popular press.[33]

For all his own journalistic enterprise, what Lockhart had in mind here was a return to the good old days, when a gentleman's home truly was his castle, proof against social as well as physical assaults. This was, however, a quixotic vision, even with respect to immediate affairs, for predictably, much excitement greeted the appearance of Lockhart's review. Willis's friends may have long harbored their suspicions, but to most British readers the *Quarterly's* article came as a surprise: the pleasant poet lately come among them had been turning hospitality to his own purposes. Few could restrain themselves from a peek at what this sneak thief of celebrity had seen, heard, and said. Who knew what juicy tidbits awaited? Ever anxious for the latest literary gossip, readers prepared for a feast. To feed their appetite, papers across the land busied themselves by extracting choice excerpts from the *Quarterly*'s review or reprinting passages from the *Mirror*, while book publishers scurried to gather up the fugitive "Pencillings," as they congratulated themselves on their good fortune.[34]

By this point, Willis could do little but acquiesce in the inevitable. Given the absence of international copyright, the letters would be published regardless. In fact, broken sets of the *Mirror* correspondence were already in press when William Macrone informed the now-notorious American traveler in late September that he intended to publish them with or without permission. Willis could either supervise the editing—and reap the profit of sensation—or loose them willy-nilly to the world.[35]

Understandably, the "Penciller" chose the former. If nothing else, this expedient offered perhaps the best hope of presenting his case favorably, though his new celebrity was now bound to be equivocal, regardless. Perhaps he was influenced as well by the prospect of providing for two. Although Willis was haunted by the memory of Mary Benjamin, his thoughts had lately turned elsewhere. "I should like to marry in England," the almost thirty-year-old traveler confided to a friend a year after his arrival in that nation, "and I feel every day (more and more) that my best years and best affections are running to waste. I am proud to *be* an American," he continued,

> but as a literary man, I would rather live in England. So if you know any affectionate and *good* girl who would be content to live rather a quiet life, and could love your humble servant, you have full power of attorney to dispose of me, *provided* she has *five hundred* a year, or as much more as she likes. I know enough of the world to cut my throat sooner than bring a delicate woman down to dependence on my brains for support, though in the case of exigency I could always retreat to America, and live comfortably by my labors.

Then, just before the storm, he finally found a girl whose father would take him: a pretty young Englishwoman of evangelical disposition by the name of Mary Leighton Stace, the daughter of the Royal Ordinance Keeper at Woolwich Arsenal. London's dissipations had evidently begun to weary her suitor, and he believed himself at something of a turning point: "I have lived the last ten years in gay society, and I am sick at heart of it," he told his new love. "I want an apology to try something else." After a brief courtship, the two were married on the first day of October 1835. With noise of the "Pencillings" rattling around the press, Willis had just time enough to strike a bargain with his publisher before heading off with his new wife for a fortnight's honeymoon in Paris. When he returned, publication of his "silly, ill-starred letters" would only further stoke the fire of controversy they had already kindled.[36]

The Problem with Personalities

For all its passion, Lockhart's righteous complaint was, in effect, a rearguard action. For one thing, the Reform Bill's recent passage had profoundly shaken the political dominion that had for so long buttressed his brand of Tory exclusivity. More to the point, the rewards entailed in catering to the growing market for celebrity had been steadily leading travel writers in particular to buck censure by dealing in all manner of familiar gossip. Indeed, impatient—as Willis was—with old-hat descriptions and emboldened by a Romantic aesthetic fascinated with exemplary character, they were, by the 1830s, fast promoting a revamped canon of report that fundamentally challenged long-standing injunctions against domestic publicity. Willis's *Pencillings* thus stood at an ethical watershed in the evolution of the culture of celebrity. Not surprisingly, the book's reception reflected its transitional position.

Once, reportorial freedoms like Willis's would have been almost unthinkable. If nothing else, Anglo-American common law judged any report tending to degrade character as libelous—regardless of truth or falsity. Traditionally, writers were thus understandably wary of printing offhand remarks upon personal appearance, habit, character, or conversation, especially as doing so almost certainly meant enduring a chorus of blame for indulging in what Willis's contemporaries commonly called "personalities." Drawing strength, in part, from an Enlightenment desire to purge public discourse of its passions, this catchall rhetoric of blame encompassed mean-spirited ridicule of habits and appearance, unprincipled plying of rumor and innuendo, and promiscuous retailing of familiar conversation—in short, anything that might be properly regarded as unfit for public consumption. For travel writers in particular, this customary proscription had always meant that domestic society was off-limits to report. Historically, even so-called public characters like Edward Bulwer—those individuals who had willfully thrust themselves before the world—could thus expect considerable protection from invasive prying and indiscriminate notice.[37]

Yet, as the circle of writers and readers steadily widened and diversified, in practice it became increasingly difficult to forestall the retailing of familiar gossip, especially as literary and social developments swelled the clamor for intimate knowledge of celebrated lives. Already, published collections of personal correspondence (like that of Alexander Pope) had begun to accustom eighteenth-century readers to the guilty pleasures entailed in opening a window into the domestic lives of those whom Dr. Johnson called the "Great." So it was that when James Boswell's wildly popular *Life of Johnson* (1791) opened the floodgates of personality to a stream of posthumous memoirs, biographies, and letter collections, readers came to think nothing of sifting through their idols' most intimate papers. Lord Byron's death in 1824, for example, spawned five major biographies fairly brimming with familiar anecdote and personal correspondence; Tom Moore's particular reliance on his deceased friend's letters and diaries was enough to convince Willis, for one, that "we know all of Byron that we could know." (In actuality, Moore had altered some letters, burned others, introduced fakeries, and systematically suppressed passages likely to offend certain living individuals.) Even where observers shrank from such immoderate disclosures, however, they were likely to endorse the general project of opening a window into private lives. When, for instance, Willis's countryman at the *Salem Gazette* removed references to living persons from portions of Byron's diary excerpted from Moore's *Life*, he knew that doing so meant burying anecdotes sure to "gratify the most lively and piquant curiosity of the reader." Still, enough information remained, he hoped, "to enlarge still further the view we have here opened into the interior of the poet's life and habits, and to indulge harmlessly that taste, as general as it is natural, which leads us to contemplate with pleasure a great mind in its undress." Others were not so careful in their prying. When, in his dunciad *Truth* (1830), William Snelling had identified Boston's most infamous dandy-poet by the farcical expedient of initials and dashes, he clearly did not plan to fool anyone by the ruse.[38]

Of course, such developments were not without their gainsayers, particularly among the "public characters" who were most susceptible to the encroachments of invasive publicity. Walter Scott evidently felt curiosity's mounting pressure as early as 1808 (soon after the publication of *Marmion*), when he confessed in what was meant to be a preemptive autobiographical sketch that "the present age has discovered a desire, or rather a rage, for literary anecdote and private history that may be well permitted to alarm one who has engaged in a certain degree the attention of the public." Two decades later, Scott's son-in-law and future biographer (the same John Lockhart who bedeviled Willis) was worried enough by the drift of journalistic practice to complain that "the ear of that grand impersonation, 'The Reading Public,' ha[s] become as filthily prurient as that of an eaves dropping lackey."[39]

By the time Willis left for Europe, however, it was not at all clear that publishing so-called private anecdotes was, as the Franco-American travel writer Louis Simond had remarked a decade before, universally regarded as an "unpardonable indelicacy." Most observers continued to maintain that domestic immunities protected common folk from indiscriminate publicity, but many were coming to agree with the self-justifying author of *Sketches of Public Characters* (1830) that "the writers of the day should speak freely of the living; as the truly great have nothing to fear, and the oftener their merits are discussed, the better for them." Such sentiments undoubtedly sent shudders through the likes of Lockhart and Scott. Still, we should not conclude that right-thinking observers universally condemned all aspects of this revolution in report. Significantly in this regard, on the eve of Willis's departure for Europe, such a pillar of propriety as Boston's Unitarian *Christian Examiner* was prepared to stand with the cause of journalistic freedom. In December 1830, for instance, its reviewer could find little wrong with the Reverend Nathaniel S. Wheaton's *Journal of a Residence during several months in London* for naming names and reporting private conversation—some individuals were "so entirely the property of the public, that a desire to learn everything connected with their persons [was] not to be harshly resolved into an appetite for scandal." In this respect, the inconvenience of notoriety that so worried Lockhart was written off as merely "one of those taxes"—the reviewer compared it to "daily" letters of introduction—"which eminence must consent to pay." This was no less than a fundamental rethinking of the ethics of report, one both eminently more conducive to publicizing celebrity and infinitely more liable to interpretation than the older model of strict excision. If domestic publicity regarding living individuals had once been universally proscribed by the charge of personalities, it was now to be provisionally legitimated to satisfy public appetites for access to the world of "undress."[40]

There was, of course, still the matter of where to draw the line; for this, the *Christian Examiner's* reviewer had a plan. First, he proposed that travelers ought not to be summarily turned away merely upon chance of their later publicizing dinner-table small talk. (With rekindled fears of British tourists swarming the United States, notebooks in hand, such a chill upon hospitality is, in fact, exactly what some Americans proposed and, apparently, practiced.) Instead, he suggested that honorable citizens should seize the moment to advise their guests of expectations governing the visit. Travelers intending to publish their adventures were to be told that no feelings would be outraged—respectable persons, after all, had nothing to fear from publicity. Only "personal peculiarities" ought to be avoided. "Reveal, if you please," the *Christian Examiner's* ideal host was made to advise his guest, "whether the favorite topics of conversation be literature or news, and how long the ladies remained at dessert; but suppress, in mercy, the mistakes which servants may commit, and any consequent irritations you may observe on the countenances of their master and mistress."[41]

This modest proposal was quite ambitious after its own fashion, for it suggested nothing less than how to reconcile expanded journalistic freedoms with the notoriously sensitive jealousies of personal feelings. Yet, as with most schemes of the moral imagination, the devil lurked in the details. The proposal was earnest enough—that, indeed, was its problem. Ritual colloquy over the terms of report was bound to be socially awkward; only a prig would habitually subject his guests to lectures upon their moral obligations. Mutual expectations were thus likely to remain unexpressed and ethical responsibilities to remain ambiguous. Neither did the proposed system offer anything but regret to those offended by subsequent report, as philosophic resignation was small consolation to the host "served up cold" for the reading world's amusement. Now, perhaps it was true, as the *Christian Examiner* admitted blandly, that such insults were unavoidable: "We are all in some degree at the mercy of every stranger who enters our doors." But in an atmosphere poisoned by steadily eroding domestic immunities and charged with national antagonisms, such a reminder was as likely to spark resentment as still misgivings. Rather than clarifying social obligations, the *Christian Examiner* had thus only succeeded in complicating them.[42]

It was through this minefield of ethical ambiguity that Willis was forced to make his way, following Lockhart's withering reproach. Considerable evidence suggests that the American traveler was keenly aware of the bind into which circumstance and his own actions had put him. While the newlywed "Penciller" was off honeymooning in Paris, his onetime host Lord Aberdeen, the Duke of Gordon, had sent along a friendly letter through Jane Porter advising the glib travel writer "*to print the Letters precisely as they were published in America*" to avoid clouding his motives. Judging solely by the *Quarterly's* extracts, Aberdeen saw no reason for personal complaint, though he objected to being gazetted as having the reputation of "the proudest and coldest aristocrat in England." He was less sanguine about the practice of reporting familiar conversation, but he admitted that his own countrymen were as guilty of the offense as anyone. Sadly, Willis shrank from this counsel: the *Quarterly's* extracts had hardly exhausted his letters' fund of embarrassing gossip. Even though British editors were industriously ferreting out much of this lacunae, its author had no wish to roil already agitated waters any more than necessary. Indeed, with Bulwer and Fonblanque in mind, Willis had already asked Blessington to strike potentially objectionable passages from the proofs, making sure that prominent individuals were identified wholly by initials and dashes. The task of answering Lockhart's rebuke he reserved to himself.[43]

On this point, Willis evidently believed a good offense to be his best defense, for there is no mistaking his preface to *Pencillings by the Way* (in striking contrast to his apologies to Blessington et al.) as anything but a performance meant to shift the weight of censure to his condescending traducer. To this end, the young American traveler could tap no greater reservoir of feeling than his own compatriots' much tweaked national pride. While now admitting that he would rewrite passages if he could (meaning Moore's table-talk denunciation of O'Connell), Willis thus stood by his contention that Lockhart was the "most unprincipled critic of the age," and his *Quarterly* the perpetrator of "every spark of ill feeling that has been kept alive between England and America for the last twenty years." To Willis's mind, neither was Lockhart the man to spout righteous indignation over personalities, having flagrantly indulged himself of the same practice in *Peter's Letters to His Kinsfolk* (1819), and then under the very noses of his subjects. It was palliation enough, the American suggested, that at least *he* had never stooped so low. More than this, Willis had a duty to his country to protest his treatment—or so he alleged. Wrapping himself in national honor, the "Penciller" thus concluded his prefatory retort with a priceless specimen of nineteenth-century bombast: "I conceive it to be my duty as a literary man—I *know* it is my duty as an American—to lose no opportunity of setting my heel on the head of this reptile of criticism. He has turned and stung me. Thank God, I have escaped the slime of his approbation."[44]

Bluster was one thing; carrying the day, another. Predictably, Tory reviewers had a field day with Willis's bravado: condemning his book's now-infamous breaches of confidence, reveling in O'Connell's embarrassment, speculating upon excised passages, and cackling over Yankee impertinence. On the way to thoroughly skewering Willis, *Fraser's* William Maginn (a notorious partisan and scandalous wit) called the egregious "Penciller" a "ninny," an insignificant bravo, a "fifty-fifth rate scribbler of gripe-visited sonnets," an unreliable gossip, an arsonist of national ill will, and, finally, a "haberdashering *attaché.*" Tory scandal rags such as the *Age* had already said worse, calling the American traveler "PIMP WILLIS," among other things. And if the Whig papers were more charitable, they generally stood with their political antagonists in deploring the unauthorized publication of "private table-talk" as an offense against good taste and domestic security: "The confidence of a dinner," one reviewer intoned, "is only less sacred than that of a woman." Coming from some of the masters of personalities, this solemnity was a bit much: few, for example, followed the principled lead of the *Edinburgh Review* by refusing to reprint the offensive passages.[45]

In a certain sense, the consonance of this torrent of condemnation misleads; many people were not in the least disturbed by Willis's brand of reportage or the culture of celebrity toward which it was pointing. The Earl of Dalhousie and his wife (who might have had reason for regret) both wrote Willis to express their thorough delight with the "spirited" "Pencillings"; Lady Dalhousie assured her young friend that the *Quarterly's* ill-natured pasquinade was met with "extreme wrath and indignation" in at least one Tory household. Willis's literary admirers

were not confined to acquaintances, either. Jane Porter later recounted melodramatically how one British mother was moved to tears by her daughter's fascination
with Willis's letters and stories. And writing to an American friend, the celebrated
Mrs. Anne Grant of Edinburgh could find "nothing offensive" in the "very resem-
bling sketches" taken of the Duke of Gordon's household—their "air of reality"
had, in fact, entertained her immensely. "I cannot see the harm of a traveler's telling
his impressions of what he saw," she reasoned matter-of-factly. "Why else do people
travel?" Even more telling was the comment of a young upcountry South Carolinian
woman upon reading the *Quarterly's* review: "Willis is very cleverly cut up here,"
she told her diary,

> but I had rather see his 'pencillings by the way' than hear talk of 'em. I think they
> must be very nice;—but perhaps I am over-partial to N. P., for how often I have been
> ready to wish with Desdemond [*sic*]
>
>> that heaven had made 'me' such a man
>
> however, as there is no 'Willis' here to 'speak upon my hint,' I suppose I must take
> the one that's nearest like him.

Even in the face of what to many looked like unpardonable breaches of conduct,
Willis's familiar letters thus found considerable favor with the general public. It was
a bet, moreover that many who condemned the messenger welcomed the message
all the same.[46]

The American was not entirely through the woods, though. Back in April 1835,
George Morris had unwittingly compromised his associate's integrity a fraction
further by appending a gossipy private communication to Willis's usual weekly
account of British society. Concerned as Morris was to maintain the gentlemanly
tone of the *Mirror*, business was business; this was neither the first nor the last time
he or his subordinates would ransack distinguished individuals' private correspondence for a juicy report. In fact, not long afterward they would justify reproducing
a private note from a celebrated American tragedian by arguing that "the opinions
of so distinguished a person are in some degree publick property." In Willis's case,
the payoff was clear: a rundown on London's latest literary and political gossip,
including what he called the "*real* prices" several celebrated authors commanded
for their books—a phenomenal fifteen hundred pounds for Bulwer, four hundred
for Lady Blessington, twenty-five hundred for the "Honourable Mrs. Norton," and
so on down to the young Benjamin Disraeli, whom Morris's glib correspondent
had heard could not "sell a book at all." By contrast, Willis told his partner saucily
that "Captain Marryatt's [*sic*] gross trash sells immensely about Wapping and Ports-
mouth, and brings him five or six hundred the book—but that can scarce be called
literature."[47]

Though struck from the London editions of the "Pencillings," this offhand remark was undoubtedly the principle goad that now prompted Captain Frederick
Marryat's once-friendly *Metropolitan Magazine* to launch after Willis. Avoiding literary matters altogether, Willis's self-appointed scourge (not Marryat himself, it
would turn out, but a zealous lieutenant) took the opportunity of his review of
Pencillings to once again slash away at the tattered shreds of the American traveler's

good name—snickering at his greenhorn pretense; demeaning his parentage; and deploring his diplomatic abuses and ill-natured backstabbing—all the while, disparaging the democratic ethos that Willis presumably represented. Lockhart may have begun the campaign to run down democracy by running down Willis, but the *Metropolitan* clearly sought to finish the job.[48]

If Willis was turning out to be the best thing for the Tory cause since Mrs. Trollope's tobacco-spitting Americans, he was also fast becoming the day's most striking reminder that, as the *Metropolitan* put it, "now-a-days three thousand miles are little more than a *twopenny post*." What should appear in its ill-natured review but the fateful sneer against Marryat that Willis had tried in vain to suppress. Judging by the remarks of the captain's hatchetman, notice of it had been sent across the sea months before by a "distinguished literary character," perhaps one of Willis's old stateside antagonists. To this obliging informant may also go the credit for the "AMERICAN tomahawk" that delivered the *Metropolitan*'s "coup de grace": certain passages rehearsing Willis's sexual peccadilloes that were drawn from William Snelling's Boston dunciad *Truth*. Youth's disrepute had thus chased the deacon's wayward son across the ocean, and finally found him. In these days of international celebrity, no distance seemed great enough to shield people from their past *or* present.[49]

Given his jealous claims upon good name and social standing, Willis was singularly ill suited to suffer this defamation silently. Lockhart's attack had already led him to brandish national honor in his defense, but histrionics had hardly given pause to his disparagers. Doubtless, this result was troubling for Willis. Still, the *Metropolitan*'s galling condescension at least presented him with a welcome opportunity to meet matters openly, and as he told his friend the countess, "once for all, I shall carry the point well through." What actually transpired, however, was less an unequivocal triumph than a telling illustration of the public follies into which modern literary celebrity could lead practitioners.[50]

For a while now, Marryat had been staying in Brussels. On the advice of gentlemen friends, Willis sent him a private letter apologizing for the inadvertent publication of what he called his "obnoxious remark," but demanding retraction of the *Metropolitan*'s unseemly sneer at his lower middling birth. For the present, Willis was prepared to be satisfied with a private apology—but not ultimately. Already he had sent lithograph copies of his complaint to seven of his most valued friends. Eventually, he intended to publish the resulting correspondence of honor to clear his name before the wider world of readers. As this audience now comprised a literary man's most consequential public, such an unorthodox scheme was perhaps unavoidable. Willis's chief advisor—anonymous to us, but in the American's estimation "one of the most distinguished officers and most accomplished gentlemen in this country"—certainly thought so. Marryat's insult had, he suggested, "lain uncontradicted on the public mind for a month," and it must be answered, tout de suite, with the captain's consent or no. Sadly, this course of action was destined to provoke the very kind of jealousies it was intended to salve.[51]

At first, Marryat was willing to explain away his hatchetman's insinuations—not graciously, it must be said, yet freely all the same. But when the captain subsequently saw his correspondence published in the *Times* against all usage in gentlemanly society, he demanded satisfaction to the tune of pistols at ten paces. Rather than face humiliation, Willis accepted. After further correspondence and considerable dickering over the site of the impending conflict, the two men's friends patched up the quarrel. Still, Marryat was not to be outdone by his literary rival: within days, he, too, took to the *Times* with his own flurry of published correspondence, including the "offensive challenge" against the Willis family honor that previous settlement had required him to withdraw.

Now it was Willis's turn to be outraged. The fight was on again. Leaving his new wife at home sick with anxiety, the young American proceeded to the harbor at Chatham, where Marryat had hurried upon hearing of the latest turn of events. There, on 27 February 1836, the two antagonists prepared to meet each other. Had the duel come off, there would have been every reason to expect Willis's death: the captain was reputedly a crack shot; his opponent rarely handled a gun. Fortunately, the necessary concessions were wrung from each of the principals and the proceedings halted before any damage ensued. Even then, the wretched affair trailed on through one more episode: only two days after returning home, Willis galloped off to London to call out one of Marryat's associates for yet another allegedly abusive circular. By this point everyone had had enough, and a mutual conciliation was arranged.[52]

For all its foolishness, this tragicomic affair was not without its advantages for Willis's cause. There was indeed some truth in Jane Porter's well-meaning prediction that the *Metropolitan*'s recriminatory spirit, like that of the *Quarterly*, "will rather increase the number of your British friends, than subtract one iota from the generally respected fairness of your name." Indeed, in reviewing the published correspondence of the Marryat affair, several observers on both sides of the Atlantic did sustain the American traveler in his dispute of honor. Even the solemn *North American Review*—no friend to the *code duello*—proclaimed some months hence that "no candid man can read the correspondence without feeling that Mr. Willis's part of it is infinitely superior to the Captain's, in style, sense, dignity of feeling, and manly honor." Nonetheless, it was hard to banish the impression that what had begun as a spirited defense of honor and the bounds of criticism had ended in anything more than a kind of public farce. The *Times* itself certainly spoke for many when it finally washed its hands of the matter. "We have a great disdain for this sort of squabbling," it confessed, "which exhibits, to say the least, an extraordinary want of judgment in the disputing parties."[53]

In truth, the spectacle of dueling authors blazing away over an incidental affront might have been almost funny had it not also been so deadly serious. This problem did not stem solely from the potential for physical harm. Marryat was more than half in earnest when he construed Willis's literary cut as a threat to his reputation. For all his self-serving logic, the bellicose captain was astute enough in observing that often "we estimate the character of a man by his writings." To those who now made their living on the literary public's good opinion, such disapprobation, if generally embraced, might prove commercially and socially disastrous. Yet as the field of honor moved inexorably into print and its compass widened to span an ocean, policing reputations had become considerably more complicated than it had once been—the dueling editors' seriocomic antics being a case in point. Not only was the field of honor as dangerous as ever, but the petty dickering and wounded vanity of jealous negotiation, traditionally satisfied by private adjudication, were now—at least for "public characters" such as Willis and Marryat—almost necessarily extended to the realm of popular print. Like invasive reportage, this burden of honor and reputation would continue to plague those who walked the shaky boards of celebrity.[54]

Legacies

Notwithstanding its problems, controversy is often good for business. In Willis's case, its rewards proved both substantial and enduring. Even at its considerable price of seven dollars a copy, demand for his *Pencillings by the Way* ran high. And success spawned success: soon after the book's publication, plans were afoot to issue a second London edition and a volume of Willis's collected magazine fiction; a U.S. edition of the *Pencillings* was in the works as well—all of which meant that Willis's long-standing debts from the *American Monthly* might yet be retired, with considerable funds remaining to start life anew with his English wife. Counting receipts of six hundred pounds for the two London editions of the *Pencillings*, nearly as much again for their author's collected tales *Inklings of Adventure*, proceeds from the American editions of each book, and Morris's annual stipend, it is clear that Willis ultimately reaped a handsome profit from his speculative journey. Even with all his troubles, he could crow not long before his return to the States, "literature has thriven with me. I am on the *riz*, as they say on the corn market."[55]

Though Willis could hardly have known it at the time, the sparkling prose and romantic descriptions of *Pencillings by the Way* were to prove central to his literary reputation for years to come. Even before the book's stateside publication, the compass of his fame was such that a waggish editor in far-off Natchez, Mississippi, could perpetrate a hoax using the celebrated traveler's name—inserting in a competitor's pages the noteworthy intelligence that "Willis, lady, child, and servant" had lately arrived by steamboat, then ostentatiously badgered his unsuspecting associate regarding the whereabouts of this "most important" of visitors announced in his paper. When Willis actually did return to the States (minus the "child"), no manner of private complaints that he danced "like a *ninny*" or that he was "notoriously destitute of principle" could keep fashionable society up and down the east coast from lionizing him "quite violently"—despite the admonitions of Lockhart, Marryat, and the like. After all, the *Mirror*'s star correspondent had, as the phrase went, *seen the elephant*—in this case, the divine Countess Blessington and her brilliant coterie.[56]

More important, he had related his experiences in language that captured the imagination of his generation. For years, Americans cherished Willis's *Pencillings* as a valuable travel companion and the stuff of dreams. No less a luminary than Daniel Webster was said to have thought the book both "instructive and amusing." Bayard Taylor, himself later to captivate readers with a career's worth of foreign adventures, would also always credit Willis's famous letters with inspiring his prodigious wanderlust. Even the expresident's son Charles Francis Adams was "amused" in spite of himself at the "affected and ridiculous" Willis. This interest did not wane any time soon. A full twenty years after *Pencillings'* first appearance, one fervent Georgia book lover who saw a "very nicely bound" copy of Willis's volumes advertised together with Bulwer's *Pelham* in an Augusta bookshop could hardly contain her enthusiasm. "I have long been anxious to see them both," she confided to her diary, "and eagerly embraced the opportunity for getting them." They would, she mused, form the nucleus of the private library of which she had long dreamed.[57]

Yet even as *Pencillings* made both Willis's name and fortune, the book's sensation saddled him with a lasting transatlantic disrepute. In Britain, critics elevated the *Mirror's* junior editor to metonymic notoriety as the embodiment of self-aggrandizing Yankee prying—a kind of tattling American Trollope whose periodic return (Willis would twice revisit Britain) unfailingly signaled the watchdogs of domestic prerogatives to their guard and satirists to their pens. William Makepeace Thackeray, who subsequently had his own troubles with Willis, used him as a model on several occasions (most memorably for the tuft-hunting John Paul Jefferson Jones in *Vanity Fair*), as did Frances Trollope herself in *The Blue Belles of England* (1842). As late as 1845, *Punch* cheekily announced the Penciller's impending return to Albion's shore with a call to aspiring authors to stand to: at no expense to themselves, the magazine predicted, dinner with Willis would see them in print—just watch your tongue. Back at home, matters assumed a similar form: for good or ill, Blessington's connection aligned her American admirer with the world of European fashion, while Willis's "silly, ill-starred letters" settled him with a fund of trespasses that enemies and critics would mine for years.[58]

The lucrative contretemps inspired by the pencillings thus decisively shaped Willis's career, particularly because it confirmed him in what would prove to be a lifelong pursuit of celebrity: his own and other's. In doing so, this episode also dramatized some of the central impulses of the emerging culture of celebrity. On one hand, Willis's experience suggests just how profoundly the commercial imperatives of travel writing were eroding long-standing domestic immunities, especially among the class of "public characters" who had lately captured the imagination of readers. Raised to general notice by achievement or station, such celebrities (as they had come to be called since the 1820s) inevitably courted publicity in the new world of popular print—many throve on it. And they were widely believed to owe the world a greater latitude of report as a consequence—not so many years later, one American observer would go so far as to suggest that such public men had no rights to a "private character" whatsoever.[59]

By subjecting even the most familiar social exchanges to the threat of indiscriminate report, Willis begged the perennial question of just where that latitude ought to end. Like his compatriots in the budding trade upon literary and fashionable gossip, he had jumped at the chance to tap the swelling interest in the domestic world behind the public scene (a fascination he himself shared), offering readers tantalizing glimpses into spheres of privilege and talent otherwise beyond their ken. By doing so, he unwittingly set himself up to play whipping boy to the considerable misgivings aroused by such invasive innovations. But even as ideological and national jealousies fed the ensuing hailstorm of reproof, his commercial fortunes were assured. In this sense, Willis came to embody one of print celebrity's most distressing yet most captivating archetypes: he was the spy who came to dinner.

The Coming Aristocracy

Father used to say that N. P. brought more true culture to America
than anyone else in the nineteenth century.

N. P. Willis's granddaughter (1966)

Upon returning to his native land in the late spring of 1836, America's newly married penciller by the way had inevitably faced the question of what to make of his situation. At first, he was inclined to retire from public notice altogether. "London is not so d——d bad," the world-weary traveler had confessed to a close friend shortly before leaving for the States, *"cependant,* I am disgusted with authorship & being now *passing rich on forty pounds a year*—more or less—I mean to hang up my fiddle and pass round the hat." Notwithstanding his smooth accommodation to the requisites of the new literary professionalism, this inclination to quit authorial labors for an older ideal of gentlemanly independence ran deep. Whenever his professional duties would let him, Willis was off to enjoy the quiet charms of Glenmary, his beloved "cottage *insoucieuse*" on the upper Susquehanna River. (It was this comfortable rural existence that the author evoked in his popular "Letters from under a Bridge" series.) For half a decade, he also chased an elusive diplomatic appointment, hoping to trade his magazinist's drudgery for a secretary's easy yoke. Yet when high living and financial reverses forced Glenmary's sale in 1842 and every diplomatic scheme miscarried, penciller Willis was obliged to concede what more than a decade of experience suggested: his surest prospects lay with the vibrant market for popular letters. He must be a literary man, or no man at all.[1]

In light of circumstances, that meant almost necessarily relocating with his wife, Mary, and their infant daughter, Imogen, to the city that was rapidly emerging as the nation's undisputed capital of celebrity. Already, New York had begun to outgrow the confines of its Knickerbocker past, as merchants, boosters, and speculators, enriched by Atlantic commerce and the Erie Canal trade, pushed residential settlement northward to accommodate new businesses downtown. By midcentury, this sprawling metropolis of over half a million people fairly pulsed with the sort of energy that, for many Americans, epitomized modernity. Driven by ballyhoo and a pervasive national curiosity, commercial attractions such as P. T. Barnum's American Museum (established in 1841) accustomed visitors to a dazzling parade of novelties and personalities, from the preposterous Feejee Mermaid to the world-famous midget, Tom Thumb. So, too, did the city's unparalleled musical and dramatic fare beckon tourists and locals alike to witness their favorites live-and-in-person, an exhibition of celebrity that the reigning "star" system of theatrical booking, with its cycle of traveling headliners, only underscored. This effect was not confined to New York alone. For those unable to make the trip, the city's powerhouse journalistic and publishing empire, sustained by papermaking and typesetting improvements, the recently introduced steam press, and a rapidly expanding rail and telegraphic system, spread news of this bustling urban world of entertainment and culture to even the nation's most out-of-the-way hamlets.

The scope and sway of literary fame, in particular, surged remarkably under the stimulus of these developments. In 1830 the average press run for works of fiction had hovered around 1,000 copies; by the 1850s, sales of select American best-sellers topped 100,000 volumes. Magazine and newspaper circulation also skyrocketed in these years, as New York–based periodicals such as the *Tribune*, the *Herald*, and *Harper's Monthly* laid claim to national audiences numbering in the tens of thousands. Moreover, with publishing houses proliferating as well as growing in size and sophistication, the bray and crow of publicity became a kind of vernacular art form. In such a go-ahead world, few successful writers could long contrive to remain anonymous, even if this were their wish.

Willis himself had much to do with setting the tone of this situation. Until lingering troubles from the *Pencillings* led to a break with Morris in December 1838, the two men had successfully carried on their *New York Mirror* as a repository of genteel culture and fashionable intelligence. Then, with Willis once again on his own, a series of high-profile commercial projects—from editing the piratical *Corsair* and *Brother Jonathan*, to supplying fashionable tales of love and society for new large-circulation ladies' magazines such as *Graham's* and *Godey's*—reconfirmed his stature as a bona fide cultural icon dedicated to hawking the talk of the town for family readers keen to feel the cosmopolitan pulse. Like his glib twentieth-century successors, Willis trafficked regularly in the "novelty and gossip of the hour," dispensing not so much fact (as he blithely admitted) but the "material of conversation and speculation, which may be mere rumor, may be the truth." Somewhat paradoxically, it was precisely these excursions into "Vanity Fair" that allowed him to assume the authoritative voice of his own fanciful "gentleman with the blue riband," a kind of au courant "ambulant dictionary" who promised to remedy a world of diffidence and embarrassment among the day's would-be cognoscenti. "How many persons of wit and spirit there are, in society, blank for lack of confidence," Willis asked, "who, with such a friend in the corner, would come out like magic-ink in the fire!" So it was that by playing to common curiosity and the social anxieties of a newly minted middle class, America's inquisitive "friend in the corner" worked to make himself indispensable to the breezy cycle of publicity and desire that was fast maturing into a full-blown celebrity industry recognizably akin to our own.[2]

In charting this course, Willis became a cynosure of the whirl and buzz he so industriously chronicled. Editorial duties at the *Mirror* and ties to the New York theater (for which he wrote several original plays in the late 1830s) had done much to establish his image as a quintessential man-about-town. This situation was only confirmed when he returned from Glenmary with his family in 1842 and took up lodgings at the prestigious Astor House. Thereafter, Willis became a fixture in the city's concert halls and theaters, in Nassau Street's "newspaper row" (where he rejoined G. P. Morris at the *New Mirror* in May 1843), and, later, among the republican celebrities gathered regularly at Anne C. Lynch's famous conversaziones. So it was that around town heads generally turned when Willis passed. No observer caught this state of affairs more delightfully than did one bemused and mildly dismayed New York journalist in the summer of 1844. "Speaking of fame," he wrote a literary friend in Boston,

> I was crossing at the South Ferry yesterday when Gen'l Morris and Willis drove out of the gate in a buggy, the latter handling the ribbons very much in the style of Bailey junior when he drove his master's cab [a jocular reference to the hard-driving cockney man-servant in Charles Dickens's *Martin Chuzzlewit*]. "There goes the celebrated Gen'l Morris," said one bystander to the ferry master. "Is it possible, well I declare," exclaimed the ferry master. "Do you know the other one?" asked another bystander. "No, who is he[?]"—"That is the great poetry man!" "My God you don't say so!" And a dozen heads were stretched out to see the phenomenon.

Perhaps Willis had not been entirely fooling himself when, earlier the same year, he had written his mother proudly, if half in jest, "My reputation keeps widening and seems to go on, without coaxing, rapidly. You will live to see me a celebrity yet."[3]

Precisely what might be achieved with such fame was another matter. There was, of course, the money. Willis himself spoke from experience when he remarked seriously enough that, in the absence of international copyright, any commercially successful American author must perforce first crack the British literary market. Only then could he or she expect to command (as Willis did for a decade or so) a transatlantic premium substantial enough to establish him as a person of means. It was this commercial achievement, as much as anything, that made him the talk of the town. Even Henry Wadsworth Longfellow (a poet and Harvard professor then doing well enough, despite the prevailing economic depression and cheap literary imports) had once been driven to lament of mustering scarcely "ten hundred" to his compatriot's princely $10,000 annual literary earnings. Nonetheless, popular letters' rewards still remained mercurial enough in this era, as the publisher's bankruptcy that forced Glenmary's sale can attest. Even for Willis, literary life remained a scramble.[4]

Yet his uncommon visibility as an author and student of society did present this admired tastemaker a golden opportunity to address a matter of special concern to his generation: that is, the problem of refining and regulating social relations in the emerging democratic ethos. Ever since the collapse of Federalist social and political hegemony early in the century, critics had bemoaned American society's headlong and rudderless quality, as money-getting and status-chasing seemed everywhere to crowd out once-common habits of self-sufficiency and deference. In these days of commercial expansion and ballyhoo politics, the question of what cultural criteria the nation was to steer by and who was to represent these republican standards figured as a perennial source of anxiety and controversy. Willis eventually hit on celebrity itself (his promiscuous assembly of "artists, authors, journalists, 'stars,' and that sort of people") as America's best hope for redressing such presumed national shortcomings. Simply put, he came to wager that taste, talent, and intellect, sifted in competition for popular acclaim and affirmed by social éclat, might yet be made to rule where station and heritage once held sway, that is, by acting as a sort of herald's college for confirming status and setting tone in a nation generally suspicious of such claims.[5]

One problem with this ambitious scheme to constitute a new republican aristocracy from the ranks of celebrity (for this result is what Willis seems to have had in mind) followed from having launched his cultural risorgimento in the orbit of commerce: in the post-Jacksonian swirl and bustle, exemplary lives would have to be made to pay as they instructed. Equally troublesome, in New York City particularly, festering class antagonisms threatened to spoil the community of feeling that was indispensable to Willis's dream of establishing a more polite and polished republican society. If sentiment and refinement yielded a recipe for sway in the print-saturated and personality-obsessed world of antebellum popular culture, so, too, did such qualities excite envy and disaffection. How zealously they could be promoted, and to whom, rated as among the era's thorniest questions.

By the late 1840s, the troubled passages of New York's cultural life would bequeath Willis—and those who set their course by his star—with more than an inkling of the difficulties posed by these problems. Before delving into such matters, however, we ought to learn more about the growth of what Willis liked to call his "literary parish." The nature of their affection will do much to explain his staying power on the American scene. So, too, will it begin to suggest why he remained as controversial a public figure as he was ubiquitous.

Sentimental Commerce

To American readers of the 1840s and early 1850s, N. P. Willis (or N. Parker Willis, as he ultimately styled himself) must have seemed a remarkably familiar, almost omnipresent figure. This situation derived not only from his voluminous literary output, fanciful prose, and irrepressible penchant for bragging about himself. (Few authors of the day wrote as frequently about themselves or with a diction that was as idiosyncratic in its use of improbable neologisms, fanciful analogies, and what one contempoary called "odd verbal combinations" and "inimitable turns of expression.") It also reflected the growing influence of the machinery of celebrity. Since the 1830s, the nation's leading journals and magazines had begun to do more than publish tales, poetry, and songs; increasingly they took to selling themselves by peddling access to their contributors through brief memoirs, character sketches, literary appreciations, and engraved and lithographed images. In Willis's case, a spate of personal profiles and likenesses that followed his first published portrait (in an 1837 issue of the *Mirror*) all served to flesh out a public character at once self-consciously stylish and peculiarly accessible. *Graham's Magazine* of April 1844, for instance, portrayed its famous curly-haired literary contributor lost in reverie, with top hat in hand, leaning casually against a fashionable neoclassical column, and the whole accompanied by a facsimile autograph promising to remain "Yours most faithfully." A subsequent woodcut engraving made this oft-reiterated invitation to intimacy explicit, as Willis (in a kind of visual pun on his longtime newspaper's name) was made to return his viewers' gaze from what was presumably a dresser-top mirror. Widely recognized as an accomplished idler by trade, this famous author and poet thus seemed to embody a sphere of easy elegance and rare, even rarified sensibility peculiarly at his readers' service. As much as anything, it was this will to please that made him a perennial player in antebellum literary circles.[6]

Unlike so many sentimentalists, however, this *deuced shrewd fellow* (as the *Literary World* once called him) was entirely happy to admit that his acquaintance came with a price. So it was that when the *Portland Tribune* took to chiding him—as so many did—for wasting his talents on "foolish fashions" and other morally and intellectually insignificant ephemera, this self-described literary "worky" parried lustily with what became a perennial defense: "We made up our mind full fifteen years ago that life was too short for any nonsense that *didn't pay!*" At the height of his commercial powers, Willis was thus gladly casting himself as a Barnumesque huckster of the new democratic market for print—others might prate of their art, but his credo would remain *"Mortality* before *immortality!"* until critics could suggest a paying alternative. Eventually, he would go so far as to proclaim himself done with conventional artistic aspirations altogether, opting instead to devote his creative energy—as he declared in *Outdoors at Idlewild* (1854)—to living "as variedly, as amply, and as worthily, as is possible . . . while upon this planet . . . and not to be remembered after [having] left it."[7]

What is most notable here is not the appeal to market values, or even the exaltation of private ambitions, though each distinguished Willis as one of a new breed of literary careerists beholden preeminently to the golden calculus of sales. It is that so many devotees failed to bat an eye at his mercenary posture. Even in an age dedicated to the proposition that commerce sullied true sentiment, brazen avidity was obviously not tantamount to sympathy's demise. Indeed, for many of Willis's most fervent admirers—principally, but not exclusively, women and girls of genteel estate and aspiration—their literary relation seemed to transcend commercial considerations altogether, often figuring as a friendship beyond reckoning, a precious correspondence of hearts, even an *affaire d'amour*. Edgar Allan Poe (himself the object of considerable female adulation) used to tease his love, "Annie" Richmond, that she was just "one of a thousand" enamored of his onetime boss; Mrs. Richmond, for her part, confessed that she longed to see "Mr. Willis more than any other human being." So, too, were the girls from a certain Virginia seminary once sufficiently smitten with their idol to press him to head their school, much to his bemusement. Such examples dramatically illustrate print's tremendous capacity to fashion affective, even erotic, ties in the absence of face-to-face acquaintance. They also suggest perhaps what most worried Willis's many critics: that mastery of the bewitching techniques of what we might call a *sentimental commerce* with adoring readers had invested him with considerable sway over the tone of antebellum culture.[8]

Considered in isolation, his attentions might seem like mere flattery, as when he advised a daughter of the Reverend Edward Payson (who herself was to become a writer) that if her future husband had a soul, he would love her for the "poetical" in her, and so she should save it for him. Yet it seems clear that Willis offered his readers—especially that class of women who, though not generally radical feminists, nonetheless imagined themselves destined for more exalted and more public spheres of intellect and emotion—something beyond honeyed words in return for their custom. As early as 1828, for instance, he was on record publicly as favoring precisely the kind of enlightened accommodation of the sexes aspired to by so many genteel souls. "Credit not the oldfashioned absurdity that woman's is a secondary lot— ministering to the necessities of her lord and master!" Willis had then proclaimed (in a representative passage from the *Legendary*):

> It is a higher destiny I would award you. If your immortality is as complete, and your gift of mind as capable as ours of increase and elevation, I would put no wisdom of mine against God's allotment. I would charge you to water the undying bud, and give it healthy culture, and open its beauty to the sun—and then you may hope, that when your life is bound up with another, you will go on equally, and in fellowship that shall pervade every earthly interest!

Often reworked and sometimes merely reprinted in new contexts, this message rang clear throughout his career. Without entirely discounting the impact of mixed motives, it thus seems plausible that one reason for Willis's extraordinary popularity was his willingness to take women, particularly literary-minded women, seriously.[9]

Of course, he could hardly marry the lot. But, as a conspicuous and sympathetic celebrity of print, he could offer his readers what in an age of Romantic ideals might be the next best thing: the semblance of an extraordinary friendship. This he seems to have accomplished most successfully by presenting himself as a kind of lay minister of true sentiment, one who was remarkably attuned to familiar affections and rarefied sensibilities, yet by no means divorced from social circles where easy elegance reigned and an idler's observation was the coin of the realm. In much of his magazine fiction, for example, Willis played less the probing psychological analyst or chiding moralist than the acute and sometimes witty spectator of the lighter aspects of human society. Like himself, his fictive heros were often social climbers with shrewd insight into the pretensions and gullibility of the modern world of genteel aspiration. Consider the American Mr. Brown, the protagonist in Willis's tale "Brown's Day at the Mimpsons." He is an ingratiating social chameleon whose instinctive adaptation to society (so the author remarks) "cleverly reflected the man and manners before him"; at the end of the day, this changeling avenges himself (and maybe his creator, too) on the snooty English Mrs. Mimpson by triumphantly procuring the tickets to Almack's she covets but cannot secure. When they were not marveling at the exclusive world Willis the magazinist opened for their inspection, readers, it might seem, were thus being invited to lift a page from the journal of one peculiarly familiar with its ins and outs.[10]

That this literary journal also divulged confidences of the heart did even more to cement an uncommon rapport with readers. It seems clear that for the countless women who dreamed of the handsome poet, for example, Willis's verse had always advertised a kind of quasi-erotic insight into its author's character. The *Pencillings*, with their emphasis on private impressions, also promised a window of sorts into the man behind the print. Even Willis's tales of European high life and American society (compounded, as they so often were, of his own thinly disguised adventures) traded on a brand of voyeurism that, at its most extreme, anticipated nothing so much as the self-promotional self-exposure characteristic of twentieth-century celebrity. It was, in this respect, easy enough to discern that a self-referential tale like the author's "Leaves from the Heart-Book of Ernest Clay" (which narrated the romantic adventures of a penny-pinched London celebrity) echoed the very same "treasures of feeling and impression" that Willis advertised in his *Complete Works* as being "secrets" from his "cave of privacy."[11]

Nowhere was this conjured familiarity more plainly articulated than in the tête-à-tête editorial letters that finally became Willis's favorite literary mode. Here, in adopting the voice of a trusted confidant, he most fully realized his trademark dictum on the value of personification—"A periodical needs to be an *individual*, with a physiognomy that is called up to the mind of the subscriber, and imagined as speaking, while he reads." The reason behind his desideratum was simple:

> An apple given to you by a friend at table is not like an apple taken from the shelf of a huckster . . . the friend's choice alters the taste and value of the apple, as the individual editor's selections or approbation gives [*sic*] weight and value to the article. The more you are acquainted with your editor—even though, in that acquaintance you find out his faults—the more interest you feel in his weekly visit, and the more curiosity you feel in what he offers you to read.

Here, also, in relating the social whirl or contemplating his own emotional or aesthetic sensibilities, he ostensibly revealed himself most completely. "Secrets we have none," this self-proclaimed sentimental exhibitionist once announced in the *Home Journal*, when illness forced him to curtail his weekly correspondence for a time, "and anything we find occasion to write about, to an individual, would be interesting, we are at liberty to suppose, to the public." Of course, commercial requisites meant that this familiar posture—and its attendant denial of a "backstage" personality—was necessarily a promiscuous exhibition designed to justify as it masked the cash transaction that underwrote commercial literary relations. This was a fact that critics were only too ready to deplore, as they often did Willis's trifling manner and eccentric prose stylings. Yet true fans rarely complained of imposture. Instead, they welcomed their favorite's periodic advent as they would the visit of a close (and particularly well-connected) friend.[12]

One woman who so welcomed him was Emily Chubbuck, a struggling Utica schoolmistress and failed author of children's stories, who in June 1844 wrote Willis as "Fanny Forester." In itself, this forwardness was not unusual for the time. Literally thousands of occasional correspondents and amateur litterateurs addressed Willis over the years, creating a press that led him, on at least one occasion, to beg his fans' forbearance. Still, it would have been bad business to stifle the flow entirely. Limited editorial assistance and a chronic shortage of capital to buy talent meant that, like many nineteenth-century periodicals, both the *Mirror* and the *Home Journal* had to indulge their readers' literary ambitions and fantasies of familiarity as a matter of course. On one hand, this open-door editorial policy certainly tended to foster sentimental attachments that can only be called hollow and illusory. Yet the sentimental mode was not *always* a cheat, even as it confounded commerce with emotional sympathies. The friendship that developed between Chubbuck and Willis bears out this contention.[13]

On one level, their relationship was business plain and simple. Strapped for cash to care for aged parents and dependent siblings, Chubbuck had wagered that Willis's imprimatur was as good as gold; if the *Mirror* paid none of its contributors ("love gets for us as good things as money could buy," the paper's junior editor once bragged), it could, in Chubbuck's words, "put me in a way of making money like smoke." This remark proved prophetic. Within months, Willis's plaudits had enabled "Fanny Forester" to contract with *Graham's* and the *Columbian Magazine* to furnish tales at five dollars a page, thereby launching a career destined for considerable heights. "Few Americans," a reviewer observed soon afterward, "have attained so much of celebrity as has 'Fanny Forrester' [*sic*], in so brief a time." Eventually, Chubbuck's sentimental sketches (collected in the "Willis-istically" entitled *Trippings in Author-Land*) caught the eye of the famous Dr. Adoniram Judson, a twice-widowed Baptist missionary lately returned from Asia. He and Chubbuck met in December 1845, worked together on a volume memorializing Judson's late wife, and were married six months later. As the new Mrs. Judson, "Fanny Forester" dutifully quit literary celebrity and its promise of economic and social independence to accompany her husband to Burma. When she died a widow nearly a decade later, publicity's glare had faded to a dull glow.[14]

By her own admission, Chubbuck had at first angled only to be "put in the way of making money." Liking her audacity, Willis had gamely encouraged a literary flirtation. So it continued, until a pellucid tale entitled "Dora' " arrested his attention. "I have just read the proof of your exquisitely beautiful outline story, my dear Miss Chubbuck," he then wrote to her (with apparent feeling), "and my heart is in my throat with its pathos, and with my interest in your genius." He asked forgiveness for "ever having spoken of [her] triflingly." Willis's motives for this professed change of heart were probably mixed; doubtless his reputation for fostering female talent stood to profit from his protégé's rising fortunes. Yet this particular tale of misunderstood "genius" consuming itself for the world's amusement evidently hit home, sparking kindred recollections of Willis's own "first fame." As he confessed to his correspondent, he also had felt the pains and burdens of celebrity she portrayed so feelingly. Henceforth, their relationship reflected this deeper understanding.[15]

Like many nineteenth-century women writers, the otherwise hardheaded Chubbuck clung anxiously to her anonymity, resisting the parade of feelings so often entailed in emerging as an author and despairing at celebrity's unwanted gossip. "I suppose no one ever dreaded becoming a professed writer so much as I did," she confided in Willis soon after her fiction had brought the two closer, "and when actually drawn into it by circumstances, I imagined that I felt the chill and the darkness and lowliness creeping about me—I felt frightened, and, without knowing what to dread, dreaded everything imaginable." Emboldened by his new under-standing, Willis rushed to assure her (from hard experience) that such anguish abated only once one learned that "genius burns darkest nearest the wick, never, *never*, appreciated by those who eat, drink, and walk with it." This advice evidently warmed Chubbuck's heart and stilled her fears. Knowing how fleeting happiness might be, yet with the keepsake daguerreotype portrait Willis had sent in her hand, she could confide in her solicitous editor, "I am *tremblingly* happy."[16]

This episode speaks volumes of the sundry modes of sentimental commerce. As Willis well knew, literary gossip often exacted an emotional toll. Yet fiction's rev-elatory aspects might also lead (as it did here with Chubbuck's semitransparent fiction) to a mutually satisfying friendship. Though she and Willis met face-to-face only once, fleeting acquaintance did not diminish the depth of their affection. In correspondence, she addressed Willis lovingly as her "dear literary godfather." So tender was *his* regard that, though blessing his protégé's impending marriage to Judson, he could not bring himself to redeem his promise to attend the newlywed couple's farewell at Boston harbor. Given the emotional trauma attending his wife's recent death in childbirth, perhaps Willis balked at witnessing the loss of another so close to his heart. Then, also, the Reverend Dr. Judson's connubial claim may have troubled the famous editor more than he dared admit. So, fittingly for two whose feelings had been expressed almost wholly on paper, Willis resolved instead to make up a parcel of books to convey his remembrance and speed the new Mrs. Judson on her way. As with so many nineteenth-century loves, theirs were bonds woven chiefly of words.[17]

It is worth noting here that the friendship with "Fanny Forester" also sheds light on another aspect of Willis's sentimental ministry—the remarkable extent to which readers were able to reconcile his (and their own) worldly pursuits with the holier impulses of religious devotion and domestic stewardship. Not surprisingly, the Rev-erend Judson's interest had inspired Chubbuck to a renewed concern for her spir-itual estate, a change of heart exhibited materially by the redirection of her literary talents. She now apparently also wished for nothing better than to save her "literary godfather," as he had helped to save her from a life of diminished expectations. "I am anxious to do him good," Chubbuck fretted to her new fiancé in February 1846, "and it seems as though I might. If he would only become a truly pious man and turn his singular talents to good." This reaction is not surprising. Among strict Christians, Willis's Pelhamite apostasy had always marked a point of distress; to uphold church discipline, Park Street's brethren had even expelled their wayward son from fellowship altogether—a formal tie to religion that he would not renew until much later in life and then, tellingly, in the high-toned Episcopal Church. Nonetheless, it is remarkable how many pious Americans, especially those like Chubbuck, who inclined toward a faith that found God in a sunset or a mother's tenderness toward her child, considered Willis to be, despite his well-publicized trespasses, eminently *worth* saving.[18]

The poet's special talent for conjuring the beauty of feelings, sacred and otherwise, had everything to do with such feelings. In the early days, even excommunication had not been enough to put off at least some of his evangelical admirers. Now, for all his self-described "worldling" excursions, Willis's "Scriptural Sketches" continued to please. Well after their author had gravitated toward more worldly subjects (returning only occasionally to mine the devotional vein of his youth), these gorgeous verses remained arguably his best loved literary work. They were, as *Graham's* proudly pointed out, the staples of American school readers and declamation days, as well as familiar accessories of the genteel parlor. It was not just flattery, then, when Willis assured his mother (in the same letter that predicted his celebrity) that the "Sacred Poems" were "as you would wish . . . my best property." Nor was it of mere passing consequence that, in response to Willis's asking whether she thought him a "very wicked man," Mary Todd Lincoln, the president's wife and a special admirer of the author, reportedly replied, "how could that be with one who wrote such exquisite sacred poems?"[19]

The memoir of one particular Yankee schoolgirl suggests just how emotionally compelling such verse could be. The daughter of a New Bedford doctor, young Elizabeth Read, prized Willis's poetical effusions above all others, copying favorite passages for her friends, measuring her brother's initial attempts at verse against Willis's standard, and cherishing her idol's volumes as "twilight companions." Judging by her letters posted homeward from the New York City female seminary where she had been sent to complete her studies, they were, in fact, nothing less than aesthetic and emotional touchstones, inspiring holy feelings and spurring Lizzie to a higher sense of purpose. "Willis'[s] poems, as usual, are before me," the teenage enthusiast wrote a friend on one occasion, "and I have been reading, for the hundredth time, (rather an exaggeration), 'Jephtha's Daughter.' Indeed, I have read them all over a number of times." Apparently the effect of this intensive study was considerable: "How strikingly beautiful all of N. P. Willis's poems are!" Lizzie observed reverently after quoting several favorite passages. "His sacred poems are peculiarly beautiful, I think." Then, losing herself in a dreamy fantasy: "I was thinking how well I should like to be a poetess:—to express my thoughts in glowing verse. Oh, the gift of the poet is great! and how good is God, to bestow such a blessing!"[20]

For young Lizzie Read at least, neither her idol's sometime mercenary posture nor his moral errantry thus seemed to matter a jot; the essence of Willis's character—and thus his suitability as a literary acquaintance—inhered in his poetry's compelling sentiments. This was no heresy against genteel Romantic aesthetics: Harvard's Boylston Professor of Rhetoric and Oratory himself had furnished the cultural sanction for Elizabeth Read's expression of delight when he lectured his undergraduates that "no poetry affected another, which had not produced a throb in the breast of the poet who wrote it." Nor was Willis's recommendation current solely among impressionable adolescents like Read. We know of Lizzie's love for her idol's verse chiefly through the posthumous attentions of her schoolmaster John S. C. Abbott, an Andover-trained evangelical pastor, educator, and author best known for his children's tales and a popular didactic tract on family government, *The Mother at Home* (1833). After a killing fever claimed his pupil's life at the early age of sixteen, Abbott set about compiling extracts of her letters and journals into a private memoir, hoping, as he put it in preface to his commemorative volume, "that these disclosures of the emotions of a generous and an affectionate heart may induce others to form their character upon the same basis of self-sacrifice." Dedicated to a practical piety founded upon gentle maternal influence, Abbott no doubt intended Lizzie Read's life to reflect the benefits of the brand of domestic pedagogy he championed with his brothers at their New York City female seminary. Certainly, if Willis's "worldling" posture had entirely discredited him from such a cause, Abbott would never have let Lizzie's panegyrics figure so conspicuously in his sentimental memorial. We can only conclude, then, that even as Willis donned the mantle of gossip's eager trumpeter and fashionable society's chronicler, he managed to maintain a foot in the camp of piety. Though he was subject to periodic attack on this front, this spiritual association would often prove a saving grace.[21]

Though few would come to cherish this minister of sentiment and celebrity as much as Read and Chubbuck, the shadow of their uncommon affection clearly lay at the heart of Willis's appeal. As it had done for many popular writers, print admitted him to homes by the thousands; there, an inventive fancy coupled with a special facility for satisfying desires for a type of higher emotional communion lodged him in many a reader's heart. This relationship was especially strong among middle-and upper-class devotees of the emotional and physical comforts of the well-ordered parlor, who (for the price of a two-dollar subscription) found in Willis both a willing ear and (as we shall soon see) a model of gracious living and elegant deportment. Ralph Waldo Emerson thus hit the mark when he included, in a notebook entry epitomizing the "rich democratic land of Massachusetts," not only houses boasting "well-dressed women with an air of town-ladies," a "clavecin & a copy of the *Spectator*," but also "some young lady a reader of Willis." When critics deplored this famous author's lexical extravagance, trifling propensities, and ethical missteps, these fans at least hung on his every word and considered him a trusted friend. Others also found much to recommend in Willis, despite his much publicized foibles: a knack for felicitous expression; an uncommon appreciation for beauty that reflected life's finer sensibilities; a reputation for fostering (especially female) literary talent; and—what would prove to be of greatest significance—a special familiarity with polite society's affairs and arcana. How far this affinity extended, and in what causes it could be enlisted, remains to be seen.[22]

Herald of Fashion

Like many of the new literary professionals, Willis shunned politics. This propensity owed partly to character. In a nation of inveterate voters, he never bothered to cast a ballot until 1856, and then, typically, not for conventional ideological reasons, but because he admired the heroic character of the Republican nominee, John C. Frémont, and thought "the Pathfinder" the right man for troubled times. Yet, celebrity worship aside, Willis's political neutrality was predominantly a matter of business; such a stance seemed to him the surest road to a national constituency. For all its success, this scheme did entail constraints: when sectional tensions worsened after 1850, for instance, the *Home Journal*'s extensive Southern circulation kept its famous editors from even mentioning slavery for fear of impairing their commercial fortunes. Still, careful nonpartisanship hardly meant that Willis lacked a social conscience or, for that matter, that his celebrity was entirely apolitical. His career as a tastemaker graphically illustrates this point.[23]

Coming into his own commercially just as technological innovation and social developments were transforming the nation's readers into an integrated but diverse national audience, Willis addressed a public eager for instruction in the fine arts of aesthetic appreciation, social conduct, and personal style, even as it distrusted certain elements of a refined program of living. Given his abiding obsession with self-fashioning and the social dynamics of distinction, it is not surprising that he rose avidly to the challenge of fleshing out the heart and sinews of gentility. As early as 1838, in fact, Willis was joking to readers that he proposed to style himself a "Capability Brown" of taste, setting up shop to tell people "what they can make of themselves," as the famous landscape designer had advised clients upon improvements to their country seats. By degrees, the jest became reality. Buoyed by intimate acquaintance with Blessington's London, the celebrated penciller ultimately emerged as the nation's most conspicuous arbiter of manners and the literary and social scene: "an oracle of fashion—the American D'Orsay—the very Dr. Johnson of dandyism," as one observer remarked grandiosely. It was chiefly in this capacity as a man "who trades upon his taste" that Willis came to press the cause that lay perhaps nearest his heart: the cultivation of what he imagined to be the coming aristocracy. Doing so once again thrust him into the vortex of American cultural politics, provoking a swirling controversy that was destined to test the limits of his sway as nothing had before.[24]

Controversy over fashion was, to be sure, hardly new in America. One need only recall Nathaniel Ward's *The Simple Cobler of Aggawam* scolding the fair ladies of Massachusetts Bay Colony for dressing like "gant bar-geese," "Egyptian Hyeroglyphicks," and "French flurts of the pastry" to realize its long and contested history. Yet following the economic upheavals surrounding the Panic of 1837, this issue attained a peculiar salience in the American republic, particularly in fast-growing cities such as New York. Here, to the dismay of disgruntled critics scandalized by the "artificial" excesses of imported fashions, scores of manufacturers and publicists—Willis chief among them—were busy transforming the national scene by marketing new social and cultural refinements to a broad public eager to remake themselves in a cosmopolitan image. Here, also, the extremes of dress and display adopted by status-conscious arrivistes refracted the nation's growing disparities of wealth and culture most alarmingly. Without the ballast of tradition or rank to leaven fortunes gained in trade, manufactures, and speculation, the new rich of the 1840s presented easy targets for satirists. Come mid-decade, for instance, New York theatergoers (and these included visitors from across the nation) howled with laughter at the antics of "Mrs. Tiffany," the parvenu matron in Anna Cora Mowatt's "Fashion" (1845) who took her cue in matters of taste from a French chambermaid.[25]

What was fun for some was deadly serious for others. In the city's increasingly stratified society, mustachioed dandies loafed on the granite steps of the storied Astor House ogling passing ladies, only yards from ragged beggars plying their trade.

So, too, did escutcheoned carriages jostle workaday omnibuses and carts on Broadway's golden mile but a short hansom ride from Five Points' notorious squalor. On one hand, such stark contrasts advertised the promise of American life. They also mocked the nation's egalitarian ideals, breeding contempt, envy, and resentment that expressed itself in a highly politicized cultural climate. Throughout the 1840s, New York's rich shrank increasingly from hoi polloi, seeking out exclusive resorts of amusement and segregating themselves in newly fashionable uptown neighborhoods. Moreover, while the urban middle classes were mortaging themselves to maintain appearances, the mass of working men and women, their ranks swelled by immigration, industrial dislocation, and the lingering effects of the late economic troubles, had to endure an often grim life shadowed by luxuries far beyond their means. The tensions arising from these volatile circumstances would find a voice in both Willis's rhetorical stance toward fashion's place in the republic and in the discordant echoes it prompted.[26]

For all his interest in fashion's role within so-called aristocratic social formations, it was not until the mid-1840s that Willis broached the problem in earnest. The particular occasion for this initiative was an extensively advertised lecture scheduled for the cavernous Broadway Tabernacle on the evening of 11 June 1844. Typically, commercial impulses lay at the heart of matters. Past lecture seasons had missed the mark, and the directors of the New York Lyceum wished to spice up their fare. Who better to kick off a new series of light and—they hoped—more popular addresses than the "American D'Orsay?" What the directors got was both more and less than they bargained for.

Willis had been asked merely to trifle, and every precedent suggested that he would fulfill expectations. Editorial advertisement for a lecture on "Fashion" seemed only to confirm that prospect. So it was that many in the modish crowd of 1,500 listeners assembled that night were undoubtedly taken aback when, after sundry preliminaries, the nation's preeminent trifler launched his uncharacteristically grave discourse. The *fashions*, he informed his listeners, were not his topic; *Fashion*, an altogether more serious matter, was—and they would soon understand the distinction. What arrested Willis's usual badinage on this particular night was a concern for nothing less than what today's scholars call *cultural hegemony:* that is, the means and politics of culture by which a dominant class asserts and extends its sway over society at large. Unlike the fashions (which even Willis admitted occasionally spawned absurdities unworthy of attention), it seemed to this cultured critic and admired tastemaker that *Fashion*—a social éclat "giving its possessor consequence in common report, value in private life, authority in all matters of taste, and influence in every thing"—could be ignored by public-spirited men only at their peril. Short of religion or constitutional law, he was even inclined to believe it the most significant issue of his generation. Surely, he implored his well-heeled audience, these questions—"Where lies power?" and "Where are the combinations that hold power?"—befit the "patriot and statesman."[27]

To Willis's eye, the condition of contemporary society only made such questions doubly compelling. Scanning the city, he could now see no single class that exercised unchallenged social authority: following the Panic of 1837, the old Knickerbocker hegemony had given way to an anarchy of rogue opinion and competing coteries.

Not wealth so much as "conspicuousness in expense" constituted the only "Fashion" the city now knew. Willis, for one, was sure that good sense and personal freedom had suffered in the process. Linked only by a mutual desire to best one another, New York's petty circles of fashion engaged in fits of extravagance and display that outraged taste and discounted economy. Even more disturbing (judging by Willis's intemperate rhetoric), "the vicious, the wilful, the ignorant and short-sighted," raised to consequence chiefly by means of the penny press, were stifling all steps toward life's embellishment by what he called an "invidious criticism and malice." "We do not live in liberty, here," the celebrated poet declared ominously, "we do not spend our money or enjoy our firesides in rational freedom. The country is free, the press is free, religion is free and public opinion is remarkably free—but the individual is a slave!"[28]

Providentially, it appeared that such a degraded condition need not last: amidst repeated bursts of applause, Willis assured his well-heeled audience that American society was yet in a state of transition, and the future still malleable. However, deliverance would come, he suggested, not by abolishing the institution of Fashion—in this regard, years of observing society had made him a confirmed realist—but by elevating a so-called natural aristocracy to its helm:

> Give us a class whose opinion is entitled to undeniable weight—a class whose judgment is made from elevated standards—a class whose favor is alike valuable to the ambitions of both sexes—a class it is important to know and propitiate if possible, but at any rate to quote as unquestionable authority—and the evil is at once abated.

In other words, with the talented, beautiful, and truly refined (those like himself, it need hardly be added) judging between "tyranny and the people," mere wealth must go begging and the vicious be driven to silence. Certainly the means to make such a class appeared to him ample enough—"discussion, enquiry, active ridicule of false pretensions, and generous approbation of that which is truly admirable," Willis ticked them off confidently. But the public must not dawdle. An American aristocracy was fast coalescing; of this, he had no doubt. "Thank God," he concluded melodramatically, "we have yet the time and opportunity to decide from what quarry it shall be hewn, and to what mortar of public sentiment it shall owe its stability!"[29]

Precisely what sparked this impassioned jeremiad is difficult to pinpoint. If nothing else, lecturing tended to summon the didact in Willis. In his maiden outing on the lyceum circuit half a year earlier, he had disappointed fashionable Baltimoreans with a grave sermon on the transcendent implications of self-culture, suggesting (with more than a hint at Hindoo transmigration) that the pursuer of refinement, whatever his earthly station, might expect to attain a higher sphere in death than the "wilful clown, or what is scarce better, the exact slave to his dollar and his prescribed duty." More to the point, since his return to New York City, urban life seems to have convinced Glenmary's onetime tenant that the nation was headed for crisis. Fresh from suing a fellow editor for defaming his good name, Willis saw trouble in the growing power of the press to straitjacket private lives. He saw it in the millionaire stoned for riding through Broadway with a mounted and liveried servant in tow, but also (it might surprise some readers) in the reluctance of ladies too "superfine" to ride in an omnibus. Most important, he saw it in what he called the accelerating "demoralization of private life." Indeed, nearly a year before his "Lecture on Fashion," Willis was bemoaning the pernicious effects of both long-term economic stagnation and the growing separation of rich and poor—beggary, he thought, being a vestibule opening into criminality, and parvenu aristocracy a recipe for ostentation and vice. Unless checked by some reconstituted social authority, these disturbing trends seemed to him destined to spiral out of control.[30]

That a so-called natural aristocracy was to provide the magic bullet to rectify this situation should probably not surprise us. Willis belonged to a generation of Whig-gish middle-class Americans who were particularly keen to reconcile their desires for standards of social quality and cohesion with their commitment to republican ideals of equal access and the free play of talent. In the immediate postrevolutionary years, faith in the existence of what Thomas Jefferson called a virtuous and talented class of natural "aristoi" had served to justify the toppling of the old exclusive political and social order. But its replacement was hardly the enlightened, nonsec-tarian democracy that Jefferson envisioned. Rather, the demise of property quali-fication for suffrage and the unleashing of common men's economic energies had only seemed to place a premium on the need for a new kind of nonexclusive gen-tility, one that was capable of arresting the anomie of modern life by tapping into the presumably universal principles of refinement, beauty, and moral fitness. Hence the interest in social formations in which the cream could be said to rise naturally to the top. For all his transcendental speculations, even a philosopher as independent as Ralph Waldo Emerson can be seen propounding this position, as when, in a lecture on manners, he advocated "unerring taste" as a necessary compliment to the all-encompassing "good-nature" and "personal force" that characterized his "self-constituted aristocracy" of self-reliance. At about the same time, the less icon-oclastic Yankee James Russell Lowell put the matter more plainly but no less forcefully: "A man gains in power," he once remarked to his friend Charles Briggs, "as he gains in ease."[31]

Willis seems to have had special reason to adhere to this brand of republican faith, for ever since bursting upon the scene at Mrs. Otis's high-toned soirees, Park Street's clever boy had been fighting to shed the onus of imposture. Lacking wealth, family connections, or even religious sanction, he had always relied upon talent, charm, and a nose for the main chance to conquer society. And conquer he did—though never sufficiently to quell his deep-seated status anxiety. Life among the British aristocracy only reinforced this abiding insecurity. As much as Willis was lionized and petted in their salons and country homes, there were always those who publicly snubbed the elegant American poet, not a few others who congratulated themselves on avoiding his acquaintance, and many who received him in society only to snicker behind his back. At least that was the report of Charles Sumner. "I find Willis is much laughed at for his sketches," the Boston lawyer wrote from Scotland several years after the publication of *Pencillings*,

> and Wilson says that he never said what is attributed to him of Lockhart and also the review of Hamilton. Some of my friends were at Gordon Castle when Willis was

there, and describe his visit in amusing colors. It was supposed that he would write a book; and the ladies all agreed to take turns riding with him, &c, so that *all* might be *equally* booked.[32]

Though this account smacks too much of wounded vanity to accept entirely at face value, its patrician condescension rings true enough, all the more so because aristocratic hauteur clearly galled Willis to the point of obsession. Years after first returning from England's rarefied literary circles, he was still harping to readers that

> there is no equality, felt or understood, between lord and author in England. . . . Through all the *abandon*, through all the familiarity of festive moments, when there is nothing named which makes a distinction between noble and simple, there is an invisible arm forever extended, with reversed hand, which the patronized author feels on his breast like a bar of iron. He never puts it aside. He never loses the remembrance of his inferiority. He is always a parasite—always a belier of God's mark of greatness, the nobility of the mind.

More than anything, this iron insult forged the underlying conviction that governed Willis's social conscience. As he liked to say, "a republican spirit must rebel against homage to anything human with which it never can compete"; in this lay the only distinction he hoped would ever "hedge in an American aristocracy."[33]

That being said, Willis was clearly savvy enough to recognize that proclaiming the sway of his natural aristocracy was not the same as seeing it happen; that would require a sustained application of what Teddy Roosevelt would later call the bully pulpit. But Willis did have reason to be pleased with the start he had made. Though the penny press was predictably unimpressed with the Tabernacle address, Horace Greeley's influential New York *Tribune* anticipated the opinions of many Whiggish observers when it declared Willis's social critique to be surprisingly "acute and faithful" and found much to commend in the lecturer's "leading idea of refining and exalting fashion into a power—the talisman of a self-sustaining, unprivileged Aristocracy, which shall furnish a counter-poise and barrier against the tyranny of Public Opinion." Within weeks, Willis was moving to capitalize on this beginning: reprising his lecture before a brilliant crowd in Albany; inquiring of J. T. Fields, a publisher, regarding prospects for an engagement in Boston; and eventually issuing the Tabernacle address for a shilling as part of the "Mirror Library," a self-publishing venture with G. P. Morris designed to sustain their combined commercial fortunes. Yet without further publicity, the impact of these initial steps was bound to be limited. Knowing this, it is easier to understand why the conversion of the *New York Mirror*, a metropolitan daily in October 1844, and Willis's subsequent christening of the so-called Upper Ten Thousand were such momentous developments. By loudly trumpeting his refurbished journal as the first resort of New York fashion while simultaneously anointing the city's upper classes as standard bearers of America's refined culture, the darling of the sentimental crowd moved decisively to consolidate his sway over an audience whose allegiance promised to be crucial to his larger campaign to rein in and elevate republican society.[34]

Notwithstanding Willis's self-confidence, the job of ministering to the circles of fashion as he reformed them was a tall order, especially as his claim to the "Upper

Ten's" custom smacked of more than a little nerve. Despite his social successes, Willis remained something of an interloper in the exclusive and money-conscious society he wished to direct. He was, after all, a working journalist when many still blanched at that profession's artisanal origins and brawling propensities. More to the point, having lately vented his spleen against two obnoxious Knickerbocker spinsters ("The Blidgimses") under an insufficient cover of fiction, Willis now found many a privileged New York home closed to him. Only weeks before the launch of his *Evening Mirror*, several Albany papers even reported rumor of a challenge of honor declined over the matter, though Willis strenuously denied the whole. Still, for all these disabilities, the *Mirror*'s editor was in a peculiarly advantageous position to furnish Gotham's fashion-conscious social elites (and those around the nation who doted on them) with perhaps what they desired most. An insider where many others felt their want of access, Willis offered unabashedly to indulge the beau monde's literary aspirations, chronicle their movements, advertise their cultural institutions, and—perhaps most significant—play their father-confessor of fashion. In return, he asked only that his patrons pay the bills and entertain his counsel.[35]

This compact readily became apparent in the revamped format and editorial line of the newspaper that now went by the name of the *Evening Mirror*. Gone were the weekly's once-trumpeted but costly and production-intensive engravings. In their stead ran an expanded digest of literary and metropolitan gossip. Within days, the *Mirror*'s junior editor signaled his new ambitions even more clearly by reprising his call for a fashionable carriage drive to supersede Broadway's bustling and dusty mile. To clinch matters, he was soon proclaiming the ten thousand people "uppermost" in New York City to be "the most moral and scrupulous ten thousand in the 400,000 of the population." If anyone doubted Willis's intentions to sustain the kid-glove crowd—intentions he would follow to varying degrees for the remainder of his life—such comments must have set the record straight.[36]

Still, he was not content merely to flatter his Upper Ten or see them lapse into exclusivity. Indeed, if anything characterized Willis's latest—and boldest—social and commercial initiative, it was a determination to ensure convenient access for the many to a range of public amusements and accommodations. This quasi-populist stance rested on a sociophilosophical creed that grounded its hope of a general refinement of habits and taste in the efficacy of salutary emulation. When S. Baptiste Mannot announced in December 1844 that his posh New York Hotel would begin specializing in room service and meals à la carte, for instance, the *Mirror*'s noted tastemaker defended the traditional American hotel practice of common dining, warning that "[w]hen the *hotel-garni* draws its dividing line through this promiscuous community of habits, the cords will be cut which will let some people UP, out of reach, and drop some people DOWN, out of all satisfactory supportable contact with society." In this regard, it was not so much social distinctions that Willis wished to head off (these were, to his mind, at once inevitable, desirable, and instructive), but the insulation of classes. A year or so earlier, in fact, the same penchant for intermingling had led him to lament the increasing reluctance of rich women to ride in omnibuses as but "another step . . . towards separating the rich from the middle classes by barriers of expense." Five years later he could still say on the subject of omnibus-riding, "We are democrat to a Tammany pitch on one point—wishing that high and low should mingle as often and as closely as can be mutually agreeable, and that rich and poor should enjoy the same conveniences of life together." Where money *was* inevitably separating classes, moreover, Willis labored to ensure that life's finer habits did not obtain exclusively behind closed doors; if wealth was to make a difference, he prayed that at least it prove itself in public.[37]

Despite these careful distinctions, it is no wonder that Willis's high-profile pursuit of New York's fashionable custom and his advocacy of a social economy of awe and emulation quickly plunged him into controversy. He was already liable to the charge of standing false idol to what many saw as a prevailing cultural declension. As one evangelical critic put it in a blast from Horace Bushnell's liberal Congregationlist *New-Englander*, the "genius" of Willis's "Scriptural Sketches" had clearly marked "what his vocation ought to have been"; instead, the dandy-journalist had followed the "general current," amusing himself and a credulous public with "mere externals, the trivialities, the barren practicalities of life. . . . It shows how strong that current must have been," Willis's detractor concluded ruefully, "when such minds as his, were not only drawn into it, but led to bend the whole of the strength of their genius and their talents, to foster and encourage the trivial, sensuous, material taste and spirit of the times."[38]

Now, the *Evening Mirror*'s revamped editorial line inflamed long-smoldering class resentments. Almost from the start, the city's cheap weeklies and penny dailies thundered at Willis for advocating the very insulated aristocracy of wealth he had warned against in his "Lecture on Fashion." "My Lord Willis," one scandalized critic suggested in the wake of the promenade proposal, was surely seeking to create a "distinction as to keep the *higha owda* from coming in contact with the *canaille*." It mattered little that his lordship pleaded to avoid just such a segregation. By first making himself into what one disgusted Kentuckian called a "walking sign-post of all that is *outré* in dandyism" (the subject prompting this particular outcry being Willis's advocacy of beards for men), and then espousing the cause of republican aristocracy so warmly, the *Mirror*'s junior editor had, in a sense, offered himself for the taking.[39]

The most telling measure of this susceptibility is the Upper Ten's linguistic and iconographic evolution. Clearly, Willis had meant to galvanize New York's disparate social elites into accepting his leadership when in November 1844 he christened them the "Upper Ten Thousand": To the extent that his neologism entered common usage as generic patois for the American beau monde, he may be said to have approached his intention. But the Upper Ten developed a life all its own, and as a stock character in the urban imagination its modes of expression were, more often than not, corrosive to Willis's cause. Put plainly, the Upper Ten figured more often as the butt of satire than as the object of emulation. Cartoonists, for instance, commonly rendered this social type as a fantastical dandy, a "man-milliner" of sorts who was most at home when making a show of himself—haunting the lobby of the plush Astor House, patronizing fashionable society's masqued balls, or parading the sunny side of Broadway sporting a whippet-thin walking stick. So, too, in the long tradition of horrible fashion, did depravity presumably lurk behind this facade of empty vanity. It was, to be sure, ominous for Willis's cause that New York's high-class brothels presently came to be called "upper tens."[40]

The minor eruption of upper-class exposés in the wake of Willis's declaration for the Upper Ten offers further evidence of this degenerate tendency. At their best, these quasi-fictive revelations were sincere, if lurid, assaults on privilege, hypocrisy, and the prostitution of true passions and sentiment. At worst, they were outright blackmail schemes. The anonymous *Revelations of Asmodeus, or, the Mysteries of Upper Ten-Dom* (1849), for instance, pointedly echoed Willis's patter in pledging (in the tradition of Eugene Sue's wildly popular *Mystères de Paris* of several years past) to raise the curtain on the "scoundrelisms and adulteries of a higher sphere of talent, character and position." It was, this modern-day scourge of Gotham promised readers, "the aristocracy of iniquity, the exclusivism of vice, the upper crust of wickedness, the *bon ton* of profligacy with which the reader must become acquainted." And so its obliging "Asmodeus" delivered descriptions of orgies at the Florence Hotel (where "elegant ladies of the *upper ten*," sodden with champagne and oysters, fell prey to reprobate companions) and dispensed unsavory insinuations against city celebrities (the impresario P. T. Barnum among them) not inclined to pay the author's price.[41]

Such sensationalist tracts, and the cheap urban theatricals that commonly echoed them, contributed to a general drift in antebellum popular culture toward confirming the city as a symbolic zone of extremes and excess, a kind of nightmare vision pointing the way toward social and moral disintegration. Over the previous several decades, the attentions of moral reformers and celebrity visitors to New York's Five Points district and its notorious Old Brewery (most notably Charles Dickens in 1842) had made such sites emblematic of degradation among the urban poor. This new rash of exposés, typified by *Revelations of Asmodeus* and Ned Buntline's *Mysteries and Miseries of New York* (1848), aimed more particularly to turn the tables on so-called respectable pretense by exposing corrupt refinement and diseased sentiment in high places. That such sensationalist excursions were also contrived to make money did not substantially discount their contribution to the demonology of Willis's Upper Ten.[42]

By unabashedly courting the custom of New York's rich, their would-be champion thus once again flirted with the taint of vice rumored to flourish in fashionable ranks. As it had been with Lady Blessington's acquaintance, this was, to be sure, an importunity Willis was ready to endure; when subsequently chided for attempting to "create distinction in the classes in the United States," he would counter that in this, of all times, he believed that he could do his country "no better service . . . than by agitating constantly the questions of relative social value." Yet, for a range of reasons, many citizens in the American republic—patrician, professional, and working-class alike—plainly balked at the serviceableness of Willis's social ideals. In the days ahead, such critics were to have an equal, even overriding, voice in resolving his campaign to transfigure the circles of fashion into an authoritative aristocracy of taste and talent capable of directing the sprawling and contentious metropolis that was New York.[43]

A Night at the Opera

No cultural development more dramatically crystallized the hopes and fears excited by N. P. Willis's fashionable campaign than the concurrent movement among entrepreneurs, impresarios, publicists, and music lovers to establish an Italian opera company in New York City. If nothing else, their exertions made this cultural enterprise the talk of the town, in a town that even then loved to talk: dandies and devotees gloried in its pomp; music critics bemoaned its uneven talent and backstage rivalries; and workingmen for the most part eyed its innovations warily. From the start, moreover, popular opinion recognized Willis as opera's majordomo. Of course, much of this was by design, as no one trumpeted the social advantages of this most glitzy of nineteenth-century urban amusements more flamboyantly than did he. Indeed, Willis told readers time and again throughout the 1840s (in a voice resonant of a newfound maturity) that opera's early hours enticed the middle-aged to venture again into society, there to temper youth's callow dominion, even as the magic of music's refining influence and beauty's pleasant company elevated the level of social intercourse. Far from an idle pursuit, a night at the opera would, he promised, function as a peculiarly effective practicum of gentility—"Grown-up society, with all its inconveniences, *does* promote taste and cultivation." So, too, did opera-going present a golden opportunity for melding what Willis would later call the "aristocracies of Brain and Pocket" (that is, the talented and the rich). It was, then, with a hopeful sense of expectancy that fashion's most assiduous trumpeter greeted prospects for a permanent Italian opera in his base of operations. Sadly, subsequent developments would do much to shake that initial optimism.[44]

Part of the problem stemmed from the sometimes-contradictory impulses of art and commerce. It was not easy to avoid these contradictions, though: in capitalist society's grand cultural institutions, art and commerce are often necessary handmaidens. The early career of New York's Italian opera was no exception to this general proposition. Without aficionados hankering after the real article, there would have been no impetus driving its importation; barring liberal patronage, there could be no hope for sustained success. In fact, several previous attempts to establish permanent opera companies in the city had failed spectacularly precisely because fans had been unwilling to pony up the price of such highbrow entertainment. But by the 1840s, lovers of operatic art could rejoice that several of the city's purveyors of culture were once again willing to bank on the prospect that refined amusements might be made to pay—this, too, in a city historically preoccupied with money-getting. For all opera's commercial potential, more than profits hinged on this enterprise: to entrepreneurs and fans alike, establishing a permanent opera would signal a coming-of-age, proving that popular tastes had advanced sufficiently to support a cultural institution worthy of New York's status as the nation's great metropolis. Yet donning what Willis called the "musical *toga virilis*" was not easily accomplished, and the steps taken toward its institution would prove socially divisive in the extreme. Understanding why this situation should occur requires deeper inquiry into the nature of opera as a commercial and social enterprise.[45]

Several difficulties faced New York advocates of an Italian opera. Expense ranked high among them. Grand opera was costly: costumes and scenery were elaborate and the requisite musicians many. If managers made do in the orchestra with local talent (much to the dismay of critics who complained of overloud instrumentation), American vocalists were out of the question. Given audience expectations, the demands of the operatic canon, and the absence of domestic training facilities, nothing short of European singers would do. Managers, consequently, had to hire foreign-born artists at premium rates. Coupled with the cost of maintaining a suitable house, these requirements meant that, to survive, a permanently housed opera company required substantially greater proceeds than did competing amusements. Only if patrons were willing to pay a high tariff for their dose of culture would such enterprises prosper.

Despite the extravagant hopes of opera lovers, moreover, experience suggested that such a class of patrons would have to be created before it could be tapped. The long economic depression of the late 1830s and early 1840s had hit theatrical establishments hard, and none harder than fashionable houses like the Park Theatre, which might once have been expected to supply an opera company's patrons. In lean times, only the cheap plebeian venues, with their steady diet of burlesques and melodramatic spectacles, seemed able to hold their own. There was some hope that the New York elite was transferring its allegiance to alternative amusements calculated to stimulate greater demand for the style of music purveyed by the opera. William Niblo, manager of the ever-evolving Niblo's Garden, had, for instance, experienced limited success sponsoring English-language vocal entertainment, with the occasional foray into foreign-language opera. In 1842, moreover, local musicians formed a Philharmonic Society that sponsored standard symphonic fare. But many of its well-heeled and fastidious patrons, and those of the city's several sacred vocal societies, would sooner forgo musical appreciation altogether than patronize even the best theatrical houses, where liquor flowed freely and prostitutes still commonly prowled the notorious third tier. Despite protracted campaigns by reformers and certain entrepreneurs (such as P. T. Barnum and Niblo himself) to refine and clean up theatrical entertainment, "respectable," particularly evangelical, opinion continued (with some good reason) to associate all forms of drama—opera included—with the demimonde.[46]

One answer to these impediments was to make both a virtue and a fashion of opera-going. This is precisely what the successful restaurateur and would-be impresario Ferdinand Palmo hoped to accomplish. Long enamored of his native Italy's music, Palmo resolved in the winter of 1843–44 to stake his considerable fortune on yet another attempt to install a permanent opera company in his adopted city. To draw a suitably fashionable clientele able to pay his price, he outfitted his "bijou" of a theater in the latest style (though its benches were generally pronounced remarkably uncomfortable) and located it nearby City Hall and the old Park Theatre, in a neighborhood remote from Bowery grogshops. The dollar admission to prime seats guaranteed that well-heeled subscribers would not have to rub shoulders with hoi polloi, though in concession to plebeian patronage, the boxes that had in the past provoked class resentment were initially omitted and seats in the tiers were priced at only twenty-five cents. To encourage the attendance of ladies (whose presence formed one of the chief reasons for fashion's assemblage), Palmo also decreed that no woman would be admitted to his Chambers Street venue without a male escort, a move designed to drive away prostitutes.[47]

For a time, this play for the "carriage" trade appeared to be a rousing success. "The mania for which the fashionable people are crowding Palmo's Opera House," reported the *Herald* in May 1844,

> reminds us of the extraordinary excitement on the first appearance of Fanny Elssler, or recently when Ole Bull turned the town upside down. By a certain class in society, the most elevated and wealthy, all other theatres are utterly abandoned for the Opera House. And the style—the elegance—the extravagance with which they dress, must be particularly profitable to the milliners and dressmakers. The brilliancy of these opera nights is beyond anything we ever saw in theatrical movements in this city. The whole house glitters with beauty and fashion, and it certainly looks more like the life, gaiety, and brilliance of the precincts of a court than the republican simplicity of a good democratic city.

Six months later, the same newspaper could proclaim that the "Opera House is beginning to assume the character of a fashionable and indispensable resort, which it bears in London—where all who wish to be thought members of *society* are compelled to appear, whether they possess a taste for music or not."[48]

All this to-do awakened Willis to grand opera's commercial and social potential. As far back as June 1843, he was arguing that a "change of the sumptuary character of Broadway" enjoined a "dress opera's establishment." Then, soon after launching the *Evening Mirror* on its campaign for the Upper Ten's allegiance, he was off again on his soapbox, counseling Palmo that no half measures would do: any successful opera house "must be a splendid affair, or a failure." With characteristic verve, Willis accordingly called for "comfort in the seats, breadth in the alleys, *boundless prodigality in the lights*, luxury in the saloons and entrances, and Alhambrian excellence in the refreshments," and to complete the scene, obligatory full dress—nothing else would lure the Upper Ten like the chance to be seen to good advantage. Nor was the *Mirror's* chief averse to employing a bit of Barnum to achieve his desideratum. "Prestige, celebrity, show, humbug and ceremony should be added to the most indefatigable real merit in the management, and then," he predicted sagely, "the shareholders would make money." In short, the *tout ensemble* must be puffed into a veritable spectacle. Taking his own advice, Willis spent the next half-decade tirelessly touting the opera's moral benefit, promoting its progress, and puffing its prima donnas. Indeed, so excessively did he admire his favorite, Rosina Pico, that William Mitchell's Olympic Theatre once ran a musical burlesque (*The Mirror of Truth*) that featured a Willis character positively thrumming in "pico-tricity."[49]

Unhappily for fans of the opera, quarrels with performers, excessive costs, and the fickle patronage of fashion doomed the starry-eyed Italian impresario's once-promising enterprise to abject failure; after several volatile seasons, Palmo was bankrupted and forced to live out his final years as a hotel cook. Yet such commercial difficulties scarcely extinguished the dream of making cultured amusement pay in New York City. Even as Palmo's was faltering, the patrician lawyer George Templeton Strong reported that "the little Chambers Street concern is quite too small";

plans, he had heard, were afoot among a group of well-to-do speculators and aficionados to build a new and grander edifice for opera uptown. In time, this became the fashionable opera house at Astor Place located near the newly built "palaces" of the city's elite clustered around Union Square. Here, Willis's injunctions to Palmo were realized in spades. To staff the company, an in-house troupe of singers was requisitioned direct from Italy, and no expense was spared to make the house the most lavish and imposing of its kind. From its "thick pictured carpet" to the silver and gold gilding of the interior facade, comfort and luxury reigned supreme. The pit (renamed the *parquette* and now dedicated to some of the best seats in the house) featured cushioned armchairs, and the balconies had sofas and "tête-à-têtes"; including in the galleries, there were some fifteen to eighteen hundred seats. Crowning the whole was a fifteen-hundred-pound cut-glass chandelier so huge that it all but blocked the stage to patrons in the upper gallery. When lit, the sixty gas jets of this "glorious chandelier" more than fulfilled Willis's call for "boundless prodigality of lights."[50]

Even more than at Palmo's, the expense of such luxuries led to exclusionary practices. Tickets, except in the upper gallery, were priced at a dollar and thus beyond the means of many middle-class and almost all working-class enthusiasts. The management, moreover, initially accorded preference to subscribers, so that the best seats in the newly "aristocratized" *parquette* and elsewhere became a monopoly of those who could afford the high tariff of season tickets. As the management were also pledged to protect visitors from all "petty annoyances and impositions" by strict policing of "improper" persons, fashion, wealth, and a certain brand of high-toned propriety came to dominate the scene both physically and socially, though critics complained that "blacklegs" and prostitutes still prowled the house unchecked. The Astor's Upper Ten character was not lost on Gotham's press. After opening night, the *Sunday Age* reported facetiously that

> the snobs . . . (and how they did swarm) exposed themselves awfully, slapping together their bunches of sausages, tightly compressed in white kids, with vulgar vehemence, instead of slightly patting the two digits of the dexter hand upon the sinister palm, shouting out *bravo*, instead of *brava*, without reference to gender or no, and always at the wrong time, at which the *cognoscenti* looked black and the *dilettanti* turned their eyes up like ducks in a thunder storm.

A year later, after the first season had failed ignominiously and another was begun under the direction of Edward Fry, Willis himself could report that the "pea-nut-ulace of public places" (that is, the common people) went "wholly unrepresented even in the gallery," which item of "progress" he took to prove that "amid the jealous equality of a republic, a place of public amusement may be *spontaneously* exclusive. (N.B.—this latter fact desirable or not, as you like.)"[51]

Though favoring these momentous innovations in popular amusement, Willis nonetheless still registered a curious ambivalence toward the progress of fashion. It should be recalled that when Palmo's was in full swing, he had zealously pressed the adoption of full dress; for precisely this reason, the social necessity of kid gloves has traditionally been laid at his door. When later it seemed to him that the opera might be placed on firmer footing, moreover, he was not above suggesting a doubling of the price of the best tickets to two dollars. Still, though Willis was widely recognized as among the first stars in the Astor's constellation of boosters, he remained at least rhetorically committed to the ideal of equal access, if not necessarily for working-class patrons, then for many below the Upper Ten. Even while first calling for a "dress opera" in 1843, he had been moved to wax eloquent over the advantages of a middle class wherein it would be "respectable to set aside certain extravagances in dress and living as not proper for a condition of life which is still far above poverty," a class (he noted parenthetically) in which "literary men" were "naturally part and parcel." This economical stance was, in fact, a corollary to his opinion that

> in this country of equal advantages, the qualities we need for the pleasantest intercourse are found in almost every stratum of society, and perhaps least in the most fashionable. . . . A man who is superfine in this country—who slights or rejects the society of men or women because they are not *fashionable*—is a shallow observer, and, to say the least, has a very limited chance of good companionship.

Just how much this democratic impulse had hardened in ensuing years is difficult to determine. Willis certainly could be dismissive of the so-called vulgar classes when he chose: recall, if nothing else, his venomous "Lecture on Fashion." Yet in the midst of campaigning for ticket increases, he could also applaud the institution of twenty-five-cent "off-nights" at the Astor, a time when what he called the "graver and more highly educated portion of New York society—elderly men, ladies who don't dress showily, musicians who listen critically, literary men who prefer not to be jostled . . . , paragons of plain respectability who would avoid any scene of open ostentation" could indulge their love of operatic art in "warm wrappers and brown gloves." Intensely aware of the tenuous nature of his own claims on society, Willis thus continued to hope that culture generally, and the opera particularly, might be made available to a fairly broad spectrum of society and, conversely, that the broad spectrum of experience be made accessible to the "cultured" classes.[52]

These seemingly paradoxical nuances were generally lost amidst the festering class antagonisms that poisoned New York society in these years. Battered by sustained economic troubles and stripped of hope for an independent future by industrial dislocation, the city's artisans and workingmen eyed the progress of fashion and its amusements with jaundiced contempt. To many urban laborers, the spectacle of the Astor Place Opera House in particular—with its exclusive boxes and *parquette*, uptown location, and conspicuous luxury—became a highly charged symbol of the growing privileges of the city's obnoxious wealth. Class segmentation of amusements played a crucial part in fostering this resentment, for as the opera and other refined amusements siphoned off the so-called respectable classes, New York's "cheap" theaters became home to an increasingly volatile workingman's consciousness. In shilling playhouses like the Chatham and the Olympic, a rough-and-ready, predominantly male clientele (cheering their favorites in melodramas and burlesques like "The Upper Row House in Disaster Place") came to see themselves as the principle repository of bedrock republican virtues—manly, democratic, convivial, forthright, and true-blue American—in contrast to the effete, exclusive, stuffy, and sneaky Europeanized "aristocrats" uptown.

This trend achieved its apotheosis in Francis Chanfrau's "Bowery B'hoy" character "Mose," who strode the boards to sustained acclaim beginning in the winter of 1848. Often cast as a butcher's apprentice, and invariably a runner in the plebeian-dominated volunteer fire companies, Mose enunciated an urban working-class consciousness as Willis hoped the "Upper Ten" would enunciate that of the cultivated classes. To polite society's dismay, moreover, Mose was (reflecting his pugilistic fans' confrontational stance) ever ready to defend his democratic rights against untoward infringement. When Walt Whitman came to sketch *his* "b'hoy of the Bowery," for instance, he pictured him puffing a "remarkably bad segar" right under the readers' nostrils, professing to be a "connoisseur in everything related to peanuts," discoursing "most learnedly about the classical performances in the Chatham Theatre," and contending "strenuously" that "Mr. N. P. Willis is a humbug—that Mike Walsh [the radical workingman's favorite politico] is a *hoss*, and that the Brigadier [Willis's partner, Morris] *ain't no where*." Whitman surmised all this, even though the "*b'hoy* in question" probably never "saw either of the gentlemen that he attempt[ed] to lampoon."[53]

Like many signs of the day, Whitman's character sketch suggests that by the late 1840s Willis and the refined urban amusement he championed had become flash points in a symbolic class confrontation pitting New York's Upper Ten against its working-class B'hoys. This was an antagonism the city's journalists were not above fueling to suit their own purposes. James Gordon Bennett, the strident editor of the *New York Herald*, was among the most culpable in this regard. Long a fixture in the city's rough-and-tumble journalistic world, Bennett had been only too glad to profit from the growth of fashionable culture, at one time even contesting the old *Mirror* for the palm in publicizing elite movements. But he was also wary of fashion as the *Mirror*'s editors never were and keenly sensitized to the potential commercial rewards entailed in playing to working-class pride and prejudice. When personal antipathy entered the mix, moreover, he could scourge aristocratic pretense with rare fury.

New York witnessed one such demonstration of this volatility when Edward Fry assumed the management of the troubled Astor Place Opera Company in late 1847. Even before Edward's brilliant but self-important brother William Henry had debuted his homegrown opera "Leonora" in Philadelphia two years earlier, Bennett had tried to run down the brothers Fry. The Astor's plan to reprise "Leonora" now only goaded him to new heights of journalistic invective. Subsequent testimony suggests that the opera's failure to contract with the *Herald* to print its bills and advertise its offerings (a custom extended instead to Bennett's inveterate enemy James Watson Webb), or even extend the usual free tickets to reviewers, may have prompted Bennett to vow to "finish" Fry once and for all, as it almost certainly led him to foment dissension among the company's refractory European vocalists. Whatever the case, over the next half-year, in a barrage that would eventually help to destroy the opera and provoke a successful retaliatory libel suit, the *Herald* blasted Edward Fry's "imbecile and weak management" on a weekly basis, devoting almost equal time to the "snobbish" opera committee's unwholesome and invidiously un-

American desire to introduce into New York what Bennett called "the conceited, exclusive, and insolent pretension which prevails in the aristocratic and worn-out circles of European society." To judge by the *Herald's* heated rhetorical sallies, this was the beginning of the end for native virtue. Should the opera culture of the "Codfish Aristocracy" prevail, Bennett predicted that its free and easy licentiousness would become the American norm. In the hyperbolic atmosphere of antebellum New York's culture wars, to stand against the opera was thus to stand for republican freedom and morality.[54]

Though Bennett could hardly have foreseen its upshot, this rhetorical escalation of the tension between Europeanized aristocratic pretense and four-square American virtue set the stage for a drama of envy, contempt, and class hatred that New York would not soon forget. A protracted quarrel between America's premier tragedian, Edwin Forrest, and his foremost English rival, William Macready, provided the pretext for this drama. In 1846, goaded by ill-treatment at the hands of pro-Macready journalists and driven by a towering temper, Forrest had hissed his rival on the Edinburgh stage—ostensibly for desecrating *Hamlet* with an inappropriate and unmanly "fancy dance." This "hiss" quickly flared into an international incident. For several months thereafter, denunciations and accusations flew hot and fast on both sides of the Atlantic. Eventually, the partisan sniping died down, only to rekindle when Macready toured the United States beginning in the autumn of 1848. Consumed with a personal grudge, Forrest played head-to-head against his rival in several American cities. And night after night, heated words and haughty pronouncements fueled the controversy and exposed its class dimensions. Forrest, his critics complained, was a no-talent ranter, and his rough-and-ready working-class supporters were yahoos and thugs; Macready, so his detractors charged, was an aristocratic snob, and his stateside advocates, Anglophile toadies. When, in Cincinnati, several Forrest partisans hurled half a sheep's carcass at Macready's feet, the spectacle of the Englishman's contemptuous glower epitomized the rising tension.

This ill feeling came to a head in May 1849 back in New York City. Here, on two separate nights, Forrest's B'hoy partisans besieged the uptown Astor Place Opera House where Macready had come to play, vowing to close this den of the "Codfish Aristocracy" and silence "English pretension." After a hail of epithets and broken chairs drove the actor from the stage on the first night, a committee of well-heeled New Yorkers headed by Washington Irving issued a public "card" deploring the precedent and pledging to protect Macready's performance. Upon the Englishman's return to the theater several nights later, shouts and hoots quickly escalated into a barrage of rotten fruit and other missiles. Scuffles followed soon after, as police waded in to collar the offenders. Finally, a flurry of hurled brickbats and flailing truncheons ensued as a full-scale riot surged in the streets outside the opera house. Before this night was through, militiamen called to the scene to restore order had fired repeated volleys into the angry crowd gathered to protest Macready's appearance. When calm finally returned to the streets, at least eighteen people lay dead and many more were wounded, four fatally. All New York—Willis included—was shocked at the violence.[55]

Postmortems

Daylight brought the inevitable chorus of blame. The signers of Macready's card and those like them who valued order and propriety—including the majority of the city's Whig press—denounced Forrest's partisans as ruffians and thugs. This "outrage" was, thought one genteel supporter of Macready, a "partially successful attempt of bullies and rowdies to establish mob law among us." Despite its populist sympathies, even the Democratic *Evening Post* called the unfortunate affair an "insurrection" against "personal liberty, against personal safety, against the right of property, altogether without provocation, and without any circumstance of extenuation." If others—most conspicuously Bennett's *Herald*—argued that there was blame enough for all (the mayor, the committee, and the rioters themselves), some ten thousand New Yorkers were sufficiently convinced of aristocratic fashion's culpability to join the mass protest called for City Hall Park on the evening following the slaughter. Then, when radical working-class and nativist agitators led fully half of these in a march on the now-shattered pleasure palace of the Upper Ten, the state of the city's social relations was made painfully clear: New York was a city divided by fashion, locked in a test of will and blood. But the revolt fizzled. Confronted by more than three thousand armed men—soldiers, police, and special deputies, with a troop of cavalry circling the opera house itself—the angry marchers eventually slipped away, reserving their frustrations and antipathies for another day.[56]

And what did "My Lord Willis" have to say of the tragedy? Not what his detractors (or even his adherents) might have expected. He did stand with law and order and reprinted the *Evening Post* editorial to prove it. But law, as he had often reminded his readers, was but one pillar of social harmony, and perhaps not the most crucial, restricted as it often was to policing extreme behavior: comity began with small considerations, and it eroded there as well. As Willis saw it now, by their sumptuary excesses, offensive manners, and monopoly of prime seats, the opera's habitués had created an exclusive fashion that the "respectable and economical" classes would not abide. Vicious brutes clearly had no place in an opera house (here we may discern the limits of Willis's democratic sensibilities), but he thought there was no sense in needlessly antagonizing the common man, especially in a republic. And it was their protest, though out of hand, that led Willis to suggest that "everywhere out of private houses" good republicans should refrain from dress, display, or acts calculated to offend fellow citizens. "What men have a right to do," he concluded, "anywhere, with the advantages of fortune, and what it is considerate and republican to abstain from doing, because it excites irrepressible envy, would put very different limits to the ostentation of luxury." To Willis, the riot's lesson was thus unequivocal: "WEALTH IN A REPUBLIC, SHOULD BE MINDFUL WHERE ITS LUXURIES OFFEND."[57]

Blazing capitals could hardly overstate this case. In Willis's eyes, much more than amusement was at stake. The opera was to him a little republic of taste, and taste taught best by example. That was why he had so assiduously answered the queries of correspondents on dress and etiquette and so tirelessly promoted his "natural aristocracy" of talent and beauty. And yet, as much as he relied on the printed word to propound his agenda, Willis knew that any leading class would come to naught unless allowed to prove itself in the republic's streets, omnibuses, hotel lobbies, steamboats—and opera houses. Nor could it do so unless its many aspirants were admitted to the refined amusements in which cultivation arguably was shown to best effect. In the wake of the riot, Willis thus took pains to remind the world (which had mistaken him before) that in this regard his "Tammany" streak ran deep. "There is a very large class of cultivated men who are compelled to live and dress economically," he had written two years previously and now recalled to punctuate his point, "and these men, below the level of kid gloves and dollar tickets, should rightfully have all the advantages, both of hearing the music and seeing the audience—forgoing *display only*, as the consideration for a cheap ticket." Even months later, when he detected a growing hostility toward the right of the wealthy to express their taste in "white gloves," "liveried servants," "mustaches," and "opera glasses"—a "needless and unreasonable" prejudice that struck hard at his cherished principle of personal expression—Willis stuck to his guns:

> *Exclusiveness*, unpopular as it is, is a republican right, subject to nothing but ridicule, when exercised in a man's house, equipage and personal acquaintance; but any privilege given, in a place of amusement, to one man above another, for fashionable preeminence merely and without competition of purchase, is un-republican and wrong, and, with that we think, the public have a right to be discontented.[58]

Opera exclusivity preoccupied Willis even more so because it threatened to undercut the very real social influence he ascribed to the "gentler sex," a class of people on which he had staked so much, both commercially and ideologically. Women in the audience had, in fact, always seemed to him the most important show at the theater. Like many of his contemporaries, he saw them as emblems and ornaments of civilized society, if not, probably, the entire political equals of men. More than most, he also courted them as a leading class, an advance guard of taste, endowed with a peculiar instrumental value to effect comity and community in the face of social antagonisms.

This was as true in the theater as it was in the realm of print. "Angrily as the discontented lower class may look upon the nabobs and dandies," Willis reasoned in his commentary on the riot,

> they gaze with softened feelings and generous admiration upon the beautiful women whom they see in the close neighborhood of the pit and boxes. To look on these is more than half the pleasure of the evening, and a link of humane sympathy with the circle to which they belong, is insensibly welded by the habit of approaching them thus nearly. Without this opportunity, they see this class of ladies only in their carriages or in the street—casually and with no possible community of feeling—and the *dangerous consciousness of a class from whom they are entirely cut off* is offensively heightened.

In other words, all that stood between viciousness and comity was a kind of sentimentalized mise-en-scène. Believing this, Willis had labored to overcome prejudice against women attending the opera, lobbied to admit prima donnas to "good society," and chastised male opera-goers for their rudeness. Now, the cloud of violence hanging over Astor Place threatened to drive genteel ladies from the opera forever. With this most crucial institution stripped of their presence, refinement would lose its best hope of effecting a cultural risorgimento.[59]

This much Willis would admit. Yet it is hard to avoid the conclusion that, in practice, the Astor Place violence spelled the death of his dream of "intellectualizing" fashion, and for reasons that struck at the core of his social vision. Put simply, taste ultimately failed to halt the slide of emulation into envy because it was neither as malleable or reconciliatory as Willis supposed. Rather than uniting people in common regard for the beauties of refined living and in admiration for "nature's nobility," his campaign to spread culture had only encouraged the very invidious distinctions he had hoped to avoid. This result was arguably not entirely Willis's fault. New York's urban working people were as susceptible to demagoguery as they were to reasonable appeals to their common predicament. Then, too, the city's Upper Ten had, in a sense, betrayed their self-appointed majordomo; though paying his price, they ignored consequential subtleties in his counsel. Still, a man also reaps what he sows—by squandering his talents appealing to high-toned prejudices and conjuring visions of cultural aristocracy, Willis profited greatly from his Upper Ten's custom. Now he would suffer their predicament as well.

In this respect, the riot underscored a dilemma that had plagued Willis's advocacy of refinement all along. Hitting on the vocation of vending taste had solved for him the immediate quandary of how to pay for life, but only to generate another problem: Was taste, as it sometimes seemed in his handling, a commodity to be sold to the highest bidder? Or was it, as he and other genteel sentimentalists averred, a transcendent ideal to be revered, whatever the cost? In short, would he give his readers what they wanted or what he believed they ought to hear? When pushed to the wall, Willis seems to have inclined toward the latter, though in the case of the Astor Place affair, at least, his answer clearly came too late for comfort. By his own admission, the riot's lesson was, sadly, an "After-Lesson." Nothing could retrieve the dead; nor was there much likelihood of restoring his—or anyone else's— hopes for the Upper Ten. This particular night at the opera was thus a calamity of multiple dimensions, and one whose repercussions would soon return to haunt Willis—and the nation—in ways he could then scarcely have imagined.

Holding a copy of the *Boston Recorder*, N. P.
Willis's father proclaims his evangelical affiliation
in this portrait by his son's friend, the celebrated
Boston artist Chester Harding. Chester Harding,
probably oil on canvas, ca. 1830. The Library
of Congress, Prints and Photographs Division,
LC-USZ62-119599. Last known owner:
Horace Bumstead.

A portrait by Harding of N. P. Willis's mother, Hannah, at the time
of her son's *American Monthly Magazine*. Chester Harding, photographic copy of original oil on canvas, 1831. Fanny Fern Collection, Sophia Smith Collection, Smith College. Original owned by
and reproduced by permission of the family of Hannah Locke
Carter.

In Willis's day, the proximity of the elegant Tremont Hotel to the Tremont Theatre across the street encouraged the patrons of the two establishments to mix in what British traveler Frederick Marryat called "a life of idleness and vacuity of outward pretence, but of no good feeling." After Philip Harry, "The Streets of Boston. Tremont Street. No. III." Tinted lithograph, Boston: Bouvé and Sharp Lithographers, 1843. By permission of the Boston Athenaeum.

Edward Bulwer, author of *Pelham* and other popular novels, is framed as a keepsake image in this American engraving. D. G. Johnson, steel engraving, ca. 1830s. The Library of Congress, Prints and Photographs Division, LC-USZ62-119598.

AN EYE TO BUSINESS.

Willis's third trip to England occasioned this dig at his brand of invasive travel reporting. Wood engraving, *Punch*, 1845. From the copy in the Davis Library, the University of North Carolina at Chapel Hill.

N. P. Willis's first wife, the English-born Mary Stace. Photographer unknown, carte de visite, probably from a daguerreotype original, ca. early 1840s. By permission of the Houghton Library, Harvard University.

N. P. Willis signs himself "Yours very truly" in this engraving after Harding in the *New York Mirror*, the author's first mass-produced likeness. After Chester Harding, steel engraving, *New York Mirror*, 1837. From the copy in the Rare Book Collection, the University of North Carolina at Chapel Hill.

Willis appeared in *Graham's* as a faithful and elegant companion. The facsimile autograph was now de rigueur for American literary magazines wishing to advertise their celebrated contributors. Archibald L. Dick after George Whiting Flagg, steel engraving, *Graham's Magazine*, 1844. By permission of the Boston Athenaeum.

"MI BOY," AND "THE BRIGADIER."

In this punning woodcut published in Charles Briggs's *Broadway Journal*, the narcissistic propensities of Willis and his longtime partner George Pope Morris ("Mi Boy" and "The Brigadier") are held up to gentle ribbing. Rodman, wood engraving, *Broadway Journal*, 1845. By permission of the Boston Athenaeum.

Emily Judson ("Fanny Forester") is idealized in this portrait engraving from a Christian hagiograph treating the lives of her missionary husband's several wives, both living and deceased. J. C. Buttre, steel engraving, in Arabella W. Stuart, *The Lives of Mrs. Ann H. Judson and Mrs Sarah B. Judson, with a Biographical Sketch of Mrs. Emily C. Judson, Missionaries to Burmah*, 1852. From the copy in the Davis Library, the University of North Carolina at Chapel Hill.

This image of Lizzie Read, the young New Bedford girl so enamored of Willis's "Sacred Poems," recalls her friends and family to the days before her untimely death. It appeared as a frontispiece to the memorial volume compiled by her teacher, John S. C. Abbott. J. Sartain, steel engraving, in *Memoir of Miss Elizabeth T. Read*, 1847. From the copy in the Davis Library, the University of North Carolina at Chapel Hill.

ONE OF THE "UPPER TEN THOUSAND."

One of the "Upper Ten Thousand" dressed to the nines and strolling New York's streets in a self-satisfied fashion, as depicted by a local engraver not long after Willis had coined the term in an attempt to galvanize the city's elite classes. Samuel E. Brown, wood engraving, in *Broadway Journal*, 1845. By permission of the Boston Athenaeum.

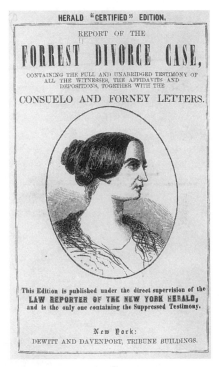

HERALD "CERTIFIED" EDITION.

REPORT OF THE

FORREST DIVORCE CASE,

CONTAINING THE FULL AND UNABRIDGED TESTIMONY OF ALL THE WITNESSES, THE AFFIDAVITS AND DEPOSITIONS, TOGETHER WITH THE

CONSUELO AND FORNEY LETTERS.

This Edition is published under the direct supervision of the LAW REPORTER OF THE NEW YORK HERALD, and is the only one containing the Suppressed Testimony.

New York:
DEWITT AND DAVENPORT, TRIBUNE BUILDINGS.

Catherine Forrest's image announces the sensational contents to be found in this Herald "Certified" Edition of the Forrest Divorce Case. Such cheap pamphlets sold in the tens of thousands following the six-week-long trial. Doubtless, this edition's unabridged transcripts of the Consuelo and Forney letters contributed to sales. Wood engraving, in *Report of the Forrest Divorce Case, Herald Edition*, 1852. From the copy in the Davis Library, the University of North Carolina at Chapel Hill.

This caricature documents the stir set off in the early 1850s as promenading Bloomers (the "Fe'He Males") challenged traditional male prerogatives to "wear the pants" in American families. "Two of the Fe'He Males," lithograph, ca. 1851. © Collection of the New-York Historical Society.

In this satirical lithograph, "Mr. Forrestini" threatens to pummel a cringing "Mr. Vanburini" unless the lawyer proves the actor's estranged wife to be one of the "Ga Hals." Ann Flowers's "kitchen testimony" lies bound and ready for use at "Vanburini's" feet. "A Scene from the Laughable Comedy of The Divorce Suit," lithograph, P. E. Abel, Bookseller, Philadelphia, ca. 1851. The Harvard Theatre Collection, the Houghton Library.

Affairs of Honor

To those whose god is honor, disgrace alone is sin.

J. C. and A. W. Hare, *Guesses at Truth*
(1827)

It is almost axiomatic that the dramas of real life are often as fantastic as those of the stage. So it must have seemed to the loafers, vendors, and passersby in New York City's Washington Square who, one evening in June 1850, turned to witness the actor Edwin Forrest thrashing N. P. Willis with the favorite instrument of imperious schoolmasters: a gutta-percha whip. Soon the attack's cause became apparent, even to those who might not have been following the two men's ongoing feud in the press. As the burly tragedian assailed his prostrated victim, whip flailing, he bellowed to onlookers, "this man is the seducer of my wife." Forrest's message—a cuckold's classic requital—was thus painfully clear: he would brook no meddling. Willis, for his part, scarcely had a chance to respond. Frantic pleas and feeble struggles aside, he was entirely overborne.[1]

Yet for all this, it would be a mistake to consider the beating as anything but a desperate play to reassert control of a situation well out of hand. Remember that these were no ordinary men, though both had risen to prominence from relative obscurity; it should not surprise us, then, that their quarrel incited extraordinary public response. Indeed, when the unwelcome press coverage that had annoyed the Forrests since the first hints of their marital trouble in the spring of 1849 redoubled as estrangement led to divorce proceedings the following February, private discord had turned swiftly into a public spectacle that mobilized Americans' strongest sympathies and deepest anxieties. Too much was known of Willis and Forrest, and too much presumed, for popular judgment to leave well enough alone. Each man had his devoted fans and inveterate detractors, and neither man's cause could be separated from the social tenets he espoused or the hopes and fears he embodied. Long before matters reached their violent crisis in Washington Square, the quarrel between Willis and Forrest had thus become, like the Astor Place riot, an affair of cultural politics as well as personal passion. Because of this emblematic dimension, the honor that Forrest sought to regain in Washington Square was largely out of his hands, as it was, more obviously, out of Willis's. When matters finally careened toward a stunning crescendo in a six-week divorce trial during the winter of 1851–52, the truth of this predicament was to be punctuated emphatically.

Coming, as it did, after several decades of unprecedented growth in the business of popular culture, this result was destined to underscore one of the new era's most salient social features: celebrities' starring role in the grand theater of American public life. Now more than ever, celebrity scandal figured, along with celebrity gossip, as an engrossing form of entertainment for an audience raised to expect insight into the sinews and heart of private character. Yet it was—as this particular case would suggest so well—diversion almost inevitably shot through with a variety of social anxieties, many of which sprang from some of the self-same emotional and commercial sources that produced celebrity in the first place. One thing that became particularly clear as the Forrest affair unfolded in its fantastic dialectic of revelation and rebuttal was the way in which Willis's brand of sentimental commerce had helped to precipitate a fundamental rift in American attitudes toward marriage and the proper relations of men and women. Such concerns alone were reason enough to lead contemporary observers to discover broad social implications in the episode. Understanding why, for nineteenth-century Americans, its lessons also encompassed matters as diverse and divisive as fashion and Fourierism and a sensational press and the so-called servant problem, will require further consideration of questions posed by the social divide separating New York's "Upper Ten and Lower Twenty." But first we must discover how Forrest came to his desperate act and what Willis did to warrant such fury.[2]

Sweetest Consuelo

Edwin Forrest had long nursed the slights that goaded him to act that fateful June evening. The trouble began with a failing marriage. After a decade of relative harmony, strains had begun to show between the American actor and his English-born wife. By the mid-1840s, Catherine Sinclair Forrest (herself the daughter of stage parents) had carried several pregnancies to term only to see the infants die soon after their birth. Not surprisingly, this unfortunate situation upset the young couple, especially as Edwin was eager to carry on the Forrest name. More upsetting still was Edwin's decision (acted on sometime in the late 1840s) to bar Catherine's sister Margaret from his Twenty-second Street home on account of her free and easy ways. In veiled defiance of this ban, Catherine continued to entertain Margaret during her husband's frequent absences on tour. Then, one evening in January 1849, with his wife away at a bon voyage party for her sister's new husband Frank Voorhies, Edwin found a love note in a locked drawer among Catherine's papers. The shock at discovering this passionate epistle, later determined to have been written by the young blackface actor George Jamieson, recalled a disturbing incident in Cincinnati six months past. Returning with an associate to his hotel room, Forrest had chanced upon his wife and Jamieson apparently close to embrace—just an innocent phrenological examination, the two had explained hastily. Nothing more was said at the time. Now, though unsure of the precise implications of his new discovery, Edwin suspected enough to give free rein to his jealous fears.[3]

That night, on Catherine's return, he confronted her in the couple's second-floor library. For several hours Edwin bitterly harangued his wife, deploring her sister's influence and growing angrier all the while as Catherine rebuked his insinuations. During one particularly heated exchange, she reportedly cried out, "It's a lie! It's a lie!" and other expressions that she later allowed were not only ill chosen but "improper." Edwin refused to suffer such impertinence, and he resolved that they must separate. Catherine reluctantly agreed. After weeks of sullenly tolerating her silent ministrations, Edwin announced in mid-April that the time had come. When he left his wife in Fanny and Parke Godwin's hallway on the morning of 28 April 1849, the great Shakespearean actor undoubtedly hoped to leave behind his torment.[4]

Circumstance would disallow so easy a solution. Though Forrest seems to have honored his wife by repelling all suggestions of her infidelity, the stony silence with which he met inquiries into the cause of separation left ample room for conjecture. In this regard, the New York newspaper that later remarked that this service had at least "saved her reputation" and "silenced gossips if it could not heal her wounds" was surely being too optimistic. Even before the separation, tongues had wagged. "Last evening I called on [Forrest's fast friend and lifelong business manager, James] Lawson," the Knickerbocker poet William Cullen Bryant told his wife in a letter of March 1849.

> He tells me that he was informed by young [Henry] Panton, as a matter which every one knew that Mr.—you will understand who [Forrest]—and his wife were to separate, and that [James] Lawson and I were to decide what allowance should be made for her maintenance. It came from Miss [Anne] Lynch, and it appears that Willis and his wife are talking in the same way. . . . Lawson quoted a saying of [Margaret Voorhies]: "My sister and he have not lived happily together for a long time, and for the last year or so, she has been perfectly reckless, but she never thought it would come to this." I am afraid that you and I know very little about the occasion of the quarrel, after all.

Whatever "reckless" meant—visits with the banned Margaret, rollicking parties, or sexual infidelity—circulation of such reports only tended to fulfill Bryant's despairing prediction to his wife that they would see this gossip "in the newspapers next."[5]

Soon after that Saturday morning when Edwin left Catherine at the Godwins', word of the separation did appear in the press. Speculation abounded regarding the reason for the split. One newspaper cited a "cause Napoleonic" (that is, lack of an heir). Another left the matter hanging, but implied, nonetheless, that responsibility lay with Edwin's monumental funk in his ongoing quarrel with William Macready—soon to issue in riot and death at Astor Place. Whatever the cause, the New York press pursued gossip thoroughly enough that a family friend later recalled that the Forrest separation had become "notorious by extracts in the papers" before he ever heard anything of it from Edwin's own mouth.[6]

Such publicity clearly tormented the husband and doubtless undercut chances for the couple's reconciliation. Though indebted to growing press coverage for their success, the nation's early celebrities were often as loath to endure scrutiny as were their latter-day counterparts—and for similar reasons. Prying made trouble, reducing intimate matters to breakfast-time banter and embroiling celebrities in annoying and potentially damaging disputes. This was especially true for choleric men like Forrest, whose temperament ran to outrage. Oblique references to his marriage troubles at the time of the Jamieson incident, for instance, had driven Edwin to snap to his sister Eleanora, "They are lying chronicles and the amount of truth they utter upon any subject might be put in a nutshell." Now, after a friend brought one particularly maddening notice of the separation to his attention, the enraged actor stormed down to New York's newspaper row to accuse its author of doing Catherine's bidding.[7]

Events ultimately bore out Forrest's worst fears. Though Lawson worked manfully to reunite the estranged couple, by December 1849 matters had reached a crisis. In a series of letters commencing on Christmas Eve, Edwin accused his wife of circulating false reports regarding the cause of their domestic troubles. Catherine denied his accusation; ugly rumor, she suggested, generated its own dynamic. This sentiment was small consolation to Edwin; besides, he did not believe her. To save a name he now considered shamefully dishonored, the great tragedian hired the prominent lawyers Theodore Sedgwick and Josiah Randall to handle his divorce. At Parke Godwin's suggestion, Catherine retained Charles O'Conor, a socially and politically conservative Irish-American Democrat and one of New York's most successful trial attorneys, to represent her interests in what was rapidly becoming a more open and acrimonious dispute.[8]

The husband had not yet abandoned hope of a quiet settlement, though. That was precisely why he (like so many of the day's well-connected and well-heeled Americans) chose to petition the Pennsylvania legislature for divorce. Having rejoined his sisters in Philadelphia after breaking up his New York home, Forrest could claim state residency by legal technicality, although he kept his nearly completed Fonthill castle on the Hudson River at Yonkers. He could also claim a native son's sentimental attachment. In this case, however, such emotions were largely a pretext. As Edwin well knew, legislative dispensations like those granted by what contemporary wags dubbed the "Divorcer-General of the Union" were relatively discreet affairs; final decisions were unavoidably public, but the essence of debate could be kept under wraps, especially if the petitioner had political connections. These the noted actor most certainly possessed, apparently of sufficient sway to persuade the state's legislators to extend an unusual measure of secrecy to his petition.[9]

At this point, however, the affair's public dimensions began to overtake private design. No mere gag rule could squelch public desire for inside report about a man as famous as Ned Forrest, especially when such appetites were whetted already by the riot at Astor Place and a spate of celebrity divorce petitions recently filed in Harrisburg (of which Pierce and Fanny Butler's was only the most notorious). Nor could that significant body of Americans leery of closed-door proceedings be expected to quash their fears that a true wife was being victimized. Over the previous two decades, a groundswell of sentiment against mercenary matches and the worst abuses of male prerogative had realized significant gains for women in the area of property rights and access to divorce, mostly by appealing to the hope that a wife's enhanced personal and financial independence would purify the institution of marriage. "Licentiousness is the effect of *enforced* relations between the sexes," argued one reform advocate at the time. "Let these relations confess the sole sovereignty of Affection, and liberty would instantly banish every disgusting form of license which now desecrates her name." To adherents of this forward-thinking social doctrine, and to certain chivalric paternalists as well, Forrest's decision to take his evidence before a secret (and presumably corruptible) tribunal, in a jurisdiction where his wife had neither friends nor a fair opportunity to plead her case, must have seemed a monstrous and morally emblematic injustice. It certainly added fuel to Pennsylvania reformers' ongoing campaign to dispense with legislative divorce altogether. So it was that the chorus of Edwin's gainsayers swelled as his petition proceeded through state house channels.[10]

In this respect, it did not hurt Catherine Forrest's cause that she seemed to fit the victim's role so admirably. Unlike her husband, she was a relative unknown. But she was young, pretty, presumably refined, and, most important, vulnerable—in short, a fair copy of the sentimental heroine of antebellum domestic fiction. Like such heroines (whose predicaments hers now mirrored), Catherine thus could expect moral advantage from the canons of Romantic womanhood, which generally served to endow middle-class ladies with a chaste aura derived from their ostensibly "passionless" nature. This was probably reason enough in itself why, at this point in the proceedings, so many high-minded and sentimentally inclined Americans considered her to be, as one unsympathetic newspaper sneered, "a suffering saint, the victim of her husband's tyranny, a lady of irreproachable character, incapable of a fault and exemplary in the discharge of every duty." Yet if Catherine now acted to encourage this sympathy—justifying her refusal to appear before the Pennsylvania legislature by pleading penury, "no fit protector to accompany" her, and an inability to enforce attendance of friendly witnesses—it was partly because she and O'Conor knew that her precarious position required every assistance.[11]

Remember that Edwin still held a trump in this game: his evidence. To avoid shame, he had initially hoped to avoid playing this card publicly. Yet, when in the face of mounting opposition legislative deliberations started to drag on and calls for publicizing the evidence multiplied, newspapers friendly to the famous tragedian began to proclaim that proof of Catherine's guilt was overwhelming. Predictably (and not implausibly), rumor spread that Edwin himself was leaking this information. Then, on the morning of 28 March 1850, a bombshell dropped: scooping its competitors, the New York *Herald* blanketed its leading pages with a full transcript of the evidence presented before the Pennsylvania legislature. Newspapers across the city and the nation quickly followed suit, as a frenzy of publicity ensued.[12]

Though the *Herald*'s revelations failed to clinch the case then and there, they certainly forced Catherine Forrest to account for some rather curious behavior and evidence. Most damaging to her cause was George Jamieson's note, the same one

Edwin had found a year earlier in his library. Swiftly dubbed the "Consuelo" letter (after the recent novel of the same name, from which it clearly drew inspiration), this communication began with this heated address:

> And now, sweetest *consuelo*, our brief dream is over—and such a dream! Have we not known real bliss! Have we not realized what poets loved to set up as an ideal state, giving full license to their imagination, scarce believing in its reality? Have we not experienced the truth that ecstasy is not a fiction? I have; and as I will not permit myself to doubt you, am certain you have.

And it closed with this aching sentiment:

> Adieu, Adieu! When next we meet,
> Will not all sadness then retreat,
> And yield unconquered time to bliss,
> And seal the triumph with a kiss!
>   Say, *consuelo?*

For many observers, this note left little to imagination; that Catherine kept such correspondence was commonly cited as proof positive of her infidelity.[13]

To this revelation Edwin had appended an exchange of letters recording the estranged couple's final break, supporting testimony documenting Jamieson's dalliance with Catherine the afternoon of the "phrenology examination" in Cincinnati, and statements from the actor's friends professing to his wife's wont to smoke "segars" and attend the theater drunk. In nineteenth-century America, cigars were a male prerogative, and then they were to be smoked in private. Boston's city fathers had even gone so far as to ban them from the street. But for a respectable woman to indulge in a smoke, even at home, outraged propriety. Public drunkenness was regarded as unforgivable in a female. To associate Catherine Forrest with such behavior was to suggest that she lacked a true woman's nice sense of discrimination, and thus to raise the possibility that her disregard of convention might be endemic.

In this respect, the "Consuelo" letter pinched even more tightly. Over the preceding decade, *Consuelo*'s internationally renowned author, the French socialist George Sand, had gained considerable notoriety by publicly puffing on cigars and donning men's frock coats, all after having left her abusive husband to pursue several celebrated love affairs. Not surprisingly, this transgressive impulse also suffused Sand's popular reform novels, which featured paeans to spiritual desire, sympathetic treatments of Fourierism, and scathing denunciations of mercenary marriage and restrictive divorce laws. For this progressive stance, she had been celebrated far and wide in American reform communities like those at Brook Farm and Red Bank. After a decade of shrill denunciations from conservative critics, however, many Americans were convinced that such overwrought sentimentality and unconventional habits led a woman not to any higher love (as Brook Farmers and their like fancied), but instead to a moral nightmare of runaway romantic sensuality, capped by the wholesale renunciation of the sacrament of marriage and fidelity. As one conservative Whig editor remarked, the troubling thrust of Edwin Forrest's evidence ought to "surprise no one who will take the trouble to think what must necessarily be the idea of persons who dote on [Sand's prodivorce heroine] Indiana and revel with *Consuelo*."[14]

To make matters worse for Catherine, her estranged husband had also gotten their servants to talk. Sometime in January 1850, Christiana Underwood—the family's former housekeeper—had come forward with a shocking disclosure: her mistress had seemingly been dallying with various gentlemen for years. Though the Scottish-born housekeeper had no hard evidence to clinch the charge of adultery, her stories of all-night revels, stolen kisses, and secret visitors were suggestive in the extreme. This startling news had sent Edwin Forrest and his friends searching for corroboration; they returned with Robert Garvin, once a manservant at the Twenty-second Street house. This obliging informant added stories of tippling and fondling to the sordid tale that was now cohering in the divorce evidence. Damning enough behind closed doors, this interesting testimony became common knowledge once Bennett's *Herald* printed the whole. And it led scandal rags like the *Police Gazette* to exult that the divorce evidence proved the existence of a "set of tinsel coteries, where manners are so liberalized, as to render acts permissible without guilt, which in chaster circles could only bear a gross construction." The servant depositions, in particular, stunned the public by confirming that the stable of alleged adulterers was both wide and celebrated: eight men in all, among them Jamieson; the Reverend Dr. Hackley of Columbia College; Captain Granby Calcraft, a British military pensioner and cousin to the Crown's postmaster general; Samuel Marsden Raymond, a bewhiskered Whig merchant and lawyer subsequently described as "inclined to fashionable dandyism"; Dr. John B. Rich, a sometime-dentist and conductor of the New York Gymnasium; Fanny Ellsler's onetime manager and supposed lover "Chevalier" Wikoff (here said to have pranced about the Forrests' hallway in a kissing frolic with Catherine); and finally, the "famous poetry man" Willis himself and his younger brother Richard, the latter just returned from six years of studying music in Germany.[15]

A private tragedy no longer, the Forrests' domestic travails thus entered a new and more public phase, as the affair moved from legislative chambers into the broader court of moral opinion. Even at this early juncture, popular judgment had already begun to divide into two camps: one, comprised primarily of social conservatives, working-class populists, and what we might call "antisentimentalists," who tended to construe Catherine Forrest as representative of the dark underside of an ideologically suspect fashionable refinement; another, drawing mostly from the Whiggish middle-and upper-classes (especially their sentimental and reformist wings), which perceived Edwin's wife as a vulnerable exemplar of genteel womanhood. What separated these camps, of course, was nothing less than a fundamental disagreement over the trajectory of American culture. Was the nation, as defenders of the sentimental impulse maintained, becoming more virtuous as it became more refined and "feminized"? Or was it drifting from bedrock republican values of manly simplicity and patriarchal order into a riot of domestic impiety and license? Though the upshot in this case remained as yet unclear, one thing might have been predicted: the introduction of N. P. Willis (a celebrity with his own peculiarly divisive history) was bound to polarize the debate.

Enter Willis

Late winter of 1850 must have been an anxious time for Willis, as it surely was for Catherine Forrest. With her husband's suit pending, their reputations hung in the balance. Only publication of the divorce evidence was needed to demonstrate how inextricably their fates—and that of sentimental gentility—were becoming entwined.

Friendship had initiated the bond that common adversity was now cementing. Ironically, it had been the up-and-coming Edwin Forrest—not his future wife—who first caught Willis's eye when the two men met at the Tremont Hotel in 1830. A decade or so would pass before their relationship moved beyond social courtesy. In the meantime, both men married English women, though Willis's "angel without foible or fault" died tragically of scarlet fever in March 1845. Soon afterward, in London, the sick and grief-stricken widower took time from his daily convalescent walks to acknowledge Mrs. Forrest's kind offers of service to his motherless daughter. Ill though he was, Willis also found energy enough to sustain Edwin in his "hissing" controversy with Macready. A "true republican" whose "consciousness of genius" made him "live in resentment" against those who would "set aside the standards of nature and dis-enoble God's men of high degree to enoble fools and pretenders" was the way the *Mirror's* editorial correspondent lauded America's premier tragedian in these days. Even as late as January 1849, during the second Macready campaign, Willis was commending Forrest for his honest emotions; in these days of "trick and management," he told his readers, a "bold and fearless dash, even of hatred, has a certain relish about it."[16]

Yet by this time it was Edwin's wife whose friendship mattered most to Willis— and to Cornelia Grinnell, a young woman from a wealthy New Bedford Quaker family whom the forty-year-old author married in October 1846. This was especially true after the summer of 1848, when the Sinclair sisters helped nurse Cornelia through a difficult illness following the birth of her first child. Thereafter, mutual friends and shared interests—in vocal music particularly—served to strengthen the relationship. So it was not surprising that after the Forrests' separation the Willises took Catherine into their own home for a time, nor that this familiarity persisted when their guest and her two sisters (Margaret and the teenaged Virginia) ultimately settled into new quarters on West Sixteenth Street in the early autumn of 1849. Then, as divorce proceedings threatened, N. P. and his wife emerged as two of Catherine's closest advisors.

This situation forced an unpleasant decision on the morally impugned husband: how, precisely, to meet Forrest's allegations? Characteristically, Willis itched for his guns, but conscience soon pointed out the path he must walk. "You will have understood, of course," he reasoned in reply to advice from his old friend Brantz Mayer,

> that, in case of conflict, the death of one of us would be next to certain, and, *with these suits untried*, an unremovable suspicion would attach to *me*, living or dead. I *must*—for my wife and children's sake—*first shew myself clear of stain, in the matter.* . . . I have had time, as you know, to get over first impulses, and act upon principle.

There would be no duel, at least not of the traditional variety.[17]

Whatever else it signified, this forbearance was ample tribute to the pressures of publicity and genteel expectation that were driving market-oriented men like Willis from the dueling ground to the courtroom in defense of their reputation. In American society's more exclusive circles, adherence to the *code duello* had once been de rigeur for most males. Now, contests of honor faced considerable objection, even well beyond the evangelical social circles that had first condemned them as unproductive and un-Christian. In reaction, a new brand of shame—one associated most closely with the ethical and emotional universe of the genteel reading public— began to overtake, if not entirely supercede, the older variety. Its demands were especially compelling for men like Willis, whose social standing, commercial wherewithal, and cultural influence depended on sustaining a respectable, family-friendly image.

In Willis's case, however, the problem of passing moral muster was complicated enormously by the erotic overtones of his worldly style of manhood, which had long threatened to unmask him as a counterfeit gentleman. Middle age had done little to resolve this difficulty. Consider the outcry prompted by his commentary on the ecclesiastical trial of Bishop Benjamin Treadwell Onderdonk. In the autumn of 1844, several women had come forth, after an interval of years, to charge this powerful Episcopalian clergyman with improprietous advances. Then, while a council of bishops deliberated Onderdonk's fate behind closed doors, heated argument raged in the press. Some observers posited a Low Church plot to rid the ecclesiastical council of its Puseyite stalwart; if this was true, then the allegations of the female informers might be so much trumpery.

At this juncture in the controversy, Willis published his "Man of the World's View of the Onderdonk Case." Here, he argued that people were naive if they believed the bishop's female accusers entirely innocent; Onderdonk may have been careless, the worldly wise "Penciller" reasoned, but in the case of assaults upon consent "every man knows—and the most vicious man knows best—that no woman is ever invaded till the enemy has given a signal from within!" Precisely why he chose this moment to remount this oldest defense against accusations of sexual harassment is difficult to determine. The New York editor Charles Briggs speculated (plausibly) that Willis was attempting, however obliquely, to acquit his younger brother Edward of wrongdoing in a recent case of assault against a woman. Subsequent commentary also showed him to be exercised over the republican tendency to blight "Eminence" with reckless accusation. Whatever the reason, close observation of the contemporary social scene now led the *Mirror's* arbiter elegantiae to assert that "[n]o woman whose virtue is beyond suspicion was ever insultingly spoken to—far less, insultingly touched,—by a man in his senses."[18]

Understandably, all hell broke loose with the publication of this tendentious doctrine. True to form, James Watson Webb's New York *Courier and Enquirer* led the charge. In a series of columns that drew their mounting spleen from Willis's testy rejoinders, its high-minded defense of womanhood quickly degenerated into rank personalities. Soon, Henry Raymond (for it was the *Courier and Enquirer's* ambitious subeditor who was hounding Willis during Webb's absence from town) and the "Man of the World" were locked in a pas de deux of character assassination. Its climax came when the future founder of the *New York Times* hauled out the dirty laundry of Willis's European trip: a trail of "slimy profliga[cy]" left in his wake; expulsion from English homes for "merchandizing" private conversation; and "libertine boasts" to shipboard messmates, among other incidental transgressions. "He has utterly forfeited the respect of every right-minded person," Raymond concluded triumphantly in his final blast against Willis, "and has made his *Mirror* the pet of pimps, and himself the crowned leader of all the profligacy that seeks a higher resting place than the gutter." In the end, Willis rescued his character only by producing what seemed like every complimentary and exculpatory note within his reach: warm letters from English peers alleged to have banished him from their homes; invitations from eminent Irishmen gathered on his second European trip; refutations of lax bill-paying, habitual intemperance, and whippings for impudence.[19]

Though this avalanche of affidavits muffled naysayers for a time, Willis could never entirely still their voices. Indeed, only months before the Forrest flare-up, public criticism had once again forced him to defend his essential probity. This time a rivalry pitting the American Art-Union against the author's favorite, the newly instituted International Art-Union and its Parisian-based sponsors, the print-sellers Goupil, Vibert, and Company, provided the backdrop to controversy. When, in a letter to the *Tribune*, a New York critic (perhaps Raymond himself) chalked up Willis's snub of the American Art-Union to spite (the organization had pulled its advertising from the *Home Journal*), and then, in the case of one of Goupil's racier engravings, tried to twist Willis's romantic espousal of the International's "more advanced state of taste" into a ratification of smut, the "Man of the World" could hardly contain himself. His friend Washington Allston had taught him long ago that when a painter aimed to "represent what is beautiful in the divine figure of woman," any imputation of "indelicacy" sprang wholly from "the mind of him who saw it." Ergo, the female figure in Goupil's risqué engraving was, then, not so much naked as *nude*—unless, of course, one was vulgar enough to see otherwise. To silence the vulgarians, Willis now defied his critics to prove him anything but "an irreproachably moral man," though he acknowledged candidly that, when young and single, he had seen what he called "every manner of life which, by general usage, a gentleman may see."[20]

Not strange to say, shaking the presumption that he protested too much only got that much harder when Edwin Forrest's sensational and career-threatening adultery charges hit the newspapers six months later. No wonder Willis sought to lay hold of every suitable weapon at his command. Despite the temptation to resort to pistols, however, the rejoinder he now contemplated was no traditional set piece at ten paces, but its rhetorical equivalent: a momentous showdown on, what was for this master of words, the familiar and relatively advantageous turf of the daily press. Forrest's evidence had appeared on 28 March. The next day the actor's bête noire posted a card in the *Herald* defending both his wife and brother. This was only a warning of things to come; the firing commenced in earnest a week later. In a four-column letter calculated to vindicate Catherine Forrest and all who stood by her, Willis thereupon proceeded to judge her husband's character, methods, and motives against what he called "the American standard of what is gentlemanlike, and the American estimate of the treatment due a lady." Time would show this chivalric salvo to be nothing short of the opening blast in what was destined to be a desperate and culturally revealing campaign to teach the world how to recognize gentility's true colors.[21]

Predictably, Willis found his rival ill-bred and black at heart. For starters, he accused Forrest of countenancing, if not actually directing, an unsavory and indecent whisper campaign to alienate his estranged wife's lady friends. If this was not proof enough that the self-styled "lord of the *American Fonthill*" was a sham, Willis also wondered aloud if nature's true nobility would employ the so-called kitchen perversions of servants to destroy their mistress' name? So long as public opinion countenanced the misinterpretations of domestics and social pretenders, he feared that no lady in New York was "safe from destruction by the easy conspiracy of vile men, nor a gentleman's house, waited on by servants, where the hospitality may not be sworn to as debauchery." But true taste would out as vulgarity would betray itself, though it adopted the airs of American nobility—or so Willis wagered. To this end, he directed his readers to recognize Forrest's marriage to the refined and beautiful English-born Catherine Sinclair for what it was: like the stage setting of the actor's nearly completed Fonthill castle, a vain attempt to play above station. Having recoiled from the cultivated society naturally drawn to his wife, and then having refused to tolerate her criticism of his conduct during the Macready troubles, Edwin, so Willis suggested, was now pursuing divorce on trumped up charges, bent on dodging the small stipend stipulated by the terms of the couple's separation. Hence, he deserved neither sympathy nor a public hearing, only the nation's scorn.

By injecting issues of taste and domestic security into a quarrel about sex and fidelity, Willis clearly hoped to enlist genteel ideals and anxieties in his own and Catherine's defense. If she could sustain her character as a sentimental heroine, he might yet rally the inestimable moral support of those Americans eager to safeguard the prerogatives of refinement, and of refined womanhood in particular. Fortunately for him, Willis believed that he exercised considerable influence over the thinking of just such a class of persons. Certainly, the toplofty correspondent who favored the *Herald* with the argument that "an ignorant housekeeper, and an equally ignorant Irish man servant, are not exactly the persons whose constructions should govern us in estimating the conduct of their superiors" echoed the author's own reasoning. So, too, did the thinking of a letter-writer in the *Tribune*, who, worrying over the plight of female innocence, begged members of her sex especially to "remember it is not Mrs. Forrest alone, but *every woman*, who is concerned in this matter." Thankfully, a lady subscriber to the *Home Journal* could report soon afterward that in "respectable" society at least, the women "all stand up for [Catherine] most warmly, and denounce her persecutors."[22]

Even granting this statement's truth, the fact remained that the contemptuous style and polemical thrust of Willis's letter once again presented his critics a rare opportunity to exploit suspicion that moral dereliction lurked within the era's refining impulse. This opening was certainly not lost on Edwin's partisans. Almost immediately, Andrew Stevens (a New York jeweler who would act as the tragedian's hatchet man throughout the long affair) answered Willis with a pair of ripostes in the *Herald.* Here, he reminded readers that Catherine's knight-errant had much to preserve by his self-styled chivalry: family reputation, a career as an "oracle of refined society," and the world's good opinion. More than this, Stevens wondered whether blood affinities might more unerringly reflect character than fancy words; had not yet another brother in the Willis clan (Edward, though his name remained unstated here) once been imprisoned in Ohio for rape? As if to underscore the thrust of this criticism, Augustus Drum, the sponsor of Forrest's bill for annulment, echoed Stevens in an hour-long harangue before the Pennsylvania Senate, responding to what one Philadelphia correspondent had called Willis's "famous letter." The text of this "forcible and bitterly sarcastic" speech is lost, but its import may be surmised: distrust tinsel prose.[23]

In the end, Drum might have saved his vitriol—constitutional scruples and disgust at logrolling ultimately sent Forrest's legislative petition down to narrow defeat—except that significant elements of public sentiment seemed to be taking up where he left off. Within days, newspaper editors and correspondents across the nation were falling over themselves to blast Catherine's defender. Having to "fight hard" to convince his wife of "virtuous attentions while visiting other ladies, as well as to convince the public of his gentility by *instinct,*" "Nat Pomatum Willis" was, thought the *Boston Daily Mail,* "in a *sorter* tight place." Many believed that the "famous letter" was actually dragging down Catherine Forrest's cause. Even advocates of the embattled wife repudiated his help. "Cannot some friend of humanity and morals prevent Willis from writing any more letters in this case?" begged one distraught supporter of Mrs. Forrest. "Will not some one occupy him with the subject of a hair ointment or a new slope to a skirt, till the case be brought to some safe point?"[24]

He was right, of course. Without adequately answering her husband's allegations, Willis's "frost work of evaporating fancy" (as the *Herald* styled the rejoinder) only more closely linked Catherine Forrest to the morally suspect world of New York fashion by seeming to be of a piece with modern elegance generally: like the Upper Ten's ostentatious Fifth Avenue mansions and Astor House fancy balls, all style and surface masking Lord knows what within. It was certainly now easier for unsympathetic critics to cast Catherine as just another idle belle of the nouveau riche, bred to iniquity on parlor intrigue and the commercialized sentimentality of boudoir gossip rags—such as the *Home Journal,* devotees of the city's sensationalist press might have said. Considering fashion's very real potential to erode true womanhood's armor of sanctity, this association was arguably among the last any embattled wife would elect to suffer. Once again, Willis's reputation as a virtuoso sentimentalist was proving an equivocal advantage.[25]

In this particular case, the populist provocateur whose newspaper first broke the Forrest evidence was destined to exploit sentiment's disabilities most effectively. A fierce social conservative, James Gordon Bennett, had, since launching his twopenny *Herald* in 1835, parlayed timely Wall Street reports, antiabolitionist hysteria, and sensationalist assaults on un-American privilege and social innovation into an extensive national constituency. And like many of his predominantly conservative working-class Democratic readers, the man reformist Whigs in particularly loved to hate was especially ready to believe the worst of Willis, polite society, and social innovation in general. With Fourierist phalanxes installed in New Jersey, spiritualists rapping in Rochester, Free Lovers ensconced at Oneida, woman advocates gathered in Seneca Falls, and the "Codfish Aristocracy" reigning in Gotham itself, traditional virtues and social arrangements seemed everywhere embattled by what Bennett construed as the impoverished morality of thirty years' reform and helter-skelter prosperity. It was his polemical genius that found in "Mr. Nincom Poop Willis" an allegorical figure to link the whole—or at least much of it—into a protean conspiracy to destroy the nation's moral fiber.[26]

In his own way, Bennett also wished to teach Americans, through the Forrest evidence, how to recognize gentility's true colors. And for him, instruction began with the specter of moral contagion conjured by the so-called Elysium of the idler— that is, modern-day Paris. When, in an 1841 treatment of George Sand's *Oeuvres*, the *North American Review* had damned the French capital as "that hotbed of civilization" where "refinement has passed into the worst form of elegant epicureanism, and debauchery is licensed by examples in high places, where the minor morals are lost sight of in the search after gain, and greater laws violated in the pursuit of sensual pleasures," it was only giving vent to commonplace sentiments. A decade later, it was possible to believe that these sins of Paris had set up shop in every major American city. While the sensational novels of Eugene Sue and Paul de Kock flooded stateside parlors with seductive portrayals of vice and degradation, madame-milliners and mustachioed fops à la Paris set the tone in fashionable uptown society. One had only to canvas the opera's kid-glove superfinery, snobbery, and carriage livery to see where such Gallic innovations were leading: to what in 1849 the *Herald* grimly characterized as the "libidinous and lascivious" polka's reign, the "shocking scenes of model artists," and raucous gambling in "splendid saloons"—a veritable gothic tableau of moral dissolution.[27]

Now, with the publication of Forrest's divorce evidence, Bennett moved to finger Willis ("the very pink of fashion") as among the most culpable authors of New York's "loose morality" and easy manners. Metropolitan gazettes like the francophile *Home Journal* and *Courrier and Etats-Unis* were, he claimed, bent on supplanting old-fashioned commonsense virtues with the slippery and self-serving criterion of "good taste." And witness the upshot: "scenes of poetic enjoyment and sentimental freedom, equal to anything exhibited by the classic socialists of Europe, of the highest and most fastidious kind." "Alas! alas!" cried Bennett piously in his initial pronouncement on the divorce evidence. "We pity Mr. Forrest—we pity as fervently Mrs. Forrest. They have both been made dupes of these new doctrines in philosophy, manners, morals, and classic socialism of the latest pattern."[28]

Most telling here is the riff on socialism, a favorite of Bennett's. At first blush, the charge is absurd, for, to be sure, Willis never espoused anything of the like, except perhaps in the peculiar sense that his critic meant the accusation. Catherine's defender was, in short, a "literary" or "classic" socialist (the two phrases were synonymous in the *Herald*'s lexicon) only insofar as he promoted what Bennett called greater "freedom of manners"—that is, liberalized social behavior, especially between the sexes. That was the imputed link between the avowed Fourierist George

Sand—whose feminist impulses had primed her to repudiate one husband—and Catherine Forrest's sentimental gallant, whose espousal of Parisian-inflected "good taste" had ostensibly led him to "dupe" another.

Given the fear of social disintegration awakened at home by the "Red Republican" revolutions of 1848, it seems clear why Bennett wished to draw just such a connection. He certainly knew—as well as did any of America's more circumspect reformers—that Charles Fourier's utopian aim to do "justice to the human passions" by freeing love from economic constraints exposed the French social philosopher and his followers to charges of licensing indecency under cover of high-flown sentiment. That is precisely why, in the early days of the movement, American popularizers of Fourierist doctrine like Catherine's friend Parke Godwin had downplayed (one could even say suppressed) Associationism's "passional" elements in favor of its economic prescriptions. Yet with prosperity's return and the general collapse of the phalanxes in the mid-1840s, calls for radical alternatives to so-called coerced monogamy had begun to filter from Fourierist circles into the broader public's consciousness by way of in-house manifestos and hostile exposés. If Bennett could now equate such "advanced thinking" about marriage with the free and easy tendency of Willis's "advanced taste," any revelations of this particular "literary socialist's" iniquity might serve to discredit liberal idealism generally. That is, "Passionalism" and the Associationist project might be pegged as "passion" run amuck.

In this sense, the *Herald*'s ultimate target in the divorce imbroglio was probably neither Willis nor Catherine Forrest, but the Fourierist, abolitionist, and labor-reform activism spearheaded by Bennett's most formidable New York competitor and greatest ideological antagonist Horace Greeley of the *Tribune*, whom the *Herald* had been working for months to discredit as a "Satanic socialist." Indeed, not half a year earlier Bennett had gone so far as to claim that

> the *Tribune* establishment, from top to bottom, has been recently converted into a socialist phalanx, and that the editors, printers, publishers, reporters, all the way from the nigger to the lesser devils, are all interested, more or less, in that delectable sheet—a sheet which has produced on public affairs and on the public mind a more deleterious, anti-Christian, and infidel effect, during the last few years, than all the publications that have heretofore appeared, from the time of Voltaire.

As with racial "amalgamation" and other kindred "infidelities" of the day, "socialism" evoked in the imagination of its detractors a world of sins, one certainly capacious enough to encompass Willis on the side. Overcoming such imputations was to be among his most difficult tasks.[29]

An Unarmed Gentleman

Following the media circus of March and early April 1850, observers of the Forrest affair might have concluded that matters had reached somewhat of a lull. After the Pennsylvania House of Representatives passed a bill for annulment, Edwin's Senate supporters could muster no better than a tie vote. That meant his petition's defeat. Still, the actor's partisans did manage to push through a compromise bill designed to allow him to press his case before the Philadelphia Court of Common Pleas. Thereafter, Forrest and his attorneys would busy themselves hatching this new legal action. Then, in late May Jamieson finally spoke from Cincinnati with a published "card" in the clearinghouse *Herald.* Here, he acknowledged responsibility for the "Consuelo" note but excused himself by claiming an imagination overstimulated by drink. This explanation satisfied no one, especially when one Henry Hunt piped up to declare that Jamieson should not be trusted. Hunt should know, as the rascal had also seduced *his* wife. Finally, in early summer, rumors surfaced of further revelations to come. The details would have to await legal hearing, but Bennett— apparently in the know—assured his readers that "the *finale* of this business will astonish some persons." Subsequent events would certainly bear out this assertion, though not precisely in the manner he presumably supposed. When readers next opened their papers to news of the Forrest affair, they were reading accounts of Forrest's punishing assault on Willis in Washington Square.[30]

As one might expect, the ink in newspaper reports was hardly dry before dispute erupted over the meaning of the incident. Debate settled quickly on the thorny question of whether the burly actor had blindsided Willis or met him face-to-face. Willis himself claimed in Horace Greeley's *Tribune* that he had been charged and felled from behind. The *Evening Post* corroborated this story; most other mercantile papers followed the *Post*'s and *Tribune*'s lead. When Forrest's partisans challenged Willis's veracity, moreover, Greeley opened his columns to several correspondents— an anonymous witness in Willis's prospective suit for damages, an incensed citizen, and "A Lady"—all of whom backed the beaten man's account. With the voice of objectivity, righteous anger, and true womanhood ranged behind him, Willis (who would himself soon lodge a legal complaint against Forrest) could thus be satisfied that "respectable" opinion was cohering around his version of events.[31]

According to these witnesses, Forrest had skulked behind trees near a gate to the parade ground as Willis strolled by, then chased down the path and jumped the surprised and unarmed "gentleman." According to these witnesses, too, the scene was brutal: Forrest, they claimed, knocked down Willis and laid about his person with a loaded whip and what "A Lady" called "vile and profane language . . . impossible to give any idea of." Two men—Andrew Stevens (Forrest's bully boy) and another trusty—were also said to have prevented bystanders from rescuing Willis from his assailant's clutches. In this regard, the apparent thuggishness of Forrest's accomplices helped to endorse Horace Greeley's speculation that subsequent testimony would prove the attack to have been premeditated. Unsubstantiated rumor already told of the vengeful tragedian's shadowing his estranged wife's door the previous evening, on the lookout for Willis. This image of Forrest the sneak was guaranteed to strike the friends of order and propriety as dangerous business.[32]

The figures each man cut before the public conspired to sustain this reading of events. By all accounts, Forrest dominated the imagination of his contemporaries as he did the stage, crowding out weaker and smaller men with his towering presence. "What a mountain of a man!" Fanny Kemble reportedly exclaimed on first seeing the famous tragedian. Years of boxing, gymnastics, and training at weights had transformed a weak adolescent body into over two hundred pounds of brawn packed into a five-foot-ten-inch frame. On stage he used his power to its full advantage. His trademark declamations often betrayed their shuddering passion in brute force, so that messengers in "Damon and Pythias" were said to tremble in fear of Forrest's hurling them into the wings to express a powerful anger. And his death scenes can only be described as monumental odes to endurance, the sort of interminable agonies that even his contemporaries, who prized grand gesture, found easy to burlesque. "If a bull could act," quipped Young America's Evert Duyckinck, "he would act like Forrest."[33]

Both on and off the stage the veteran actor reserved his sharpest scorn for what he regarded as unwarranted pretense. Having risen from humble beginnings as the son of a struggling Scottish immigrant, Forrest came by his radical democratic convictions naturally. He loved to play the common man's deliverer, and once even flirted with a career in Locofoco Democratic politics. There was, as one of his partisans remarked, "no upper ten about him." In tune with this populist character, Forrest had nothing but contempt for hereditary aristocracy and its admirers. "What a glorious baptism of blood was that in Paris!" he wrote his wife of the French Revolution of 1848. "Did I not say they should have killed every remnant of royalty? What are the lives of such moths, compared to the life of one honest industrious man?"[34]

Given such pronouncements, it seems likely that few of his contemporaries would have accused Forrest of bucking a challenge. Yet the Macready controversy of the late 1840s *had* raised troubling doubts about the American actor's capacity for self-control. Indeed, so possessed with hatred for his polished English rival had Forrest come to seem by the time of the Astor Place affair (precisely the time of separation from his English wife, as well) that certain observers wondered if he had not lost his senses. If nothing else, many held Forrest's feverish rhetoric and fury at least partly responsible for precipitating the tragic riot; not a few observers (Whigs especially) saw his hand at work among the Bowery toughs and nativists who had driven the "damned Englishman" and his kid-glove partisans from the opera house. Given this history of muscular heroics, populist sentiment, and rampaging passion, it was now easy to imagine that jealousy and rage had run away with Forrest and set him on the "aristocratic" Willis with little regard for decency or fair play.

Next to Forrest, Willis seemed puny. Although he was almost six feet tall—and, to modern eyes, an imposing figure—witnesses of the Washington Square incident consistently remarked on Willis's inferior size and bearing. He was, to one observer, "a slight, delicate-looking gentleman"; another called him "the smallest and weakest person" of the alleged adulterers. All agreed that Willis had seemed helpless beneath the rain of blows that drove him to his knees. Semi-invalidism may partly explain this perception. Never really healthy since what doctors called "brain fever" had struck him in 1845, Willis recovered after a lengthy convalescence, only to suffer an attack of rheumatic pleurisy in early 1848 that prostrated him for months. From then on, chronic ill health (due most likely to the effects of epilepsy, compounded by a tubercular disorder) weakened his constitution, caused seizures, and periodically obscured his sight, undoubtedly contributing to his fragility that June.[35]

Yet there was more at work here than delicate health could explain. Having made himself into a walking embodiment of New York's pretensions to refinement, Willis had suffered all manner of damaging appropriation. But now as a victim, his so-called effeminate elegance was to be made to speak, if not necessarily for him, then certainly against the rampages of his bull-like assailant. Those who most recoiled from their sense of Forrest's brutality were the same ones who now insisted most vigorously on the moral significance of disparities of size and force. In their minds Willis's prostration served as a chilling metaphor for refinement's vulnerability amidst the rough-and-ready working-class bustle of New York. Staged, as it was, among the Greek Revival terraces and shade trees of one of the city's most exclusive uptown parks, the beating must have seemed to many friends of order an Astor Place Riot writ small, a curious replay of that frightening moment when hypermale violence rose up to reject fashionable pretension. As it had then, the fear of being unable to walk the streets safely—literally true the night of the theater riot—raised the specter of a city given over to thuggery. Was no place safe, many asked. Alive to such threats, genteel New Yorkers now generally deplored Forrest's violence as a base and cowardly expedient, as they had earlier condemned the actions of his partisans at the opera house.[36]

To realize their own—and Willis's—worst fears of culture buckling before over-weening force, and to turn that fear to gentility's service, such observers had only to identify Forrest's victim with refined society's most precious and vulnerable jewel: a lady. This proved remarkably easy, especially as Willis's whole career had been preparing him for the association. Detractors of the tendencies of his literary style had from the start urged him toward "manly" prose and matters. Yet, when he failed them, they turned in disgust to insinuations and accusations of effeminate weakness. "Namby-Pamby Willis," a critic had once called him; "an impersonal passive verb—a pronoun of the feminine gender," quipped another. Willis's well-known affinity for women, beauty, and feminine prose only encouraged this common identification. Given the proper circumstances, however, what could damn could also serve. "If Mr. Forrest *believes* these charges against his wife," one of Forrest's gainsayers now argued, "and possesses one spark of manhood, why did he pass by the *able-bodied, full-sized* Mr. Jamison [*sic*], whom he believes he caught in *delictu*, and select only a *woman*, and a man *half his size*, and against whom he had no proof, for the object of his vengeance[?]" Contrast with the strapping "Jamison" thus implicitly suggested to at least one observer that it might as well have been a man beating a woman out on the square. In a society wedded to the doctrine of separate spheres, the moral valences of such a beating could only hurt Forrest's cause. In this respect, it seems that Willis shrank physically in the estimation of many in part so that his assailant might shrink morally.[37]

This moral diminution had important consequences for the fate of the affair's principle antagonists. In his so-called famous letter Willis had explicitly cast himself as protector of the weak and refined against the rampaging mendacity of a parvenu vulgarian. Forrest's brutal assault now seemed to confirm that ugly character. If nothing else, the tragedian's evident ferocity and alleged stealth mobilized a chorus of condemnation from the *Tribune* and other Whig papers; even Forrest's old Lo-cofoco comrades at the *Evening Post* swelled the chorus. In fact, great portions of the "respectable" press that had previously embraced Willis's cause merely in def-erence to Forrest's embattled wife now began to think better of him, if only because his accuser had begun to look worse. As the *Louisville Daily Courier* remarked,

"Mr. Willis no doubt has his faults, but he is a man of tried courage, and he unquestionably intends to redress his wrongs at his own time and in his own way. Mr. Forrest, we heard long ago on good authority, is a coward, and we consider his attack upon Willis a proof [of] it." Coupled with the residuals of literary affection, this was strong physic. "I know nothing of Willis's morals," remarked one upstate New Yorker privately after hearing of Forrest's assault:

> [I] should suppose him above anything mean, or what would render him justly ame-nable to the censure of those who have long admired him as a leading and charming writer. It is a sad, sad day for a man or woman who have made themselves (*sic*) a home in thousands of hearts, and ministered to us in our holiday hours, when he or she stoops from that admired eminence, and becomes a thing for scorn to point its finger at. I will not believe this of Nathaniel Parker Willis—the author of a thousand gems of thought which he has scattered up and down in my memory like spring flowers.[38]

If Edwin Forrest thus probably sensed (quite correctly) that his advantage was slipping away, he was not without recourse. Support among his populist fans ran deep. And with Jamieson's note and the servant depositions still unanswered, his manly honor—and that of common republicans generally—might yet be salvaged. But that outcome would require a new campaign in the press.

Such assistance was not long in coming. Andrew Stevens spoke first. His swift retort to Willis's testimony—printed concurrently in the *Herald* and *Tribune* on 19 June—related that Forrest had "stepped quickly in *front*" of his former friend, looked him steadily in the eye, shook a fist in his face, and addressed him forth-rightly, though Stevens confessed he could not hear distinct words from his vantage fifty yards off. Then, when Willis's hand moved to his coat as if to draw a gun (subsequent police search revealed none), Forrest struck the cringing poet—with his fist and, only afterwards, with the whip. No doubt this "deliberate fist" was calculated to recapture the moral high ground, as was Stevens's claim that Forrest's cry of "seducer" had spontaneously halted interference from bystanders. When this rebuttal proved inadequate, Forrest himself took to John Wien Forney's *Pennsyl-vanian*—a Buchananite Democratic newspaper that served as the actor's mouth-piece throughout the divorce matter—to charge that Greeley's "A Lady" was obviously Willis, and thus a liar as well as a changeling. Forrest claimed pointedly to disdain such vile subterfuges; indeed, he now appeared before readers as he wished them to believe he had confronted his tormentor. "I most solemnly aver," he de-clared histrionically, "that when I first struck N. P. Willis, I stood before him, face to face, and with my hand alone felled him to the earth."[39]

Forrest knew that he must sustain his version of the confrontation or forfeit public sympathy regarding the more significant question of provocation's role in justifying assault. To believe him blackguard enough to fell an unarmed man from behind was to believe him capable of fabricating stories of a wife's adultery to serve sinister motives. Grant this possibility, and his entire case began to unravel. Enter-tain his version of the incident, however, and matters changed dramatically. In the face of underhanded collusion, moral outrage, and every provocation, Forrest might be said to have defended not only his rights as a husband, but the integrity of the institution of marriage and the patriarchal order it buttressed. Among American jurors, an unwritten law already licensed cuckolded husbands to kill their wives' paramours should they catch the offending couple in delictu. This precedent is precisely why many more tradition-minded observers especially were now prepared tentatively to applaud the beating as a righteous rebuke to philanderers everywhere. As one armchair judge of honor remarked, should adultery ultimately be proved, any "court of morals" would surely forgive Forrest for taking "the law into his own hands and annihilat[ing] the seducer."[40]

Others were prepared to sanction retribution on the spot. Characteristically, the *Herald*, seconded by a pack of penny papers, led the charge by resuming its tocsin against the threat of "fashionable socialism." By late August, Bennett would go so far as to suggest that in the pending assault case against Forrest the chief point at issue was whether "Willis and the *Home Journal* are creating a revolution in manners and morals throughout society, by introducing the blessed Blessington creed among the fashionable people of New York." Now, though Bennett called Forrest's attack ill-advised, he maintained that the *Home Journal*'s editor had long ago forfeited his immunity to assault. Greeley quickly blasted his rival for inciting violence, but Forrest's supporters decried the condemnation. And when a sarcastic Philadelphia editorial heaped ridicule on Willis's pretensions to persecution, Bennett reprinted it. One especially enterprising printmaker even issued a brace of caricatures entitled "Upper-ten-dom entering Washington Square" and "Upper-ten-dom leaving the Square at 30 minutes past 6, [P].M." Those who plunked down their dollars for such engravings were presumably happy to share a laugh at Willis's expense. More important, they were encouraged to believe that the supercilious refinement he had come to embody was getting its long-awaited comeuppance. All "the ladies" may have been "on the side of Mr. Willis," as one anonymous New York correspondent remarked after the cowhiding, "but the ungallant masculines and those who don't live 'bove Bleecker come out strong for the tragedian."[41]

Given all that had transpired since Willis's return to the United States in 1836, it certainly did not take the Washington Square incident to establish the disturbing reality that New York was becoming a city increasingly at odds with itself, ruptured (as this last correspondent suggested) along a class divide. Yet this particular incident did underscore what we might call the gender dimension of this situation: that is, the propensity in mid-nineteenth-century American public affairs for ladies, especially those from "'bove Bleecker," to range themselves against the city's so-called ungallant masculines. Edwin Forrest's stature as a working-class hero and N. P. Willis's standing as a sentimental icon only helped draw out and amplify this division, which tapped sources that ran deep in American society. Celebrity's coming trials would offer further evidence of the extent of the fault lines.

Trials of Celebrity

Lawsuit, n. A machine you go into as a pig and come out of as a sausage.

> Ambrose Bierce

The Forrest affair's spectacle of passion made compelling public theater not just because many in the audience at large believed, as Willis surely would have wished, that they knew its celebrated principles intimately. As we have come to see, this imbroglio also rehearsed a riveting drama of cultural anxieties that took in such prickly matters as the proper relation of husband and wife, the propriety of fashion and refinement, and the prerogatives of honor. The affair assumed this significance, moreover, in light of an intense glare of commercial publicity that had become national, even international, in scope. As early as six months into the proceedings, the *Georgia Journal and Messenger* reprinted a humorous vignette that suggested the unprecedented dimensions of this development. A traveler approaching a hut "fifty miles from anything in the Western Prairie," so the story went, had asked its tenant of his opinion of a notorious murder case, the so-called Golphin claim, and the Forrest divorce suit. When he replied that he knew nothing of such matters, the stranger reportedly "burst into tears" and resolved to stay with the farmer for three weeks, that being the time news took to travel to this remote quarter. What was the reason for this outburst? So the account joshed: "He was a man who had been bored into madness by reading newspaper discussions on the three cases." Of course, such complaints did little to arrest the march of publicity and probably only served to underscore the general preoccupation with celebrated legal actions that gripped the nation in the early 1850s. It was here, as much as on the concurrent political maneuvering surrounding the issue of slavery, that public interest settled in these early days of mass popular culture.[1]

134

This public dimension had important implications for the outcome of the imminent legal ordeal. Barring material evidence that irrefutably clinched the case either way, the fate of the Forrest affair's leading characters hinged principally on the cogency of competing interpretive narratives developed by their respective counsels, narratives that necessarily drew their inspiration and persuasiveness from prevailing beliefs and prejudices. Eventually, of course, such rival stories would have to carry the day in court, before a judge and jury. But following the Washington Square incident, several highly consequential preliminary acts in this melodrama of domestic travail still remained to be played before the public. As before, Willis—and his controversial style of manhood—was to figure crucially in the course of events.[2]

Turning the Tables

Even after the miscarriage of her estranged husband's legislative divorce petition, Catherine Forrest's prospects still looked bleak. Willis, her would-be champion, had tried to convince good people to stand by a true woman wrongfully accused. But his "frost work of evaporating fancy" only convinced many of fashion's hand in the wife's corruption. The beating on the Washington Square parade ground only partially undercut this reading of events. In the months ahead, however, several important developments would begin to turn the tables against Edwin, and in ways calculated to illustrate some of celebrity's more treacherous pitfalls.

The first of these developments was probably most crucial to the course of legal affairs, bearing as it did on Edwin's culpability in the Forrests' domestic troubles. As early as May 1850, Willis was reporting privately that Catherine had sufficient evidence of her own against her husband that she would have no trouble "throwing him over." First, however, Edwin's pending Philadelphia Court of Common Pleas suit for divorce had to be halted and money raised for the impending legal battle. Willis, it appears, went about satisfying the second need by sending a confidential round-robin request for donations among New York's Whig gentlemen; Charles O'Conor satisfied the first by obtaining a restraining injunction in September 1850. Two months later came Catherine's counterattack: a suit for absolute divorce, filed in New York Superior Court on grounds that her husband had committed adultery in and out of sundry brothels and hotel rooms with "divers women," including a "certain play actress, now deceased"—subsequently identified as Josephine Clifton.[3]

This was a momentous turn of events, not merely because the alleged assignations ran to half a column of newsprint. "The Magnificent Josephine," a six-foot-tall Amazonian beauty, had once been an international celebrity in her own right, sufficiently renowned to have commanded a $1,000 premium for an original play written by America's brightest new playwright—none other than N. P. Willis himself. But she was also notorious as the daughter of an alleged brothel-keeper, a scandalous connection that still echoed in the theatrical world when Edwin Forrest first engaged Clifton as his leading lady for a nationwide tour in 1842–43. Having died suddenly in 1847, however, she could scarcely be expected to reply to the charges that now assailed her reputation.

Alternatively, Edwin and his attorneys could, and did, reply to the allegations and attendant depositions with which Catherine and her attorney flooded the courts in late fall of 1850. In response to these sundry presentments, the now-embattled tragedian proceeded to drag his sister-in-law's name through the mud with depositions alleging that Margaret Voorhies had manipulated her marriage date to antedate the birth of a child conceived out of wedlock and had generally led the life of a loose woman. Forrest and his lawyers also kept up their assault on what the *Herald* called Willis's "coterie of male dandies," a clique of bounders whose leader Edwin now alleged had alienated his wife's affections over a number of years by "arts and address which he acquired in foreign society," introducing "habits of debauchery" into his household that no American could countenance. In this respect, it became clear that Forrest and Bennett were now reading off the same page, as the *Herald* often scooped its competition with salacious rumor and inside information. Two could apparently play at advocacy journalism.[4]

This strategy was probably at least partly the work of John Van Buren, son of the former president and now Edwin Forrest's chief counsel since Theodore Sedgwick's withdrawal in early fall on grounds of ill health. A celebrated dandy and Democratic politico who graduated from Yale the year following Willis, Van Buren had earned the derisive nickname "Prince John" for having waltzed with Britain's future queen Victoria during his father's ill-fated days visiting the English court. For all this, he shared at least some of his client's Locofoco leanings, as he did Forrest's dander. In 1848 the eloquent Van Buren had led the Barnburner bolt to the antislavery Free Soilers, only to return to the Democratic Party fold a year later. At the moment, his political fortunes were thus dicey. In the field of law, however, he stood at the peak of his career. As New York's attorney general, he had recently prosecuted one of the upstate Anti-Rent rioters in a donnybrook of a trial (Van Buren himself had pummeled the opposing counsel) and seen the brawling Tammany politico, Captain Isaiah Rynders of the Empire Club, acquitted of charges of having instigated the Astor Place Riot. Forrest's choice of counsel thus set the stage for a monumental test of legal skill, one that was destined to spill over in personal as well as professional antagonism.[5]

Yet for all his forensic skills, the one thing Van Buren could not seem to do was rein in his client's towering rage. Once, Forrest had seemed a man chastened, worried, and driven by circumstances; now, his periodic outbursts made it harder for even sympathetic observers to think of him as a victim. The assault on Willis in Washington Square was only a start. Wherever New Yorkers went in the ensuing months, the city's most conspicuous thespian could be seen browbeating or menacing people involved in the case. In September 1850 it was Granby Calcraft (the postmaster general's relation) whom Edwin accosted below Fulton Street with cries of "When are you going to England?" A month later it was Catherine herself, in a crowded omnibus on Broadway, browbeaten with contemptuous remarks about her "paramour" Willis and threats of sending her to "State Prison." When the affidavits of November and December were published, these and other interesting revelations came to public attention: how in February of 1850, Edwin had met his wife in the street and told her, "You ought to die"; disturbing new details of a late-night showdown with Samuel Raymond; and tales of the club-wielding actor prowling the streets around his wife's rented home. Then, soon after the New Year, the *Tribune* featured yet another exchange of "cards" between the notorious Washington Square disputants. If Greeley's readers had not personally seen the action on Fifth Avenue and later at the opera, they could now read all about what Willis characterized as the "loud and offensive braggadocio and conspicuous gestures and head-shakings" with which Forrest had taunted him and "annoyed and terrified" Mrs. Willis, and how Willis had allegedly slunk away when Forrest had accosted him with the words, "You infernal scoundrel, liar and coward! This is the first time I have seen you since the horse-whipping I gave you in June last. Don't turn pale, I will not lay violent hands upon you!" Even Catherine's crackerjack lawyer, Charles O'Conor, was not immune to her estranged husband's wrath. One morning in July 1851 the two men apparently exchanged coarse insults before a crowd of bystanders on Hammond Street.[6]

In light of this behavior, it seemed increasingly conceivable that Edwin's own terrible temper and jealousy had twisted appearances of impropriety into what passed for incontrovertible proof. Perhaps he was, as some observers now suggested, "insane" with rage. If so, his wife might well be the chaste victim she had always represented herself to be. When the opportunity to confute her claim, by rehearsing again the tale of seduction, came and went in May 1851 with further postponement of Willis's assault and battery suit, Edwin's best chance to repair a reputation for marauding was lost. Clearly the great tragedian's temper did him no favors.[7]

By this time, the principal character in this domestic melodrama who was looking increasingly victimized was not Edwin Forrest but N. P. Willis. This rehabilitation of character hinged chiefly on yet another fantastic development in the saga of this author's sentimental commerce with the world. As might be expected, his measured response to his antagonist's ranting at the opera in January had built on the sympathy generated by the previous June's beating, though at least one Forrest partisan still insisted that even if the tragedian acted at times like a "ruffian, or rather like a madman," this did not make Willis an "innocent sufferer." Yet now, only a day after walking away from the deferred assault case in Superior Court, Catherine Forrest's chief defender was forced to face yet another crisis of reputation when an old nemesis assailed him anew from an entirely different quarter. And what Colonel James Watson Webb broached before the world in May 1851 had the potential to blast Willis's character once for all—and with it, most likely Catherine Forrest's, too.[8]

Newspaper politics and personal enmity spurred Webb's attack. In December 1849 Willis had printed an open letter in his *Home Journal* protesting the colonel's nomination to the position of minister to the Hapsburg court on grounds that his character and manner unfit him for that sensitive post. (The Austrian Empire was, at that time, seeking to crush several democratic revolts within its borders.) When the *Times* of London drew on Willis's uncomplimentary note and another in the New York *Day Book* to discredit the *Courier and Enquirer*'s protectionist trade policies, Webb apparently resolved to strike at both his English and American critics by publicly assailing the *Times*' sources as a pair of scoundrels. Willis took most of the abuse in this newspaper drubbing, as past peccadilloes were dredged up for yet another run through the mud. Webb first recalled Blessington's coterie ("the most immoral in London") and Willis's betrayal of genteel codes of hospitality, then dragged out Henry Raymond's triumphant reproach from the Onderdonk tiff to be reprinted in full. Even more outrageous, Willis's antagonist now also alleged that while the self-proclaimed "Man of the World" was editing the *Mirror*, he had lured a young female admirer to his bed and that discovery of this foul act had driven her father to the grave. Webb also claimed to have the girl's letters to confirm the dirty deed. Here at last might be the proof of sexual depravity that Willis had time and again challenged his slanderers to produce.[9]

One reason these charges probably sounded plausible was that Willis had recently taken to coining commercial advantage from the sentimental desire for emotional voyeurism entailed in just such correspondence of the heart. A series in the *Home Journal* featuring "Returned Love Letters" had drawn considerable fire from critics enraged by its exploitation of what ought to be private affections. These were none "but Willis's own unlovely cogitations," one detractor spat, "for nobody but just such a man as he is, ever wrote any such letters." The fact was, however, that many Americans probably *had* engaged in writing such letters disclosing a heart's burdens. And for a world that prized the transparent legibility of private expression, they assumed an aura of "authenticity" that promised to substantiate a sin of the flesh echoing the metaphorical sin that many already laid at Willis's door: the seduction of their daughters through print.[10]

Still, there remained the thorny question of how the letters had come into Webb's hands. To honor a father's wish to hide his daughter's ruin, Webb now claimed to have recovered them from Willis in the company of a family friend, George Buckham. Why then was Webb dishonoring his dead friend's request by parading them before the world? That is precisely what Willis asked in a "card" printed in the *Tribune*. The letters he remembered, but no seduction, only (as he explained it to his readers) "the irregular outpourings of a heart and mind overflowing and impatient of silence" and yearning for "literary fame." He now suggested that such billets-doux were, simply, occupational hazards. "What sentiment in them was addressed to myself," Willis confessed, "I never twice thought of—for it is such as is addressed often to those who are the supposed gate keepers of celebrity and appreciation. An Editor's drawer is full of such propitiatory compliments, and he is indeed silly if he consider them as anything but the toll to the pathway of fame."[11]

This was not explanation enough to satisfy Willis's critics (who continued to wonder aloud "how such a man is encouraged in his career of crime"), but it may have seemed persuasive to those predisposed to his or a young girl's case. Many had probably seen such correspondence, or written it themselves. Even so, no young woman wanted her personal letters arrayed willy-nilly before the world. And though Webb had mentioned no names, it was (according to one New York editor) almost immediately "current in the mouths of thousands" that the "murdered man" was the artist Henry Inman, and the seduced girl his only daughter, now Mary Inman Coddington. Indeed, only a day or two transpired before she chimed in from Rahway, New Jersey (where she now lived with a husband and three children) to dispute Webb's right to her letters. Now he looked the indelicate cad. Despite Webb's attempt to placate critics by calling for private inquiry into the letters, the newspapers blasted him left and right. One of his most vicious detractors even remarked that for his perfidy the colonel deserved to be shot down in the street like a "dog." Only Bennett reminded readers pointedly that Willis's conduct also could not be "lauded to the skies" but was, in fact, "that of a vain, silly male coquette, leading a youthful schoolgirl into a clandestine correspondence." In the end, Mary Coddington would have her letters back, though it took court action and Buckham's testimony to having more than once unsuccessfully requested their return from Webb to pry them away.[12]

This was a close call for Willis. Regardless of the true nature of those letters (and Webb plainly ached to have a panel of respected clergy, or even George P. Morris if not the public at large, attest to their character), it was clear from this incident just how vulnerable celebrities had become to the unsolicited attentions of admirers. Mary Inman had sent her letters off to a Willis she contrived of a dreamy imagination and seductive magazine prose; by keeping them, their real-life recipient demonstrated the dangers attendant in such flights of fancy (if indeed that is what they were).

This was not only a situation to worry sentimental celebrities. Saddled with Jamieson's flights of fancy, Catherine Forrest doubtless recognized this reality. So did the Congregationalist *Independent*, which now suggested that all public characters who cherished their good name should be concerned that Webb had menaced Willis with a letter addressed *to* him, not *by* him. Clergymen, after all, had their flocks as Willis had his; who was to know what passions moved parishioners' hearts? Echoing the defenders of Catherine Forrest, the *Independent* now complained anxiously that "there is not a name in the land so pure, so elevated, so free from every suspicion of the stain, that it could not be brought into disgrace in an hour" should such evidence be countenanced. A month later, even the "matter-of-fact, beef-and-potato-eating" Pittsburgh abolitionist Jane Swisshelm was concurring with such sentiments. It was humiliating, to be sure, that Willis had to play the "old coxcomb" when once his poetry had stirred her blood with its "pathos, and beauty, and sublimity," but she cautioned that even she had received "similarity-of-the-soul" familiarities that approached those she had heard prevailed among New York's Upper Ten. To many genteel Americans, the Coddington letters thus once again raised the specter of ignorance, envy, or mendacity misconstruing refinement into vice. It is a measure of the level of anxiety that almost universal condemnation greeted Webb's revelations. Although proof of seduction would have been sufficient to expel Willis from good society and probably wreck his career, his persecutor's methods were so repugnant—and so potentially devastating to a sense of domestic security—that the charges were given no chance of proof among the world at large.[13]

Rather than damning Willis, Webb's gambit thus actually may have buttressed the poet's case, especially since the *Home Journal*'s editor used the occasion to reprise his call for gentlemanly standards to safeguard the reputations of American women. Given this country's go-ahead and protean social state, it was, Willis now argued, fine for public men to endure personal attack: "In the building of almost any fame, public attention is the inadhesive lime which the dirty water of ill-will and slander converts into mortar; and the slanderer is but the hod-carrier, who . . . leaves strengthened by his base of toil the pyramid which he seemed climbing to disfigure."

Nor was he arguing against these "unconscious helpers to celebrity—these enlisters of partisans and defenders—these bubbles in the wake that chronicle the speed they strove to hinder." No, he now declared forthrightly: "Let the men who are worth slandering be slandered, if the republic please." Women were another matter. Nothing, he suggested, was easier in "our country than to destroy the good name of a lady." The law was certainly not a fit remedy for such attack: "It is a year of torture, expense and notoriety, and of ingenious vilification by false witnesses and 'eminent counsel,' with the falsehoods and the abuse daily immortalized in journals and legal reports." Neither was there redress in a duel "by husband or brother" at a "cost of state-prison or exile, and complete wreck of family and support." The sole remedy seemed to him to lay in a social code that charged gentlemen with rebuking hearsay and false assertion until guilt was proved. By standing for "the sacredness of a lady's reputation," Willis thus once again yoked his fortunes to a higher civility, one calculated (not surprisingly) to appeal to the waverers remaining in gentility's ranks.[14]

After such remarkable developments, it now remained only for Edwin Forrest to set the stage to permit the final drama to begin. Delay followed delay through the summer of 1851 as the affair's principals decided to abandon the Philadelphia courts and consolidate the New York suit to reflect each side's charges. Then there were further depositions to be gathered and Anna Flowers, a new servant witness, to be recalled from New Orleans and then Galveston, where she had fled, seemingly to escape further interrogation. All this activity meant a trial postponed until October at the earliest, perhaps even December. Before that, Edwin planned to return to the stage for a limited engagement, beginning with "Damon and Pythias" at the popular Broadway Theater. It would be his first performance in two years, and everyone knew that the play was merely prelude to his inevitable curtain call.

In this respect, Forrest did not disappoint his loyal fans. Having returned to acknowledge their thunderous applause after playing that evening's role, he avowed that the night's full house gratified a heart taxed almost beyond limits—by the press, Macready's partisans, that "mendacious dungeon lawyer," and a "certain fashionable clique" that aimed to cover its shame and escape justice. "Why is all this?" Forrest asked rhetorically. "I will tell you why. It is because I would not tamely submit, which perhaps, it is their wont to do in that very refined circle— because I would not tamely submit to the most infamous of all wrongs—the dishonor of my house." At this flourish, the predominantly male working-class audience reportedly erupted in "cheers, and cries of 'You were right.' " It was a scene to stir hearts and rally spirits. Whatever had been lost, there remained these loyal friends, and with them, confidence in vindication. The common people's favorite would see justice done—justice to his character, to his persecutors, and to the good opinion of all those who stood by him in defense of manly honor and true American virtue.[15]

After a most lengthy preliminary, the final act of the Forrest affair was thus set to begin. Like many a well-crafted play, precisely whose tragedy it would prove remained to be determined.

Sportive Tricks and Infamous Plots

The six-week-long divorce trial that opened in December 1851 was destined to be one of the nation's most engrossing spectacles to date. Given the lengthy preliminaries, few Americans had not at least heard of the Forrests' domestic troubles. Indeed, four juror candidates of the sixteen interviewed felt themselves so prejudiced by the past eighteen months' newspaper reports that they asked to be excused; another candidate had "read the charges and refutations" but reckoned that he could judge fairly and was thus impaneled. Once begun, moreover, the trial riveted the nation. Spectators packed the court daily, while the curious observers denied entrance followed the case in their daily papers. Not a few of the old-style mercantile sheets refused to publicize the proceedings; even the recently launched *New York Times*, conscious of its pretensions to respectability, dispensed with much of the lawsuit's more sordid disclosures. But the *Herald* and the penny papers were glad to oblige their working-class readers with detailed courtroom reports. (Indeed, so thorough was Bennett's court reporter that even Judge Oakley checked his own notes for accuracy against the paper's account.) Both the *Herald* and *Police Gazette*, moreover, promised complete editions of the transcripts ("with pictures to match") immediately upon the trial's conclusion and expected to sell tens of thousands of yellow-paper-bound copies at twenty-five cents a copy. Louis Kossuth, the celebrated Hungarian freedom fighter, may have been feted up and down Broadway during these days, but, according to one newspaper, the often salacious Forrest testimony outdrew even "The Nation's Guest."[16]

If the most avid scandalmonger could scarcely have asked for a more titillating trial, neither could a historian ask for a better rehearsal of many of the period's more contentious social issues. As adultery tended to elude direct proof, each attorney had to strive to suggest a character for the opposing defendant that would admit not only the possibility, but the probability that adulterous opportunities had been acted on. What could not be proved directly was to be carried by inference and innuendo. In this pursuit, adultery's presumable accessories—on one side: fashion, "socialism," late hours, and fallen womanhood; on the other: vulgarity, theater morals, and "kitchen testimony"—were invaluable aids to argument. Without them, there was no "proving" moral proclivities, either in the courtroom or on the street. With them, inquiry was free to exploit the strongest prejudices and prepossessions of a watching world.

The opposing counsels grasped this situation from the beginning, and in squaring off, their rival legal strategies served to underscore the central issues at hand. Simply put, each attorney sought to exploit the manner in which adultery constituted a symbolic defilement of perhaps *the* central institution of antebellum society: marriage sanctioned within the single-family home. By regarding adultery as an actionable crime against the state, as well as a sin against sacred decree, nineteenth-century Americans had already demonstrated, as a body, compelling interest in safeguarding matrimonial ties. That is why antebellum law generally denied divorce to adulterous mates. It was thus possible, should both Catherine and Edwin Forrest be found guilty of adultery, that the State of New York would force the couple to continue their unhappy marital estate as punishment for their mutual sins. This possibility, and the spectacle of this domestic morality play performed on a national stage and starring the day's most famous public characters, made for compelling viewing.

In directing jurors to consider Edwin Forrest's version of events, his counsel, John Van Buren, began where James Gordon Bennett left off. Van Buren evidently knew that proving Catherine Forrest's adultery would not be an easy task, especially with what he called a "sickly sentimentality" inclining jurors to doubt refined women capable of animal passion. But by moving early and often to indict the "sportive tricks" and "looking-glass amblings" of Willis's fashionable "literary clique," Forrest's chief counsel hoped to nullify any advantage presumably inherent in Catherine's sex. Notorious lotharios and infamous libertines might then, in effect, be made to so dominate the scene that observers (the all-male jury in particular) would be led to conclude that true womanhood could never have suffered the association. By playing to fears that fashion and its sensual impulses were home-wreckers, Van Buren hoped to win the day for his client, even should Catherine's adultery not be positively proved. In this respect, his case, like the *Herald*'s campaign that preceded it, resembled nothing so much as an indictment of the morally free and easy society Willis and his devotees were reputed to have instituted among New York's bon ton.[17]

In great measure, prospects for Van Buren's courtroom strategy hinged on the elaborate social codes that made antebellum Americans such sticklers for appearances. As urban society spread, the public face of propriety had become all the more central to its regulation. Wary as antebellum Americans were of the promises of appearance, still, those who hoped to sustain the march of refinement as the path to social virtue had little choice but to accept the proposition that "seeming" bore some relation to "being." Indeed, the etiquette of polite culture was dedicated to legislating this correlation. This was as true of homes as of people. Apart from the convenience of restricting the hours necessary to receive callers, highly evolved rituals of gentility such as visiting hours and calling cards aimed to regulate contact with the world so as to conform to a middle-class model of propriety. Social calls were to be made in broad daylight and through front doors, with servants and family alerted to their best behavior. To flout such convention was to invite neighbors to talk. And talk they did, often with devastating consequences.[18]

In pressing his case, Van Buren exploited a common prejudice that construed untimely visits as unseemly visits. To this end, his witnesses were repeatedly coaxed to tell of calls beyond "respectable hours": the 10 P.M. visits of Dr. Rich, for instance (whose only offense, it might appear to modern readers, was in attending to Catherine's aching tooth at too late an hour); or Willis's early morning calls, especially as Catherine was reported to have received her friend in "undress" or from her bed. More rewarding still for Van Buren were accounts of the overnight visits of Samuel Raymond and Granby Calcraft, as well as Richard Willis's alleged three-day hideout in an upstairs bedroom. Considered in light of the new urban exposé novel and its burden that antebellum America's moral underworld coursed remarkably close to the decorum of polite society, Van Buren's suggestion that upright citizens might not be what they seemed gained even greater credence. Perhaps positive proof of adultery could not be sustained, but it was clear that a married woman had entertained men in her husband's home without his say or ken. That such men allegedly skulked from kitchen doors to avoid notice only further suggested the rogue behind the would-be gentlemen.[19]

Such comings and goings might have been summarily dismissed had they not also been coupled with reports of rollicking parties in Edwin's absence. This is where servant testimony came into its own. No class of observers was better situated to disclose a private home's dishonor than those who daily plied its corridors and chambers. Domestics saw what others did not, and while employers normally suppressed their servants' testimony as tending to disrupt domestic harmony, courtroom imperatives often authorized their speech in the greater interest of justice. Symbolically marginal to the kin-based sentimental family (though in practice often crucial to its economic maintenance), domestic servants thus here assumed a central role in policing the institution that so often sought to deny them. In this particular case, both Garvin and Underwood now told of free-flowing liquor, ladies smoking, and easy society: the all-night songfest of Cornelia Grinnell Willis, her brother-in-law Richard, Catherine Forrest, and her sister Margaret; ladies in the Forrest house puffing on "little paper segars" (or "cigarettes") à la George Sand; Catherine dandled on Granby Calcraft's knee and "so tipsy she couldn't carve"; Calcraft and Voorhies stumbling upstairs with a tray of glasses. Doubtless blame would have settled on the man of the house had such revelry occurred under his watch. In this instance, however, Edwin Forrest's absence from these celebrations was conspicuous. Nor, presumably, was it lost on the all-male jury when Van Buren remarked in his closing statement that he doubted whether any of *them* would have permitted such a "frolic" in their homes. Doubtless this unchaperoned conviviality added weight to the more serious charges of sexual inconstancy that Edwin had leveled against his estranged wife.[20]

In this regard, the jury had much to consider. Van Buren's quartet of servant-witnesses—Underwood, Garvin, Anna Flowers, and a new deponent, N. P. Willis's onetime stableboy John Kent—related stories of a half-dozen years rife with sexual encounters ranging from stolen kisses to outright venery. Garvin, for instance, claimed to have caught Catherine and N. P. Willis "lying on each other," and afterward found some hairpins and a garter in the sofa. Anna Flowers, Catherine's onetime chambermaid, swore that she had once found her mistress bedded down with Captain William A. Howard, yet another alleged cuckolder named by Edwin Forrest since his initial presentment. Taking the offensive to enemy territory, John Kent told of how his celebrated former employer—dressed in only a shirt, pantaloons, and slippers—had once passed the room of the visiting Catherine Forrest saying the words "goodnight dear." Other damning secrets were broached as well: how Garvin had caught Samuel Raymond and Margaret Voorhies in carnal embrace (the same Margaret who had previously conceived a child out of wedlock with her present husband); how Captain Howard had twice pressured Anna Flowers to have sex with him (to the point of rape), and later a child was born, and its maintenance paid by Catherine Forrest to forestall Flowers's threat to swear out a complaint against Howard. Van Buren even found a backlot neighbor who was willing to testify that he had once seen Willis and Catherine Forrest embracing by the library window of the Twenty-second Street house before retiring to the darkness. Given these domestic shenanigans, it was only a small step for Van Buren to suggest that after leaving her husband, Catherine and her sister had all but turned prostitute in their rented Sixteenth Street house. It mattered little that this last charge was destined never to be sustained; to defenders of a patriarchal order, even allegations of such free and easy behavior were proof enough of a wife's moral dereliction, and the name "prostitute" a mere formality.[21]

To pinch her tighter, Catherine's own words suggested how a Bennettesque "fashionable socialism" might have conspired to lead her astray. By this point in the proceedings, everyone had presumably heard of the infamous "Consuelo" letter—"a witness that cannot lie," Edwin's counsel called it. But Van Buren now also produced for the court a highly interesting note that his client's wife had sent James Lawson in 1848. Among other things, this "Fourier" letter sketched out Catherine's ideas on the institution of marriage. Mixing personal experience with Associationist doctrine (perhaps gleaned in conversation with her friend Parke Godwin, a leading American authority on Fourier), she therein blamed much domestic unhappiness on women's continued social and intellectual dependence on their husbands. In itself, this position was hardly shocking or even unduly feminist, being only a variant on the by-then-common preference for companionate ideals. Catherine had, in the letter, even agreed with her friend Lawson that she hardly wished to "outrage the laws of nature" by "running out of her own sphere." What followed, however, was at least guaranteed to raise eyebrows, as well as the hackles of her husband and the enemies of "fashionable socialism." By calling marriage a "galling yoke" wholly unfit to restrain "forever every feeling and passion," Catherine opened herself to the full weight of contemporary anxieties on that most controversial of modern institutions. Even the self-described "sacrifice" of indulging a husband "his fancies" rather than forcing him into an "unhappy life of self denial and unrest" became, to those who wished to make it so, a badge of potential degradation, a sign that she could countenance infidelity in one whom God's law and society's injunction had pledged her to love and obey. More ominous still was Catherine's complaint that though society's laws could not now be "openly brave[d]," its despotism could not last forever. In the meantime, she expressed the hope that "those whose minds soar above common prejudice, can, if such be united, do much to make their present state endurable." To unsympathetic readers, this suggestive passage could mean but one thing: carnal liaison with Jamieson. The only drawback in this bonanza for Van Buren was Catherine's postscript that she had read her letter to Edwin and that he approved its sentiments.[22]

In light of the supporting allegations and fears about the sins of Paris erupting in American parlors, there was perhaps no evidence better calculated to confirm social conservatives' fears that Fourierist "passionalism" was just a cover for sexual license. If nothing else, complaints about being the victim of a "conventional marriage" commonly elicited retorts to the effect that speakers were giving evidence of their own iniquity. "There may be, as yet, nothing of what the world calls crime on their part," one scandalized observer remarked on another occasion, "but there is a screw loose somewhere in the machinery of their morals." With the recent proliferation of women's rights conventions and the appearance of Amelia Bloomer's Turkish trousers in many Northern cities, it was easier than ever for disparagers of reform to charge that radical women particularly wished to unsex themselves by assuming the prerogatives of male desire. In the case of bloomers, the *Herald* even went so far as to rave that this style of dress had been for "twenty years . . . worn in disreputable houses as a lure to the imagination." This was precisely the kind of object lesson the nation's traditionalists also drew from communitarian experiments like those at Oneida, Brook Farm, and Red Bank. While few reformers seeking to liberalize congress between the sexes had, by 1851, actually come to repudiate marriage altogether, insinuations that ideals of common property were to extend to persons and free manners to lead to free love were hard to shake. Read in this context, Catherine Forrest's "Fourier" letter challenged right-thinking jurymen to stanch the moral hemorrhage by returning a guilty verdict. Doing so would presumably reaffirm the moral authority of the patriarchal gender relations Van Buren invoked when he argued, as he did before the court, that it was a wife's duty to conform to the husband's style of life. In this respect, James Gordon Bennett could not have improved on Van Buren's courtroom strategy.[23]

But John Van Buren was not the only attorney capable of marshaling evidence to suggest domestic nightmares of a virtuous home and family shamefully dishonored. Nor did Edwin Forrest's attorney possess a monopoly on public prejudice. More to the point, Van Buren's client was in his own way as vulnerable as his estranged wife. Edwin was, after all, both a man and an actor; each estate bordered on disrepute. By common assent, men were expected to yield to their sexual passions unless restrained by domestic influences; on the road, Edwin effectively had no "home." More damning still, the humble origin of many players daily threw him into suspect company. So it was not entirely outrageous when Charles O'Conor alleged before the court that an extraordinary intimacy had once existed between Edwin and his former leading lady, Josephine Clifton. To support this charge, Forrest's former costumer "Dummy" Allen was brought forward to testify to having seen Ned Forrest and Clifton "kiss and embrace" in a hotel room in which they spent the night. Another witness claimed to have seen Forrest in Clifton's room in an Albany tavern wearing nothing but "his linen and a cloak." Furthermore, one Doctor Hawkes—a druggist, really—was brought forward to describe what he characterized as the immediate aftereffects of an "abortion" on the train from Utica to Rochester. To add to this litany of shame, a witness named William Doty chimed in with an involved story of a shared stateroom and a single mattress on a steamboat run to Albany in 1843. Though these last two charges ultimately failed to pass muster—Hawke's pretension to medical expertise was soon discredited by several practicing physicians and Doty's story was blasted, as staterooms had yet to be installed on the Albany line at the time of Forrest's alleged indiscretions—the resulting questions concerning Edwin's fidelity were hard to resolve.[24]

Even more valuable for O'Conor was evidence suggesting Edwin Forrest's propensity to frequent brothels. And if Caroline Ingersoll refused to admit on the witness stand any more than that the great tragedian had occasionally lodged in her rooming establishment for three-hour stints, most people undoubtedly saw through her feigned ignorance to the likely use of the many "chambers" she rented. In this respect, O'Conor did not have to push Ingersoll; he had other ways to establish the character of her house. During the trial, a parade of policemen were run past the jury to report it as a "suspicious place" and a reputed "upper ten"—that is, a high-class whorehouse. So, too, did a local butcher testify to having seen a woman "put her finger to her nose to a gentleman who was passing by"—obviously a common sign of love for hire. None of this testimony proved Edwin's infidelity conclusively, but it must surely have set jurors to thinking. As for the character of Ingersoll's boardinghouse and its indoor activities, O'Conor left that matter to their consideration; he merely suggested that Forrest had probably not gone there "to say his pater noster."[25]

Like his wife, Edwin Forrest thus fell victim to a social geography that reinforced a host of unsavory imputations. As O'Conor surely knew, antebellum reformers of all stripes agreed that, along with drink, prostitution most threatened the sanctity of respectable home life. Indeed, no other vice so mocked the marriage vow, for men who exchanged money for sexual satisfaction engaged in an illicit economy of love whose site—the house of prostitution—symbolized all that a true home ought not to be. The very streets that surrounded such establishments consequently assumed a bad name. With all the tales about Clifton and the bawdy houses, it now seemed conceivable that Edwin Forrest had all but abandoned his wife years before he had thought to even ask for a separation. In light of this possibility, Forrest's well-known and very considerable exertions to divorce his wife began to look more and more like a dastardly plot.

That was precisely what O'Conor hoped to prove. In this regard, he had letters of his own to produce. Several days into the proceedings, testimony revealed that as Forrest had been preparing his case before the Pennsylvania legislature he had relayed the alleged cause of separation to John Wien Forney, an old friend and political crony. Then, whether on his own or at Forrest's direction it is not clear, Forney had written George Roberts of the *Boston Times* to ask for help in obtaining "in some way an admission from Jamieson." Alcohol, Forney suggested, might loosen the glib actor's tongue. Luckily for Catherine, Roberts bristled at this commission, or so he later claimed; in any case, no drunken confession ever surfaced. Sometime later, O'Conor had obtained a copy of Forney's fateful letter—through Roberts, no doubt, who evidently had since fallen out with his old confrères. Now Catherine's counsel produced it before the court to illustrate the depths to which her husband's associates had descended to serve their friend. More damning still, though Edwin had never seen the note, the tragedian had, by Forney's own reluctant admission under oath, approved of the errand.[26]

The actor's camp was not above blackmail either, judging by the questionable means used to procure perhaps the trial's most crucial witness—Catherine's onetime serving girl Anna Flowers. In June 1850 an advertisement in the *New Orleans Picayune* had promised this young Irish immigrant that she would "hear something to her advantage" if she applied at the newspaper's office. Flowers—now married in New Orleans with a child of her own—had gone there apparently expecting to "get a fortune." Yet, as she later plaintively told the court, she "got nothing at all"—nothing, that is, except the insistent attentions of Forrest's agent, Henry Dougherty. By whatever means, he convinced her to travel to New York to testify against her former mistress. With Lawson paying her expenses, Flowers was then put up in several New York City hotels while Forrest, Theodore Sedgwick, and others pumped her for information. All this and more emerged from courtroom testimony.[27]

Perhaps most important, in his cross-examination of Flowers, O'Conor compelled the former serving girl to own to a letter sent to her former mistress on that initial visit to New York. It read:

> Dare Mrs. Florrist I have just arrived from New Orleans, and I want to see you very much before I see anybody else. I am going to Brookling this morning, but I will be hear at half past 5 this afternoon. Do pleas com and see me for I have so much to tell you. I don't want to be seen hear until I see you. Call at 142 Mercer Street, Willson's hotel. Please send answers by the barer.

As Catherine's attorney triumphantly pointed out, this note lied shamelessly. Forrest and his cronies had already interrogated Flowers for two days running when the letter was sent. The onetime serving girl's pretensions to wanting to see Catherine *first* were then so much deception. When O'Conor produced a second disingenuous note, accompanied by a misleading card planted in the *Herald*, Flowers broke down and admitted that she had lied "to deceive Mrs. Forrest," though she pathetically maintained that she meant no harm. Edwin Forrest, on the other hand, apparently did. Many observers felt that the card in the *Herald* bore all the marks of his hand.[28]

Even this revelation did not exhaust O'Conor's bag of surprises. Though observers were not to know the import of the testimony until the summing up, Ellen Lawless, an employee at Wilson's Hotel, was presently brought forward to testify that Flowers and an unnamed man (doubtless one of Edwin's handlers) had, during the former servant's initial return to New York, rented a backroom for an afternoon and fitted its windows and doors with black muslin curtains. If Catherine had done as Flowers was alleged to have suggested—that is, come to this place deep in the brothel district for their interview under escort of someone like Professor Hackley, the Columbia professor then under suspicion in the Forrest suit—and then conveniently been discovered with that man in midafternoon by one of Edwin's stooges, it would have been hard to discredit the appearance of prostitution. As Van Buren himself remarked, Anglo-American law looked on a married woman's presence at a "bawdy house" as strong proof of adultery. Had such a scene been enacted on Mercer Street in the summer of 1850, Edwin Forrest might have demanded divorce from his wife on almost any terms he named.[29]

While Forrest may have commenced legal proceedings to save his name, he was now in danger of being caught by his own devices. And what was often a celebrity's greatest asset—the financial resources that fame could now bring the famous—only encouraged this possibility. As early as the spring of 1850, rumors were rife of cash flowing in the backrooms of the Pennsylvania State House. Eighteen months later, critics surmised that Forrest's pretrial return to the stage had been driven by a need to satisfy monumental expenses as well as overweening pride. Such speculation did not end with the trial's commencement. Along with the Mercer Street shenanigans, jurors now learned that Andrew Stevens (Forrest's perennial mouthpiece in the war of words with Willis) had spent nearly a year and a half tracking down witnesses, compelling them to testify, and dispensing cash where needed.[30]

This information bore hard on the credibility of Forrest's witnesses. The stable-boy John Kent, for instance, seemed to have received a consideration for his troubles. After leaving Willis's employ in July 1850, he had been chronically underemployed, losing the few jobs he had to what he described as wage disputes. It was, then, probably welcome attention when Stevens searched him out to testify, loaned him money here and there, and employed him to run odd errands relating to the Forrest case. Later, when Willis came looking for Kent, Stevens instructed his errand boy to deny having told Forrest anything to Catherine or Willis's detriment. Nor was Kent the only witness who seemed unusually beholden to those who counted on his testimony. Anna Flowers had certainly been enticed to testify with purposefully misleading, if effective, promises of reward. And though she found no fortune awaiting her, her passage to New York and expenses were paid from Forrest's accounts. In itself, such payment was not unusual (following common practice, both sides paid witnesses for their time) except in its extraordinary exertions and the intimation of strong-arm tactics used to compel testimony. When coupled with the doubts raised earlier about Underwood's motives, further confusions raised during the trial over when Underwood had told Lawson what, and troubling inconsistencies in Garvin's testimony—precisely how, for example, had he seen Willis and Catherine Forrest coupled in the library when the blinds were shut and the room dark?—the hints of bribery and bullying served to discredit Forrest's witnesses, especially as this result was precisely what genteel Americans expected from so-called kitchen testimony.

Further revelations about Flower's history only corroborated such presumptions. By her own admission, the onetime servant girl had admitted Captain Howard to her bed (first under threat of violence, and subsequently upon "promises") and then borne a child out of wedlock. After this transgression landed Flowers in an angry dispute over the maintenance of her child with Samuel Raymond (of all people), the girl's family had ostracized her, a brother even threatening to kill her if she returned north. Now, though the embattled exchambermaid maintained her innocence in the episodes of seven years past, a parade of witnesses suggested otherwise. Her first employer told an interested jury of having money stolen by his young maid and a watch purloined from a neighbor, offenses that landed Flowers in New York City's House of Refuge (she called it a "boarding school") for some months. More than this, another employer now swore that "he would not place a straw in her word," while his nephew told of the young girl's once promising "any favor" for fashioning a corset board. As it had with Catherine Forrest, Flowers's sexuality thus proved a weakness. It would ultimately prove her undoing, for Howard, it seems, was not the only man the teenaged servant had slept with. In this regard, the Forrests's former cook told the court that years ago she had caught Flowers in bed with Barney McCabe, once a lower servant at the Twenty-second Street house. Flowers now frantically denied the charge, calling McCabe a "small, dirty boy." But when O'Conor summoned him to the stand, the "dirty boy" owned that he had engaged in sexual intercourse with Flowers several times only days before Howard had come to her bed. "Miserable looking, ill clad, [and] shirtless," as the *Herald*'s court reporter described him, the inarticulate (and perhaps inebriated) McCabe was clearly of the most hopeless class; his connection to Flowers stamped her character as an indiscriminate wanton. No one, O'Conor suggested, ought to believe such a fallen woman.[31]

They should not believe Edwin Forrest either, his wife's attorney added, especially when tales of the actor's bullying were not yet exhausted. Though O'Conor had initially cajoled McCabe to depose to sleeping with Flowers (probably paying him for his trouble as well), Forrest's henchmen had thereafter apparently sent a trusty from the police force to pressure the reluctant Irish laborer to retract his statement. After being "driven around" by several of Forrest's boys, the semiliterate McCabe was convinced to sign a paper swearing that he had been drunk at the time of his first affidavit. He was then given a dollar and sent off. The weight of these sundry intrigues (strong-arm tactics; bought witnesses; the "Forney" letter; the "Mercer Street Plot") O'Conor now offered to the jury as evidence of a conspiracy extending back through whippings, beratings, and roughshod bullying of senators to the whispering campaign against Catherine, a fiendish plot of such proportions and resources that its mastermind could be none other than Edwin Forrest. The "sportive tricks" of literary coteries could not hold a candle to such home-wrecking.

Of course, O'Conor still had his client's innocence to prove. Here again, genteel prepossessions were to prove crucial to the trial's outcome. In this regard, Judge Oakley said perhaps more than he knew when he told jury members that this "is not a case which depends upon a minute examination of the testimony but on the credibility or non-credibility of the witnesses." Despite Van Buren's claim that the "Consuelo" letter was a "witness that can not lie," no evidence had surfaced to establish adultery conclusively, only the testimony of witnesses who, as Oakley had hinted, *could* lie. And with all the trial's fantastic charges and revelations, separating dissemblers from truth-tellers was tricky business. Under the circumstances, justice might have to rest, as it did in Flowers' case, on a reckoning of essential character. By its very nature, this game of substantiating character favored Catherine's cause. On one hand, many people in "good society," at least, fully expected Edwin's servant witnesses—like all domestics—to lie. On the other hand, though battered by damaging revelations, Catherine's female virtue continued to draw strength from genteel presumptions.[32]

This does not mean that O'Conor did not have considerable suspicions to allay in his client's defense. There were conspicuous absences among her compatriots—George Jamieson in St. Louis, Margaret Voorhies off to Italy on a "musical" tour, Captain Howard plying the Sandwich Islands, Parke Godwin gone to Europe after brief testimony. Though Edwin's working-class partisans in particular took these absences (probably rightly) as attempts to avoid embarrassing courtroom disclosures, further damage to Catherine's cause was effectively forestalled. Those who remained could at least deny their complicity. This they did, with varying degrees of effectiveness. To his dismay, Richard Willis got confused about how many nights he had spent at the Twenty-second Street house, and Granby Calcraft squirmed to avoid Van Buren's inquiries into his failed marriage to an "ex-actress." Nonetheless, each of Catherine's alleged paramours swore to her innocence (and theirs). In addition, none was forced to face incontrovertible proof of their guilt.[33]

In this regard, Willis's much anticipated appearance on the stand was particularly significant to the course of the trial. He certainly had much to lose in the bargain. Every one of Edwin's servant-witnesses had testified to the famous author's dalliances with Catherine. To make his client's case, moreover, Van Buren had ridden his fellow Yale graduate hard throughout the trial, once even quizzing him on his church affiliation, when he knew full well that Willis had been excommunicated long ago. Yet as with Webb's attack and Forrest's assault, Van Buren's badgering may have done more harm than good for his client. Particularly in his closing remarks, O'Conor was able to exploit canons of fair play to present Willis as an ill-used man. Furthermore, by taking the stand, Willis finally had a chance to restate his case. In doing so he categorically denied kissing, lying on, or embracing Catherine Forrest. So, too, did he explain his frequent evasion of Forrest's mates as resulting from distaste for "their very vulgar habits and conversation"—supercilious testimony, to be sure, but hardly out of character. To cap matters, Willis dismissed John Kent's ominous "good night, dear" as the benediction of a loving father to his daughter.[34]

Perhaps nothing better underscored this comforting image than the frequent courtroom attendance of Cornelia Grinnell Willis. In their initial sketches of each day's proceedings, court reporters often noted Mrs. Willis's presence at Catherine Forrest's side; nor was this fact lost on jurors, who might be expected to conclude that her stoic attendance elevated the cause of her husband's friend. That was certainly the intent behind including Willis's wife in the courtroom tableau and on the witness stand. A lady of indisputable connections, Cornelia Willis required—and received—kid-glove care. There was, for instance, none of the wiseacre in Van Buren's cross-examination; later in the proceedings he even complained to jury members that he had failed to get in his full licks against her husband in deference to Cornelia's presence in the courtroom. This complaint was convincing evidence that gentility deflected inquiry. As graphic as examinations often got—and even the *Herald* occasionally could find no suitable euphemism to stand in for the trial's racy testimony—certain matters were not fit to discuss with a lady. Thus the former servant girl Anna Flowers might be quizzed on her sexual habits, but she was a drudge, after all, and trailed her lowly character like a comet's tail. Cornelia Willis was another matter. The one incident that might have led to her debasement—the all-night songfest—was probably redeemed by her testimony that nothing untoward had gone on that evening. Similarly, Kent's "good night, dear" story was also effectively discredited by his mistress's disclosure during questioning that she herself had summoned Catherine to help care for the newborn child who lay beside her in the sickroom.[35]

If jurors were tempted to believe that N. P. Willis and Catherine Forrest had carried on a long and shameless liaison, Cornelia Willis's faithful courtroom attendance on both her husband and bosom friend suggested otherwise. More than this, Mrs. Willis's example provided Catherine's attorney with yet another golden opportunity to bend sympathies toward his client's cause. Summing up before the twelve men who would decide Catherine's fate, O'Conor was moved to muse on what he supposed must have been Edwin Forrest's feelings as Cornelia Willis had confronted his so-called kitchen witnesses: "My God, how I must appear before this community! Am I not like some obscene animal which has escaped from its slough and looks out from its place of concealment at the refined and delicate society from which he shrinks, lest his presence should contaminate it?" This was no idle exercise in courtroom mimicry. Ultimately, all O'Conor asked of jurors was that they ratify this visceral reaction, restoring genteel virtue to its rightful prerogatives and confining animal impulse to its deserved fate.[36]

So matters stood as the jury prepared to deliberate a verdict, with each side accusing the other of heartless and long-standing perfidy but neither able to sustain its case unquestioned. On that Saturday afternoon of 24 January 1852, it remained only for Chief Justice Oakley to define the case that presented itself to the jury. His instructions probably did much to determine the eventual verdict. Regarding Edwin Forrest's adultery, Oakley pronounced two witnesses untrustworthy but maintained that most others had raised suggestive evidence of intimacy between Clifton and her onetime leading man. The jury must decide the import of this relationship, as it would judge the stories of visits to Caroline Ingersoll's many-roomed boarding-house. As for Catherine's Fourierist sympathies, Oakley cautioned jurors about concluding guilt of adultery from "theoretic notions about social life and relations." Nonetheless, he remarked that preserving the "Consuelo" note was, at the very least, an unusual step. Beyond this, Oakley regarded the case against Calcraft, Raymond, and Richard Willis as abandoned. That left the actions of N. P. Willis, Howard, and Jamieson to be judged. Based on discrepancies in their testimony, the chief justice had some reservations about Garvin's and Kent's testimony against Willis. Regarding Flowers, he was more certain: the Mercer Street affair was an "unworthy plot"; the jury must assess her charges against the perfidy of this act.[37]

With these instructions, Judge Oakley dismissed the jury to their deliberations at 4:55 P.M. Two hours later, their foreman returned to ask if frequent visits to houses of prostitution were sufficient proof of adultery; that question, he affirmed, was the jury's sole point of disagreement. Oakley sent him back to find the answer in his own conscience. In an hour the jury sent word not to hold the court, and the judge declared the trial adjourned till Monday morning. Legal decision, so long prolonged, would have to wait a few more days.

What Kind of Justice?

When the jury asked Judge Oakley to dismiss the court early Saturday evening and then, only a few hours later, sealed their verdict, they almost guaranteed that thousands of excited citizens would greet the ruling of justice the following Monday morning. And why not? The Forrest affair had been a fascinating drama of domestic violation that played to the nation's profound anxieties over prevailing sex roles, the place of fashion and sentiment in society, and the state of domestic morality. Now, having followed the ins and outs of this tortuous affair through many months, the public at large was keen to know which version of events the law was prepared to sanction: Would it sustain the authority of manly honor against the blandishing seductions of foreign fashions intent on dishonoring a husband's home? Or, would it stand against rampaging manhood bent on tyrannizing refined womanhood? With the future of not one but two of the nation's most famous celebrities hanging in the balance, for many people these were all-consuming questions.

By ten o'clock, when Chief Justice Oakley took his seat on the bench, the court was packed with expectant faces while crowds thronged the city park outside the courthouse, eager for the verdict. They did not have long to wait. News of Catherine Forrest's complete vindication and $3,000 alimony award, as well as her husband's utter defeat, spread quickly. When Edwin emerged from the courthouse, bewildered but undaunted, a crowd of supporters—many of them his loyal working-class fans—cheered him "halfway up Broadway." But that was only one part of the story. On the other side of the building, similar emotion greeted Catherine and her attorney as she stepped into a waiting carriage on Chambers Street and he made his way through cheering throngs to his office on Nassau Street. Throughout town, talk of the trial monopolized conversation. "In every public house, in every barroom, on the ferry boats, in the cars, in the omnibuses, and in every hole and corner of the city, amongst all kinds of society, from the literary coteries and codfish aristocracy down to the merest jabberers on the Five Points," the *Herald* reported, "the facts, the incidents, and above all, the verdict, were freely discussed." But though there had been a legal decision, there was no consensus on the matter of guilt. Nor were the contentious social questions broached by the trial easily dismissed. In some respects, the trial's repercussions would echo for years.[38]

Precisely why the jury reached its conclusion is impossible to say. In their estimation, Edwin Forrest was guilty as charged, if not in the case of Clifton, then certainly by frequenting whorehouses; evidently, O'Conor's comment on Edwin's "pater nosters" had struck a chord. As for Forrest's wife, Oakley had done her a great favor by effectively ruling out half her alleged paramours and then questioning the reliability of the opposition's key witnesses. Under such instruction, the jury presumably had been unable to banish its "reasonable doubts" regarding her guilt. In this respect, the degraded character of the "kitchen witnesses" seems to have been at least partly at fault. Then, too, evidence of willful deceit and outrageous bullying made it difficult to believe the word of any of Forrest's witnesses; Willis and Howard, as a consequence, were saved. That left only Jamieson for the jury to consider. Under the circumstances, to convict Catherine of heinous adultery solely because of a letter sent *to* her must have seemed unreasonable. Though they might heartily disapprove of her prudence, the jurors were not ready to consign her to what amounted to social death. By their word, Catherine Forrest was innocent.

This verdict was hardly what one might have predicted when her husband began preparations for his legislative divorce suit in February 1850. Then, Jamieson's note and the testimony of servants bore hard on Catherine. Willis's "famous letter" also probably did her more harm than good. But time and a masterful defense turned the tide, at least in the legal arena. After failing to carry his legislative suit, Edwin Forrest's obsessive temperament goaded him to adopt unwise methods to demonstrate his estranged wife's guilt. And though the length of pretrial maneuvering subjected each side to damaging scrutiny, Catherine was perhaps better situated to weather the storm. As Van Buren understood, both her sex and her social class pleaded for special consideration; buttressed by canny and resourceful counsel, such inherent advantages eventually stood the test against Edwin Forrest's rampaging populism.

Any satisfaction arising from legal decisions would, however, prove fleeting. This was as true for Willis as it was for the rest of the affair's leading characters. In the days immediately following the trial, all his trouble and expense, as well as the ordeal's toll on his health, had seemed justified; by declaring Catherine innocent, the law had pronounced him honorable. But, as many celebrities in his day and beyond would learn, one triumph of law does not necessarily safeguard a good name. For Willis, the situation was especially touchy, given that his much postponed assault suit against Forrest was finally scheduled for trial in March. Eventually, the jury pronounced Forrest's attack unwarranted but awarded Willis only $2,500 of the $10,000 asked in damages—doubtless small compensation for enduring yet another round of insults and innuendoes at the hands of his old nemesis John Van Buren. First, there were sundry digs at Willis's manhood. Then, in the summing up, Van Buren joked that six-and-a-half cents plus interest should suffice to cover damages—all this after Willis had bowed respectfully to the opposing counsel upon first entering the courtroom. Yet with the assault case won and Catherine's defense behind him, the affronted poet no longer felt compelled to suffer such indignity. Apparently, he challenged Van Buren to a duel, though nothing came of this abortive trial of honor but rumors and the snub of seeing the affair's correspondence printed in the *Herald.* "It seems a hard case," Bennett joked, "that Willis cannot get somebody to shoot him in the settlement of this business." Yet, it is no wonder that Willis again sought out the certain danger of pistols at twenty paces rather than the shame that two years of invasive notoriety had heaped upon him. If one lesson could be drawn from his ordeal, it was that a reputation once given over to the press and common report was hard to rein in. This lesson was made especially bitter when the hard-won damages of Willis's assault suit were later reduced on appeal to a mortifying $1 award.[39]

Edwin Forrest could also testify to the trials of celebrity. The courtroom defeat, after so much heartbreak and trouble, galled him immeasurably. "A great wrong had been done," he declared to his notebook shortly after the trial, "and to prevent a repetition of it—the offenders should be scourged and what scourging is so effective as to keep the names of these ermined tyrants a mockery and a scorn forever in the mouths of men." This calling was to prove a lifelong burden, as the great tragedian relentlessly pursued his animus through the courts. Keeping after Willis over the *Home Journal* libel until 1859, Forrest ultimately collected $500 in damages. The actor was less fortunate when it came to his former wife. Though he fought the alimony through repeated legal battles, the New York courts eventually forced him to relinquish over $60,000 in back payments after his final appeal failed in 1868. Still, obsession died hard. In these later years, any rumor, no matter how wild—a tip that someone had seen Jamieson in flagrante delicto with Catherine and still retained reward used to quiet him; reports of a deathbed confession that the divorce jury had been packed—would send Forrest off to his lawyers to press for yet another appeal. Nor could he ever forgive those whose opposition hurt him so. When news reached Forrest in October 1868 that George Jamieson had been killed by a railroad train near Yonkers, his fellow thespian observed grimly that "God is great, and Justice, though slow, is sure—another scoundrel has gone to Hell, I trust forever."[40]

Of course, Forrest could know none of this in 1852; at that times, he still had hope, and more: the continued support of his loyal fans, especially among New York's b'hoys. Upon his return to the Broadway Theatre on 10 February to reprise his starring role in "Damon and Pythias," they were there in the hundreds, led by the Empire Club's Isaiah Rynders, to greet their hero with "huzzas" and, later in the evening, a banner inscribed "This is the People's Verdict." Great was the noise when Forrest returned to the stage to acknowledge his fans' applause as evidence that justice would yet be done. So it might have seemed, judging by their undiminished affection. For sixty-nine nights—an unprecedented run—his adherents flocked to see their hero. Still, while it was indeed a great vindication by popular acclaim, all of New York could hardly have been expected to crowd into the Broadway Theatre; the absence of those who stayed away was pointed. After the trial's disclosures, genteel New York closed its doors for good to the nation's great tragedian. As the *Times* observed:

> We cannot conceive it possible that Mr. Forrest should retain with the public any degree of character and respect. He may possibly continue to crowd the galleries of our second-rate theatres, and to receive the applause of the reckless mob. But his character is gone. The revelations of this trial, with the inferences which they render necessary, will follow and brand him to the end of his days.

And so they did.[41]

For a time, polite society had others to acclaim. Foremost among the honored ones was Charles O'Conor. As yet, he had taken no payment for his services and was said to have spent $6,000 out-of-pocket. More than this, his defense of the "defenseless" Catherine Forrest was widely regarded as both masterful and magnanimous—"the most remarkable exhibition of professional skill ever witnessed in this country," one judge called it. The New York Bar concurred in this conclusion by hosting an honorary dinner. To cap O'Conor's triumph and proclaim their sympathies, thirty ladies joined together to present the now-famous trial attorney a silver vase for his service to womankind.[42]

Judging by the presentation silver, many in polite circles took Catherine's acquittal as a great victory for virtuous womanhood over marauding male brutality. Though she herself might have been expected to share in the triumph, her subsequent actions only worked to dampen sympathies presumably awakened by her ordeal. Needing money and without reliable income (the alimony remained undelivered and subject to reversal), Catherine had resolved, even before the trial, to try the stage. Only days after the lawsuit's close, she opened at Brougham's Lyceum as "Lady Teazle" in *The School for Scandal*. This was, to many minds, a remarkably apt—if inopportune—character. Although in assuming this role Catherine pledged her alimony to charity, vowing to live only by her own efforts, the theater's general disrepute gave her supporters second thought. Sympathetic as they might be to the plight of a single woman, many people now regarded her choice of the stage as most unwise. This "most absurd step" (as George Templeton Strong put it) did much to alienate the genteel world that had so recently hailed her acquittal. After a moderately successful, if uninspired, theatrical career that eventually took her to Australia and England and an unprofitable stint at the helm of the Metropolitan Theatre in boomtown San Francisco, Edwin Forrest's former wife retired in 1859 to a quiet life, punctuated periodically by what were undoubtedly unwelcome bursts of publicity that accompanied her husband's persistent court appeals. Never again would Catherine Sinclair's fame rival that of the winter of her domestic discontent.[43]

If the leading characters in the Forrest affair suffered much in its ordeals, many judged that society had suffered as well. All around, observers agreed that the case had harmed public morals. In his charge to the jury, Judge Oakley called on the New York legislature to safeguard equal justice by prohibiting publicity of such trials until their conclusion. Horace Greeley hoped furthermore that such testimony would be published only at the legislature's discretion. "One such trial should suffice for a lifetime," he concluded. In calling for private trials, Greeley joined others who believed that this parade of kissing and hugging, drinking and smoking, license and deception could not but excite common minds. Printing such details was merely to pander to the public's degraded appetites. This, indeed, was the seamy side of press freedoms for which Americans otherwise liked to commend themselves. And it was a sign of Greeley's concern over the disturbing march of publicity that he could be moved to renounce the right of free reporting that he held so dear.[44]

Detractors of the verdict did not stop with such objections. To many minds, the lifestyle the decision ostensibly endorsed capped the enormity of the miscarriage of justice, for the verdict was liable to be regarded in many circles as what one paper called a "premium paid to licentiousness." Or, as another editor lamented (this one from far-off North Carolina),

> Forrest is a rude, arrogant, uneducated, and somewhat brutal man; coarse, vulgar, unrefined, and purse-proud, but it fairly admits of a question whether even he be not preferable to such a broken down roué as Capt. Calcraft, or such a dawdling, heartless, man-milliner as N. P. Willis, companions whose company Mrs. Forrest would persist in keeping although opposed to her husband's wishes, and although they spoke contemptuously of that husband in her presence. No "positive" iniquity may have been proved upon her, but no one can recognize a person who would so act, as a true wife or a pure woman.
>
> If the revelations made pending this trial present any thing like a true statement of the actual position of society among the would-be "upper tens" of New York, then the Lord preserve us, if we ever get married, from New York upper-tendom; for most assuredly few of the dames who figure in the picture, come quite up to Caesar's standard in a wife—of being above suspicion.

Not surprisingly, this was precisely the lesson Bennett wished to draw from the trial. Unlike his rival Greeley, the *Herald*'s editor could not endorse Oakley's call to privacy, if only because his business hinged on drawing readers to just such trial reports. Even now, the *Herald* edition of the trial notes was selling like hotcakes. There was also something dodgy about closed-door justice. Without the prying of papers such as his—and the *Herald* had been in the thick of the unfolding story throughout—the "rapid progress of fashionable ideas under the auspices of Willis's philosophy, and Fourierism taught by Greeley and Company" that Bennett wanted so desperately to discredit would have remained hidden. Now, perhaps even worse, they had seemingly been granted legal imprimatur. New York, as the *Herald* put it, had been "pronounced a Fourierite city."[45]

Judging by such declarations, the cultural antagonisms that the trial had excited promised to continue plaguing public debate, as would the disturbing questions raised by the trials of celebrity generally. For some, it was not so much that one side or another had triumphed, but that the spectacle had happened at all. Prompted by legal inquiry and press speculation, noted and respected persons—celebrities even—had faced embarrassing examination, slander, and ridicule, with ill results all around. Forrest, the nation's foremost actor, and Willis, its foremost aesthete, were reduced to discounting tales of brothels and repudiating charges of having dishonored a wife sick in bed across the hall. And though there may have been some small consolation in revealing cultural heroes as "just like us," the "us" revealed was often petty and vindictive.

The progress of justice was equally disconcerting. Americans generally prided themselves that free inquiry and adversarial jurisprudence offered the best path to truth. Yet here, more often than not, it was a truth many would rather have avoided. Seemingly indiscriminate questioning had exposed not only Edwin and Catherine's connubial torments, but also the foibles of their domestic circle: Margaret Sinclair's bastard child and her liaison with Samuel Raymond; John Forney's misguided scheming; the checkered past of a piteous servant girl ravished by one of her "betters" and spurned by her family; and a shirtless and bedraggled Barney McCabe, barely able to answer questions. To gain this dubious victory, servant had been pitted against employer, friend against friend, husband against wife; the desire to please—polite society's desideratum—was replaced by the desire to discredit and destroy.

As further evidence of a general social unraveling, personal enmity and class antagonism had once again threatened to lead New Yorkers to riot. Mayor Kingsland, worried about a repeat of the bloody Astor Place affair, felt compelled to post police and troops to safeguard the theatrical openings of both the great tragedian and his former wife against disturbance: tragedy had struck over seemingly pettier quarrels before; there was no reason to suppose it might not again. Luckily, both nights passed without undue incident, despite the tremendous crowd (B'hoys and gentlemen alike, but few ladies) who gathered to witness the spectacle, though an especially tense moment ensued when police hustled a drunk from the gallery at Brougham's Lyceum after he had tried to lead "three groans for Mrs. Forrest" and accompanied his call with remarks that Anna Flowers was "as good a lady" as her mistress. This had been the signal for a reprise of what Greeley's *Tribune* called "groans" against Macready, Willis, the *Tribune*, the "d——d English pimp," the mayor, the police, and "almost everything"; and cheers for Edwin Forrest, Ned Buntline (a hero of the Astor Place rioters), the *Herald*, the Bowery boys, and "all such folks." After that, the "mob" (as the *Tribune* put it) dispersed and "slunk into the rum holes which they frequent." Such had cultural antagonisms become in midcentury New York. Perhaps America had not come so far as many had thought or hoped.[46]

And where was the honor in all this? Perhaps nowhere. Concern for vindicating his good name before the world had initially led Edwin Forrest to seek a dispensation to divorce his wife, then pressed Catherine and her champion Willis to counter the charges. But legal remedy precluded quiet settlement, and the ensuing rumor, misinformation, and innuendo sparked by cultural politics, personal antipathy, and an intrusive press mocked the conceit that the reputations of honorable persons were always theirs to lose. This was especially true of celebrities. As courtroom justice had shown, it was rather more what one *heard said* than what one *knew* that determined "general character." Once private life became revealed to so many and in such terms as it was by the Forrest case, often little could be done to retrieve a name dishonored. It was ironic, in this respect, that Willis's desire for public access to the lives of noted personages should redound so savagely against himself and those he celebrated. However self-serving, his happy conclusion that intimate knowledge of the day's great personalities would enrich and ennoble society had reflected a general hope for a more polite and civilized community. Once again, events had proved this hope to be misguided.

Outrageous Fictions

No man is truly himself, but in the ideal which others entertain of him.

William Hazlitt, *The Plain Speaker*,
no. 12 (1826)

As should be clear by now, the literary lions of the antebellum age—like celebrities generally—assumed a public character only at their audience's sufferance. No doubt talent and the resources of print endowed such figures with considerable sway over their public image; there is, for example, no gainsaying fiction's power to establish the ruling conception of the man and—increasingly as the century wore on—the woman behind the prose. Nonetheless, maintaining a paying and congenial image remained tricky business even for literary celebrity's most adept practitioners. Over the years, N. P. Willis, for one, had proven himself a master at fashioning a persona calculated to reward his efforts. Yet this professional currency had been bought only at the price of persistent contempt—he sold his books all right, but often in spite of his public persona. Never was this vexing condition clearer, and perhaps more perilous, than in the wake of the Forrest troubles. When in August 1853, as a young man in Ohio, the future President James Garfield purchased an edition of *Hurry-Graphs*, he confided to his diary what must have been a common reflection of the day: "Willis is said to be a licentious man, although an unrivaled poet. How strange that such men should go to ruin, when they might soar perpetually in the heaven of heavens."[1]

No doubt the object of Garfield's meditations itched to put such mixed reviews behind him. How could he not? Apart from the dictates of honor, he had his career to consider; even for Willis, there was such a thing as too much notoriety. For all its flirtation with transgression, his *Home Journal* aimed squarely at the family trade; like other self-styled "respectable" journals of the Victorian era, its prosperity required that appearances be maintained and high-minded sympathies preserved. This requisite was reason enough in the 1850s for its chief to rededicate himself to the proposition he had always taken great pains to maintain: that he was, as he had protested during the Onderdonk imbroglio, a "good citizen, a good husband and father, and a moral and capable editor."[2]

One way that Willis sought to express and exhibit these sterling qualities was to retreat to a rural setting. The decision to do so was not pure window dressing; often weakened by sickness, he suffered increasingly from periodic blindness, recurrent vertigo, and a wracking and bloody cough throughout the long months preceding the Forrest trial. By the time of its conclusion, the hour for delay was long past. So it was that, as soon as he could free himself from the legal entanglements of his assault and battery suit against Forrest, Willis embarked on an extensive "health trip" to the Caribbean. This journey was memorialized with yet another series of letters in the *Home Journal,* collected in 1853 as *A Health Trip to the Tropics.* But when the worrisome cough persisted on his return, doctors ordered him from the city into the bracing air and picturesque surroundings of the Hudson Highlands. Here, at a country home he named Idlewild, the onetime "Man of the World" was destined to work out his life's final chapter in a long strategic retreat from the complications of epilepsy and consumption. More to the point, in a series of weekly letters to the *Home Journal* that made Idlewild one of the most famous homes of the mid–nineteenth century, he was to counter the damaging assumptions of the Garfields of the world by trading urbane frippery for the sympathetic disposition of a convalescent country gentleman. Notwithstanding its trials, arcadian invalidism thus held out the possibility that Willis might effect not only a physical convalescence but a moral renovation.

Such a pastoral character was not new to his repertoire. Fifteen years earlier, a younger and heartier Willis had charmed a generation with his bucolic "Letters from under a Bridge." Sent cityward from the Susquehanna Valley farmstead Glenmary, these New World echoes of Charles Lamb's "Elia" were some of the best loved of Willis's occasional prose, establishing him as a connoisseur of nature and nature's sympathies. Tender souls recalled his leave-taking "Letter to the Unknown Purchaser and Next Occupant of Glenmary" with special fondness. As with the familiar maternal odes of Willis's youth, this heartwarming appeal to an ideal of domestic stewardship and rural husbandry blunted complaint, lending substance to Willis's perennial contention that criticasters had misunderstood his essential character. If facile talent repeatedly seduced him into ornamental excess, his admirers could still comfort themselves that the glow of home fires presumably revealed the authentic measure of the man whose sentiments they so often clearly cherished.

Romantic theories about home life's offering a peculiarly legible index of the private man, coupled with a trend toward enshrining the nation's cultural elite as a domestic treasure, contributed to this effect. Consider Washington Irving's Sunnyside at Tarrytown on the Hudson: by midcentury, the architectural character of this much publicized Anglo-Dutch "snuggery" was commonly said to exhibit the inner architecture of its bachelor-proprietor's endearing and much beloved personality. At Willis's Idlewild, nature itself apparently conspired to abet this salutary domestication. The mountain jaunts and "pig-tight gates" of his rural letters seemed miles away from Broadway's promiscuous bustle and courtroom scandal, as did Idlewild's rekindled sentiments of place and family. In such hallowed precincts, ugly rumor came only as an unwelcome intruder.[3]

However, the warm glow of this idyll was not always proof against outsiders' attack. Tucked away at his country home, Willis might, as America's foremost convalescent, once again resolve to write himself into his readers' hearts. But in this new world of popular print he could scarcely keep others from contesting the genial domestic character he sought to embody. In this regard Willis labored, more than most, under a peculiar vulnerability dictated by the very terms of his success. As he himself had learned to great profit, gossip could be a golden commodity. Soon he would find out it could also be profoundly subversive—especially when couched in the authoritative idiom of domestic fiction.

A Sister Scorned

Before the 1850s, there is little reason to believe that Willis had ever contemplated the old misogynist chestnut "hell hath no fury like a woman scorned." Male jealousy and contempt certainly plagued him from the start. Yet the women in Willis's life—his faithful readers foremost among them—sustained him even while he was most beleaguered. It must then have been with some chagrin, even trepidation, that in the months following the Forrest trial their idol came to notice stirrings of discontent from the very quarters he might have thought most secure—and from a blood sister, no less.

In part, this unwelcome quickening reflected the culture of print's growing capacity to transform lives, as a survey of the Willis family fortunes will suggest. We are already acquainted with N. P.'s career, and that of his father. It is also worth recalling the work of the deacon's youngest son, Richard Storrs Willis, who capitalized on his musical training in Germany by editing New York's *Musical World and Times* in the early 1850s on the way to a long career publicizing the cause of classical and sacred music. (Today he is best remembered for composing the music to "It Came upon a Midnight Clear.") Notable among the Willis girls was N. P.'s spinster sister Julia, who busied herself by supplying her brother's *Home Journal* with anonymous book reviews and (according to at least one source) ghostediting her father's *Youth's Companion.* But it was Sara, N. P.'s youngest surviving sister, who was destined to make the greatest mark on her times. It was also this sister who, in the guise of the newspaper columnist "Fanny Fern," was to cause the Willis clan—and brother N. P. in particular—considerable distress by demonstrating, in no uncertain terms, print's spectacular potential for unmaking as well as making families.[4]

Understanding the extent to which this development both reflected and helped inflame the social and sexual hostilities that smoldered beneath the surface of sentimental literary culture requires further inquiry into Sara Willis's personal history. Like her eldest brother, she seems to have made her own way in the world—to the perennial frustration of those who would clip her wings. As a young girl, Sara's headstrong ebullience had once moved Nat himself to entreat her, in a verse entitled

"To My Wild Sis," to "be still, thou wayward girl." Deacon Willis, for his part, despaired of ever disciplining his daughter to her prescribed place in evangelical society. Even several years at Catharine Beecher's Hartford Female Seminary failed to break Sara's restive spirit: against stories of stolen pies and hair curled with leaves of a geometry text, the headmistress could report to the Willises only that "religious influence has greatly improved her character"; Lyman Beecher's eldest daughter held out little "confidence" in her student's "piety." Later developments would reveal this obstinacy as emblematic of a larger will to independence: like brother Nat, Sara resisted her father's crabbed faith till her dying day, and she joined the church only when maternal duty seemed to demand it.[5]

For a period of six years after leaving school, Sara Willis had continued to chafe at the domestic lot expected of her. Then love intervened, and she was married (quite happily, it seems) to an ambitious young bank cashier, "Handsome Charlie" Eldredge. Despite the day's prevailing economic doldrums, which ruined many a businessman, the Eldredges were evidently doing well enough by May 1838 to purchase a home in Brighton, outside Boston. With an eye toward the future of their growing family (three girls were eventually born into the fold), other investments followed, including participation in an ill-advised project to raise an imposing brick structure on Tremont Street—ultimately the home of the Boston Museum of Fine Arts. Then tragedy struck. Beginning in February 1844, Sara's youngest sister, mother, and eldest daughter all died in quick succession of various causes; brother N. P. lost his first wife in the same months as well. To heap calamity upon tragedy, typhoid fever claimed Charles Eldredge's life in October 1846, and legal troubles stemming from failed real estate speculations—having already forced the sale of the Brighton house—left his estate insolvent. Not surprisingly, Sara Willis Eldredge's comfortable world was shattered.[6]

As if unwilling to confront their financial predicament, the Eldredge family had been lodging at a resort hotel in Salem in the days before Charles's death; now there was no escaping cold reality. In this era of limited economic opportunities for women, the lack of an ample inheritance would have weighed heavily on any widow's prospects. Yet, when Sara threw herself and her surviving children on the goodwill of their relations, aid was granted only grudgingly. Over the years, Charles Eldredge's parents had evidently soured on their determined daughter-in-law, now perhaps even unconsciously blaming her for their son's unhappy fate. More important, neither family was keen to bankroll a daughter they apparently supposed guilty of improvidence or at least failure to temper a husband's speculative fever. To supplement her family's meager largesse, Sara Eldredge thus tried her hand at a series of humble occupations. But when, after several years of trying, nothing could keep her little family afloat, at her father's urging and apparently for the sake of her surviving children, she wed Samuel P. Farrington, a local merchant, widower, and Park Street communicant years her senior.[7]

The union was a disaster. Sara could never love her new husband, and she apparently told him so. He was intensely jealous—perhaps even to the point of threatening physical violence—and ultimately accused her of infidelity. After only two years of marriage, the Willises' "wayward girl" left her troubled home in January 1851 for the Marlboro Hotel and initiated divorce proceedings. A month later,

Farrington repudiated his estranged wife by newspaper card and quit Boston for parts west, ultimately resurfacing in Chicago two years hence to claim his own divorce on grounds of desertion. Meanwhile, distressed at the shameful conduct of their refractory "girl," the Willis and Eldredge families apparently kept her at arm's length. Disgraced in the eyes of the world and forsaken by her family, Sara's fortunes plummeted. Amidst ugly recriminations, deepening privation forced the distraught mother and her girls into ever seedier rooming houses. At rock bottom, Sara succumbed to the unthinkable and sent her eldest daughter to live with her first husband's parents, whom she had grown to despise. Such humiliation was a bitter pill.[8]

It was to escape such desperate straits that N. P. Willis's younger sister sent off her maiden contribution to the newspapers. As with so many women of her generation and class who were educated to an ornamental domesticity and denied gainful work, she considered this expedient the last resort of the distressed: as Sara herself would later put it, "no happy woman writes." Yet if women's writing was often a trade upon despair, by the 1850s it was not one without a future, as Susan Warner's fabulously popular best-seller *The Wide, Wide World* (1850) was then so dramatically demonstrating. Few authors attained such heights, but still the potential was there. Those who labored in the shadow of such giants could, with luck and talent, wrest a serviceable though precarious income from their exertions. In this regard, Sara Farrington was lucky: she had experience composing and editing for her father. She was talented, too, with a natural flair for the kind of discursive prose suited to newspaper paragraphing. Finally, her own late trials provided ample material to win the hearts of a popular audience. After several newspapers picked up her initial contribution to the press, two Boston-area family papers retained her services: the Reverend Thomas Norton's *Olive Branch* and (after November 1851) William Moulton's *The True Flag*. To disguise her frequent contributions, the unfortunate Mrs. Farrington assumed several pen names; only late in 1851 did she settle upon the nom de plume destined to make her fortune.[9]

In these dark days, any steady income was welcome; still, all the heartening acceptance at the *Olive Branch* could not change the fact that Sara's receipts (like those of so many of the day's fledgling women writers) remained pitifully small and hard-won. Yet again, she was—or appeared to be—lucky, for she had a famous and well-connected literary brother known for sponsoring female talent. If the two had seen little of each other in late years, still she had reason to count on his affections. In happier days, regard for her eldest brother's first wife had led Sara Eldredge to name her firstborn after the pleasant Englishwoman who had won his heart. And when the much lamented "English Mary" had died in childbirth, it was to the Eldredge home that the still-grieving husband had sent his motherless child while readying himself to embark on one last swing through Europe. More than this, Nat's "Wild Sis" seems always to have reserved a special place in her heart for the dashing elder brother of her youth. (Perhaps she is the one referred to in "Jephthah's Daughter," where the poet talks of having been "a sister's idol" who knows "how full / the heart may be of tenderness to her!") So it was that late in 1851 Samuel Farrington's estranged wife looked hopefully to the only well-placed man who had not previously deserted her, sending him samples of her work as well as entreaties for assistance. Surely her elder brother would do what he could.[10]

His reply came back as a bombshell: he would not help her. Complaining of an aching tooth, Willis begged off with the excuse that the *Home Journal* (as his sister would remember) paid no contributors whatsoever; as for New York's literary prospects, that was the "most overstocked market in the country." This contention was true enough, as probably was Willis's claim that he had "tried to find employment for dozens of starving writers, in vain." But his excuse merely prefaced deeper concerns: clearly, Willis doubted the entire advisability of his sister's plan. "Your writings show talent," he conceded in palliation, "but they are in a style that would only do in Boston. You overstrain the pathetic, and your humor runs into dreadful vulgarity sometimes." Nor was this the whole of it: "I am sorry that any editor knows that a sister of mine wrote some of these which you sent me," he lectured ungraciously. "In one or two cases they trench very close on indecency. For God's sake, keep clear of that." This being said, he imagined her only chance lay with the religious papers (which paid for a "certain easily acquired kind of writing"); in all other branches of literature, Willis predicted with monumental inaccuracy, "I see no chance for you—unless, indeed, you can get employed by the editors you write for already." No doubt this was chilly counsel but, he ventured, frank enough: "I would not keep you on a mistaken track." And so, with apologies for any curtness occasioned by his throbbing tooth, he closed hopefully as "Your affectionate brother."[11]

In some respects this reply was probably an honest (if mistaken) reflection on Sara Farrington's prospects. Historically, amateur literature had been, as her brother put it, a most "broken reed" to "lean upon for a livelihood," especially for one of his sister's literary temperament. No doubt, she did at times "overstrain the pathetic" (though in this age of sentimental affections that trait was no certain bar to success), and her tart, sometimes scandalous humor *was* ill calculated to please the genteel audience that had learned to treasure her brother's more measured literary talents. But it was the specter of indecent association, coming as it did at the height of his own legal trials, that probably most spooked the ultramontane Willis into the unkindness of his refusal. Already, Forrest's lackeys had beset Willis's honor (and, with it, his credibility) by advertising his younger brother's conviction for rape. Now, caught in a vortex of scandal, with skeletons from his closet emerging with maddening frequency, the cause of an abandoned, suspect, and disgraced sister must have been the last this embattled celebrity was eager to assume. In these circumstances, he could never puff Sara, as he had so many other deserving and not-so-deserving lady protégés, without risking the taint of her disrepute. Nor, strapped as he was by the expense of the Forrest business (in all, $2,000 by later reckoning), could he probably have employed her at the *Home Journal,* even had he wished. Whether he also felt diminished by her talents and scandalized by the prospect of his sister's parading herself before the public, as her most recent biographer has suggested, it is impossible to say.[12]

One thing is certain: Sara's shock at this repulse was immediate and intense, sparking resentment that burned like vitriol. There is today no record of any immediate reply. Years later, however, when Fanny Fern's papers came down to her descendants, her brother's peevish note appeared therein tagged with this pathetic indictment: "From Nathaniel Parker Willis when I applied for literary employment at the Home Journal office[,] being at the time quite destitute. *My* house having been his child's refuge for months after the death of his mother." So, too, was there a scorched copy of "To My Wild Sis," apparently cast into the fire in a fit of rage, only to be retrieved at the last moment when its sacrifice could not be borne. But these exhibits were posterity's testament. In all likelihood, N. P. Willis did not at the time realize the depth of pain he had caused his sister.[13]

Then a remarkable thing happened: her last hope rudely shattered, Sara Farrington dug grimly into her considerable reserves of determination and resolved to make it on her own. In truth, she had little choice otherwise. Happily, brother Nat was dreadfully wrong about at least one thing: her salability. From the start, Fanny Fern's tart humor, headlong prose, and sentimental pathos caught the public fancy. America's new middle-and working-class readers were particularly taken with her fervent defense of children and fearless, often satirical, interrogation of hypocrisy in high places. By the summer of 1852, she was a genuine hit. So impressed was one New York editor—Oliver Dyer of the *Musical World and Times*, the very same paper that employed Richard Willis—that he forthwith sent off to Boston to offer this "Fanny Fern" twice her present salary if she would agree to write exclusively for his paper. This was undoubtedly a delicate maneuver, as it involved snatching away the prize columnist of both the *Olive Branch* and the *True Flag*, but Dyer, who seems to have been a persuasive man, had considerable funds to back up his dramatic offer. After a trip to Boston, he also had remarkable news to tell his unsuspecting business partner: Fanny Fern was none other than Richard Willis's sister! Stunned though he was by the news, Richard warmed quickly to the idea of Fern's vocation, in marked contrast to his more famous elder brother.[14]

Under Dyer's stewardship, Fern steadily realized an even greater measure of her commercial promise. In December 1852, he released the *Musical World*'s star contributor from their exclusive agreement when her former editors grumblingly agreed to double her previous salary; now Fern was writing steadily for three papers. The following spring, Dyer helped steer her toward the publishing firm of Derby and Miller, which had offered liberal terms for the rights to her collected newspaper columns. The resulting *Fern Leaves from Fanny's Port-Folio* (1853) sold nearly 100,000 copies in its first year alone, a phenomenal figure for the time. This stunning success catapulted Fern to a celebrity rivaling even her famous brother's and—more importantly—remedied Sara Farrington's long-standing financial woes.[15]

To all the world, this meteoric triumph must have seemed the most remarkable of success stories. Appearing on the national scene just months earlier, Fanny Fern had stormed to the top of her profession with astonishing speed, doing her part to show why the 1850s was destined to prove the decade of so-called scribbling women. But her achievement was even more improbable than the general public then realized, for with penury almost literally driving her to write, the unfortunate Mrs. Farrington had resolutely forged a new independence from print's rewards when every patriarchal guarantee had failed her. In doing so, she found a voice tempered to express her grievances as well as her fancy—grievances, moreover, whose depth the world, and her family most of all, was just beginning to glimpse.

Calling Things by Their Right Names

It is, of course, impossible wholly to recover the complex play of emotions that *Fern Leaves*'s publication and swift success in June 1853 must have stirred in its author. Yet, all extant evidence suggests that the experience left her with a profound and heady new sense of empowerment. Buoyed by soaring prospects, Fern had already terminated her strained relationship with the *True Flag* several months earlier (evidently provoking its resentful editor, William Moulton, to vow revenge); now, emboldened by the first wave of hefty receipts from *Fern Leaves*, she cut ties with "bigoted" old Boston altogether, dispensing with the *Olive Branch* soon after removing to New York City in June 1853, accompanied by her youngest daughter. Within weeks, Fern would also reclaim her eldest child from the clutches of her recently widowed and much despised mother-in-law, but not before launching what was to prove a momentous experiment in fictional insurgency. Just as *Fern Leaves* was introducing a growing audience to the pleasures of its author's literary company, unspent rancor and the pangs of injustice drove her to escalate the unprecedented campaign of discursive reprisal she had long waged covertly against her offending relations, a campaign destined to culminate eighteen months later in the sensational issue of her first novel, *Ruth Hall* (1854). Though she could scarcely foresee it at the time, the unintended consequences of this initiative would demonstrate how profoundly subversive such fictive complaints could be in the new culture of celebrity.[16]

Central to Fern's literary campaign of redress was a faith in the efficacy of "calling things by their right names," a conviction shared with abolitionists and other social reformers that public witness to injustice (right naming) would move people to rectify that injustice (right action). This was no simple matter, in Fern's case or in any other. For one thing, embarkation upon her discursive initiative meant assuming the traditionally male prerogative of naming, as she had already appropriated the traditionally male occupation of author. To do so was thus to venture into perilous territory. Yet whatever her misgivings, Fern was evidently ready by the summer of 1853 to test the powers of her newfound authorial autonomy. Ironically, it would take the masquerade of fiction to deliver the full weight of her burdens.

In one crucial respect, masquerade had always lurked at the very heart of Fern's literary progress, for though she was generally forthright to a fault, there was at least one "right" name Sara Farrington had steadfastly shrunk from proclaiming: her own. Such penchants for disguise were common enough; many women of Fern's generation and class recoiled from the spectacle of parading themselves beyond their appointed sphere. Yet this writer's motives were clearly more immediate: Samuel Farrington's mortifying slanders and her own brazen independence had marked her for scandal, and it was both a professional requisite and a personal desideratum that the world be kept from linking the disgraced character of her failed second marriage to her present literary prospects. Consequently, the fledgling author clung fiercely to her pen name, binding knowing editors to secrecy and resisting all pressure to divulge her true identity to the world. At times, this determination verged on obsession. Even months after her darkest days, Fern agreed to reveal herself to her new publishers Derby and Miller only when there seemed no alternative ("I had much rather be shot than tell!" she fretted in February 1853), and then only by swearing them to absolute secrecy. Nonetheless, in time a newfound sense of independence allowed her to take distinct pleasure from disguise, especially when mounting curiosity sent the public scurrying fruitlessly after the key to her identity. Not long after the first flush of *Fern Leaves*'s success, for instance, its author delighted in telling readers how she had met an unsuspecting bookseller hawking her new volume. "Who wrote it?" she asked the lad. "Don't know," said he. "She's first this person, and then that: now a man, and then a woman; somebody says she's everybody, and everybody says she's *some*. Here's your *Fern Leaves*," she reported him saying, "forty thousand sold in sixty days."[17]

Confounding gender expectations was clearly a source of great delight for Fern. But nothing compared to the grim satisfaction she undoubtedly derived from the liberty disguise granted to rebuke those whom she believed had done her wrong. Like her famous brother, Fern drew almost exclusively from experience. And with cold shoulders and desperate penury plainly wounding her to the quick, she unburdened herself in cathartic torrents that left many a fugitive newspaper column laden with her own bitter history. Indeed, in her weekly columns she often changed little beyond names to disguise a contempt grown malignant. So it was that the father whom she blamed for pressing a disastrous second marriage on her, then stinting her at every turn, appears in several early newspaper sketches as a parsimonious hypocrite divine; the estranged husband is reproached for jealous conniving in another; and her famous elder brother is pilloried in several more—most egregiously in the *Musical World* itself, under the inimitable moniker "Apollo Hyacinth." Issued a mere fortnight after publication of *Fern Leaves* made its author the talk of the town, this last sketch would play a particularly decisive role in escalating Fern's familial insurgency.[18]

If nothing else, "Apollo Hyacinth" suggests precisely why Fern captured the popular imagination as she did, and why fiction was to prove such a potent weapon in her hand. At mordant character sketches, she arguably had no equal in her day; the task was often done with such consummate skill that her victims might be thought to have incriminated themselves. Consider, for instance, her modern-day Apollo, a self-styled connoisseur of the beautiful who appears as the walking repudiation of his own pet conceit that refined sensibilities are the keenest test of moral excellence: professing concern, he shuns responsibility; worshiping the codes of civility, he neglects their substance; worst of all for Fern, imposing upon affections, he spurns them when they threaten his social ambitions. "Let their good name be assailed," Fern warned those who might still cherish such a one, "let misfortune once overtake them, and his *moral excellence* compels him, at once, to ignore their existence, until they have been extricated from all their troubles, and it has become perfectly safe and *advantageous* for him to recover the acquaintance." Apollo Hyacinth is, in sum, the very kind of man who would abandon a blood sister in her distress—the very sort totally undeserving of the ill-gotten affection that so conspicuously surrounds him. Indeed, he is, in Fern's gendered lexicon of censure, no man at all. By assuming the prerogative of the male judgmental voice to rebuke her brother in this fashion, Fern had in effect administered the literary equivalent of Edwin Forrest's famous horsewhipping. No wonder certain critics had already taken to deploring what they saw as the "irreverent" and "masculine" edge of her columns.[19]

As Fern must have known, such pen portraits were nothing if not explosive. Readers might be expected to pass by the father and husband as of a type, but Sara Farrington's celebrated brother was a bona fide original, and widely recognized as such. Fern, moreover, had sketched him in such a memorable fashion (even to the point of travestying his extravagant diction) that readers were bound to catch the likeness and wonder at its author, especially as the unkind portrait appeared in his own brother's paper. If this were not enough to raise eyebrows, the pointed animadversions of "Apollo Hyacinth" followed hard on the first hints at Fern's true history since the *Musical World and Times* had informed its readers months earlier that she was a lady living "eight hours from New York." In late April 1853, its glowing review of the forthcoming *Fern Leaves* (perhaps penned by the obliging Oliver Dyer) disclosed the startling news that the book's real-life author had endured wrenching privation and familial neglect—on occasion even toiling well into the dawn to succor sick babes—before lately regaining the comfortable station to which she had been born. No doubt, this revelation was meant both to shock and to stir sympathy. But more than this, it now became possible for astute observers to conclude that Fern's trademark long-suffering widows and their dastardly persecutors sprang from a deeply personal sense of victimization at the hands of skinflint and sanctimonious relations. And with "Apollo Hyacinth" abroad upon the land, some readers undoubtedly began to put two and two together.[20]

This disturbing possibility was not lost on N. P. Willis. After he had dashed his sister's hopes, the two apparently lost all contact: preoccupied with his own financial troubles and failing health, Idlewild's famous convalescent had no time for her troubles, if indeed he ever realized their full extent. Sara's literary identity may even have remained a mystery to him until his brother Richard's epiphany in late 1852. From then on, the *Home Journal* added its refined voice to the swelling chorus of acclaim; in private, its convalescent editor could even be quite gracious with his praise: "Fanny Fern improves," he confided in Richard on one occasion. "She is eminently readable, and I rejoice in her having the Public by the Ear." That was before either the *Musical Times'* review of *Fern Leaves* or "Apollo Hyacinth" had registered with the public. Now, horrified that his brother would so foolishly lend credence to the picture of penury and neglect sketched (however covertly) of Sara's history, and disturbed at the possibilities this development posed for his own career, N. P. moved quickly to contain the damage. "I wish her success not only with all my heart, but with all my *pride*," he lectured Richard in a letter surviving from the incident, one saved out of what was evidently a more extensive exchange of family correspondence that included another sister, Lucy Willis Bumstead, as well. "The higher she rises, the more she honors us," N. P. continued. "But (my brother!) *we* were *not* honored by your publishing the account of her excessive poverty and starving babes, and nightwatchings, and desertions by friends, & c—*no word of which* (Lucy says) *was in the least true.* I, for one, contributed when money was blood-drops," Willis complained angrily, "& when creditors (as now) were screwing *sops* out of my very vitals. *You* help'd her. *Lucy* took care that her children never suffer'd. Father did something—did he not?" The *Home Journal* would praise Fern where praise was due. But, N. P. entreated his brother, "let us not be thus *gammon'd* out of our respectability as relations, by false pictures authenticated by being given to the world under our own hand and seal."[21]

In N. P.'s case, there was special reason for this concern: as he reminded Richard, of all the members of the family his "more conspicuous name and fame" was most susceptible to the conditions of Sara's new celebrity. This disability was particularly pointed in light of N. P.'s reputation as a protector of women. He could, therefore, scarcely have been pleased that reports of Fern's "excessive poverty & starving babes, & night watchings, and desertions by friends & c" had been followed soon after by the damning (and thinly veiled) sketch of himself as "Apollo Hyacinth." But Willis was in a ticklish position. Now that his sister had hold of the public's ear (a steamboat had in fact just been named in her honor) and her whisper campaign of insidious pathos was well under way, she could scarcely be silenced without broadcasting a family quarrel he was determined to squelch. Evidence suggests that, in his distraction, N. P. may have asked his sister Lucy to dissuade Fern from her course, to no avail, and he almost certainly forbade his subeditor James Parton from further publicizing the most damaging of Fern's stories—a demand that probably led to Parton's precipitous resignation in favor of the woman whom this future dean of popular biographers would marry three years hence. Yet partly because of N. P.'s own cherished status as womankind's special protector, he could do little more to keep Fern from emulating the advice she had given only weeks before to victims abandoned by their relations: "get your head above water, and then *snap your fingers in their pharisaical faces!*" From the look of things, she was certainly getting the hang of that trick and, even more ominous, showing signs of becoming cavalier with her anonymity. In August 1853, for instance, her readers were asked cheekily just what *did* people do before the advent of newspapers to answer such pressing questions as "whether Fanny Fiddlestick was Napthali Wilkin's sister?" The old fear of exposure seemed to be fading fast.[22]

By the summer of 1853, Fern's newfound independence was thus revealing itself in remarkable ways, and newspaper tales of hers such as "Are There Any Men among Us?" (wherein the moral weakness of "milk-and-water husbands and relations" forces a wrongly defamed woman to unsex herself by shooting the offending male gossip in the throat) suggest just where that independence was taking her. But to this juncture, anonymity and the intermittent issue of her most pointed tales had blunted the impact of Fern's familial revolt. Soon, skyrocketing celebrity would enable her to see what more concentrated effort might accomplish. In February 1854 the Mason Brothers of New York (Oliver Dyer's new associates and the sons of Park Street's onetime choir director) engaged the now-celebrated columnist to write a first novel, published ten months hence as *Ruth Hall.* Advertised as a "domestic tale of the present time," it proved to be the most transparent of autobiographical fictions: a heartbreaking rendition of the trials and tribulations that fate and betrayal had forced its author to endure on the way to triumphal success. In great part because of the way it divulged (and concealed) its burdens, this novel would test the capacity of Fern's fictive complaint to redress real-life injustices as nothing had before.[23]

Like many of Fern's newspaper columns, *Ruth Hall* was no idle trifle designed solely to make money—though it would certainly do that. Instead, it aimed at nothing less than the complete mortification and overthrow of those who had grievously hurt or offended her. It was, in other words, a "snap of the fingers" of prodigious proportions. Given Fern's bitter resentments, as well as the signal celebrity of some of her relations, it is not surprising that this concatenation of bile and autobiography worked on several levels. Like much of her writing, its composition may have been therapeutic: neglect and disregard clearly cut deeply, and the chance to tell her story (albeit cloaked by fiction) must have been remarkably cathartic. Beyond this, the luxury of extended composition gave Fern a rare opportunity to spin credible and peremptory testimony to the cruel hypocrisy of kinfolk who professed to value familial ties above all. Redolent of hard luck and domestic troubles, her life already resonated with the strongest myths of the day; cast as a sentimental melodrama wherein she figured as both long-suffering victim and triumphant avenger, it offered unparalleled opportunity to express her complaint. By taking her own story upon the hustings of domestic fiction, while at the same time suppressing elements of her experience calculated to spoil the effect (such as the unsavory associations of her unhappy second marriage), Fern crafted her life to appeal to readers' sympathies in an extremely powerful way.

But the novel was not entirely self-serving: like the most ambitious of sentimental fictions, *Ruth Hall* implored its readers to turn right feeling into right action on a stage beyond the merely personal—in this case, to repudiate reigning male prerogatives (and perhaps even the prevailing gender system itself) that permitted hapless widows and their helpless children to slip through the cracks of patriarchal protection. While trying men first on scales of traditional male responsibility, Fern thus also advanced toward the more overtly feminist stance she would later assume in her newspaper columns. As always, however, her feminism was profoundly and desperately bound up with the personal. For one thing, given the novel's dynamics, her public's change of heart could happen only if sympathies long extended to her famous brother (and to a lesser extent, to her father) were transferred to Fern herself. In this sense, *Ruth Hall* was, finally, a revealing record of desire: the imaginative fulfillment of its author's profound wish to supplant her family in the theater of public affections, coupled with the projection of her fervent hope to quit past troubles for a sunnier independence.[24]

In writing her novel, it might thus be said that, in both a figurative and fundamental sense, Fern married manful assertion to womanly fortitude. On one level, her melodramatic tale follows the struggles and triumphs of "Ruth Hall" quite literally: the joy of ideal marriage; the sorrow of widowhood; the cruel hypocrisy of scheming relations; the depths of despair; and, finally, the sweet triumph of success. Yet the book's familiar progression can also be read as an altogether more subversive allegory of a woman's travels toward what Fern called the "Port of Independence." Ruth begins as a sentimental victim, but with a difference: her identity, echoing the fortitude of her Old Testament namesake, marks her as extraordinary. Perhaps most important, like Ruth of old, Fern's heroine is transformed by hard experience into a new woman, uniting the best of both sexes. Touched by adversity, Ruth Hall understands compassion for the lowliest sufferer. Yet like the true man the novel's inquisitive fans are made to detect in her literary persona, she also has "courage" enough "to call things by their right names."[25]

One "right name" Fern clearly intended to trumpet loudly was her famous brother's; he is, in fact, the linchpin in the tangled scheme of redress, reform, and revenge that is *Ruth Hall.* In the guise of the *Irving Magazine's* effeminate, lickspittle editor "Hyacinth Ellet" (a pointed echo of "Apollo Hyacinth"), Willis pales beside his alter ego's kid sister Ruth. She is faithful and forthright; he is feckless and fulsome. She is eminently worthy of sympathy and respect; he, of nothing but disdain. Never is this unflattering contrast clearer than in Hyacinth's self-serving dealings with Ruth: he spurns her when she is down and recognizes her only when it suits his ambitions, even as he schemes at every turn to run down her celebrity. In this regard, Fern's novel is as much a ringing denunciation of her brother's way of doing business and living life as a celebration of her own triumph against adversity.

Yet *Ruth Hall* also exhibits the extent to which that selfsame brother had alienated the affections of a sister who claims to have been prepared to cherish him as did so many women of her day. N. P.'s spirit haunts the novel with a kind of pathetic vengeance, ofttimes displacing even the professed objects of Fern's affection. In the opening scene, for instance, it is Hyacinth, not her faultless fiancé, whom Ruth recalls wistfully on the eve of her wedding—the same brother who once called her "awkward" and "very plain," who ignored her girlish attentions, and who visited her at school with a hopelessly self-absorbed "kiss me if you insist on it, Ruth, but for heaven's sake, don't tumble my dickey"; the same brother, nonetheless, whom she admits to having loved "just as well as if he were worth loving." Born, like the author, into a household shrouded in emotive restraint and orthodox pieties, Ruth longs for unfettered affection; Hyacinth, for all his foppery, is her special idol. Perhaps he, too, like Ruth, "thrilled" at the "sweet strain of music" or "a fine passage in a poem" when all about was solemn; perhaps he, too, shared a sense of what Fern calls her "twin-soul." Nor should we conclude that such romantic musings were necessarily mere adolescent fancies: even these many years past her youth, Fern could still disclose to her readers (and perhaps to herself as well) that Ruth wished her brother "would love her a little."[26]

In the novel (as in real life), intolerable rejection changes all that. "I have looked over the pieces you sent me, Ruth," Hyacinth is made to reply to his sister's request for employ, in words retouched from the original to radiate even greater malignancy than was perhaps intended:

> It is very evident that writing never can be your forté; you have no talent that way. You may possibly be employed by some inferior newspapers, but be assured your articles never will be heard of out of your own little provincial city. For myself, I have plenty of contributors, nor do I know of any of my literary acquaintances who would employ you. I advise you, therefore, to seek some *unobtrusive* employment.

At this heartless rebuff, Ruth boils; the novel's long and triumphal denouement is, in some sense, this fury spent. "No talent!" Ruth shrieks at the indignity; she would show Hyacinth. Enacting the melodrama of endeavor that circumstance and temperament has made of her life, Fern steels her heroine for the arduous literary labor ahead: "I *can* do it, I *feel* it, I *will* do it. . . . *Hyacinth shall yet be proud to claim his sister.*" Proud and (it might be added) mortified, as well.[27]

We might ask ourselves how anyone could conceive that such a book as Fern had been driven to write might make her brother proud. Yet, by a kind of tortured logic, she could have intended the novel to do just that. Having failed to elicit his assistance—and his esteem—in her moment of need, she now moved to exact satisfaction by impressing him in the only forum he could not ignore: the theater of public affections. And what better way to demonstrate her worth than to eclipse her brother's literary achievements with a prodigious flourish? As part of Fern's campaign to see herself installed in the hearts and minds of Americans, an impressive sale could confirm her at the top of her field, a popular phenomenon even in this dawning age of best-sellers. Widespread sympathy, moreover, might also spell an end to her family's pretensions to respectability, even as it cemented their "wayward girl's" return from the degrading embarrassment of having fallen so low in the world's estimation. In this sense, the screaming italics of the novel's crisis scene merely proclaimed what was manifest throughout: Fanny Fern itched to top her famous brother at his own game, and *Ruth Hall* itself was her trump card. With it she aimed to raise up one celebrity on the moral ruin of another.[28]

Considerable evidence suggests that Fern was telegraphing this desire all along. As "Ruth," she had already staked out a new identity as an independent woman, but was this enough? Did she wish to assume—if only figuratively—her brother's name as well? Perhaps so. In the novel (if not, as we shall see, in real life), Ruth successfully conceals her identity from the public with the pen name "Floy," a feminized echo of N. P. Willis's own early incognito. Soon letters are deluging this "Floy," begging autographs, expressing admiration, even proposing marriage, with each one faithfully reproduced for Fern's readers in a flood calculated to swamp the real-life idolatry that had once engulfed the young "Roy" and still on occasion beset him to that day. If Fern was savvy and self-possessed enough to discount nine-tenths of this outpouring, still, such tokens of fame had their value. Most important, Ruth's fictive (but presumably genuine) testimonials served both to establish and proclaim Fern's popularity in the most public of forums.[29]

With *Ruth Hall,* Fanny Fern thus aimed simultaneously to rehearse and enact the rupture of the sentimental congress that had long sustained her brother's literary fortunes. Yet, her triumph would be incomplete without displaying evidence of the fraternal regard for which she apparently deeply longed. Significantly, such sympathies are awakened in the novel not by some new husband (the first, Fern is at pains to show, was too saintly for succession, and of a second—the despised Farrington—there is no mention), but by a brother-editor who is ever anxious to celebrate and promote her genius. Knowing journalists as she did, Fern had long been unsparingly critical of that trade. The editors in *Fern Leaves* are, for example, all layabouts, scoundrels, and backbiters, poaching off the talents of their assistants and contributors.

This was not so in *Ruth Hall,* however. Balancing the savage caricatures of brother, father, and Fern's ingrate former editors at the *Olive Branch* and the *True Flag* are Horace Gates, long-suffering subeditor at Hyacinth's *Irving Magazine,* and

John Walter of the *Household Messenger.* Tellingly, these last two characters are the only ones who, like Ruth, are man enough to call things by their right names. In the novel, Gates—like his model, Fern's future husband, James Parton—trumpets Ruth's talents and exposes Hyacinth for the shallow and mendacious manipulator that he is. Walter does more. He alone among Ruth's readers sees the "bitter life experience" in her fiction; "it is a wail from her inmost soul," he soliloquizes at one point. More than this, he is prepared, as no other person is, to encourage Ruth in the manner best calculated to touch her heart. In stark contrast to Hyacinth (and by extension his real-life model, N. P. Willis), Walter celebrates Ruth's genius and tirelessly, selflessly, and faithfully works to promote it. His reward is most precious: to him alone "Floy" reveals her true identity, pouring out her "long pent-up feelings" as if Walter were the brother she had never truly had—the "real, warm-hearted, brotherly brother" long denied her. In this sense, the novel is a heartfelt tribute to the trust and affection the real-life Walter (Oliver Dyer) had reawakened in Fern after so much betrayal, succor gratefully acknowledged previously by dedication of the second series of *Fern Leaves* (1854). It is, as well, the final ouster of one brother of the flesh by another of the heart.[30]

With *Ruth Hall,* Fern had decisively cast off the once-beloved brother of her girlish imagination. How this familial ouster would play in public remained to be seen.

The Trouble with Fiction

Ruth Hall concludes with a dream of desire so strikingly American that it hurts. After every indignity, the long years of selfless trial distribute their just rewards, not least to Ruth herself. Following a hairsbreadth escape from the nightmare of a tenement fire, Fern's heroine is delivered into a more lasting security by the arrival of Mr. Walter with a package. It is, he announces, the stock certificate her literary genius has earned, all $10,000 of it a substantial guarantee of the independence previously withheld by fate and rancor. In *Ruth Hall,* money really does buy peace of mind, especially when abetted by a reverie of sentimental reunion. Accompanied by her new brother of the heart, Ruth is last seen conveying her daughters to their father's grave one final time before leaving "this part of the country" to rendezvous with her future. Predictably, old memories press upon her, meaningful glances are exchanged, and when a lark trills upon the little company's leave-taking, Walter commends the providence to his sister-companion: "Accept the omen, dear Ruth. . . . Life has much of harmony yet in store for you." And so Fanny Fern hopefully wrapped up her bitter broadside with a sweet prayer of mutual sympathy secured by the comfort of money in the bank.[31]

It was a bit naive to think that this moment of fictional bliss could hold in real life. The part about riches does not necessarily count: that promise had already been redeemed to some extent. But the dream of platonic brotherly accord would soon seem an extravagant fancy. The long-awaited publication of *Ruth Hall* in December 1854 (postponed several days by its publishers to accommodate the expected demand) thrust Fern's private exorcism into a new sphere. Quickly, reviewer after reviewer saw through the thin veil of fiction to the autobiography below; good manners alone kept many of the rest from authenticating the discovery at once. So it was that, after all the coyness, the real-life Fern emerged to face her public and her domestic enemies, a situation whose upshot was destined to prove far from the harmonious dream projected in her fiction. Calling on sentimental polemics was one thing; commanding them was quite another.[32]

Despite subsequent disclaimers tendered by Fern's advocates, it is hard to believe that *Ruth Hall*'s author had no inkling of what she was doing—and not only because mortifying her relations (N. P. in particular) required public recognition of family ties. As noted, the novel almost begged to be read as a transparent record of her life. Yet there is a simpler measure of her designs: by the time of *Ruth Hall*'s issue, many clued in to the literary scene (especially around Boston) already knew precisely who Fanny Fern was—and they could guess why she wrote with such fire. Repeating a by-then-familiar ritual of literary celebrity, rapid sales of *Fern Leaves* had escalated the inevitable round of speculation upon its author's identity—until publication of "Apollo Hyacinth" some had even suggested brother Nat was behind the Fern phenomenon. Soon afterward, at least a few were hitting on the truth. A full fifteen months before the release of *Ruth Hall*, the hypermasculine *Democratic Review* was sure enough in its contempt of what it called Fern's literary "humbug" to sneer that "she *is* said to be N. P. Willis's sister," gossip that echoed in London's *Athenaeum* in October 1853. Six months later, rumor had become common knowledge, at least in Fern's home city. The *New York Tribune* might still proclaim the futility of conjecture, but the remarkably casual reference in the *Boston Transcript* to Deacon Willis's three celebrated children—N. P., Richard Storrs, and "Mrs. Farrington (Fanny Fern)"—suggests how common such knowledge was. It was all the more so when the *Home Journal* reprinted the notice for its far-flung readership in April 1854. Some months earlier, in fact, an autograph hunter had sent to N. P. Willis for both his and Fern's signatures; having satisfied half the man's request, Willis had forwarded the solicitation to his now-famous sister. It should not surprise us, then, that even one of the earliest of *Ruth Hall*'s reviewers could report without blinking an eye that " 'Fanny Fern' is well known to be the sister of N. P. Willis, who, on being left a penniless widow, is said to have been neglected by her brother and other relatives." Nor should it surprise us to conclude that Fern herself knew exactly what she was doing when she contracted with Mason Brothers to furnish a manuscript. With this in mind, *Ruth Hall* can only be called a calculated gamble designed to court sympathy and promote outrage at the threat of inviting potentially disruptive inquiry into its author's own private affairs.[33]

Above all, it was this willful calculation that allowed Fern's publishers to crow so confidently that her novel was destined for "sensation." They were not taking any chances, though. Calling upon the machinery of literary celebrity developed in recent years, the Mason Brothers very ably set about orchestrating their spectacular "sensation" with a massive newspaper campaign. This blitz featured the usual pastiche of congratulatory puffs, spiced with the suggestive promise that *Ruth Hall* would "enlist the sympathy of every American" to a "reform which has no enemies." But Fern's publishers need hardly have bestirred themselves: the novel's domestic polemics were its own best advertisement. The portrait of Hyacinth alone was calculated to set tongues wagging. Much of this situation was due to Fern's wicked talent for playing to the prepossessions of a public fed upon a diet of backstairs gossip and literary backbiting—the sordid side of celebrity. Little of what she essayed to divulge had not already been at least rumored before. But here it was, brazen as brass beneath the thin gilding of fiction, authenticated by none other than Hyacinth Ellet's flesh-and-blood sister. Who in fact had not already heard him called, as Ruth's father-in-law did, "a mincing, conceited, tip-toeing, be-curled, be-perfumed popinjay?" And where had it not been whispered that N. P. Willis had married women for their fortunes and squandered his money on "distressed actresses?" Public response to this scandal-mongering was predictable. Just one week after *Ruth Hall's* release, a Boston correspondent reported that Fern's new book "is so deliciously personal, *so jolly malignant*, and the characters hit hardest are so well known here, that everybody has a copy." Celebrity thus carried the seeds of its demise. "Where a man as eminent in fashionable society as N. P. Willis is the overturned idol," another onlooker remarked, "there must be many thousands to gather around and witness the iconoclasm."[34]

Fern probably enjoyed the uproar at first. As predicted, the book was selling phenomenally well—some 70,000 copies, ultimately—a flood to swamp her brother's recent sales and mark her return from the shame of having sunk so low in the world's estimation. Then, too, there was delicious irony in the spectacle of N. P.'s considerable celebrity, once refused a downtrodden sister, now involuntarily enlisted in effecting its own overthrow and her vindication simultaneously. Months of hints and innuendo had already accustomed Fern's readers to sympathize with her past estate. Now with *Ruth Hall's* publication, the burden of persistent rumor found compelling corroboration in the novel's affecting vignettes of privation and injustice. As a woman, she may have had an advantage in this regard: at the time, female writers were widely regarded as more likely than men to write from the heart. John Hart, for instance, had only recently observed in *Female Prose Writers of America* (1852) that women's "own likes and dislikes, their feelings, opinions, taste, and sympathies are so mixed up with those of their subject, that the interest of the readers is often enlisted quite as much for the writer, as for the hero, of a tale." The response to *Ruth Hall* was also testament to the sway of its author's sentimental aesthetics, and that of the sentimental mode generally. As Fern must have hoped, those who recognized truth's hand in the tale rushed to confirm her as the blameless and suffering widow she and her publishers had made her out to be. The "conservative and high-toned" *Philadelphia North American*—so called by Mason Brothers in their gleeful advertisement of its review—spoke for many when it read sober truth in the author's emotional artistry: "No one but a mother who has loved and suffered could write as she does of children. No one but a sister who has borne wrong and contumely at the hand of a brother could write as she does of Hyacinth." Across the nation of readers, small-town editors and concerned citizens alike echoed similar sentiments. Here was the sympathetic response for which Sara had long prayed—and prepared.[35]

With the aura of verisimilitude thus seeming to confirm the novel's essential truth, N. P. could do little to stay the scandal unleashed by his sister's subversive fictions. Given his long public history as womanhood's would-be defender, it would scarcely do to take her down too strongly. Even if he could prove Fern's claims to penury exaggerated and her venom misguided, the shame of a family row would still reflect badly on all involved. And if he spoke out against her character as a wronged woman, he might only be inviting observers to conclude that she had indeed struck home, confirming the moral burden of her novel. In this respect, the fictional projection of Fern's victimage served to stay the hand of the brother who had once hurt her so.

Nonetheless, the *Home Journal*'s chief was not without recourse. By introducing domestic quarrels into public consideration, Fern had, in fact, laid herself open to several criticisms, especially ones concerning the indelicacy of a woman even broaching such matters in a public place. Then, too, if she raised the specter of filial negligence to her brother's discredit, he could at least protest his rectitude. As luck would have it, another familial tragedy soon gave him his chance. After fire ravaged his father's office, Willis was quick to respond with a filiopietistic verse addressed "To My Aged Father" and published in several papers with ties to the *Home Journal*. Even where his fellow editors demurred from noting it, the contrast between dutiful son and parricidal daughter was clear. At this point, Richard Willis also seems to have closed ranks: though he had formerly allowed his sister the forum of the *Musical World*, advertisements for *Ruth Hall* were as conspicuously absent from his paper as the signal inclusion of his elder brother's filiopiety was conspicuously apparent. One domestic apostate was evidently enough for the Willis family.[36]

When it came to his faithful readers at the *Home Journal*, N. P. had to content himself with a show of philosophical resignation intended to express regret without admitting culpability. "We outline, with a certain sadness of affection, the path we can never re-travel," he confided in a New Year's message intended, among other things, to limit further trespass upon his private life. "Much of that retrospect is for our own eyes only. None but ourselves can see the by-paths doubted, the steeps hard-climbed, the lures rejected, the gulf avoided." But this he could declare: "*The Home Journal has not willingly or knowingly given pain to any one.* Answers to the malignity and injustice which are never without new shapes, have been sometimes difficult to forbear—but we have forborne them." At least outwardly they did, for this rueful avowal was accompanied by a more enigmatic statement printed only a page away: an excerpt from Willis's old play "Tortesa, the Usurer." It was common enough for the *Home Journal* to contain such samplings from its editor's oeuvre, but this passage is so incongruous at first glance that it could only have been intended for Fanny Fern. Where many readers probably turned away puzzled, Willis's "Wild Sis" was surely meant to see herself in Zippa, the glover's daughter whose sisterly love for Angelo, the "poor but gifted painter," is finally disabused by a jarring epiphany. "I see! I see!" Zippa wails in words that, now recalled, may have been meant to rebuke Ruth's plea for Hyacinth to "love her a little." "His *soul* was never mine! . . . No! No! he never loved me!"[37]

By themselves, such half measures promised only limited satisfaction. For one, they addressed neither Fern's damning allegations nor her manifold motivations. In this sense, Willis's wistful regrets probably resonated among readers far less than, say, his chivalric retort to Edwin Forrest's "kitchen testimony." Still, the comparison is not entirely uninstructive. As they had during that recent ordeal, the fortunes of celebrity rested as much upon prevailing ideological prejudices, especially those surrounding the state of gender relations, as on any intended design. In this respect, the *Ruth Hall* episode resembled nothing so much as yet another trial of honor, this time played out on the plain of Romantic fiction, with scandal and titillation the chosen weapons. One thing was certainly clear: the world that received *Ruth Hall* was neither the perfect universe of spontaneous sympathies Fern had projected on her novel nor her brother's ideal congress of refined hearts, but something altogether more intractable.

The extent of this refractory condition becomes clearer with further inquiry into the dynamics of *Ruth Hall*'s reception. As we have seen, Fern crafted her novel to evoke compassion as well as outrage; plenty of each ensued. But however compelling *Ruth Hall* may have been as a record of a good woman wronged, its most affecting scenes of woe proved insufficient to the task of displacing the loyalties of Willis's most zealous fans. Some were unwilling even to credit the novel, let alone countenance its slurs.

One such devotee of N. P.'s was "Annie" Richmond, a Massachusetts housewife with a passionate fondness for books and their authors. Shortly before his untimely death in 1849, she had carried on a brief affair with Edgar Allan Poe, whom she had met during one of his lecture tours. Yet Richmond's coincident idolatry of Poe's perennial defender and former boss arose wholly through the offices of print, and it was no less fervent for want of face-to-face acquaintance. "You know," she once told Poe's mother-in-law (whom she called "Muddie"), "I longed to see Mr Willis more than any other human being—how dear Eddie used to laugh at me, & tell me I was only *one of a thousand* who were in love with him." In this respect, Richmond's regard could only have been strengthened by the kind and steadfast support Willis had lent to her beloved and often beleaguered "Eddie." No wonder news of *Ruth Hall* drove her to distraction. "Oh Muddie, dear Muddie," Annie wrote plaintively upon hearing of the novel's issue:

> How I do pity Mr Willis, & I am sure, I *love* him more than ever—oh how I wish I were his *sister*, and I would love him, *so dearly* that he would forget, all the unkindness of her, who does not deserve the name—"Ruth Hall" I have not read, *nor do I intend to*, since I find it abuses one of my *idols*[.] . . . Would it were in my power to do *something* to atone for that *woman's* (for I will not call her by the sacred name of *sister*) unkindness not to say *cruelty*—I cannot bear, that he who has ever touched the most sacred & the deepest recesses of *my heart*, should have *his* torn & lacerated, & I not allowed to do *something* for him—I do, *pray for him*, & pray Heaven to send him comfort, & to surround him with gentle & loving spirits, such as he knows *so well*, how to appreciate & enjoy.

Annie's heart clearly had room enough for only one victim of outrage, and no taletelling adventuress was going to displace the beloved convalescent of *her* print-inspired dreams.

> I hope dear Muddie when you see [Willis], you will do all you can, to cheer him, & make him forget his sorrows—I am so fearful, this schock [*sic*] will kill him, he is so feeble & has so little strength just now[;] oh *then*, (when she finds she has brought

him to an early grave), will she not repent in dust & ashes!—God pity her, for she will have to suffer yet, more than she has ever done before—Don[']t you think so?[38]

Richmond's partisanship was an extreme case, but it does suggest how sentimental loyalties founded in print might upset the best laid of sentimental insurgencies. Though Annie responded to the spectacle of unwarranted abuse as might any good sentimentalist—with prayers, pity, compassion, and a resolve to assume another's suffering—she blanched at Fern's claim to victimization and sisterly presumption, chiefly because no true sister would stoop so low. In the end, Annie's loyalties to the "great poetry man" were stronger than any outrageous fiction might hope to sunder.

Though few harkened to N. P.'s side with as much fervor as Annie, her distaste for *Ruth Hall*'s bitter familial politics was hardly singular. Many weighty reviews and popular journals condemned the novel and its author outright, even as they admitted that the book would sell tremendously. Ever decorous, *Godey*'s refused even to review it. Other pillars of literary correctness—from the *New York Times* to the *Southern Quarterly Review*—pronounced it common, mean-spirited, and not a little dangerous. Even admirers of Fern's style and conviction blanched at her umbrage. After praising the novel's striking and affecting intensity, the *Tribune*'s reviewer was reduced to a hopeful (if scarcely convincing) proverbial allusion to the effect that "domestic misunderstandings . . . are ill brought out of doors, and seldom affect the opinion of the public in regard to the parties concerned."[39]

Nothing could have been farther from the truth: *Ruth Hall*'s "personalities" had everything to do with the dynamics of its reception. Like the spectacle of the Forrest trial, Fern's novel had drawn her brother into a public quarrel and thus, if nothing else, forced the world to take sides. This in itself was a considerable achievement for someone once discounted by gender conventions generally and N. P. Willis in particular, and it suggests the kind of emotional and social rewards fictive complaint could offer to women and other marginalized Americans. Yet Fern's use of her novel was hardly an unmitigated triumph. In an age ill at ease with, if not outright hostile toward, outspoken women, few observers were willing to excuse Fern's venom unless it arose from authentic and self-denying suffering. And much in her bitter life portrait suggested truth's distortion as much as its epitome.

First, there was the matter of characterization. Even among those enamored of melodramatic contrasts, moral monsters such as Hyacinth and Old Man Ellet seemed to many the impossible exaggerations of a diseased and overwrought fancy, as unlikely as the remorseless nobility of Ruth herself. Others found all too much relish in the evisceration of Nat Willis's celebrity to accept the spotless character Fern had assumed for herself. This suspicion was partly a function of the narrative strategy she chose to employ: having invoked the pathetic assumptions of sentimental fiction, Fern could not overstep its bounds without undermining the powerful compassion it could evoke. Public displeasure also drew strength from reigning gender assumptions: on the field of honor, a lady could see her persecutors horsewhipped, but she must not seem to relish the spectacle. Because Fern so obviously did enjoy it, she must be, prima facie, no lady at all. In time, this very judgment became a common refrain in the press and in parlors across the nation.

And it had significant consequences, not least, the forfeiture of a lady's immunities from direct public assault. As the *New York Times* remarked in its chiding review, "FANNY FERN has a sharp pen. Being abundantly competent to take care of herself, we feel no disposition to apologize."[40]

But while it is true that many reviewers ignored or discounted the burden of Fern's denunciations (both personal and social) to blast her gender transgressions, we must not conclude that sexist anxiety alone explains the storm of criticism that greeted *Ruth Hall.* In fact, it was as much how and where Fern unburdened herself as what she chose to say that eventually ranged so many against her. In particular, those polite souls who hoped to reserve the province of fiction for generic (and thus, transcendent) truths found the spectacle of print given over to domestic quarrels profoundly disturbing, even nightmarish in its threat to privacy and propriety. In this regard, it hardly mattered which sex sinned against good taste. Had Fern's famous brother taxed the public with his own jaundiced tales of familial injustice, no doubt he too would have been roundly condemned for abusing authorial privilege. In his case, however, the thrust of censure would probably have assumed a shape tailored to his sex, as it had with the cries of "puppyism" that greeted the social transgressions of *Pencillings by the Way.*[41]

An exchange in the feminist press makes this point clear. Reviewing *Ruth Hall* for the *Una* in February 1855, Elizabeth Cady Stanton lauded Fern's novel for its fearless witness to patriarchal abuse—calling it as worthy and credible a record of oppression as any ex-slave's narrative, and thus as righteous an endeavor as these bold exercises in true naming. For this reason, above all, she had rebuked her male compatriots at the *Anti-Slavery Standard* for their chiding review of Fern's proto-feminist manifesto. "This is but a beginning, gentlemen," Stanton warned the world portentously—no more mealy-mouthed sentimentality from the pens of long-suffering Woman, but the long-awaited real story of gender injustice. Under the circumstances, this feminist reading is not surprising: Stanton was especially ready to believe women in the battle of the sexes, and Fern's heartrending denunciation appealed to those who yearned to witness against male cruelty and injustice.[42]

Yet dissent arose even in the ranks of true believers. Only a month after this literary summons to arms, the *Una*'s associate editor Caroline Healey Dall respectfully demurred from her friend. "It is not because she is a *woman*," Dall insisted firmly, "but because she is a human being, that Fanny Fern has been so severely censured." To Dall, *Ruth Hall* seemed no credible autobiography at all, but rather a jaundiced version of events primarily reflecting its author's emotional turmoil. Proper Bostonians familiar with Fern's previous history would understand. Like her "far more gifted brother," she was, as Dall saw it, incapable of leading a "consistent life." And having bewildered her friends and provoked her kinfolk, if not actually having committed any "real sin," Fern now confounded an ideal self with the history of her troubles. In doing so, she served neither truth nor comity, nor, it seemed, the women's rights movement that Dall was coming to support. In this stance, the *Una*'s editor did not wish to be mistaken: "Let no one think us indifferent to her sufferings; we feel for them deeply; but Heaven shield the cause from making a reformer, conscious or unconscious, out of a Fanny Fern."[43]

Dall's comparison of N. P. and Sara Willis is instructive: like her brother, Sara projected her character upon the public conscience; also like him, she experienced the maddening appropriations that marked the new culture of celebrity. Such appropriations were, in fact, to be even more extensive than Sara Willis might have imagined. Fern's relations were not the only degenerates she had denounced; *Ruth Hall*'s "Mr. Tibbetts" (her old editor at the *True Flag*, William Moulton) came in for his share of abuse, and he had it within his power to revenge himself on this strong-willed woman who had first wangled higher wages from him, then left him for a better deal. Through the early weeks of January 1855, the *True Flag* blew Fern's remaining cover wide open by publishing an authoritative "key" to *Ruth Hall* and promising to reveal more: how her claims to penury were so much poppycock and why she had failed to disclose the marriage to Farrington in her autobiographical novel. Armed with this volatile information, Moulton was prepared, as N. P. Willis was not (at least not publicly), to claim that he alone knew the "real" Fanny Fern. And it was not long before Moulton had moved decisively to unmask his former contributor with a self-styled "authorized" biography featuring early "Fern Leaves" drawn from his files, on-the-spot "interviews," and the so-called true story of her divorce and onetime financial circumstances. Clearly, (at least) two could play at this game of subversive lives.[44]

If nothing else, the release of Moulton's *Life and Beauties of Fanny Fern* in 1855 hopelessly complicated the task of identifying the *real* Fanny Fern—or the *real* N. P. Willis, either. To the charges of filial negligence, willful exaggeration, and poor taste leveled against the real-life "Ruth Hall," Fern's critics could now add malicious prevarication, for beneath her pose of artless Romantic sincerity, readers were invited to witness the hand of calculating design, an artifice of the worst sort. These charges put Fern in a bind. Short of enlisting the testimony of former boardinghouse keepers or dissident family members (neither of whom ventured to come forth), she could do little to contradict Moulton's charge that she had been living quite well on his salary, except to pray for fair treatment from the public. More damning still, *Life and Beauties* made it impossible to deny the disastrous marriage to Farrington, and it was hard work for Fern to explain why this troubling episode had been withheld from her otherwise well-documented life-story. The pathetic alibi that *Ruth Hall* was true fiction through and through was no excuse at all. Granted, the spirit of revenge many detected in the anonymous *Life and Beauties* tended to discount its revelations—someone even spread a rumor that N. P. Willis had conjured the whole travesty. But under the circumstances, Moulton's fast-selling counterbiography was no less believable as an accurate measure of character than *Ruth Hall* might claim to be. As the *Boston Post*'s New York correspondent suggested of Fern's novel disdainfully, "believe as much of that $15,000 story as you like."[45]

Fanny Fern's calculated sensation thus exploded upon the American scene with even greater force than she could have anticipated. But to what end? Having sallied forth to disrupt the sentimental attachments that sustained her eldest brother's cultural and professional sway, Fern could claim at least partial success: if he was not hopelessly discredited, his cachet was certainly considerably diminished in *Ruth Hall*'s wake; even many who condemned the messenger admitted that her bitter anger bespoke some heinous crime of the heart. In other respects, Fern's fictional insurgency paid off even more handsomely. *Ruth Hall's* phenomenal success led the editor of the upstart *New York Ledger*, Robert Bonner, to engage Fern as a regular and extravagantly paid columnist. This was quite a coup for the ambitious Bonner, who once worked as N. P. Willis's foreman and copy editor at the *Mirror*. And though Fern initially balked at stooping to lend her name to a cheap weekly (the *Ledger* sold for three cents a copy), she did ultimately relent—and profit. By the crude measure of the 180,000 readers this engagement brought her by 1856, she can fairly be said to have eclipsed her famous brother in the race for public affections. Certainly she addressed a more heterogeneous—some said common— audience than he did in his high-toned *Home Journal*.[46]

In effect, the fight on the field of honor was also a struggle for authorial fame and power in the new mass marketplace; on that field, Fern won hands down. But the stakes of celebrity were such that she could scarcely retire from the field. Head bloodied but purse full, Fern turned next to her second husband: her final novel, *Rose Clark* (1856), revisited the disastrous second marriage whose conspicuous absence had so marked its predecessor, and here Farrington (in the character of John Stahle) fared even worse than *Ruth Hall's* dastardly villains. This fictive recourse seems to have been, in part, a defensive measure: after *Ruth Hall*, every sympathetic partisan was matched by another ready to stigmatize Fern as "Ruth-less Hall," the insufferable virago. Such disdain was especially current among genteel readers, scandalized by the undignified spectacle she had made of her life. Fern's tarnished character thus may have been fine for selling books and contracting with cheap story sheets like the *Ledger*, but it in no way restored her to the universal regard that she had so hopefully projected in her fiction. Nor did fictional release ease the pain of having to endure the kind of public scrutiny that evidently tormented her. Only once after *Ruth Hall's* publication did its author publicly address in any extended fashion the spiraling sensation unleashed by the novel. When the *New Bedford Mercury* circulated the claim that readers would find her "real" story in *Life and Beauties*, Fern riposted quickly. "I have never authorized it," she complained ruefully in an open letter to its editor. "I have never been consulted with regard to it. . . . I am, and have always been, opposed to any such work, my life having been a humble one, in no way of any interest or concern to the public." She had a point here about biographical ethics, but to insist on it while mouthing patent absurdities about her unassuming bearing was to confound moral precepts with the bitter contest of celebrity into which she had irrevocably cast her lot. In this world, skewering reputations was evidently easier than sustaining them unspotted.[47]

Anatomy of a Weakness

In its day, *Ruth Hall* was certainly among the most spectacular exemplifications of the capacity of print—and fiction in particular—to intervene materially in the fortunes of celebrity. Yet we should recognize that this novel was neither singular nor unprecedented in its day. Many American readers themselves readily recognized in Fern echoes of Lady Rosina Bulwer, whose roman à clef *Chevely; or, The Man of Honour* (1839) had, fifteen years earlier, shocked the reading world with its fictive assault on her famous husband, Edward, for crimes against the marriage vow. Indeed, this novel was only a glimpse of things to come. Throughout the 1840s and into the 1850s, British and American presses churned out title after title of a new brand of texts aimed expressly at swaying opinion toward the era's renowned and notorious public characters; Thomas Dunn English's *1844* (1846), with its savage caricature of a drunken Poe, was an early and particularly virulent American example of this literary genre. A decade later, the very same season that saw publication of Fern's familial insurgency also featured her future husband James Parton's contemporary biography of Horace Greeley, the notorious "Chevalier" Wikoff's exculpatory *My Courtship and Its Consequences,* and P. T. Barnum's self-promotional *Autobiography*—all served up for the Christmas trade.[48]

Taken together, this remarkable confluence of print, puffery, and sensationalist exposé registered what can only be called a significant transformation in the function of biography: no longer strictly postmortem retrospect, by the 1850s American tales of lives (both openly professed and disguised by fiction) had become potent auxiliaries in the running contest of celebrity. Yet as *Ruth Hall*'s fate suggests, such interventionist lives were, by nature, profoundly refractory—and never more than when they essayed to establish any sort of "authentic" character.[49]

If we want to find corroboration that by the mid-1850s the cumulative effect of this trend had begun to tell, we can do no better than to turn again to N. P. Willis—and not only because of *Ruth Hall.* Well before that book's appearance he could already have seen himself travestied in fiction several times. The coming months brought additional—and more disturbing—appropriations. Chief among these was the ineptly crafted but nonetheless incendiary book *The Match-Girl; or Life Scenes as They Are.* Published in November 1855, this sensational novel revisited the Forrest imbroglio with a vengeance, and though it was issued anonymously, its sympathies ran clear. The book's villainess, "Caroline St. Maur Oakwood" (a thinly veiled Catherine Sinclair Forrest) is the most despicable of creatures, a sex-crazed opportunist whose overweening ambition leads her first to cuckold and finally to divorce her innocent husband on trumped-up charges. Along the way to imagining herself the "Aspasia" of the fashionable world, she resorts to all manner of dissembling to achieve her "self-exultation"—press manipulation, briberies, "bought witnesses," blackmail, even chloroform. (Just so none missed the point, at one juncture in the book Caroline Oakwood is made to dream of mounting a balcony to receive the hosannas of a crowd proclaiming her the "most virtuous and the loveliest of women!") Willis himself, as the dandy-devil editor "Bazaleel Wagstaff Bayes" of the *Fireside Gazette,* is little better: having once dallied with Caroline, he shamelessly orchestrates the sentimental publicity campaign that poisons public sympathies against her long-suffering actor-husband. In true melodramatic fashion, such scheming gets its comeuppance. Bayes is quickly forgotten. Mercurial opinion also tires of Caroline's pretensions and libidinous antics; increasingly ignored, she becomes a wanton, a drunkard, half mad, a "hopeless wreck." Though crushed by his former wife's lack of remorse, Edgar Oakwood reappears as the novel winds down to save her from a jeering crowd. Remanded to his care, she dies broken and pathetic;

wearied by cruel adversity, "this demi-god, this strong and powerful giant, this genius of his age" reaps a bittersweet vindication.[50]

Clearly this was spicy stuff, and *The Match-Girl*'s Philadelphia publisher was right to think that his sensational advertising would find its mark among scandal's devotees. Several papers noted that the novel sold briskly, and consistently enough to go into a tenth edition printed in Boston. In an atmosphere already thick with domestic double cross and trial reports rivaling the most sensational fictions, more-over, the wildest flights of fancy readily assumed truth's mantle and even the most improbable of conjectures seemed credible. One Boston matron, for instance, was only too eager to credit her daughter's surmise that "The Match-Girl may be written by Fanny Fern," as the "caricature" of N. P. Willis seemed "worthy of Fanny" herself. When instead Willis's former paper the *Evening Mirror* (now run by Poe's old nemesis Hiram Fuller) subsequently identified the novel's author as Catherine Forrest's estranged chum Madame Julie de Marguerittes, the plot thickened: scandal's hawkeyed votaries might now recall how, not long after the close of the initial divorce trial, Bennett's meddlesome *Herald* had forecast that the two women's discord would produce further revelations.[51]

Of course, nothing here was guaranteed to ruin Willis's reputation or, for that matter, Catherine Forrest's. (As evidence that it did not, Edwin's upcoming date in court—which may have had something to do with the timing of *The Match-Girl*'s release—ended only in further frustration for the tortured actor.) Much of this was due to the fact that the novel's clumsy plot offered little of *Ruth Hall*'s aura of verisimilitude, and its cardboard characters were even more outrageous than Fern's. Nor did anyone of stature stand forth to authenticate the novel's picture of conspiratorial depravity, though privately Charleston's William Gilmore Simms (who had heard the inside scoop from James Lawson) was satisfied that this "trashy book" presented "a truer version of the Forrest parties that anything that has yet been given to the public." Still, the *Match-Girl*'s guttersnipe allegations threatened to pile rumor upon rumor until, by the accumulated weight of insinuation, Willis and his circle were convicted of deep-dyed depravity. As with *Ruth Hall*, little could be done to check such insidious affronts: one could hardly horsewhip an anonymous assailant. Legal redress also presented significant problems. Libel suits targeting the novel might well founder on the difficulty of authenticating its author. Even if successful, such post facto remedies inevitably left much of the damage done: in the court of public opinion, instructing observers to disregard ill-gotten testimony was often as futile as it was in legal courtrooms. Perhaps the safest—if not the most satisfying—option was to ignore such provocation altogether. In any case, this seems to have been the choice made by both Catherine Sinclair and her embattled pro-tector.[52]

Hard experience was thus yielding a compelling lesson: it was not enough for celebrities to invite gossip; they must also hold it within bounds. And this was a task that for Willis, at least, seemed increasingly beyond his power. Rather than gossip's creator and purveyor, he was becoming its chronic victim, recalled (more often than not) as "Caroline St. Maur Oakwood's" lackey or the heavy in his sister's familial melodrama—anything but the genteel convalescent conjured by Idlewild's Arcadia. But how did one recoup one's fortune in this refractory world of shifting character and interventionist literature, where sexual hostilities ran high and sentimental impulses could be used to undercut as well as foster emotional ties? Willis seems to have cast his lot with the familiar. Not long after the *Match-Girl*'s appearance, the *Home Journal* began featuring its editor's *own* serialized semiautobiographical novel, published in its entirety in November 1856 as *Paul Fane; or, Parts of a Life Else Untold*. Following his sister's lead, he thus prepared to fight fiction with fiction.[53]

In some respects, Willis's *Paul Fane* was only the latest in a long series of revelatory fictions that featured its author in thin disguise. It certainly was promoted that way. "The characters, the publishers are at liberty to state, are drawn very literally from life," promised one advertiser; "manifestly autobiographical—idealized history of the youth of the author," noted another. Commercial advantages aside, this was precisely the kind of narcissistic display that had time and again goaded critics to dismiss Willis's literary work (with some reason) as shallow self-publicity. Still, *Paul Fane* appears in several respects to have been crucially removed from its trifling forebears. First, it *was* a novel—Willis's maiden effort in that genre. For years critics and partisans alike had been pressing him to redeem his early promise with a sustained imaginative effort; now this might be the author's last best chance to leave behind a statement exhibiting his genius and essential character. Nor was the book as easily scribbled as was Willis's earlier poetry and short fiction. Sickness plagued him throughout *Paul Fane*'s composition; early on, the ominous portent of chronic hemorrhaging and recurrent vertigo had even moved his doctor to forbid him to write altogether or risk sudden death. But Idlewild's famous convalescent would not be deterred: "I have slept upon my death-narrative," he informed Morris early in 1856, "and have concluded to meet it half way—that is, to take the best cure I can of my health, and [trust in] my novel and with Providence to do what is best with me." This grim resolution speaks volumes of the compulsion that must have underwritten *Paul Fane*. Indeed, every evidence suggests that Willis saw this novel as much more than his usual self-described "rubbish"; it was to be his life's work, as well as a necessary vindication.[54]

Certainly he labored long and hard—harder than he ever had before—to craft his account of the early life of "Paul Fane," a hypersensitive Boston-born artist afflicted with what his chronicler subsequently called a stubborn, if ultimately curable, case of "pride-measles." For it is, first and foremost, the sting produced by a visiting English gentlewoman's hauteur that drives this ambitious son of an "orthodox hardware merchant" to Europe on a pathological quest to gauge his relative rank in the world's first circles. New England Calvinist roots and an urge to travel were not the only reasons to associate this brand of republican anxiety with the well-publicized past of the author. On the road to his eventual assimilation into Florentine society, Fane encounters several characters of the type Willis's readers doubtless imagined to have peopled his Italian adventures. Among these are Mildred Ashley herself (she of "that look" of exclusion) and her brother Arthur, two thoroughbred aristocrats whose snobbery confounds Fane inordinately; Sybil Paleford, the beautiful daughter of a British military pensioner, whose love Fane pursues for all the wrong reasons; and Princess C——, a romantic black-eyed *improvisatrice* who, in the tradition of Italian nobility (and defiance of American convention) lives

apart from her run-of-the-mill husband. To these objects of Paul's desire and ambition is eventually added Mary Evenden, the American artist's childhood admirer,
who shows up to remind him of the charms of home. In every case, the interplay
of these fanciful characters allowed Willis the luxury of spinning out theories on
the nature of art and the appreciation of genius, all the while illuminating the "secret
mouldings" of Fane's "genius and character which *were else untold.*"[55]

Mirroring the novel's larger burden of telling heretofore undisclosed and (presumably) authentic tales, *Paul Fane*'s plot turns on the veiling (and fortuitous recognition) of its characters' inner natures. Not coincidentally, the book thus
reproduces celebrity's perennial preoccupation with plumbing surfaces for essences,
as well as its fantasies of personal communion. Along these lines, the protagonist
himself proposes a pet theory about "two or more souls inhabiting one body,"
whose serviceability Willis investigates exhaustively. Most prosaically, in the novel
this dual character reflects practical needs. At home in Boston, Paul must conceal
from his stern and businesslike father a consuming passion for art; in the Fane
family the boy's mother—his special idol and confidante—alone aids and abets this
secret pursuit of beauty and taste. Then, while he is in Europe, Fane (as Willis
had done in real life) assumes the beribboned character of a diplomatic attaché,
the better to make his way in the masquerade world of "good society." Still,
at heart, Fane fancies himself less a social adventurer à la Pelham than an artist
of the beautiful, one whose peculiar talent—a "genius," Willis terms it—lies in
recognizing, and then portraying in pencil strokes, the essential character of his
sitters.[56]

It is worth noting here, apropos of the author's claims to special emotional
rapport with his "literary parish," that this spiritualist aesthetic approximates the
one Willis attributed to Samuel Laurence, the English portrait painter who, it
seemed to him, caught not just the likeness but the "soul" of a man. All of this had
prepared the *Home Journal*'s editor to muse, "What a luxury it would be if there
were a school of *soul-painters*, so that one could choose between having such a
portrait of a friend as *the world* would recognize, or a portrait of the face as *we* see
it, with eyes stopping not on the surface." In the novel, it is precisely this sort of
sympathetic insight that eventually wins Paul Fane social acceptance from the Ash-
leys, as well as the affection of Sybil Paleford, whom Fane concedes shamefully to
having once loved "wildly and passionately," even as he ultimately gives her over
to another suitor (Arthur Ashley himself). It also admits him to the secret life of
Princess C——, a devotee of beauty who, like Fane, must disguise her artistic
calling—in this case by literally masquerading as a man, "Signor Valerio." The
peculiar friendship that develops between these two artists of the soul—the cross-
dressing aristocrat and the Woman-revering republican—lies very much at the heart
of Willis's message.[57]

In light of the gossip generated by the Forrest scandal, it is easy to see how the
conclusions Willis drew from this particular friendship might readily assume the
shape of an apologia. It is not preeminently as *lover* that he finally extols Woman
(this voluptuary relation would merely confirm his critics' bad opinion), but as
virginal *soul-mate*. At first, passionate impulses combine with jealous pride to drive
Willis's fictional alter ego to pursue the love of both Mildred Ashley and Sybil

Paleford. Sexual yearning also inspires Fane's budding intimacy with his artist-princess. Yet only after this ordeal of desire is bested (chiefly by a maternally instilled deference to Woman's better nature) does a higher sympathy entail, a kind of sympathy equal to the wants of genius. As the princess remarks (doubtless speaking here for the author himself):

> I am inclined to think that genius could (better than other natures, and certainly better for itself), do without what is called *love*, altogether. The main portions of the sympathy it needs might be found in intimacies which could correctly and irreproachably be called *friendships*; and its motives and conduct are often misunderstood, because it requires, from these friendships, a tenderness of mental sympathy which seems, to common observers, possible only with love.

As if to demonstrate the proposition that "the intellectual world would breathe its more native and proper element" if love's instincts were "subdued" while the "sympathies of the mind" were "declared to be of no sex," it is neither Miss Paleford nor Miss Ashley whom Paul Fane is eventually made to marry, nor even Princess C—— (whose extraordinary friendship remains a precious memory), but it is instead Mary Evenden, the American artist's "mind-idol" and "genius love." Reflecting her symbolic serviceability, she evokes, by name, both the universal woman ("Eve") and, more particularly, Willis's beloved first wife, Mary Stace (and perhaps even his lost fiancée, Mary Benjamin). So, too, it is Mary Evenden's chaste appreciation of Paul Fane's genius that eventually leads him to voice the sentiment in the novel best calculated to disabuse Willis's real-life critics: put simply, that "the *mind's love* . . . is the best worth securing and living for."[58]

If *Paul Fane* thus served implicitly as a veiled defense of Willis's familiar relations with women, especially the possibility of a companionate amity unstained by baser passions, it also affirmed his democratic impulses and essential Americanism. After all the social climbing, young Fane is, finally, a self-confessed republican at heart: content, he claims, to "yearn for the appreciation of those who are not *grand folks*" and, to all appearances, cured of his diseased obsession with rank by the recognition that " 'the hell of social life, and of all life, is false position.' " Having long found himself valued chiefly for his "familiar acquaintance with great people" (the celebrity hunter's perennial complaint), Fane now wishes merely for the "liberty not only of sinking to where, by the laws of specific gravity, I belong, but of being looked at, after I get to that level, *through one pair of eyes at a time*." That is, as Willis now saw it, the possibility of being judged by "simple individual opinion, without class condescension, class servility, or class prejudice," appeared to be "American only." Doubtless this was special pleading, but coming from one who had long aspired to be numbered among the better sort (at home and abroad), it was at least a start on the road to Damascus.[59]

In fact, it is hard to avoid the conclusion that *Paul Fane* was meant to be one of the most heartfelt statements of Willis's long and well-documented career, not least because it tasked his jealous pride to confess publicly to his own shortcomings. As he himself admitted shortly after the book's publication in November 1856, its protagonist was more "patient" than hero. One can thus appreciate the depth of Willis's distress when, instead of a therapeutic sympathy, widespread disdain greeted its appearance. "The critics are all down upon my novel," he moaned to an old friend not long after the reviews had begun appearing. "It seems strange that they do not see my *purpose*. *Paul Fane* is the careful anatomy of a *weakness*—not the ideal of a hero. It is (as the title page says) the *part of a life else untold*—a revelation of its transition stage, like a physician's statement of scarlatina or a measles." And then he added, trailing off in anguished complaint: "They only half read my book." This last comment approaches the crux of the matter. In the ensuing weeks, Willis even took to the *Home Journal* itself in an attempt to teach the world how to read his book. But sadly, nothing could change the fact that many still chose to receive his avowed confessional of youthful failings outgrown as just another self-promotional conceit. Given such a reading, far from justifying supposed trespasses, Paul's unattractive self-absorption only corroborated old charges against his delineator's character. "It is the favorite fancy now-a-days to see in the fictitious sketch of the hero the likeness of the author," the *New York Times* observed mordantly in one of the reviews that probably pained Willis most. "But we trust there can be no resemblance in this instance. For in truth Paul Fane is a most miserable snob."[60]

It seems, then, that the "weakness" *Paul Fane* best anatomized was one that Fanny Fern herself surely understood: in the volatile world of popular print, pressing claims to authenticity was necessarily tough going; for celebrities it was doubly so. Granted all their extensive self-promotional resources (fiction prominent among them), every public character remained, finally, beholden to a circuit of judgment comprised of interventionist detractors as well as dyed-in-the-wool fans, all of whom confronted a world plagued by personal rivalries, class tensions, and gender hostilities. It was, in this respect, not enough to trust, as the sentimental gospel suggested, to the benignity of spontaneous sympathies. In these days of factual fictions, who really knew where the genuine left off and the counterfeit began?

With this situation in mind, perhaps it is best to close our extended inquiry into the outrageous fictions of the 1850s with a bit of droll ventriloquism perpetrated in the antebellum press. "I heard recently a story of N. P. Willis, who was an ardent spiritualist, that was eminently characteristic of the man," joked an anonymous contemporary of the convalescent author. "He was in a spiritual circle, when his mother's spirit, or what [was] assumed to be such, was announced anxious to communicate with him. Willis, though believing fully that it was her spirit, appeared entirely indifferent to her, but said he would be delighted to hear from [the French dandy Alfred] D'Orsay." Given the Victorian age's devotion to the moral primacy of mother love—and regarding someone who clearly idolized his mother—it is difficult to imagine a more damning dismissal of cultural and personal pretensions than this final corruption of domestic affections by the corrosive influence of worldly fashion.[61]

Echoes

There is no person in the world but Willis, Willis, Willis, from the
one end to the other.

> Newspaper clipping in Willis's scrap-
> book (elsewhere attributed to Mordecai
> Noah, *Sunday Times*, ca. 1845)

Silence is thus our vestibule to death.

> N. P. Willis to John O. Sargent
> (1 November 1865)

Boston was suitably somber that day. Death had come at last, after protracted
suffering. Now, in the gray January noontide, a phalanx of literary compatriots bore
the mortal remains of N. P. Willis from the solid walls of St. Paul's Episcopal
Church. Throughout the city, bookstores ceased their bustling trade to honor his
passing. Old friends and associates also hastened to pay their last respects: chief
among them, the poets Henry Wadsworth Longfellow, James Russell Lowell, and
T. B. Aldrich; Drs. Oliver Wendell Holmes and Samuel Gridley Howe; the publishers E. P. Whipple and James T. Fields—pallbearers all. It was, in sum, just the
sort of public homecoming long denied Willis in his prime—the prodigal welcomed
at last, if only in memoriam.

In his day, controversy, condemnation, bitter resentment, and commercial opportunity had driven Deacon Willis's clever boy to undertake all manner of passages:
literary, social, and peripatetic. Now there was but one short journey left. As the
flower-strewn casket lay awaiting its hearse, Holmes plucked a bloom for his remembrance (or so he would have us believe). Soon afterward, the slow procession
began its journey toward Mount Auburn Cemetery. There, on the twenty-fourth
day of January 1867, as friends and family bade their last farewells, Boston consigned
its wayward son to the comforting confines of tradition.[1]

Truth be told, the man whom the *New York Times* reckoned as "for so many
years the most-talked-about American author" had to some extent already outlived
his fame. "Ten years ago it would have been almost supererogatory to write a sketch
of the life of N. P. WILLIS," the paper remarked in his obituary, "but in this busy

age the man who withdraws from the whirling currents of active life is speedily forgotten." Tucked away at Idlewild, Willis had seen the world start to pass him by, his weekly convalescent reveries more often touching already converted hearts than firing new imaginations, his only serious literary work disdained or ignored. Then came the war, with its frightful dislocations and accelerations. Almost overnight, the *Home Journal*'s subscription list was devastated and its editor reduced to trailing after Mary Todd Lincoln and her entourage for his copy. To pay the bills, Willis's beloved Idlewild was rented for a time; at rock bottom, Cornelia Willis returned with the children to run the house as a girls' school. Often sick and exhausted, her husband labored on resolutely for his family and remaining subscribers, even after seeing his partner Morris dead and buried in 1864. But the penciller's voice had ceased to matter in any but the most nostalgic sense. When it finally went silent forever on the afternoon of his sixty-first birthday, its echoes had already begun to fade from popular imagination.[2]

As if to underscore the point, when Annie Richmond learned several months later of her idol's passing, she admitted to her beloved "Muddie" that "for the last few years I have known little of him, yet it is sad to feel we shall never again see that name among the list of 'our contributors.'" Seventeen years later, a writer in the *Atlantic* could remark of Willis that "the present generation knows him not, or knows him vaguely." Having hitched his star to ephemeral fancies, the once-famous celebrity offered succeeding generations little on which to hang a literary reputation: a few fugitive tales of a bygone era, the surprisingly fresh *Pencillings*, and the poems of his youth. These last writings seem to have persisted longest in public memory: twenty years after their author's death, they were his only literary works still in print. But most other signs mirrored his diminution. For a time, the New York lawyer who purchased Idlewild from Willis's cash-strapped widow reportedly found it necessary to post the "pig-tight gate" against trespass. This he did to forestall liberties taken almost weekly by visitors keen to see the home of "the dude-poet of the Hudson," as local old-timers called Willis. Yet eventually the intrusive footfalls up the great hill to Idlewild ceased; the warning signs came down; and Willis's name was heard no more.[3]

By century's end it would seem that the once-celebrated author had achieved at least the backhand portion of the personal desideratum laid out in *Out-doors at Idlewild*: "to live," as he put it then, "as variedly, as amply, and as worthily, as is possible to his human faculties, while upon this planet . . . and not to be remembered after he shall have left it." In part, this posthumous obscurity proceeded from the trajectory of Victorian literary tastes, which were moving steadily beyond the quaint-seeming literature of the past generation toward a more robust realism. It also reflects the tenuous existence that might be called celebrity's half-life. Inevitably, death marks a boundary between two distinct economies of fame: that of those who can speak for and of themselves, and that of those who must rely on posterity to enunciate their enduring value. Granted his success in the first case, Willis has proved to lack the sort of cultural capital likely to sustain him in the second.[4]

Of course, such a bankrupt legacy does not foreclose the brand of rediscovery and reevaluation that has been this study's task. Yet having reanimated certain forgotten debates initiated in Willis's wake, we are now left to ask what should be made of such a life. For one, concluding, as Henry Beers did, that it was "comfortable that there should have been a Willis" misses much of the point of his life. Granted the man's affinities with the idealized ease of the antebellum parlor, it is precisely because he was such a dynamo of controversy that Willis illuminates the tangled passages of his generation. Particularly in the realm of taste, which so many of the famous author's contemporaries dreamed would ultimately herald a more enlightened republican persuasion, Willis's example crushed many hopes, even as it excited others. Certainly for many, it was harder, following his death, to trust to the salutary workings of a democratic marketplace or to count on the sincerity of sentimental literary representation.[5]

Yet if the "American D'Orsay" often distressed contemporaries, neither was it always "comfortable" to have *been* Willis. James Parton evidently understood this uneasy condition when he declined a publisher's offer to write his estranged brother-in-law's memoir. Though claiming to be the "only person living who could truly expound him," Parton begged off the task professedly to spare Willis's family the discredit unvarnished account must bring to light. "He was one of the millions of victims of the baleful thing called evangelical religion," Fanny Fern's husband concluded sadly. "His old dad was one kind of victim; the son, another kind." What Parton probably meant here was that, in fleeing the constraints of a crabbed piety, his talented but temperamentally prickly onetime employer had hastened straight into the arms of a seductive though ultimately unsatisfying and morally enervating creed centered upon the pursuit of fashionable eminence. Julia Ward Howe certainly thought so. "Thus ends a man of perhaps first-rate genius," she confided in her diary after returning from the funeral at St. Paul's, "ruined by the adoption of an utterly frivolous standard of labor and life. George IV and Bulwer have to answer for some of these failures." In this respect, both Parton and Howe recognized Willis as simultaneously a victim and a perpetrator of some of their generation's most disturbing cultural dimensions.[6]

The upshot of this vexed estate emerges most plainly in the field of celebrity journalism, the characteristic Victorian enterprise that Willis did so much to enunciate and promote. Observers in succeeding generations certainly recognized his pioneering role in this pursuit when they dubbed him the progenitor of their own special correspondents, interviewers, and society reporters. Yet by century's end, prying journalistic enterprise, newly fortified by technological advances such as mass-produceable images, portable Kodak cameras, and flash photography, had so transfigured the public sphere that it was possible to look back at Willis's innovative brand of invasive familiarity and wonder about the fuss. True, conventional set-piece interviews had to some extent begun to formalize claims on eminent personality. It was equally true that, as such developments added yet another technique to the arsenal of self-promotion, they also forced celebrities to calibrate their self-presentation to public expectation in an ever expanding range of circumstance. The English author Maria Edgeworth had predicted as much a half-century earlier: "We shall only see minds like Byron in prepared undress," she lamented wistfully in the mid-1830s, "and we shall never get the real likeness." Those who might once have hoped to revel in the genuine article thus had ample reason for despair. So, too, did celebrities themselves, who, as the new century loomed, complained more than ever of renown's impositions approaching intolerable proportions. In 1883 Oliver Wendell Holmes even joked rather grimly of establishing a new "Association of Authors for Self-Protection." His sentiments undoubtedly found favor among a wide range of public figures.[7]

This concern was not strictly a matter of gallows humor. Indeed, checking the intrusive excesses of the frenzied pursuit of celebrity was the chief aim of two young Boston lawyers, Samuel D. Warren and Louis D. Brandeis, who together in 1890 would make legal history by promulgating the doctrine of privacy. To this point in the passage of the American republic, its citizens could claim no "right to be let alone" distinct from protections against libel and trespass. Prompted immediately by galling accounts of Warren's own private entertaining, but more generally by the distressing march of journalistic invasion and technological innovation spear-headed by Willis and company, Warren and Brandeis's famous and influential ar-ticle "The Right to Privacy" sought to establish a legal distance between the public and the objects of its fascination. This legal protection was meant to cover not only the physical facts of domestic life, but also its "thoughts, emotions, and sensations," so that citizens might claim what the two men called an "inviolate personality." For a time, this innovative doctrine went some way toward arming courts with the rationale to restrict disturbing trespasses upon domestic security, at least for those who could afford to sue. Nonetheless, by excluding from privacy's legal protections any individuals whose persons could rightly be construed as of "public or general interest," Warren and Brandeis left open the door to some of the very excesses they had hoped to remedy. Once *Corliss v. E. W. Walker Co.* (Massachusetts, 1894) established the notion that a nebulously defined class of so-called public charac-ters—that is, statesmen, authors, artists, and even inventors—effectively renounced their claim to privacy as the price of their cultural station, the way was clear for the stalking paparazzi of our own times. In the end, Warren and Brandeis did not so much rein in publicity as pave the way for a world in which public encroachments upon private life spiraled in ever wider orbit, taking in all that "public interest" might notice.[8]

The roots of this situation lay at least partly in the central paradox of the sen-timental culture that drove much of antebellum America's preoccupation with "public characters." Dedicated, as it was on one hand, to preserving and celebrating the value of an inviolate private experience, Willis's generation was also moved by the pleasures of sentimental desire toward an unprecedented commercialization of intimacy. Somewhat paradoxically, this trend was destined to make this emotional state increasingly precious as it became all the more shot through with contradictory impulses. Not content, that is, with building domestic havens safe from the cares of the outside world, nineteenth-century Americans trusted that a "harmless" and morally instructive view into lives might be opened without imperiling the security of their cherished domestic affections. They slaked part of this hunger for insight into the "authentic" through domestic fiction's dramas of sentiment and trial, which promised familiarity and fellow feeling at the cost of a library subscription. Yet, as we have seen, fiction was not immune to the designs of celebrity. Neither were celebrity's guilty pleasures easily curbed, especially when they were sanctioned by the nation's foremost purveyors of "good taste." If the most cocksure Victorian advocates of gentility liked to think that the impulses of a sensation-mongering press sprang wholly from vulgar quarters, N. P. Willis and his personality-hungry readers suggested otherwise.

Perhaps it is fit that those like Willis who profited most from the marriage of gossip and sentiment also suffered most by it. Following the success of *Pencillings*, he stood tall by staunchly defending the propriety of his brand of familiar portraiture; the problem, Willis insisted forcefully on a number of occasions, inhered only in excesses, not in the pursuit itself. In a sense, he was right, for who could complain when exemplary characters were exhibited in exemplary fashion, and particularly when those characters included himself? Yet having opened the door to domestic speculation, Willis found closing it on demand to be a difficult task, especially as new voices and new self-promotional techniques proliferated in the wake of the rapid articulation of a commercially driven popular culture. By the time of his death, he knew only too well the vanity of empowerment and adulation that celebrity promised its practitioners, having suffered the trials, insult, and dishonor of sensational legal actions and outrageous fictions as much as anyone of his generation. Because Willis brought much of this trouble on himself, we can quibble only over the justice of his desserts.

Today, of course, celebrity's apparatus has proliferated to such an extent that a nineteenth-century person like N. P. Willis would surely find the frenzied spectacle of self-promotion and commercial aggrandizement bewildering, to say the least. In recent years, Hollywood, satellite television, and franchise endorsement have brought a multimediated culture of celebrity to the masses around the globe. In the process, the dogged energy of tabloid journalists, fueled by commercial profiteering, has made prying imposition modern fame's almost inescapable burden. So, too, have the frontiers of privacy been pressed until there is next to no "private matter" we do not discuss today. Yet the social and emotional impulses driving these characteristically modern developments are certainly those that a citizen of Willis's print-saturated generation would have recognized, perhaps even applauded. Could they now be magically resuscitated, such nineteenth-century Americans might well take perverse comfort from the fact that many of the sentimental assumptions that enlisted so much of Willis's creative and commercial energies remain alive and well. In charting his generation's uneasy love affair with celebrity, we are thus plumbing the wellsprings of our own obsessions.

NOTES

CHAPTER ONE

1. Beers, 7.

2. *NYTi*, 22 January 1867, p. 4.

3. Briggs, "Laurence Sterne and Literary Celebrity in 1760," 251–73.

4. Rivington and Brown quoted in Wolf, *Book Culture of a Colonial American City*, 190. For the colonial culture of print, see Shields, *Civil Tongues and Polite Letters in British America*.

5. Postlewait, "Autobiography and Theatre History," 250.

6. Boswell is quoted in Braudy, *Frenzy of Renown*, 389, but see also 371–89.

7. London booksellers began catering to the market for signatures not long after Sotheby's auctioned off the first self-described collection of autograph letters in 1819. See Munby, *Cult of the Autograph Letter in England*, and Thornton, *Handwriting in America*, esp. 86–88, 114–15.

8. Morgan's early use of "celebrity" is documented in Stevenson, *Wild Irish Girl*, 236–37. See also a suggestive though undatable passage in Morgan, *Passages from My Autobiography*, 282; Buckley, "To the Opera House," esp. 501–9. For recent forays into the history of the culture of celebrity, literary and otherwise, see Fay, "A Modest Celebrity," and Gabler, *Winchell*.

9. For Willis's early use of "celebrity," see NPW to [Charles] Summer, Glenmary, 25 December 1841, bMs Am 1.9 (10)–1, MH.

10. Bushman, *Refinement of America*.

11. My preference for the phrase "sentimental persuasion" (adapted from Marvin Meyer's "Jacksonian Persuasion") follows from what I consider to be certain intractable problems associated with terms such as "sentimentality" and "sentimentalism." Most troubling is their pejorative connotation, which tends to overdetermine scholarly analysis. "Persuasion," on the other hand, avoids the trap of construing sentiment as inherently pathological (or, for that matter, invariably radically transformative), while underscoring the way that, among nineteenth-century Americans and others, sentimental impulses forged

a loose but powerful "interpretive community" united by a common language and guided by an authoritative aesthetic.

12. The most influential modern exposition of Stowe's sentimental power is Tompkins, *Sensational Designs*, esp. 122–85. This work may be profitably supplemented by Camfield, "The Moral Aesthetics of Sentimentality," 45. For kindred spirits, see Taylor and Lasch, "Two 'Kindred Spirits,' " 23–41.

13. Smith, *Life of Ole Bull*, 67.

14. "N. P. Willis," *Arthur's Home Magazine* 4 (September 1854): 239.

15. For fame's history, see especially the magisterial Braudy, *Frenzy of Renown*.

CHAPTER TWO

1. Percival to George Hayward, New Haven, 9 January 1828, reprinted in J. Ward, *Life and Letters of James Gates Percival*, 288–89.

2. For Ware's review and its influence, see [Henry Ware Jr.], "Sketches," *Christian Examiner* 4 (November–December 1827): 530; and NPW to GJP, Andover, 14 January 1828, NNC(NPW).

3. Collins, *Profession of Letters*, 172.

4. Buell, *New England Literary Culture*, ch. 7; Buell, "Literature and Scripture in New England between the Revolution and the Civil War," 1–18.

5. "Follies and extravagances" comes from James Walker's Phi Beta Kappa oration and is quoted in Howe, *Unitarian Conscience*, 181.

6. For Dwight's "Dissertation on the History, Eloquence, and Poetry of the Bible," see Silverman, *Cultural History of the American Revolution*, 222–23.

7. As a boy, Nathaniel Willis apprenticed with his father's paper on the frontier in Winchester, Virginia, before returning east in 1797 to finish his training in Boston. For his years as a Republican political operative, see Fassett, *History of Newspapers in the District of Maine, 1785–1820*, 107–39.

8. Note this telling measure of the city's plight: in 1806, Portland levied customs duties on $342,909 worth of imports; in 1808, $37,633. For Payson, see Cummings, *Memoir of the Reverend Edward Payson, D. D.*, 142–43.

9. For Nathaniel Willis and the Park Street Church (where he became a deacon in 1828), see Englizian, *Brimstone Corner*; Park Street Church Records, MBC. "Brick house" quoted in Holmes, "A Mortal Antipathy," in *Works of Oliver Wendell Holmes*, 7: 3–4.

10. For Nathaniel Willis's family government, see Ethel Thomason Parton, "Fanny Fern: An Informal Biography" and Beers, *Nathaniel Parker Willis*, 10–15.

11. S. Parton [Fanny Fern], "The Prophet's Chamber," in *Fern Leaves from Fanny's Port-Folio*, 216 (in which Payson appears as Mr. Temple); Warren, *Fanny Fern*, 6–7, 14. See also Greenwood, "Fanny Fern-Mrs. Parton," in J. Parton, *Eminent Women of the Age*, 67. For more about the Willis-Payson connection, see also Edward Payson Papers, MBC; Prentiss, *Life and Letters of Elizabeth Prentiss*, 1–18, 87–90; Cummings, *Memoir of the Rev. Edward Payson, D. D.*, esp. 240–54.

12. NPW, *Paul Fane*, 10; Beers, 14.

13. For adolescent conversion, see Kett, *Rites of Passage*, 62–85.

14. As for Adams, whom the trustees eventually forced out for his antiquated ways, Josiah Quincy the younger (class of 1817) later remembered how, after a four-hour session one Sunday, the headmaster had said, "There will now be a prayer-meeting; those who wish to lie down in everlasting burning may go; the rest will stay." Quoted in Fuess, *Old New*

England School, 173. N. P. Willis remembered Dwight in Sprague, *Annals of the American Pulpit,* 2: 669–74.

15. Most quotations are reproduced in Beers, 24–29. For "house of prayers" and "rebellion against God," see Nathaniel Willis to the Reverend Edward D. Griffin, Boston, 22 February 1823, PHi(G).

16. For the ministry, see Jane Porter to Robert Ker Porter, Coughton Court, 4 August 1835, CtY(KP).

17. NPW to Louisa Willis, New Haven, 15 February 1825, NjP(CS); "Roy" [NPW], "To My Mother," *BR* 8 (1 February 1823): 20.

18. Hawes quoted in Cross, *Horace Bushnell,* 8. Beecher quoted in Sklar, *Catharine Beecher,* 88–93.

19. "Roy" [NPW], "Misanthropic Hours," *BR&T* 10 (16 August 1825): 136, (9 September 1825): 146; and (16 September 1825): 152; "Prize Poem," *BR&T* 11 (24 February 1826): 31.

20. "Prize Poem," *BR&T* 11 (19 January 1827): 11. Both "The Sacrifice of Abraham" and "Jepthah's Daughter" were later reprinted in Willis's *Sketches.* Dewey is quoted in Conforti, "Edwardsians, Unitarians, and the Memory of the Great Awakening, 1800–1840," 43. The problem of language suffused antebellum evangelical religious culture. Horace Bushnell, himself destined to pioneer a suitable vocabulary to express changes in religious sensibilities among antebellum Congregationalists, felt out of place at Yale for just such reasons of language. "I was brought up in a country family," he later remarked, "ignorant of any but country society, where cultivated language in conversation was unknown." This quotation appears in Cross, *Horace Bushnell,* 5.

21. "Poetry and Poets," *BR&T* 10 (5 March 1826): 40; "Religious Novels," *BR&T* 13 (8 February 1828): 24; and "To the Patrons of the *Recorder,*" *BR&T* 15 (7 July 1830): 106.

22. "Philagathos" made his point in "On Fictitious Narratives Employed to Convey Religious Instruction," *BR&T* 11 (7 April 1826): 53.

23. Bryant's quotation appears in his review of "Hadad, a Dramatic Poem," *New York Review* 1 (June 1825): 2. For Hillhouse and Willis, see NPW, *Dashes at Life with a Free Pencil,* 222–23.

24. "The Miscellaneous Poems of Wordsworth," *NAR* 18 (April 1824): 356; Holt, "A Medical Student in Boston," 372; Emerson, *The Journals of Ralph Waldo Emerson,* 108–9; Richard Henry Dana Sr., "Hazlitt's English Poets," *NAR* 8 (March 1819): 319. A decade later, however, Willis's early love for Wordsworth would sour. See "Willis on Wordsworth," *New Yorker* 10 (30 January 1841): 317.

25. For rejoinders to "Misanthropic Hours," see Pray, "A Study of Whittier's Apprenticeship as a Poet," 26. For N. P. Willis on New England religion, see "The Poetry of Religion," *AMM* 1 (August 1829): 293.

26. The quotations are reproduced in Beers, 43–44, from letters since lost.

27. Ibid., 59.

28. Ibid., 44.

29. Ibid., 45–46. Unfortunately, little additional evidence remains to flesh out the relationship between N. P. Willis and his sister Julia, the woman whom Henry Beers called the poet's favorite sister.

30. "Lawless" quoted in Meredith, *Politics of the Universe,* 34–35. "Human nature and human depravity" quoted in Woolsey, "Theodore Dwight Woolsey, 253. Though, as one modern scholar has pointed out, many New England colleges were moving toward educating a larger percentage of older students (most aged in their midtwenties), Yale

and Harvard lagged behind in this regard. See Allmendinger, *Paupers and Scholars*, esp. 116.

31. For Willis in New York (including quotations from letters since lost), see Beers, 54–57.

32. For Van Schaick, see NPW, "The Remainder," *NM* 3 (13 July 1844): 239–40. A lawyer by trade, Van Schaick also dabbled in newspaper editing with his brother-in-law Simeon De Witt Bloodgood (who had been De Witt Clinton's personal secretary) and contributed short stories to several literary publications. The quotation about Pumpelly comes from the dedication to Willis's *Fugitive Poetry*.

33. Beers, 57.

34. The quotation describing the spread of gift-books appears in Branch, *Sentimental Years*, 114–15. For Goodrich, Willis, and the changing culture of print, see Goodrich, *Recollections of a Lifetime*, esp. 2: 252–78.

35. For examples of Willis's canned verse, see "Saturday Afternoon" and "Psyche, before the Tribunal of Venus," both in *The Token* of 1829.

36. An agreement with Goodrich dated 4 December 1827 (held today in the N. P. Willis Collection at Yale University's Beinecke Library) guaranteed Willis $200 for a year's editing of *The Token*, with further compensation for his prose and verse contributions. On the obverse is a note that Willis was also charged with superintending *The Legendary*—preparing matter for press, reading proof, and writing two original articles for each volume.

37. The other "callow bards" were Rufus Dawes, George Lunt, William Crosby, Frederick Hill, and Charles G. Greene. The quotations appear in *HJ*, 22 February 1858, p. 2; NPW to GJP, Boston, [26 November 1827], CtY(NPW); and NPW to GJP, Boston, 24 May 1828, NNC(NPW).

38. For Willis's frenetic social activities, see any number of letters to George Pumpelly or J. B. Van Schaick from this period. "Pale of Unitarianism" quoted from NPW, "The Elopement," *AMM* 2 (May 1830): 104.

39. "[There] are women who confide in you utterly after you have once struck one of their secret feelings," Willis reported to Van Schaick, "and my knowledge as you know is all in that line. I can philosophize upon 'feelings' till the candle goes out." NPW to JBVS, Boston, [postmarked 27] April [1829], PHi(G). For other quotations, see NPW to GJP, New Haven, [ca. spring 1827], NNC(NPW); and NPW to JBVS, Boston, 29 January [ca. 1828], PHi(G). This is not to say that Willis was anxiety-free. "My forte is sober and tête-à-tête conversation," he admitted to Van Schaick after meeting his friend's brother-in-law for the first time, "& for this I had no opportunity—I do not know how to put my mind in undress, and at table & in the two or three brief moments of meetings in the parlor I could not start a subject. . . . Of course I played dumby, and left a stupid impression." NPW to JBVS, "Steam Boat," Long Island Sound, "Wednesday Evening" [postmarked 24 August 1827], PHi(G).

40. NPW to GJP, Boston, 2 October [1825], NNC(NPW). We can guess the year from a passing reference to the "canal celebration," probably the one convened in November 1825 for the completion of the Erie Canal.

41. NPW to JBVS, *n.p.*, 12 April, [ca. 1829–31], PHi(G); NPW to JBVS, *n.p.*, 20 April [ca. 1829–31], PHi(G). In later years Willis liked to tell stories about these adventures that reflected, more or less humorously, on his youthful sense of fashion. One friend remembered that the poet recalled once being mistaken for a burglar by a watchman late one night outside the Willises' Atkinson Street house. After arguing without success to be allowed to pass, the deacon's son finally sought to clinch his case by recourse to the quality of his clothes. "Do you suppose that a housebreaker would wear trousers like this?" he reportedly said, pointing to his fine broadcloth. See Tuckerman, "Some Old New Yorkers," 443–44.

42. NPW to GJP, Andover, "Tuesday" [postmarked 2 May ca. 1828], NOwHi.

43. For Miss Woolsey, see NPW to GJP, New Haven, [ca. spring 1827], NNC(NPW); NPW to GJP, Boston, September [1827], NNC(NPW). For "Genevieve," see NPW to GJP, Boston, "Tuesday Night" [ca. September 1827], CtY(NPW); NPW to GJP, Boston, 26 November[1827], CtY(NPW); and NPW to F[rancis] Alexander, Andover, *n.d.* [ca. 1827], with mss. sonnet, CtY(NPW). Willis's love was probably related to the clan headed by the prosperous New York and New Haven hardware merchant William Walton Woolsey (Timothy Dwight's brother-in-law), whose son Theodore held a position as tutor during Willis's years at Yale. A younger William Woolsey also appears in one of Willis's letters home from New York City. See Beers, 56.

44. NPW to GJP, Andover, 14 January [1828], NNC(NPW). This was a poem ("my *immortal*") Willis apparently never was to complete, though in December 1828 he was telling Van Schaick, "It will get me a name I doubt not—but that is not money. My plan pleases me and surprises me. I did not know there could be a poem so unlike any thing I ever saw. I shall finish it by March I trust." NPW to JBVS, Boston, 4 December [1828], PHi(G).

45. NPW to GJP, Boston, 15 June [1829], NNC(NPW).

46. NPW, "The Editor's Table," *AMM* 1 (December 1829): 646–47. For Willis's comments, see NPW to JBVS, Andover, 1 May [1828], PHi(G); NPW to GJP, [Boston], 24 May 1828, NNC(NPW).

47. Edward Beecher's troubles at Park Street are documented in Snyder, *Lyman Beecher and His Children*, 70–73. For an accounting of Park Street membership and disciplinary action in this period, see Cayton, *Emerson's Emergence*, 263.

48. "Crowded" quoted from NPW, "The Female Ward," *NM* 2 (28 October 1843): 58–62.

49. NPW, "Unwritten Poetry," *The Legendary* 1 (May 1828): 36–52. Willis's identification with Paul Lorraine was evident to at least one perceptive reader. But the author himself rushed (more or less disingenuously) to assure his compatriot John Neal that he had no intentions of "painting [his] own portrait!" NPW to John Neal, Andover, [ca. 1828], bMs Am 1949 (344), MH.

50. NPW, "Unwritten Poetry," 36–52.

51. For the bizarre footnote, see NPW, "Unwritten Poetry," 37. For the eternal spirit, see NPW to JBVS, Boston, 29 September [1828], PHi(G). See also NPW, "The Poetry of Religion," *AMM* 1 (August 1829): 295, in which he finally contended that for a Christian the ravishment of natural beauty inspired the "deepest and highest" meaning "of which his nature is capable."

52. NPW to JBVS, Boston, 29 September [1828], PHi(G). Goethe's memoir is mentioned in NPW to GJP, Andover, "Tuesday" [postmarked 2 May ca. 1828], NOwHi.

53. For the quotation on the prospect of church discipline, see NPW to JBVS, Boston, 29 September [1828], PHi(G). See also NPW to JBVS, [Boston], 23 November [1828], PHi(G); and Park Street Church Records (6 February 1809–1 February 1834), MBC.

54. The rise of evangelical print is discussed in Rabinowitz, *Spiritual Self in Everyday Life*, esp. 138–65.

55. The *Boston Recorder* may no longer have solicited "Roy's" poems (as the newspaper once had), but it gladly reprinted them from the likes of the *New England Baptist Register* well into 1831. Stowe's comments appear in a preface to "The Leper," *BR&T* 15 (14 July 1830): 112.

CHAPTER THREE

1. NPW to JBVS, Boston, 15 September [1828], PHi(G).

2. NPW to JBVS, Boston, 15 September [1828], PHi(G); NPW to JBVS, *n.p.*, February [1828], Atcheson Laughlin Hench Autograph Collection (#6435), ViU; NPW to GJP, [Boston], 4 February 1829, NNC(NPW).

3. For Federalist literary culture, see Simpson, *Federalist Literary Mind*, esp. 3–41; Buell, *New England Literary Culture*, 23–55.

4. "Scientific and elegant" in *Bower of Taste* 2 (2 May 1829): 285. For the *New Monthly* and its American vogue, see Sullivan, *British Literary Magazines*, 331–39; NPW to GJP, Boston, [ca. early 1829], Special Manuscripts Collection Typographical, NNC; NPW to JBVS, *n.p.*, September [1828], PHi(G).

5. [NPW], "Unwritten Music," *AMM* 1 (April 1829): 5–15; NPW, "Unwritten Philosophy," *Legendary* 2 (1828): 235.

6. NPW, "Unwritten Music," 10–12.

7. Ibid., 12–15.

8. The "Hymn" to temperance appeared at least twice in religious newspapers. [NPW], "Hymn," *BR&T* 15 (10 February 1830): 24; *Boston Watchman-Examiner*, 19 February 1830, p. 4.

9. For "Elia," see Cecil, *Portrait of Charles Lamb*, esp. 149–57. For *Blackwood's* and the "Noctes," see Allen, *Poe and the British Magazine Tradition*, 19–39; NPW, "Keeping Diary," *NM* 2 (2 December 1843): quote 138.

10. [NPW], "Editor's Table," *AMM* 1 (December 1829): 620.

11. [NPW], "The Scrap Book," *AMM* 1 (November 1829): 556. Charles Lamb's *Specimens of Dramatic Poets, Who Lived about the Time of Shakespeare* (1808) was among the most influential books to spearhead this nineteenth-century fashion for seventeenth-century poets. See Jack, *English Literature, 1815–1832*, 393–405; Amavasinghe, *Dryden and Pope in the Early Nineteenth Century*, esp. 126.

12. [NPW], "Minute Philosophies," *AMM* 1 (November 1829): 519; [NPW], "Editor's Table," *AMM* 2 (July 1830): 273. As with much of Willis's epicurean creed, this last sentiment had its origin with the editor's friend J. B. Van Schaick. See NPW to JBVS, [Boston], 30 October [1829], PHi(G).

13. G. Curtis, "Reminiscences of N. P. Willis and Lydia Maria Child," 718.

14. [NPW], "Editor's Table," *AMM* 1 (November 1829): 579–86.

15. Ibid., 560.

16. Part of this bragging owed to the shameful specter of failure. As Willis told Van Schaick in June 1829, "I have been boded so much, + condoled with so provokingly, + left so much to do every thing myself that I should die of mortification if I should fail." NPW to JBVS, Boston, 5 June [1829], PHi(G). For the magazine's prospects, see "American Monthly Magazine," *Bower of Taste* 2 (2 May 1829): 285; NPW to GP, Boston, 15 June [1829], NNC(NPW).

17. NPW to Richard Henry Dana Sr., Boston, 3 February 1829 [misdated 1828], National Park Service, Longfellow National Historic Site, Cambridge, MA; Clark to [Summer A. Fairfield], Philadelphia, 7 December 1829, reprinted in Clark and Clark, *The Letters of Willis Gaylord Clark and Lewis Gaylord Clark*, 26. "True magazine flavor" is quoted in Holmes, *John Lothrop Motley*, 14.

18. Fuller, *Letters of Margaret Fuller*, 6: 125, 155, 170, 214. "I *will* admire him," Fuller wrote of Willis, "notwithstanding his cloak, patronizing airs to the daughters of *highly respectable families*, and his devotion to the Misses Cain." Greeley quoted in Beers, 293–94.

19. Reprinted in the *Boston Statesman*, 13 June 1829, p. 1, excerpted from Samuel Kettell's *Specimens of American Poetry*.

20. Federalist critical techniques are suggested in the anonymous article "The Reviewer as Executioner" and Joseph Stevens Buckminster, "The Polity of Letters," both reprinted in Simpson, *Federalist Literary Mind*, 176–84.

21. *New England Weekly Review*, 30 June 1828, p. 2.

22. For worries over women reading, see Douglas, *Feminization of American Culture*; Kelley, *Private Woman, Public Stage*; and Baym, *American Women Writers and the Work of History, 1790–1860*, 14–24.

23. *Salem Gazette*, 24 July 1829, p. 2; *New England Weekly Review*, 28 December 1829, p. 2; *American Traveller*, 26 March 1830, p. 3; *American Traveller*, 23 February 1830, p. 3.

24. [NPW], "Editor's Table," *AMM* 2 (June 1830): 206–7; *New England Galaxy and Boston Mercury*, 21 May 1830, p. 2; *New England Galaxy and Boston Mercury*, 18 June 1830, p. 2.

25. The literary career of Letitia Landon (L. E. L.) is chronicled in Blanchard, *Life and Literary Remains of L. E. L.*, esp. 51–57. "For pet slut," see the *Boston Courier*, 2 August 1830, p. 1.

26. Boswell, *Life of Johnson*, 4: 191; Snelling, *Truth*, 12–15.

27. Willis's promise appears in [NPW], "Prospectus," *AMM* 1 (April 1829): ii. For his retorts, see [NPW], "Editor's Table," *AMM* 1 (January 1830): 721–23; [NPW], "Editor's Table," *AMM* 1 (February 1830): 803. For Child and Willis (who allegedly once carried on a brief flirtation), see Karcher, *First Woman in the Republic*, esp. 50, 133–35.

28. NPW to JBVS, Boston, 3 March 1829, PHi(G); [NPW], "The Literary Remains of the Late Henry Neele," *AMM* 1 (April 1829): 27–38.

29. Blair, *Lectures on Rhetoric and Belles Lettres*, vi. Blair's impact on American culture is discussed in Gabler-Hover, *Truth in American Fiction*, 35–58.

30. For the scope of social anxieties in the early republic, see Watts, "Masks, Morals, and the Market," 127–49; Cayton, *Emerson's Emergence*, 3–32. "Life of idleness" is quoted in Williamson, *American Hotel*, 118–19. For Willis and the Tremont, see [NPW], "Scribblings," *AMM* 2 (June 1830): 162.

31. For a sampling of the theatrical controversy, see "The Rapid Progress of Sin," *BR&T* 12 (16 March 1827): 42; "Theatre," *BR&T* 13 (11 January 1828): 6; *American Traveller*, 3 July 1829, p. 2; "Concealment of Opinions," *BR&T* 15 (15 September 1830): 145; "The Theatre," *BR&T* 15 (13 October 1830): 164; *Boston Statesman*, 9 October 1830, p. 2; *Boston Courier*, 14 October 1830, p. 1; *Boston Courier*, 29 November 1830, p. 1.

32. *Rhode Island American and Providence Gazette*, 15 February 1828, p. 2.

33. Crawford, *Famous Families of Massachusetts*, 2: 243–44; NPW to GJP, Boston, 23 November [ca. 1830], NNC(NPW); "Masquerades," *BR&T* 14 (23 April 1829): 67.

34. *Boston Courier*, 6 May 1830, p. 2. "The Fashions" is quoted from the *Providence Daily Journal* in *American Traveller*, 31 July 1829, p. 1.

35. The genre is chronicled in Rosa, *Silver Fork School*, and Adburgham, *Silver Fork Society*. For Henry Colburn and the Regency publishing scene, see Sutherland, "Henry Colburn, Publisher," *Publishing History* 19 (1986): 59–84. For the social measure of Almack's in Boston, see NPW to GJP, Boston, 13 November [ca. 1830], NNC(NPW).

36. Bulwer's *Pelham, or, the Adventures of a Gentleman*, edited by Jerome McGann, is the best modern edition of *Pelham*, containing McGann's helpful introduction, the text and preface of Henry Colburn's second (1828) edition, and the preface to the 1840 edition. In later editions Bulwer edited the book to make it less objectionable. All citations hereafter will refer to this edition. For Bulwer (who later became Lord Lytton and was then referred to as Bulwer-Lytton), see Sadleir, *Bulwer*, and Harvey, *Men in Black*, 23–39. For

postrevolutionary dreamers, see Silverman, *Cultural History of the American Revolution*, 490.

37. Bulwer, *Pelham*, 30, 180.

38. "Kitchen maid's literature" appears in the Evert Duyckinck Diary, 25 January 1839, Duyckinck Family Papers, NN. For Willis and *Pelham*, see NPW to JBVS, Boston, 27 November [1828], PHi(G); NPW to JBVS, Boston, 4 December 1828, PHi(G); NPW to JBVS, Boston, 25 July [1829], PHi(G); NPW to GJP, Boston, 4 February [1829], NNC(NPW); NPW to JBVS, Boston, n.p., 3 February [1829], PHi(G); NPW to JBVS, Boston, 13 and 20 March [ca. 1830–31], PHi(G); NPW to Henry Greenough, Boston, 28 March 1830, in F. Greenough, *Letters of Henry Greenough to His Brother*, 58–61.

39. Bulwer, *Pelham*, xxxiii. The most famous British attack on the Pelham school of novels came in Thomas Carlyle's *Sartor Resartus* (1836).

40. Bulwer, *Pelham*, xxxiv.

41. The problem of Bulwer's brand of "mixed characters" is discussed in "Novels," *Christian Examiner* 15 (May 1829): 177.

42. John G. Whittier to Mrs. L. C. Tuthill, Hartford, 24 [April] 1831, bMs Am 1838 (935), MH.

43. "Mr. Dewey's Oration," *Christian Examiner* 9 (November 1830): 229.

44. "Literature vs. Fashion," *Bower of Taste* 3 (23 January 1830): 54–55.

45. NPW to Hannah Willis, [England], 12 September 1835, quoted in Beers, 99.

46. For quotations concerning Willis's financial status, see NPW to GJP, Boston, 29 March 1829, NNC(NPW); NPW to JBVS, Boston, 15 September 1828, PHi(G); NPW to JBVS, Boston, 16 June 1829, Atcheson Laughlin Hench Autograph Collection (#6435), ViU; NPW to JBVS, Boston, 11 January [1830], PHi(G); NPW to GJP, Boston, 14 May 1830, NNC(NPW). For additional evidence, see also NPW to GJP, Boston, 19 May [1829], NNC(NPW); NPW to GJP, Boston, September [ca. 1829], NNC(NPW); NPW to JBVS, Boston, [12 October 1829], PHi(G).

47. Initially, Willis had hoped that literary fame would solidify his marriage prospects. "I have folded my arms & got a new cushion for my chair, and determined to be a Benedict for two or three years longer," he informed Van Schaick in November 1828, "& by that time I hope my reputation will be enough to prepare the way for me." NPW to JBVS, Boston, 23 November [1828], PHi(G). For other quotes, see NPW to GJP, [Boston], 14 May [1830], NNC(NPW); NPW to GJP, Boston, 21 October [1830], NNC(NPW).

48. For quotations treating of Willis's amorous adventures and their social consequences, see NPW to JBVS, Boston, 5 April [1829], PHi(G); NPW to GJP, Boston, January 1830, NNC(NPW); NPW to JBVS, n.p., 20 February 1831, PHi(G). See also NPW to JBVS, Boston, 16 June 1829, Atcheson Laughlin Hench Papers, ViU; NPW to GJP, 14 May 1830, NNC(NPW); NPW to JBVS, n.p., 20 January [1830], PHi(G). This bad blood ultimately exploded publicly in the fall of 1836 with a tit-for-tat literary exchange prompted by Park Benjamin's critical assessment in the new *American Monthly Magazine* that Willis was "the most compete quack known in *our* Republic of Letters." Willis riposted with an ill-natured "Dramatick Fragment" that blasted the physically and morally crippled "Pedro" (Park Benjamin was lame from a childhood illness) as unworthy of the love of his beautiful sister Giulia (Willis's onetime fiancée Mary). See [Park Benjamin], "Mr. Willis's Poems," *American Monthly*, (series 2) 2 (October 1836), 348; and NPW, "Dramatick Fragment," *NYM* 14 (29 October 1836): 140.

49. NPW to GJP, Boston, 21 October [1830], NNC(NPW); NPW to JBVS, Boston, 22 April 1831, PHi(G). For Willis's "liberal bargain" with Morris, see NPW to George Lunt, n.p., [postmarked 22 August 1831], Nathaniel Parker Willis Papers, Pennsylvania State University Libraries.

CHAPTER FOUR

1. For Willis's early days in Britain, see NPW to Julia Willis, [London], [4 June 1834], reprinted in Beers, 139–41; and NPW, "Pencillings by the Way," *NYM* 12 (21 March 1835): 297.

2. For quotes about Willis in Britain, see Mitford to Miss Jephson, *n.p.*, 23 July 1834, reprinted in *The Friendships of Mary Russell Mitford*, ed. the Reverend A. G. L'Estrange, 191; NPW to JBVS, London, 25 June 1834, PHi(G); NPW to Blessington, Gordon Castle, 23 September 1834, reprinted in Madden, *Literary Life and Correspondence of the Countess of Blessington*, 2: 176.

3. Willis's sexual progress was, of course, sub-rosa. "For God's sake," he closed a note to Van Schaick, "don't show my letters." NPW to JBVS, London, 21 January 1835, PHi(G); NPW to JBVS, London, 25 March [1835], PHi(D); NPW to Hannah Willis, [England], 22 July 1835, reprinted in Beers, 162–63.

4. For Morris's bragging, see "Mr. Willis and His Commentators," *NYM* 11 (30 November 1833): 175; and "The Foreign Correspondence of the Mirror," *NYW* 11 (24 January 1835): 279.

5. The most complete book-length text of Willis's letters is the 1853 edition of *Pencillings by the Way*, though even this volume omits phrases and paragraphs that appeared in the original. Reliance on the initial published correspondence in the *Mirror* is the only way to know what readers read and when they read it.

6. For the etiquette of introductions, see Spiller, *American in England During the First Half-Century of Independence*, 16–18.

7. For the Greenough correspondence, see "Letter from Italy," *American Monthly Magazine* 1 (August 1830): 345–48. In April 1830 Willis had begged Henry's pardon for writing him, "knowing you as little I do." Willis was more intimate with another brother, Alfred, and a sister back in Boston, who arranged to send communications to Henry in Italy through the traveling editor. NPW to Henry Greenough, Boston, 28 March 1830, enclosed with Alfred Greenough to Henry Greenough, Boston, 1 April 1830; Alfred to Henry Greenough, Boston, 22 August [1830]; and Alfred Greenough to Henry Greenough, Boston, 7 September 1831, reprinted in F. Greenough, *Letters of Horatio Greenough to His Brother, Henry Greenough*, 56–61, 65, 72–73.

8. For Cooper's role in Paris's American expatriate community, see Spiller, *Fenimore Cooper*, 162–88. As for Howe, perhaps he was repaying social courtesies Willis had extended him during a brief sojourn in the United States on behalf of Greek independence in 1828. See NPW to GJP, Boston, [1828], NNC(NPW); NPW to JBVS, Boston, 22 April 1831, PHi(G).

9. For Willis and Carr, a man who, according to one American sojourner in Paris, had "killed two or three of his compatriots in duels & talks with perfect nonchalance of putting a man to death," see Brevoort, *Letters of Henry Brevoort to Washington Irving*, 249–51.

10. Despite his Parisian social successes, Willis did leave some ill feeling behind him. "To help a countryman in distress," Cooper evidently lent Willis (whom he later claimed to have seen but "ten times in [his] life") $150 to quit the city in the spring of 1832. In return, Willis gave him a draft ("without interest even") drawn upon Morris in New York. To Cooper's dismay, it was initially protested but finally paid with interest six months later. Cooper to Peter Augustus Jay, Paris, 17 October 1832, reproduced in Cooper *Letters of James Fenimore Cooper*, 6: 317.

11. NPW, *Pencillings by the Way* (1853), 437; NPW to Hannah Willis, Florence, 20 January 1833, quoted in Beers, 124. Horatio Greenough eventually soured on Willis, de-

ciding he was "not a man after my heart" but instead "corrupt." See Greenough, *Letters of Horatio Greenough, American Sculptor*, 118, 125, 128, 130, 142, 156.

12. Willis and Porro quoted in Beers, 119–20.

13. Landor to Blessington, [Fiesole], [May 1834], reprinted in Morrison, *Blessington Papers*, 103–4; Blessington to Landor, London, 9 June 1834, reprinted in Madden, *Literary Life and Correspondence of the Countess of Blessington*, 2: 355–56; Beers, 131–35 and 141. Willis was well aware of the magnitude of Landor's service to his cause. Blessington "is my lodestar and most valued friend," he wrote his benefactor from England in January 1835, "for whose acquaintance I am so much indebted to you that you will find it difficult in your lifetime to diminish my obligations. I thank you from the bottom of my heart." The friendship even survived Willis's casual handling of his friend's volumes, which sent them inconveniently to New York for a time. Only when the British author eventually returned to England to find that his letters of introduction had caused further mischief did he publicly reprove his cavalier courier. After attempting to apologize by post—Landor, now in high dudgeon, haughtily refused the letter—Willis eventually explained himself in the *Mirror* and satirized Landor in "Lady Jane," a Byronic verse after "Don Juan." For Willis and Landor, see NPW to Landor, *n.p.*, 23 January 1835, reprinted in Forster, *Walter Savage Landor*, 2: 314; Landor to NPW, [Italy], [ca. spring 1835], reprinted in Beers, 134–35; Landor to Blessington, [2 April 1836], in Morrison, *Blessington Papers*, 118; NPW to Landor, Royal Arsenal, Woolwich, 6 April [1836], reprinted in Morrison, *Blessington Papers*, 231–32; NPW, "Letters from under a Bridge," *NYM* 16 (13 October 1838): 124. A detailed discussion of the episode appears in Super, *Publication of Landor's Works*, 56–60.

It is, however, perhaps wrong to conclude (as have several of Landor's biographers) that Willis's May 1834 meeting with Landor was their first. Willis later implied that he had visited Landor several times; as early as 1832, in fact, the American traveler was mentioning Landor in his foreign correspondence, though not specifically any interviews. This circumstance may help to explain Landor's confidence in him.

14. To obviate some of the problems attendant upon the reckless issue of introductions, by the 1830s certain merchants had taken to affixing "secret devices and signs" to modify the express tone of recommendations. See Tasistro, *Random Shots and Southern Breezes*, 1: 163–64.

15. "Tame after-philosophy" in NPW to Henry Greenough, Boston, 28 March 1830, in F. Greenough, *Letters of Horatio Greenough to His Brother*, 60. Willis's views on travel writing are most cogently expressed in his "Review of the Travels in the North of Germany, in the Years 1825 and 1826, by Henry E. Dwight," *AMM* 1 (June 1829): 241–49, quote 249. Yet it appears that Willis hit upon the idea even earlier in his career. As early as 1828, he was telling Pumpelly that only James Gates Percival's "fickleness" had kept the Connecticut poet from visiting Europe with an $800 advance on a "new species of book—of *first impressions* (something like a Ramble in Germany). . . . This I can do—and my reputation will sell the book, [Goodrich] says—so what prevents?" NPW to GJP, [Boston], [ca. 1828], NNC(NPW).

16. NPW, *Pencillings by the Way* (1853), 65, 121–30, 156–61; *(New York) Spirit of the Times*, 2 June 1832, p. 2, and 16 June 1832, p. 2.

17. NPW, "Pencillings by the Way," *NYM* 12 (7 March 1835): 281–82. The several letters that make up the initial batch of correspondence from Seamore Place were probably written at the same time, which may account for Willis's assurance that his English letters would contain the familiar descriptions and anecdotes promised in the first letter.

18. NPW to Mitford, Traveller's Club, 22 February 1835, reprinted in Mitford, *Friendships of Mary Russell Mitford*, 193. For the note that prompted this reply, see *New York Evening Post*, 18 September 1835, p. 1.

19. For the state of American literature in England, see Gohdes, *American Literature in Nineteenth-Century England*, esp. 19–20 and 47–70.

20. For Willis's British progress, see Beers, 129–30; NPW to JBVS, Boston, 13 and 20 March [1831], PHi(G); NPW to JBVS, Boston, 13 December [ca. 1828–30], PHi(G); Mitford to Miss Jephson, *n.p.*, 23 July 1834, reprinted in Mitford, *Friendships of Mary Russell Mitford*, 190–91.

21. For evidence of growing British interest in American periodicals, see especially the *(New York) Evening Star*, 26 May 1835, p. 1, and 17 October 1835, p. 2. The *Liverpool Journal* connection is an intriguing one. Its resourceful young editor, Robert Shelton Mackenzie (1809–81), was, like Willis, poised to profit from both the popularization of literary culture and the late surge in transatlantic literary interest. The son of a British army officer and sometime poet, Mackenzie had made his way by vending his poems in British magazines and annuals, penning biographical sketches, and editing provincial newspapers like the *Liverpool Journal* (whose helm he assumed in 1834). He later claimed that his engagement with the *Evening Star* effectively made him the first British correspondent to be retained permanently by an American paper. His articles appeared in the *New York Mirror* as well. Eventually, Mackenzie immigrated to the United States, where he worked the literary trade till his death in 1881. See Baker, "Robert Shelton Mackenzie," in *American National Biography*.

22. By January 1835, Morris had laid up a goodly cache of letters; Willis's columns would be printed well into October without exhausting the supply penned a year earlier.

23. *C&E*, 29 April 1835, p. 2, probably quoting the *(New York) Evening Star*.

24. Ibid.; *C&E*, 27 March 1835, p. 2, 3 October 1835, p. 2, and 16 September 1835, p. 2. This was, in fact, part of an extended newspaper battle between the *Mirror* (with its English-born literary editor Joseph Price), the *Evening Star*, and, eventually, Jane Porter on one side, and Webb's *Courier and Enquirer* and John Inman's *Journal of Commerce* on the other. See also *C&E*, 17 September 1835, p. 2; *(New York) Evening Star*, 21 October 1835, p. 2; NPW to JP, Athenaeum, [ca. summer 1835], CtY(KP); Diary of Jane Porter for 1835, 13 and 15 July 1835, Folger Shakespeare Library, Washington, DC; NPW to JP, Athenaeum Club, [postmarked 22 July 1835], CtY(KP); *New York Evening Post*, 18 September 1835, p. 1; and *New England Galaxy*, 3 October 1835, p. 2.

25. NPW, "Pencillings by the Way," *NYM* 12 (7 March 1835): 281–82; *C&E*, 29 April 1835, p. 2. With Moore, matters were even more touchy than either Willis or Webb probably suspected. Immediately before Willis's arrival in England, publication of a supplement to Moore's *Irish Melodies* had precipitated a rift between the poet and O'Connell. The quarrel hinged on the implications of a lyric entitled "The Dream of Those Days," which questioned what Moore saw as O'Connell's self-aggrandizement of the "Catholic Rent," a levy meant to sustain the Repeal Movement. See Moore, *Journal of Thomas Moore: 1831–1835*, 4: 1609–12, 1620–23, 1625, 1633–35, 1689; L. Strong, *Minstrel Boy*, 251–52.

26. *C&E*, 29 April 1835, p. 2. Born Sally Power in Tipperary in 1789, Marguerite Blessington was at age fifteen given into marriage for financial considerations, only to flee her abusive husband after three months to return to her drunken father's household. Soon, she escaped with a Captain Jenkins, with whom she lived until he effectively sold her in 1816 to Lord Blessington for ten thousand pounds sterling. It was while traveling with her new husband—the first having since died—that the couple met the young Count Alfred D'Orsay, Webb's "French Adventurer." In time, D'Orsay was convinced to marry the Earl of Blessington's fifteen-year-old stepdaughter Harriet Gardiner to secure a large bequest from his patron's estate. The earl died in 1829, but the girl never reconciled herself to the match; she and her new husband were barely civil. And even before the widowed countess returned from the Continent, the *Age*'s blackmailing editor Charles Molloy Westmacott had begun spreading rumors that the D'Orsay-Gardiner match was wholly a convenience designed to

cover an illicit connection between D'Orsay and Blessington. After D'Orsay squandered his inheritance and his wife left him in 1831, such rumors erupted anew in the press and society. See Sadleir, *Strange Life of Lady Blessington.*

27. For Edgar Allan Poe's "Lionizing," see Thomas and Jackson, *Poe Log*, 159, 193; Paulding to Thomas W. White, New York, 3 March 1836, reprinted in Paulding, *Letters of James Kirke Paulding*, 173–75; Benton, "Poe's *Lionizing*," 239–44; Daughrity, "Poe's '*Quiz on Willis*,'" 57–62.

28. NPW, "Pencillings by the Way," *NYM* 12 (14 March 1835): 292.

29. Ibid., 292; [Edward Bulwer to NPW], *n.p.*, 28 April 1835, reprinted in Madden, *Literary Life and Correspondence of the Countess of Blessington*, 3: 173–74. Concerning the incident, Henry Crabb Robinson later recollected, "Fonblanque told me that Willis had apologised to him for some remarks on his dress, such as no man likes. In answer to his letter, Fonblanque wrote: *Sir, your apologies are as indifferent to me as the scurrilities that render them necessary.* Bulwer, on the other hand, *preached* to him." Willis told Mary Longfellow soon afterward that he had barely escaped dueling over the unfortunate affair. For these comments, see Robinson, *Henry Crabb Robinson on Books and Their Writers*, 1: 445. For Longfellow and Bulwer, see Richards, "Longfellow in England," 1129–30.

30. Hall, *Travels in America*, 12–15; NPW to Blessington, *n.p.*, [ca. late April–early May 1835], reprinted in Madden, *Literary Life and Correspondence of the Countess of Blessington*, 183–84. Willis repaid Blessington's constancy with admirable loyalty. Years later, after the countess's death opened the floodgates to salacious memoirs, he continued to defend this "good and gifted woman ['s]" character (and D'Orsay's) from ill-treatment; her life, Willis suggested in 1855, should be remembered primarily as a drama of "society and its Tyrannies Defeated." *HJ*, 5 May 1855, p. 2.

31. According to Mackenzie (who was the clearinghouse for the information on Hewitt as well), at least one London paper the *(Spectator)* excerpted paragraphs from Willis's "Pencillings" in the several weeks prior to publication of Lockhart's review. For intelligence on Willis in England, see *(New York) Evening Star*, 26 October 1835, p. 2; Richards, "Longfellow in England," 1136; *Spectator* (London) 8 (14 August 1835): 303–4. Morris (who had direct contact with Mackenzie in these days) noted the *Liverpool Journal* praising Willis's description of Moore. "This sketch of Moore is one of the best written articles we have ever read . . . we are gratified to find that these papers are copied far and wide in the English Journals, who acknowledge the correctness of the portraiture and the elegance of the pencilling." "Mr. Willis's Letters from England," *NYM* 13 (11 July 1835): 15.

32. Sumner to Sarah Perkins Cleveland, Edinburgh, 17 September 1838, in Sumner, *Selected Letters of Charles Sumner*, 1: 47; Lockhart to Walter Scott, November 1828, reproduced in Lang, *Life and Letters of John Gibson Lockhart*, 2: 37; NPW, "Pencillings by the Way," *NYM* 12 (31 May 1835): 388. Lockhart's animus probably drew strength from his dislike of Bulwer and his Radical political associates, whom Willis had celebrated.

33. [John Lockhart], "Willis's Pencillings by the Way," *Quarterly Review* 54 (September 1835): 455–69.

34. For British suspicions, see Mary Mitford to Miss Jephson, 23 July 1834, reprinted in Beers, 142; JP to NPW, Royal Arsenal [Woolwich], 6 October 1835, NjM(NPW).

35. As Willis remembered it in a preface to a subsequent edition of *Pencillings*, Macrone's offer came on the day before his marriage. NPW, *Pencillings by the Way* (1853), vii.

36. NPW to Mary Skinner, *n.p.*, [ca. summer 1835], quoted in Beers, 161–62; NPW to Mary Stace, *n.p.*, [ca. late September 1835], quoted in Beers 173–77.

37. By the mid–eighteenth century, the term "personality" had already come to express the notion of distinctive character attributes. Yet even into the late nineteenth century it was more often used in the plural to reprove journalistic invective and license. "Personality,"

Oxford English Dictionary, 11: 602. For common law libel, see Wickwar, *Struggle for the Freedom of the Press, 1819–1832*, 18–28.

38. For the history of gossip and private letters, see Spacks, *Gossip*, 66–91. For Lord Byron's posthumous fame, see Walker, *Byron's Readers*, 132–34, 150–85; Elfenbein, *Byron's and the Victorians*, esp. 47–89. Quotations appear in [NPW], "Galt's Life of Byron," *AMM* 2 (November 1830): 594; *Salem Gazette*, 16 March 1830, p. 1.

39. Walter Scott, "Ashetiel Fragment," 26 April 1808, quoted in Lockhart, *Memoirs of the Life of Sir Walter Scott, Bart*, 1: 1; John Lockhart, *Quarterly Review* [ca. 1825], reprinted in *New England Galaxy* 10 (30 March 1827): 4.

40. Simond, *Journal of a Residence in Great Britain*, x–xi; *Sketches of Public Characters* reviewed in the *American Traveller*, 25 June 1830, p. 1; "Wheaton's *Travels in England*," *Christian Examiner* 9 (December 1830): 306–7.

41. "Wheaton's *Travels*," 309–10.

42. Ibid., 309.

43. For all his private advice, Lord Aberdeen had no wish to champion Willis publicly or to accept the dedication Willis proposed. He did not object to Porter showing her young friend the letter if she saw fit, but he made it clear that there should be "no printing either in England or *America*." Aberdeen to JP, Haddon House, Aberdeen, 18 October 1835, then forwarded to NPW, NjM(NPW).

44. NPW, *Pencillings by the Way*, 2d British edition (1836), 1: xi–xvi.

45. For attacks on Willis, see [William Maginn], "Willis's Pencillings," *Fraser's Magazine* 13 (February 1836): 195–203; *Age*, 4 October 1835, p. 316; *Literary Gazette and Journal of Belles Lettres*, 21 November 1835, p. 741; "Pencillings by the Way," *Edinburgh Review and Critical Journal*, American edition, 63 (January 1836): 184–90.

46. The Dalhousies are quoted in Beers, 190–91. For other quotations, see JP to NPW, 15 Montague Square, 20 August 1839, NjM(NPW); A. Grant, *Memoir of Mrs. Grant of Laggan*, 1: 273; Moragné, *Neglected Thread*, 17.

47. NPW, "Pencillings by the Way," *NYM* 12 (18 April 1835): 332; "Private Communications," *NYM* 12 (16 May 1835): 364–65. Willis's excuse that this offensive comment was never meant for publication, and was added without his leave, is borne out by its presentation in the *Mirror*. His catalog of *on dits* is clearly distinct in its tone, font, and, most important, in its timing from the rest of the letter with which it appeared. Though the whole was published in April 1835, the first half of the column (an account of an evening at Lady Blessington's) dates from the summer of 1834. On the other hand, the concluding remarks (among them, the fateful sneer at Marryat's works) are dated 22 February 1835. Accounting for posting and the vagaries of transatlantic travel, this evidence suggests that publication was decided upon almost immediately after its receipt.

48. "Mr. Willis's Pencillings by the Way," *Metropolitan Magazine* 15 (January 1836): 74–79.

49. Ibid., 77, 79. Judging by the *Metropolitan*'s wording of Willis's sneer, neither Marryat nor his editor probably ever saw the original column from which it came, though they could have gotten their information from reviews like that in London's *Athenaeum*, which had called *Truth* a "tomahawk sort of satire." See Holmes, *Works of Oliver Wendell Holmes*, 7: 5–6.

50. NPW to Blessington, Manor House, Lee, Kent, 18 [January 1836], reprinted in Madden, *Literary Life and Correspondence of the Countess of Blessington*, 3: 188.

51. NPW to Marryat, Manor House, Lee, Kent, 10 January 1836, Joseph Regenstein Library, University of Chicago, Chicago, IL.

52. The naval yard at Chatham was finally chosen for the hostile meeting because Marryat's new second, Edward Belcher, was stationed there. Beers, 197–206, provides the most

accessible account of the tangled affair. All published correspondence appeared in the *Times* of London between 29 January and 1 March 1836.

53. JP to NPW, Shirley Park, 18 January 1836, NjM(NPW); [C. C. Felton], "Willis's Writings," *NAR* 43 (October 1836): 408–9; *Times* (London), 1 March 1836, p. 4.

54. *Times* (London), 29 January 1836, p. 3.

55. NPW to BM, Royal Arsenal, Woolwich, 5 April [1836], CtY(NPW).

56. The Natchez episode was reported in the *National Gazette,* quoted in the *Baltimore American and Commercial Daily Advertiser,* 23 January 1836, p. 2. Other quotes appear in Henry van der Lyn to Mary [van der Lyn], Washington City, 13 January 1837, (BV van der Lyn), NHi; Fisher, *Diary of Sidney George Fisher, 1834–1871,* 13–15.

57. Lawrence Shaw Mayo, "The America that Used to Be from the Diary of John Davis Long," *Atlantic Monthly* 130 (December 1922): 727; *Life and Memorials of Daniel Webster* (1853), 2: 119, quoted in Allibone, *A Critical Dictionary,* 3: 2756; Adams, *Diary of Charles Francis Adams,* 7: 171; Thomas, *The Secret Eye,* 137.

58. "To Authors about to Publish," *Punch,* 9 (1845): 25.

59. For the loss of privacy among public men, see (*Philadelphia) Public Ledger,* 16 August 1850, p. 2.

CHAPTER FIVE

1. NPW to BM, Woolwich, England, 5 April [1836], CtY(NPW); NPW, "Letter from the Dollar: Number Three," *Dollar Magazine* 1 (September 1841):258.

2. NPW, "Jottings," *NM* 2 (14 October 1843):31; NPW, *Complete Works,* 230–31.

3. Charles F. Briggs to James Russell Lowell, Bishop's Terrace, New York, 9 July 1844, William Page and Page Family Papers, microfilm reel D312, Archives of American Art, Smithsonian Institution, Washington, DC; and NPW to Hannah Willis, n.p., 20 January 1844, NjP(CS).

4. Longfellow to George Washington Greene, Cambridge, 28 May 1840, in Longfellow, *Letters of Henry Wadsworth Longfellow,* 2:229–30. For American authors' constricting financial prospects in the late 1830s, see Greenspan, *Walt Whitman and the American Reader,* 18–19.

5. *HJ,* 23 February 1850, p. 2.

6. For Willis's distinctive diction (which became a kind of genteel parlor vernacular), see "Our Contributers, No. XI," *Graham's Magazine* 25 (April 1844): 146–47. Characteristically, Willis was concerned about the image projected in his portraits. "I wish . . . that you could get an artist to remove the two *side twists* of the moustaches," he once complained to an editor, "which none but a fool who does not know what else to do with his hands, even wears on his face. This would remove much of the ludicrousness of the character of the picture." NPW to unknown, New York, 21 September [1847], Nathaniel P. Willis, Misc Mss, NHi.

7. Review of "People I Have Met," *Literary World* 6 (26 January 1850): 81–82. "Worky" appears in NPW to Joseph Boughton, Glenmary, 7 June 1842, 12230, New York State Library, Albany, NY, and NPW, "The Cabinet," *NM* 3 (7 September 1844): 367. "Foolish fashions" appears in NPW, "Coming down Salt River," *NM* 2 (2 December 1843): 143–44. For Willis's desideratum, see NPW, *Out-doors at Idlewild,* vii.

8. Edgar Allan Poe to "Annie" Richmond, Fordham, 16 June [1849], reproduced in Poe, *Letters of Edgar Allan Poe,* 2: 448; "Annie" Richmond to Maria Clemm, *n.p.,* "Thursday Afternoon" [ca. January 1855], in Poe, *Edgar Allan Poe,* 56–58.

9. Prentiss, *Life and Letters of Elizabeth Prentiss,* 35. Willis's companionate manifesto

appeared first in "Unwritten Philosophy," in the *Legendary*, 2:242, and later, somewhat reworked, in a column on "Women and Marriage" for the *New York Tribune*, 12 February 1842, p. 4.

10. NPW, "Brown's Day at the Mimpsons," NPW, *Complete Works*, 275–78.

11. NPW, "Leaves from the Heart-Book of Ernest Clay," in NPW, *Complete Works*, 251–68; and NPW, "Preface," in NPW, *Complete Works*.

12. NPW, "Ephemera," in NPW, *Complete Works*, 650; *HJ*, 17 June 1848, p. 2.

13. This is not to say that all correspondence was equally welcomed. Requests for autographs, Willis once wrote, were "very much like asking the postman to take a walk for pleasure." Ultimately, he developed a lithograph form letter to deal with routine and unsolicited requests that stated that "a private letter" was "the last ounce that broke the camel's back." For Willis's comments and the printed reply, see, for instance, NPW to F. B. Sherford, New York, 2 November, *n.d.*, Special Mss Collection PB, NNC; and NPW to [Mr. Hurst], New York, 17 January 1851, Atcheson Laughlin Hench Autograph Collection (#6435), ViU.

14. Much of Chubbuck's correspondence with Willis and her friends is reprinted in Kendrick, *Life and Letters of Mrs. Emily C. Judson*, 92–125, but see also Brumberg, *Mission for Life*, 118–44. For Forester's celebrity, see "Trippings in Author Land," *Broadway Journal* 2 (29 November 1845): 322.

15. Kendrick, *Life and Letters*, 106–9, 118. An artist friend of Willis was so pleased with one descriptive passage in "Dora' " that he expressed a wish to paint the figurative protagonist. As a token of his affection, Willis commissioned the portrait, paid for it, and sent the finished picture to Chubbuck in Utica.

16. The quotations appear in [Mrs. Emily (Chubbuck) Judson] to NPW, *n.p., n.d.*, Emily Judson Collection (#9274), Clifton Waller Barrett Library, ViU; and Kendrick, *Life and Letters*, 106–8, 117–19. For evidence of the hard-headed side of Chubbuck's character, see Brumberg, *Mission for Life*, 130.

17. [Mrs. Emily (Chubbuck) Judson] to NPW, *n.p., n.d.*, Emily Judson Collection (#9274), Clifton Waller Barrett Library, ViU; and Kendrick, *Life and Letters*, 210–11. When Chubbuck did finally meet Willis in the early summer of 1845, she called him a "noble fellow and the very best friend I have got." Emily to Wallace Chubbuck, 2 July 1845, quoted in Brumberg, *Mission for Life*, 129.

18. Brumberg, *Mission for Life*, 270. For Willis's mature religious sentiments, see "Editor's Table," *Knickerbocker* 24 (October 1844):398; and *HJ*, 2 September 1848, p. 2, in which he called himself an "intense spiritualist" who found echoes of God's love most manifest in the beauties of nature. For his Episcopal connections, see NPW to C. W. Thornton, Washington, 28 February 1862, MeWC.

19. NPW to Hannah Willis, n.p., 20 January 1844, NjP(CS); and Grimsley, "Six Months in the White House," 68–69.

20. Read, *Memoir of Miss Elizabeth T. Read*, esp. 58–60, 66, 125. Born into the family of Dr. Alexander and Sarah Willis Read on 30 August 1830, Elizabeth Read was, by all accounts, a precocious and avid reader, especially of religious material: by three years of age, she was said to have read the Bible fluently and memorized hymns. Nathaniel Willis's *Youth's Companion* was said to have "afforded her great delight."

21. "Throb in the breast" quoted in Howe, *Unitarian Conscience*, 196. The significance of Willis's figuring so prominently in Lizzie Read's memorial is only compounded when we realize that poets generally were not John Abbott's cup of tea. His work *The Mother at Home* (1834), for instance, featured Lord Byron as exhibit number one of the disastrous effects of improper mothering.

22. *Emerson, Journals and Miscellaneous Notebooks*, 13:177.

23. Galvanized by the impassioned rhetoric of the elegant Republican stump speaker George William Curtis, Willis publicized his support for Frémont in an open letter published first in the *Evening Post*, then reprinted in the *New York Times*, 8 October 1856, p. 2. See also NPW to [Mr. Gray], Idlewild, 9 October 1856, Special Manuscript Collections Typographic, NNC; NPW to J. A. C. Gray, Idlewild, 4 October 1856, and NPW to Gray, Idlewild, 22 October 1856, MeWC.

24. For Willis as tastemaker, see NPW, "Letters from under a Bridge," *NYM* 16 (18 August 1838): 60; "Nathaniel Parker Willis," *New-Yorker* 9 (18 April 1840): 77.

25. N. Ward, *Simple Cobler of Aggawam*, 26.

26. According to the indefatigable labor advocate and founder of the National Reform Association George Henry Evans, wages declined by one-third to one-half between 1838 and 1843, and the business upturn of the early 1840s did not result in increased earnings for most working men and women. He estimated that, in 1844, one in seven of New York City's dwellers were paupers. Noted in Branch, *Sentimental Years*, 83.

27. NPW, *Lecture on Fashion*, 1–3, 13.

28. Ibid., 6–13.

29. Ibid.

30. NPW, "Coming Down Salt River," *NM* 2 (2 December 1843): 144; NPW, "Slip-Slopperies of Correspondence," *NM* 2 (30 December 1843): 208.

31. Emerson, "Manners," in *Collected Works*, 2:75; Lowell to Charles Briggs, Boston, 30 January and 4 February 1846, in Lowell, *New Letters of James Russell Lowell*, 18. My thinking about the role of "aristocracy" in American society has been most influenced by Wood, *Radicalism of the American Revolution*, esp. 229–369.

32. Sumner to George S. Hillard, Lanfire House, Ayrshire, 24 September 1838; Sumner to Hillard, Traveller's Club, [London], 1 March 1839, in Sumner, *Memoir and Letters of Charles Sumner*, 1: 361–62.

33. NPW, "Professed Table-Talkers," *NM* 1 (1 July 1843): 199; NPW, "Author-Life Abroad," *NM* 1 (2 September 1843): 345.

34. *NYTr*, 12 June 1844, p. 4.

35. "The Blidgimses" (actually, two sisters by the name of Bridgens) had been plaguing Willis since his days in Italy. "I am not *quite* the reprobate some people think me," Willis wrote Van Schaick in 1834. "Those bloody Bridgens's [*sic*] are the worst of liars and I hear from them constantly in some disagreeable shape or other, and all because I cut them for slandering a sweet woman who was a d——d sight better than they. But let that go." NPW to JBVS, London, 25 June 1834, PHi(G). See also NPW, "The Remainder," *NM* 2 (13 July 1844): 239–40; NPW, "Two or Three Little Matters," *NM* 2 (20 July 1844): 254–55. Willis's mean-spirited tales ("Those Ungrateful Blidgimses" and "Ernest Clay") ultimately appeared in his *People I Have Met* (1850).

36. *EM*, 9 October 1844, p. 2; *EM*, 11 November 1844, p. 2; NPW, "The Upper Ten Thousand of New-York City," *WM* 1 (23 November 1844): 122.

37. *EM*, 2 December 1844, p. 2; NPW, "Jottings," *NM* 1 (2 September 1843): 350; *HJ*, 20 May 1848, p. 2.

38. For Willis's detractors, see "Manners and Society," *New-Englander* 1 (July 1843): 372.

39. *EM*, 10 January 1845, p. 2; NPW, "Coming Down Salt River," *NM* 2 (2 December 1843): 143.

40. Willis first introduced the "Upper Ten Thousand" in the *Evening Mirror* of 11 November 1844. Several weeks later James Gordon Bennett's *New York Herald* and other penny papers picked up the lingo. By 1859 John Bartlett's *Dictionary of Americanisms* was

illustrating entries for the "Upper Ten" and "Uppertendom" with examples drawn at random from the popular press. None from Willis was needed to canvas the phrase's usage, so indispensable had the term become to the vernacular. *NYH*, 8 December 1844, p. 1; Bartlett, *Dictionary of Americanisms*, 494–95.

41. *Revelations of Asmodeus, or, Mysteries of Upper Ten-Dom.*

42. Buntline [pseud. E. Z. C. Judson], *The Mysteries and Miseries of New York*. For Five Points and the development of this new literature, see Gilfoyle, *City of Eros*, 36–46, 143–57.

43. *HJ*, 12 May 1849, p. 2.

44. *HJ*, 26 December 1846, pp. 2–3; and *HJ*, 23 February 1850, p. 2. As with so many of Willis's cultural stances, his advocacy of music was not subject to a foolish consistency. In 1845 he wrote from Germany that the opera in the United States was primarily for the wealthy and refined; "like the exotics in greenhouses, these expensive importations bring but little of the soil in which they sprang, and produce nothing for the 'many.' We want 'American' music to give national fragrance to 'American' feeling, enthusiasm and religion. . . . War aside, national music is the true nurse for love of home and love of country, and in a general taste for music lies one of the greatest levers which can be brought to bear on religion and devotional feeling." NPW, "Invalid Rambles III," in *Rural Letters*, 264.

45. *HJ*, 4 November 1848, p. 2.

46. For the business of music and theater, see the encyclopedic Lawrence, *Strong on Music*, 1:22, 94–130.

47. For the opera's progress at Palmo's, see Lawrence, *Strong on Music*, 1: 250–69, 429. Even the fastidious Horace Greeley, who as a rule condemned theatrical amusements, was moved to laud Palmo's initiative, primarily for his barring of so-called assignation rooms.

48. *NYH*, 1 May 1844, p. 2, and 14 December, p. 2.

49. NPW, "More Particularly," *NM* 1 (10 June 1843): 160; *EM*, 9 November 1844, p. 2; *HJ*, 3 March 1849, p. 2. "Pico-tricity" is quoted in Lawrence, *Strong on Music*, 1:346–47.

50. For the Astor Place Opera House, see Lawrence, *Strong on Music*, 1: 454–505. Willis reprinted a description of the new opera house and its frequenters, wherein he figured preeminently, in the *Home Journal* of 20 May 1848.

51. The *Sunday Age* was quoted in the *NYH*, 1 December 1847, p. 2, and the passage is reproduced in Lawrence, *Strong on Music*, 1:456; *HJ*, 4 November 1848, p. 2; and *HJ*, 11 November 1848, p. 2.

52. For Willis and the opera, see *HJ*, 4 November 1848, p. 2; *HJ*, 13 November 1848, p. 2; *HJ*, 2 December 1848, p. 2; *HJ*, 11 November 1848, p. 2; NPW, "More Particularly," *NM* 1 (10 June 1843): 160; *HJ*, 25 November 1848, p. 2; NPW, "Superfinery," *NM* 1 (23 September 1843): 416. See also *HJ*, 19 January 1850, p. 2, where Willis argued that it "is the lesson we have picked up from travel and philosophy, that, by occupying the central plane, one may reach what is good that were else below him and what is good that were else above him. The man lives but half a life who has no friends but the fashionable—as he does who has no sympathies but with the vulgar; and, to be known for only an exponent of the opinions of either class, would soon put our self-respect, as it would the waxing circulation of our paper, on the wane." According to Bayard Taylor, Willis assumed an "affectation of aristocratic elegance in his writings; yet, in his life, he was as natural a democrat as Walt Whitman, gentle, considerate, and familiar with the lowest whom he met, and only haughty towards ignorant or vulgar pretension." Taylor, *Echo Club, and Other Literary Diversions*, 87.

53. For the B'hoys and the theater, see Buckley, "To the Opera House," esp. 139–61, 294–409; Dorson, "Mose the Far-famed and World Renowned," 288–300. Whitman's

sketch of the "B'hoy of the Bowery" (published initially as "The Habitants of Hotels," *Daily Crescent*, 10 March 1848) appears in Whitman, *Uncollected Poetry and Prose of Walt Whitman*, 1:194–95.

54. For Bennett versus the brothers Fry, see *NYH*, 22 February 1849, p. 2; *NYTi*, 6–19 December 1853; Lawrence, *Strong on Music*, 1:563–67 and 2:258, 594–600. Lawrence can discern no obvious reason for Bennett's animus, though she guesses that a tiff with the Fry brothers' father, a Philadelphia journalist, during Bennett's early 1830s stint in the Quaker City may have been at fault. William Fry was also the New York *Tribune*'s Paris and London correspondent for a time in the late 1840s; this connection to Bennett's rival paper may also have contributed to the contretemps. See E. Robinson, "The Public Ledger: An Independent Newspaper," 45.

55. Lately, analyses of the riot have become a cottage industry among American cultural historians. The earliest and most extensive historical study is Moody's *Astor Place Riot*, but see also especially Buckley, "To the Opera House," 1–83.

56. E. S. Gould to Evert Duyckinck, 18 Clinton Place, [ca. May 1849], Duyckinck Family Papers, NN. *Evening Post* is quoted in *HJ*, 19 May 1849, p. 2.

57. *HJ*, 26 May 1849, p. 2, but see also *HJ*, 19 May 1849, p. 2, and 12 May 1849, p. 2. In this last article, Willis suggested that "Forrest is the injured man in the quarrel—but we wholly disapprove of his intemperate methods of expressing his anger. We detest the rotten egg hostility to a gentleman, which was three-fourths of the feeling at the riot—but we think there should be some sort of American recognition of MR. MACREADY'S selfishness and ingratitude."

58. For Willis on fashion and exclusivity at the opera, see *HJ*, 27 February 1847, p. 2; *HJ*, 6 October 1849, p. 2; *HJ*, 20 October 1849, p. 2.

59. *HJ*, 24 February 1849, p. 2; *HJ*, 3 March 1849, p. 2; *HJ*, 26 May 1849, p. 2. The *Home Journal* generally struck what might be called a moderate domestic feminist stance on the woman question, calling, for instance, for an end to laws that stripped women of their property rights upon marriage. Yet, in arguing against extension of the franchise, Willis suggested that women's greatest dominion lay not in political activism but in the power to give or withhold favor from men, thus determining social position. On the other hand, see the author's friend Elizabeth Oakes Smith, a noted feminist lecturer who remembered: "Refined as he was and admiring Woman as he did, [Willis] accepted the advanced ideas of suffrage for her, her entire equality under the law, with no mean vacillation. His respect and admiration for her was his reason for this. He would place her upon no ignoble throne, where the robes of only the few could be saved from defilement, but where she should be royally acknowledged: an equal in her own right of graciousness and divine appointment." Quoted in Kirkland, " 'A Human Life,' " 289.

CHAPTER SIX

1. Some said that Forrest beat Willis with his own cane as well. A review of Forrest's assault, relating its particulars, as well as some feeling for conflicting accounts of the conduct of its participants, is most readily accessible in *NYTi*, 3 March 1852, p. 3, and 4 March 1852, p. 4.

2. The best account of the Forrest affair is Moody's *Edwin Forrest*, 245–334. It differs from mine by relegating Willis to a relatively minor role in the drama. Given the subject of Moody's study, the choice is understandable. Slighting Willis, however, underplays the important role the famous poet played in the demonology of tormentors Forrest constructed in the course of his campaign for divorce and, more important, ignores the wider controversy that, for cultural historians, is perhaps the most instructive aspect of the affair.

3. Edwin claimed to have barred Margaret from his home in 1846, while Catherine swore that only in autumn 1848 had her husband forbade her sister's visits. See *NYH*, 29 November 1850, p. 2, and John Van Buren's notes on Catherine Forrest's affidavit, PU(EF).

4. Precisely what Catherine denied when she branded Edwin's accusations a lie—his charges against her sister or the accusations concerning Jamieson—remains unclear to this day. This question would prove critical to the subsequent divorce action.

5. The quotations appear in *(New York) Weekly Universe*, 9 March 1850, p. 2; and William Cullen Bryant to Frances F. Bryant, [New York], 20 March 1849, in Bryant, *Letters of William Cullen Bryant*, 2: 545–46.

6. For press notices of the separation see *NYA*, 29 April 1849, p. 2, and 7 July 1850, p. 2; *NYH*, 30 April 1849, p. 1; and *Cumming's (Philadelphia) Evening Bulletin*, 30 April 1849, p. 2. The family friend was the Reverend Elias L. Magoon, a Baptist minister at New York's Oliver Street Church; he made the comment at the subsequent divorce trial. *FDC*, 70. The edition of the trial report I consulted had an idiosyncratic pagination. After page 119, the numbering returned to 81, then proceeded anew. I have identified pages from this anomalous second numeration with the prefix "b."

7. "Lying chronicles" is quoted in Moody, *Edwin Forrest*, 247–48.

8. The letters were subsequently published as part of Edwin Forrest's divorce evidence.

9. Catherine Forrest initially agreed to this course of action. But when a draft of her husband's petition mentioned criminal acts inconsistent with the marriage vow, she had O'Conor withdraw her assent. "Divorcer-General" appears in *(Philadelphia) Sunday Dispatch*, 3 March 1850, p. 2.

10. The companionate reformer was probably Henry Tuckerman. *NYTr*, 1 April 1850, p. 1. As for the campaign to limit legislative divorce, only days before Forrest brought his petition to Harrisburg Senator Muhlenberg had read a remonstrance from Philadelphia citizens against the practice and the Pennsylvania Supreme Court had ruled that divorces granted by the legislature for causes within the court's jurisdiction were unconstitutional. See *Pennsylvania State Senate Journal*, 1:607; *NYH*, 3 February 1850, p. 1, excerpted from the *(Philadelphia) Public Ledger*, 1 February 1850; and *(New York) Weekly Universe*, 23 March 1850, p. 2.

11. Cott, "Passionlessness," 219–36; *(Philadelphia) American Banner*, 13 April 1850, p. 2; and *(Harrisburg) Pennsylvania Telegraph*, 16 March, 1850, p. 2.

12. Precisely how the *Herald* obtained the transcript is unclear—perhaps from a partisan legislator or Forrest himself. Pamphlets detailing Edwin's case were certainly circulating after it looked as if his divorce petition would meet opposition. Certainly the news appeared at a critical juncture for his case: just after the Pennsylvania Senate had dashed a prominent South Carolinian's hopes for divorce 25 to 7 and just as an amended bill was coming before that body that would have allowed Forrest to press his case before the Philadelphia Court of Common Pleas.

13. *NYH*, 28 March 1850, pp. 1–2.

14. *New York Morning Express*, 29 March 1850, p. 1. *Consuelo* was first translated into English by Francis G. Shaw of Roxbury, a Brook Farmer, and appeared in the Fourierist community's official organ the *Harbinger*. Idealistic liberals like young George William Curtis were enthralled; it is a "great novel," he wrote a friend at the time of its appearance, "for after [Goethe's] *Wilhelm Meister*, I know none superior." See G. W. Curtis, "Some Early Letters of George William Curtis," 367.

15. *Police Gazette*, 6 April 1850, in newspaper clippings, M-HTC. Christiana Bedford ended her longtime service to the Forrest family when she married a Sixteenth Street neighbor, the so-called male laundress Joshua Underwood, on 25 November 1849. The new Mrs. Underwood's willingness to come forward with her revelations two months later may thus

212 • NOTES TO PAGES 122–128

have stemmed from an enhanced sense of domestic and financial security (her husband was said to be worth $12,000). To avoid confusion, I shall refer to her throughout as Mrs. Underwood, since that is the name most frequently used by her contemporaries during the trial. See *NYA*, 1 December 1850, p. 2.

16. Death of Willis's "angel" is quoted in Beers, 276. For Willis's subsequent loneliness, see NPW to BM, [New York], [postmarked 18 May 1845], CtY(NPW); NPW to GPM, [Liverpool], 18 July [1845], CtY(NPW); NPW to BM, Astor House, [17 March 1846], MiD(BM); and NPW to BM, New Bedford, 5 August 1846, MiD(BM). Other quotations appear in NPW, "Letter from London," *WM* 1 (29 March 1845): 386; *HJ*, 6 January 1849, p. 2.

17. NPW to BM, [New York], 17 February 1850, CtY(NPW).

18. *EM*, 19 January 1845, p. 2; *WM*, 18 January 1845, p. 226; Briggs to J. R. Lowell, *n.p.*, 6 January 1845, William Page Papers, Archives of American Art, Smithsonian Institution, Washington, DC. For an overview of the Onderdonk affair, see Cohen, "Ministerial Misdeeds," 35–57. Edward Payson Willis, about whom little is known today, later acted for a time as the traveling agent of the controversial danseuse Lola Montez, before he died prematurely in 1853 at the age of thirty-six.

19. *EM*, 7 January 1845, p. 2. Raymond's campaign drew explicitly on the history of slander levied against Willis. A surviving letter to the Philadelphia editor Rufus W. Griswold, for instance, requests some "facts" used eight years previous in a "savage" article against Willis, and it ends with the sentiment, "If you do this, I'll meet any expense you may incur, and will repay the obligation any way you please." Raymond to Griswold, Knickerbocker Office, [11 February 1845], reprinted in Griswold, *Passages from the Correspondence and other Papers of Rufus Wilmot Griswold*, 164.

20. *HJ*, 27 October 1849, p. 2. Willis's critic may well have been Henry Raymond again (who served on the Art-Union's Committee of Management), judging by an undated yet suggestive letter Willis sent to Horace Greeley at the *Tribune*. It began, "You misunderstand me. I object not to argument, but to gross personalities. My part of what you call *the controversy* is free from them. Your correspondent is a coarse slanderer, and if I had dreamed it was Raymond, whom I convicted of a string of slanderous falsehoods years ago, I certainly should never have replied to them." NPW to Greeley, Home Journal Office, *n.d.*, Horace Greeley Papers, NN, also held in typescript at the Horace Greeley Papers, DLC.

21. The second letter was printed in both the *NYH*, 4 April 1850, p. 1, and *HJ*, 6 April 1850, p. 2. It had a powerful effect on Forrest. A friend of the actor later recalled how only interference from friends prevented him from rushing to New York and "braining his slanderer on the instant." *PP*, 25 June 1850, p. 2.

22. *NYH*, 2 April 1850, p. 1; *NYTr*, 13 April 1850, p. 2.

23. Stevens's letters appear in *NYH*, 30 March 1850, p. 2, and 6 April 1850, p. 6. Drum's speech is noted in *NYTr*, 18 April 1850, p. 4.

24. *Boston Daily Mail*, 11 April 1850, p. 2. Catherine's "distraught supporter" (in an article of 13 April 1850) is to be found among the newspaper clippings concerning Edwin Forrest in M-HTC.

25. *NYH*, 18 April 1850, p. 4.

26. "Nincom Poop Willis," in *NYH*, 23 April 1849, p. 2.

27. Jones, *America and French Culture, 1750–1848*, 282; "Oeuvres of George Sand," *NAR* 53 (July 1841): 110; *NYH*, 22 February 1849, p. 2.

28. On "fashionable socialism," see *NYH*, 7 March 1850, p. 2, and 28 March 1850, p. 2.

29. In the wake of the Astor Place Riot, Bennett even went so far as far as to attribute difficulty of getting criminal convictions in recent years to the efforts of Fourierist socialists

and their disciples to remove the restraints of law, morality, and religion that had previously checked "the vicious and badly inclined portion of the community." *NYH*, 18 September 1849, p. 2. For Fourierism in the United States generally, see Guarneri, *The Utopian Alternative.*

30. *NYH*, 15 June 1850, p. 2. Edwin Forrest ultimately filed his Philadelphia Court of Common Pleas suit on 9 August 1850.

31. Commerce even made its way into such an unlikely situation. Soon after the attack, Dr. Felix Gouraud advertised that the "Lady" who sustained Willis's cause was not only among the "fairest and most beautiful women of the city," but also a user of his "Italian Medicated Soap and other delicious cosmetics," all of which could be purchased at his shop on Broadway. *(New York) Morning Star*, 26 June 1850, p. 2.

32. *NYTr*, 22 June 1850, p. 1. Greeley's surmise proved correct. Forrest himself admitted during subsequent legal proceedings that on 15 June 1850 he had visited his wife's neighborhood and watched her door, believing that "the worst enemy of his domestic happiness, and the most unscrupulous calumniator of his character, was in the house." Instead, Forrest met Samuel Raymond—another of the New York eight accused of adultery—coming from her house and proceeded to browbeat him with what one paper called "the lowest and most profane language." See *NYH*, 29 November 1850, p. 3, 30 November 1850, p. 1, and 22 December 1850, p. 1; *Cumming's (Philadelphia) Evening Bulletin*, 23 December 1850, p. 2; and *Boston Daily Mail*, 25 December 1850, p. 2.

33. Fanny Kemble is quoted in Moody, *Edwin Forrest*, 77. Moody also tells of a burlesque "Spartacus," complete with giant padded calves à la Forrest, playing the greater part of his death scene with a thicket of daggers plunged into his legs. When someone finally pointed them out, he dropped to the floor and writhed in anguish. "Bull" quoted in Yannella and Yannella, "Evert A. Duyckinck's *Diary: May 29–November 8, 1847*," 234.

34. For "no upper ten," see the *(Philadelphia) Pennsylvanian*, 6 April 1850, p. 1. For "baptism of blood," see Edwin to Catherine Forrest, *n.p.*, 16 July [1848], reprinted in *FDC*, b123. For Forrest's appeal among Jacksonian Democrats, see Mallett, " 'The Game of Politics,' " 31–46.

35. *NYTr*, 22 June 1850, p. 1, and 20 June 1850, p. 1. Willis himself contributed to this impression by describing himself as "not a fourth part of [Forrest's] strength or health." *HJ*, 29 June 1850, p. 2.

36. Over the nineteenth century, genteel expectation came to demand increasing expressive control in the street and marketplace. For the relationship of passion, restraint, and expression to antebellum social geography, see Lystra, *Searching the Heart*, esp. 18, and Kasson, *Rudeness and Civility*, 112–81.

37. "Willis's Pencillings," *Fraser's Magazine* 13 (February 1836): 195–203; Willis Gaylord Clark to James Lawson, Philadelphia, 2 September [*n.y.*], South Caroliniana Collection, University of South Carolina, Columbia, SC, quoted in Silverman, *Edgar A. Poe*, 223; and *NYTr*, 20 June 1850, p. 1.

38. *Louisville Daily Courier*, 24 June 1850, p. 2; and John E. Robinson to A. Leah Fox, Rochester, 21 June 1850, reprinted in Underhill, *Missing Link in Spiritualism*, 146–47. Thanks to Barb Ryan for bringing this last item to my attention.

39. Steven's card was printed concurrently in the *NYTr*, 19 June 1850, p. 4, and *NYH*, 19 June 1850, p. 2. Several papers, including the *(Boston) Evening Transcript*, 27 June 1950, p. 2, reprinted Forrest's card in *PP*, 26 June 1850, p. 2. It seems that Stevens also trumpeted a "pronunciamento" about town to the effect that Forrest would whip any editor who had "aught to say about his pending domestic difficulties." Forrest himself apparently responded with unbridled anger to newspaper accounts of the assault. Filled with rage, he confronted Parke Godwin on Broadway over his report of the beating (a "damned lie") in the *Evening*

Post; as for Willis, Forrest seethed to Godwin that he had "meant to cut his damned heart out." Beers, 313; *NYA*, 23 June 1850, p. 2, and 7 July 1850, p. 2. Rumor noted (plausibly) that Forrest was one of the "real" owners of the *Pennsylvanian* and had lent its editor, John Forney, five thousand dollars to cover expenses. Certainly the two men were chummy enough to also have spawned rumors that together they planned to start a New York journal dedicated to advancing "fierce democracie" in politics and the theater. See *(Philadelphia) Sunday Dispatch*, 28 May 1850, p. 2, and 2 June 1850, p. 2; *NYH*, 27 September 1849, p. 2; Robinson, "The *Pennsylvanian*," 350–60.

40. For the "court of morals," see *NYA*, 23 June 1850, p. 2. For the unwritten law, see Ireland, "The Libertine Must Die," 27–44; and Hartog, "Lawyering, Husbands' Rights, and the 'Unwritten Law' in Nineteenth-Century America," 67–96.

41. *NYH*, 19 June 1850, p. 2; *(Philadelphia) Public Ledger*, 19 June 1850, p. 3. As for the caricatures, the only extant evidence is a report from the editor of the New York *Atlas* that he had received anonymous copies several weeks after the assault. He called them "strictly personal," designed to "injure the reputation and the sensibilities of Mr. N. P. Willis," and he would have nothing to do with them. Still, he surmised that the cartoons were not Forrest's doing but the work of a "print seller" out to profit from interest and feelings in the matter. *NYA*, 10 November 1850, p. 2.

CHAPTER SEVEN

1. *Georgia Journal and Messenger*, 31 July 1850, p. 4.

2. For narrative and the cultural dimensions of nineteenth-century trials, see Korobkin, "The Maintenance of Mutual Confidence," 1–48; and Bernard S. Jackson, "Narrative Theories and Legal Discourse," in Nash, *Narrative in Culture*, 23–50.

3. "Throwing him over" appears in NPW to BM, [New York], 4 May 1850, MiD (BM). For the circular request, see NPW to Samuel B. Ruggles, Cornwall, 5 August 1850, reproduced in Stokes, *Memorials of Eminent Yale Men*, 1: 157–59.

4. *NYH*, 20 September 1850, p. 2.

5. For Van Buren, see Beck, "John Van Buren," 58–70, 202–13, 318–29. The opposing counsels' antagonism is discussed in Bigelow, *Retrospections of an Active Life*, 1: 81–87; Bigelow, "Some Recollections of Charles O'Conor," 729–31.

6. Information on Forrest's rampages appears in *NYH*, 13 September 1850, p. 1; 29 November 1850, p. 3; 22 December 1850, p. 1; 23 December 1850, p. 4; and 27 December 1850, p. 3. The new exchange of cards between Willis and Forrest is in *NYTr*, 9 January 1851, p. 4, and 10 January 1851, p. 4. The sole extant account of the O'Conor-Forrest meeting that I have been able to locate is an affidavit sworn out by Henry McKee for a case against O'Conor that probably never came to court. Given Forrest's loathing of O'Conor (only a month after Catherine had retained his services, Edwin was accusing him of forgery to sustain her case) and the fact that McKee was Edwin's witness (the affidavit was among the actor's papers), we must take its pro-Forrest sentiments with a grain of salt. Henry McKee affidavit, PU(EF).

7. For "insane," see *Cumming's (Philadelphia) Evening Bulletin*, 23 December 1850, p. 2.

8. *(Philadelphia) American Banner*, 1 February 1851, p. 2.

9. *C&E*, 15 May 1851, p. 2. Bennett, who detested Webb even more than he despised Willis, printed the whole of Webb's broadside and the *Day Book*'s column in a triumphant article entitled "New York Journalism of the Respectable and Fashionable Class, as Described by Themselves," in *NYH*, 16 May 1851, p. 2.

10. *(Macon) Georgia Citizen*, 5 April 1851, p. 2, quoting the *New York Mirror*.

11. Willis's "card" appeared in *NYTr*, 17 May 1851, p. 5.

12. "Webb vs. Willis," newspaper clipping, Edwin Forrest Collection, M-HTC; *NYA*, 8 June 1851, p. 2; *(New York) Sunday Times and Noah's Weekly Messenger*, 8 June 1851, p. 2; *NYH*, 5 June 1851, p. 4.

13. "New Rules of Evidence," *(New York) Independent* 3 (12 June 1851): 98; *Pittsburgh Saturday Visitor*, 5 July 1851, p. 2.

14. For Willis's reasoning, see *HJ*, 5 June 1851, p. 2, and 14 June 1851, p. 2.

15. *NYH*, 16 September 1851, p. 1.

16. *FDC*, 1; *NYTr*, 12 January 1852, p. 1.

17. *FDC*, b156.

18. For etiquette and appearance, see Halttunen, *Confidence Men and Painted Women*; Kasson, *Rudeness and Civility*.

19. *FDC*, 24–25, 34, 38–45, b147.

20. *FDC*, 33, 39, b89, b120, b148.

21. *FDC*, 40–41, 49, 70, 80, 99.

22. *FDC*, 96–97, b149. For Bennett's gleeful response to the "Fourier" letter, see *NYH*, 3 January 1852, p. 2.

23. *Cumming's (Philadelphia) Evening Bulletin*, 7 December 1850, p. 4; *FDC*, b84; *NYH*, 11 June 1851, quoted in Fatout, "Amelia Bloomer and Bloomerism," 367.

24. *FDC*, 15, b81. Ultimately, Doty was tried on charges of perjury but was found innocent, much to the distress of Edwin Forrest, who charged the jury with corruption.

25. *FDC*, b82–83, b87–88, b113–14, b161.

26. *FDC*, b103–4.

27. *FDC*, 47–61. The timing of Flower's initial arrival in New York (15 June 1850) may help to explain why Edwin Forrest was driven to flog Willis on Washington Square several days later.

28. Ibid.

29. *FDC*, b147.

30. So considerable were Stevens's out-of-pocket expenses that when the trial had ended his demand that Forrest repay such a large amount precipitated a falling out that had Forrest crying extortion and Stevens publicly charging his former associate with bankrolling the Astor Place Riot and seeking divorce for ulterior motives. See Stevens, "Secret History of the Astor Place Riot," printed concurrently in the *Police Gazette*, 3 April 1852, and in an extra edition of the *Boston Daily Times*.

31. *FDC*, 50–60, b100–1.

32. *FDC*, b181.

33. *FDC*, b88–92, b94–99, b108–9.

34. *FDC*, b110–12, b176.

35. *FDC*, b105–7, b172.

36. *FDC*, b177–78.

37. *FDC*, b182–84.

38. *NYH*, 27 January 1852, p. 6; *NYTi*, 27 January 1852, p. 4.

39. *NYH*, 13 July 1852, p. 4. As in the divorce trial, Forrest's counsel repeatedly and pointedly joked about Willis's manhood. He told the judge that whereas before he had proposed to prove criminal adultery against a woman, now he would "try the cause as against a man, or to speak more properly, who was not a woman." The crowd laughed heartily at this impertinence, but the judge was not amused, and he warned Van Buren against further such remarks. See *NYTi*, 2 March 1852, p. 3; 3 March 1852, p. 3; 4 March 1852, p. 4; and Tuckerman, "Some Old New Yorkers," 442–43. There is evidence that Willis also challenged Forrest to a duel but was refused. See NPW to [George Rex] Graham, *n.p.*, 25 January 1853, PHi(D).

40. Forrest quoted in Moody, *Edwin Forrest*, 324, 365–67.

41. *NYH*, 10 February 1852, p. 4; *NYTi*, 26 January 1852, p. 2.

42. The judge's opinion appears in Curtis, *Memoir of Benjamin Robbins Curtis*, 167.

43. Strong, *Diary of George Templeton Strong*, 3: 84. In 1868, when the court finally compelled Edwin to relinquish the back alimony heretofore frozen in legal battles, Catherine pocketed only $15,000 of the $68,000 award. O'Conor took $38,000, and his assistant Nelson Chase, who had been running the case since 1865, took almost $15,000. Catherine felt cheated; she believed O'Conor had agreed to defend her gratis. In 1875, in a last-ditch effort to regain her lost money, Catherine's brother-in-law filled five columns of the *New York Times* accusing O'Conor of duplicity. To clear himself, the famous lawyer demanded— and got—an investigation that exonerated him of any wrongdoing. When Edwin died soon afterward, however, his widow negotiated with her former husband's executors for release of her dower right, which, with interest, equaled $95,000. Agreement of Catherine Forrest and James Lawson, James Oakes, and Daniel Dougherty, 15 December 1874, Box 23, PU(EF).

44. *NYTr*, 26 January 1852, p. 4.

45. *National Democrat*, 27 January 1852, reprinted in *NYH*, 29 January 1852, p. 6; *Wilmington (North Carolina) Daily Journal*, 2 February 1852, p. 2; *NYH*, 28 January 1852, p. 2. Not surprisingly, this viewpoint was soon represented by pamphlets contesting the decision, including the anonymous pro-Edwin *Review of the Forrest Divorce*, which promised to reveal the "Secret doings" of the jury.

46. *NYTr*, 3 February 1852, p. 5.

CHAPTER EIGHT

1. Garfield, *Dairy of James A. Garfield, 1848–1871*, 1:216.

2. *EM*, 10 February 1845, p. 2.

3. As with so many cultural trends of the day, America's sentimental quest for the domestic associations of genius found inspiration in British models. Parlor show books such as *Homes of American Authors* (1853) undoubtedly took their cue from the likes of William Howitt's *Homes and Haunts of the Most Eminent British Poets* (1847). The most accessible record of Willis's particular brand of literary arcadianism is his *Out-doors at Idlewild* (1855).

4. The most complete and reliable source of information on Sara Payson Willis is Warren, *Fanny Fern*. This biography can be profitably supplemented by Desmond, "The Widow's Trials." For Julia Willis's reviewing, see the *True Flag*, 27 January 1855, p. 2; and NPW to [T. B.] Aldrich, *n.p., n.d.*, bMs Am 1429 (4698–99), MH.

5. Catharine E. Beecher to Mr. and Mrs. Willis, Hartford, 27 May 1829, MNS-S(FF). See also E. Parton, "Fanny Fern at the Hartford Female Seminary," 95.

6. N. P. Willis eulogized his sister's husband as a "robust, joyous and generous looking specimen of manly beauty" who found time from his duties at the Merchant's Bank to cultivate a "fine taste in the arts," an inclination that expressed itself in the "poetical and reflective" bas-relief commemorative monument he had recently erected in memory of his deceased daughter. *National Press*, 24 October 1846, p. 3. For Charles Eldredge's tangled investments, which included assuming the financial obligations on the Tremont Street project of his brother-in-law Joseph Jenkins (Mary Willis's husband), see Warren, *Fanny Fern*, 66–73.

7. For Farrington's Park Street connections, see W. E. Parton to [J. P. C. Winship], Newburyport, 28 February 1899, MNS-S(FF).

8. Farrington's disgust with his wife is evident in his newspaper card printed in the *Boston Daily Bee*, 25 February 1851, p. 3, newspaper clipping, MNS-S(FF). For his estranged

wife's side of the story, see her daughter's letter, Ellen W. E. Parton to [J. P. C. Winship], Newburyport, 28 February 1899, MNS-S(FF). Ellen Parton reports that Samuel Farrington went so far as to encourage the children to spy on their mother. More than this, *Rose Clark* (1856), Sara Willis's second semiautobiographical novel, tells of sexual abuse endured for the financial security often possible only in patriarchal marriage; ignored by day and forced to submit to unwanted sexual advances at night, Gertrude Dean (one of the novel's central characters) comes to loathe her spouse.

For the dire effects of penury, see E. Parton, "Fanny Fern," and Warren, *Fanny Fern*, 88, 106–7. There is some reason to question the extremes of this picture, particularly its portrait of Sara as entirely hemmed in by circumstance. Difficult though her days were in the Washington Street boardinghouse, Fern managed to save at least a few tokens of better days; years later she reported a silver service dating from her first marriage as part of the goods stolen from her New York City townhouse. So too does the matter of her daughter's domicile reveal at least a trace of autonomy left Sara Farrington. One of the reasons she evidently agreed to send her eldest daughter, Grace, to live with the Eldredges was that in mid-1851 Sara's father-in-law agreed, ultimately, to divide his property among the two girls so long as Grace stayed with his wife until her death. For Sara, this deal was acceptable, if still distasteful, only because she believed her mother-in-law's death to be imminent. Two years later Sara was telling her publisher that her first husband's mother was "over eighty and her physicians say cannot live many months." But old Mrs. Eldredge hung on for several years more—long enough, it turned out, to disinherit her son's family entirely. For such matters, see Desmond, "The Widow's Trials," 181; FF to J. C. Derby, ca. 1853, quoted in Derby, *Fifty Years among Authors, Books, and Publishers*, 211.

9. For the situation facing women writers in the 1850s, see Coultrap-McQuin, *Doing Literary Business*, esp. 1–26.

10. In 1845 Willis had meant to leave his surviving daughter, Imogen, with her aunts in Boston but could not bear to part with her, and eventually took her along with his daughter's longtime nurse, the escaped slave Harriet Jacobs. See NPW to BM, [New York, 18 May 1845], CtY(NPW). "Jepthah's Daughter" was first published in *BR&T* 11 (21 July 1826): 116.

11. NPW to Sara Eldredge Farrington [FF], *n.p.*, [ca. late summer 1851], MNS-S(FF). Precise dating of this letter is difficult. Warren is probably correct to suggest summer or early autumn of 1851. After all, N. P. Willis's sister claims therein to write for "several editors," although she is still looking for permanent employ.

12. I agree with many of Joyce Warren's speculations on the reasons for Willis's refusal to help his sister. But that he was jealous enough of his sister's talents to attempt to silence her for this reason alone seems unlikely. At the time Sara sent him her work, he was generally regarded as a master stylist. Willis's sister's talents, on the other hand, were both unknown and in many respects manqué. More likely, Willis genuinely disliked her tone, as did many genteel souls who blanched at its headlong and often transgressive bite. Yet if Willis often advised starry-eyed aspirants not to count on making a living from their pens, he did occasionally offer to aid. For the precariousness of N. P. Willis's finances and the state of the *Home Journal* in the early 1850s, see NPW to GPM, 25 April 1853, IaU; and NPW to [Mr. Hirst], New York, 17 January 1851, Emily Judson Collection, Clifton Waller Barret Library, (#9274), ViU.

13. NPW to Sara Eldredge Farrington [FF], *n.p.*, [ca. late summer–early autumn 1851], along with ms. poem, "To My Wild Sis," MNS-S(FF).

14. For Fern's progress, see Warren, *Fanny Fern*, 97–105.

15. A volume of tales for children, *Little Ferns for Fanny's Little Friends*, and a second series of *Fern Leaves* followed soon after.

16. At the very least, Fern was relieved to be finally free of the onerous necessity of incessant newspaper paragraphing. "I am so glad my book has done so well," she confided to her publisher in mid-June 1853. "I feel now as though I could lie back to sleep without feeling that it was a waste of time—on waking up in the night thinking over an article for the next morning at the bidding of some Editor." Later that summer Fern also finally obtained her divorce from Farrington. As for Moulton, judging by *Ruth Hall,* he may have threatened to sabotage Fern's newfound fortunes when she moved to leave him; but if so, she was not cowed. Of "Dear Old Boston," she wrote venomously in late June, "You know that you are bigoted, and opinionated, and narrow-minded (and like all who revolve in a two-pint measure), given to meddling with what is lawfully none of your business." Fern was last published in the *True Flag* on 23 April 1853 and in the *Olive Branch* on 25 June 1853. The most useful edition of Fern's first novel is Warren's *Ruth Hall and Other Writings,* which includes selected newspaper columns as well. For Fern's movements at this time, see Derby, *Fifty Years,* 211–13; Warren, *Fanny Fern,* 109–113, 334. The subversive potential of nineteenth-century women's fiction is discussed in Harris, *Nineteenth-Century American Women's Novels,* esp. 111–27.

17. FF to Derby and Miller, 8 February 1853, quoted in Warren, *Fanny Fern,* 108; *MW&T* 6 (13 August 1853): 229. Sara Farrington used her legal name (Mrs. S. P. Farrington) professionally only once in the early months of her literary career, under a piece of didactic sentimentalism written for *The Mother's Assistant.* When she left Boston in June 1853, Fern lived with her daughters at the New York Hotel under the name Payson. Warren, *Fanny Fern,* 99; Desmond, "The Widow's Trials," 235.

18. For Fern's compositional method, see Parton, *Fanny Fern,* 55. Fern's subversive newspaper tales are most accessible in *Fern Leaves* (which includes "The Widow's Trial," "No Fiction," "A Page from a Woman's Heart; or, Female Heroism," and "Uncle Jabe") and in *Fern Leaves, Second Series* (which includes "Critics," "How the Wires Are Pulled," and "Apollo Hyacinth").

19. FF, "Apollo Hyacinth," *MW&T* 6 (18 June 1853): 98. For masculine trespass, see "Fern Leaves," *Putnam's Magazine* 1 (July 1853): 103.

20. "Fanny Fern," *MW&T* 5 (2 October 1852): 67; review of "Fern Leaves," *MW&T* 6 (28 May 1853): 52. Although Warren suggests (plausibly) that Richard Willis wrote the *Musical World*'s review of *Fern Leaves,* I think greater evidence points to Dyer as its author. "Just look in the *Musical World and Times* this week, will you," Fern wrote J. C. Derby at about this time, "and see what Dyer has written. Isn't he *keen*? . . . he's *good* and sincere and *independent* and *dare say* what *he thinks*—I like *that*; I hate pussy cats!" FF to J. C. Derby, [ca. early June 1853], quoted in Warren, *Fanny Fern,* 110.

21. As N. P. Willis's congratulations on his sister's literary achievements come in the context of praising his brother's paper, the remark seems likely to date from April 1853; that is the only April during which the *Musical World* published Fern consistently. NPW to RSW, Idlewild, 18 April [ca. 1853], NjP(CS). It is possible that George Morris was instrumental in the *Home Journal*'s public support of Fern; in an obituary notice, Fern later remarked that he had welcomed her to New York in 1853, even inviting her to his Hudson River home. This support is noted in Desmond, "The Widow's Trials," 285. There is every reason to believe that Willis's account of his financial woes is accurate. For example, see NPW to GPM, Cornwall, 25 April 1853, IaU, in which Willis asks for forbearance of his friend's loan, as the double burden of unrecovered expenses from the Forrest affair and depending solely on his income after years on credit have left him living hand-to-mouth. See also NPW to H[enry] C[arey] Baird, Cornwall, 25 January 1853, H. C. Baird Papers, Baird Section, Gardiner Collection, Historical Society of Pennsylvania, Philadelphia, PA.

As Joyce Warren points out, N. P. Willis's second note to Richard is evidently one letter from a flurry of family correspondence that greeted Fern's disclosures. But Warren is probably mistaken in dating it 2 June. For one thing, only several days separate the date of the letter from the publication date of the *Musical World* review of *Fern Leaves* to which it alludes. Given both N. P. Willis's distance from New York City and the likelihood that this letter was part of an ongoing exchange of correspondence, it seems improbable for it to have been written so soon after the events to which it refers. More than this, an easier answer exists: the letter is dated 27 June, not 2 June. This seems likely when one compares the shape of Willis's "7s" in other letters (see, for instance, NPW to [his publisher], New York, 17 March *n.y.*, Fred Lewis Pattee Library, Pennsylvania State University Libraries, University Park, PA) to that of the letter in question. Both feature peculiar curlicues that distinguish Willis's hand from others.

Though Warren thinks not, moreover, I believe it highly probable that Willis alludes to the "Apollo Hyacinth" article of 18 June in his 27 June letter to Richard. "There are some things," he told his brother, that Sara "herself has written which I would give much to expunge." On the strength of *Ruth Hall*, Warren also suggests that N. P. Willis may have entreated Lucy Bumstead ("Louisa Miller" in the novel) to try to dissuade Fern from her course. This is possible, even likely, though he may have begged Fern to stop the insinuations rather than cease writing altogether, as the novel (and Warren) suggest. NPW to RSW, Idlewild, 27 June [ca. 1853], NjP(CS); Warren, *Fanny Fern*, 94, 333.

22. FF, "Don't You Believe It," *MW&T* 6 (7 May 1853): 5 (copied from the *Olive Branch*); FF, "Newspaper-dom," *MW&T* 6 (6 August 1853): 211. The Parton incident probably happened as follows. In 1852, with Willis an invalid up at Idlewild, Parton had assumed most of the daily editorial chores at the *Home Journal*. Taken with Fern's talents but unaware of her relation to his superior, he began clipping her tales for publication in the *Home Journal*. This went on for some time, until Willis arrived one day in the New York office and forbade his subordinate from copying any more of Fern's articles into the *Home Journal*. (Perhaps it was merely one particularly offensive article, as Fern's columns occasionally appeared in the *Home Journal* even after Parton's departure.) At this demand, Parton reputedly stormed out in a rage, never to return. As he had, by the summer of 1853, personally met Fern (Oliver Dyer introduced the two on Sara's removal to New York City), Parton's hair-trigger dudgeon may have sprung from a new understanding of Fern's former predicament. In any case, Parton would have nothing further to do with his former boss. In May 1854 he wrote Horace Greeley that he had not seen Willis for several months, nor would he speak to him if he did.

Fern and Parton later married, having signed a prenuptual agreement reserving the wife's earnings to herself alone. Parton went on to a long career as the nation's foremost biographer. For Parton's responsibilities at the *Home Journal*, see NPW to GPM, Idlewild, 14 March [1853], IaU. For "Fern Leaves" copied into the *Home Journal* after Parton's departure, see *HJ*, 21 January 1854, p. 1; 29 April, 1854, p. 1; and 19 August 1854, p. 1. James Parton to Horace Greeley quoted in Flower, *James Parton*, 27–28. For a general overview of the situation, see Warren, *Fanny Fern*, 105–6, who dates the breakup—accurately, it would seem—to early autumn 1853.

23. Fanny Fern, "Are There Any Men among Us?" *MW&T* 7 (24 September 1853): 29–30. Oliver Dyer parted ways with Richard Willis in November 1853 and soon connected himself with both the *Musical Review and Choral Advocate* and the Mason Brother's Publishers (Daniel and Lowell Jr.). He was, remembered a third Mason brother (the pianist William, whose concert tour Dyer publicized), a "man of action, and possessed [of] good literary ability." William Mason, *Memoirs of a Musical Life*, 184–85, quoted in Lawrence, *Strong on Music*, 2: 507, but see also 2: 240, 458.

24. Joyce Warren has shown how many incidents in *Ruth Hall* had their foundation in actual experience. Yet we should be wary of taking Fern's fiction as an entirely authentic report of real life. It seems likely that its "sensational design" (to borrow Jane Tompkins's phrase) was affected by Fern's psychological state, as well as by her conscious intent to subvert patriarchal prerogatives. For a provocative interpretation of Fern's use of the "female complaint," to which my own analysis is broadly indebted, see Berlant, "The Female Woman," 429–54.

As for the sources of Fern's feminist impulses, it is safe to conclude that they arose primarily from grim experience. Some evidence suggests that they may also have stemmed from a kind of nineteenth-century "consciousness raising." In a reminiscence, the eighty-six-year-old Boston dry goods dealer William Endicott later recalled how, as a young clerk in the late 1840s, he had once boarded at a house on Columbia Street run by the former housekeeper at Brook Farm, a Mrs. J. B. Hill. With him in this "atmosphere of idealism" were former Brook Farmers John S. Dwight (the Fourierist music critic) and Charles A. Dana (eventually to be editor of the New York *Sun*), as well as "Mrs. Eldredge, a widow with two little daughters, sister of N. P. Willis the poet." If this reminiscence is accurate, the "very jolly times" had among the impecunious radicals may have taught Fern more than how to economize and still have a good time. The only problem with this scenario's placing Fern among the company of cultural reformers in the years between her first and second marriages comes in its corroboration. Secondary sources fail to name the Boston boarding-house resorted to by Dana and his new wife in the months before their removal to New York City in February 1847. Dwight seems to have spent time after Brook Farm at an "associationist" boardinghouse on High Street, before eventually moving to a "combined house" on Pinckney Street, run by a Mrs. Parsons, mother of a Brook Farm well-wisher. See Endicott, "Reminiscences of Seventy-Five Years," 215; Cooke, *John Sullivan Dwight, Brook Farmer, Editor, and Critic of Music*, 129–30; and J. Wilson, *Life of Charles Anderson Dana*, 58–61.

25. *Ruth Hall*, 133. Joyce Warren suggests that Fern's "Ruth" may have been inspired by the British novelist Elizabeth Gaskell's sympathetic treatment of "fallen women" in her own *Ruth* (1853). I think it as likely to have been inspired by Fern's own evangelical education in the story of this biblical "gleaner," or perhaps a reading of Wordsworth's "Ruth" (in *Lyrical Ballads*) or George Crabbe's "Ruth" (in *Tales of the Hall*), both of which emphasize their protagonists' innocence, loneliness, and alienation from their families. Warren, *Fanny Fern*, 138–39; E. Stoddard, "The Genealogy of Ruth," 204–37.

26. *Ruth Hall*, 13–17.

27. Ibid., 116.

28. Ibid., 179.

29. Ibid., 130. Ann Douglas recognized "Floy's" provenance but did not explore its significance. Wood, "The 'Scribbling Women' and Fanny Fern," 21–22.

30. Fern's next novel, *Rose Clark*, also spoke of her desire for a brother to protect her, as he did Gertrude from the predations of her divorced husband. Warren, *Fanny Fern*, 87, 158–61, 140–47, 149–52, 170–80, 201–3, 210–11; *Ruth Hall*, 133, 143, 151–52.

31. *Ruth Hall*, 208–11. I agree at least partly with Lauren Berlant, who argues in "The Female Woman" that Fern's experience had led her to "repudiate patrifocal family as a site of female fulfillment, although she desires intensely to live in a family made up of mothers and daughters." I would add that perhaps Fern had not given up on men entirely, but yearned also for brothers—true brothers—and perhaps even true fathers.

32. To document the certitude with which reviewers identified the nature of the book, see, for example, the *Boston Post*, 14 December 1854, p. 1. Those denying the novel's autobiographical content were often reduced to wishful thinking. As one editor could not

imagine that any author would parade his or her experience in such a fashion, he counseled readers that the book had "better be read, without anxious inquires as to who may be meant by particular characters." *Boston Daily Advertiser*, 12 December 1854, p. 2.

33. For inklings of Fern's true identity, see "Fanny Fern," *Democratic Review* 33 (August 1853): 188; *Athenaeum*, 22 October 1853, p. 1254, noted in Desmond, "The Widow's Trials," 243; *NYTr*, 26 May 1854, newspaper clipping, MNS-SFF; *HJ*, 1 April 1854, pp. 2–3, quoting the *Boston Evening Transcript*; NPW to William J. Gilbert, Idlewild, 15 November 1853, Seymour Library, Archives and Manuscripts Collection, Knox College, Galesburg, IL; *Cumming's (Philadelphia) Evening Bulletin*, 16 December 1854, p. 17. It is, of course, possible that Fern saw neither the *Transcript*'s article, the *Home Journal*'s reprint, nor the request for her autograph. But she must have been aware of the career of rumor, and there is considerable evidence that she had been telegraphing her identity all along. In November 1853, for example, Fern was quoted in her paper of the moment, the *Saturday Evening Post*, proclaiming (much as she would in the crisis scene of *Ruth Hall*) that "I felt that I *would* succeed—and I DID succeed." More than this, the scenario that suggests that *Ruth Hall* was written at the insistence of Fern's publishers and against her better judgment probably began with Fern herself, and with her granddaughter, Ethel Thomason Parton. Subsequent scholarship (including the pioneer work of Elizabeth Bancroft Schlesinger) then repeated the assertion. Most recently, Joyce Warren has argued that Fern's "carefully guarded secret identity" was not exposed until William Moulton's "Key" to *Ruth Hall* appeared in the *True Flag* on 30 December 1854.

Given new evidence, revision is, I think, justified. Ethel Parton had her reasons for maintaining that her grandmother's bitter fusillade had been meant for family eyes only: as a young girl, she had gotten the information straight from her beloved grandmother (who died when Ethel was ten years old, and who never divulged her second marriage to her granddaughter); then too, believing so made Fern a wholly innocent victim of Moulton's spite. For hints, see *(Philadelphia) Saturday Evening Post*, 5 November 1853. For the career of this interpretation, see Ethel Parton to Mrs. Willis, 20 September [1931], Newburyport, NjM(NPW); E. Parton, "Fanny Fern: An Informal Biography"; Schlesinger, "Fanny Fern," 501–19; McGinnis, "Fanny Fern, American Novelist," 1–37; Adams, *Fanny Fern, or, a Pair of Flaming Shoes*; Warren, *Fanny Fern*, 121–23.

34. *Ruth Hall*, 70, 83, 178–79; *NYH*, 23 December 1854, p. 3; *Cumming's (Philadelphia) Evening Bulletin*, 16 December 1854, p. 7. For "reform" and the "sensation" predicted, see Mason Brother's initial advertisements in *NYTr*, 15 November 1854, p. 1, and 16 November 1854, p. 1; *NYTi*, 15 November 1854, p. 5, and 16 November 1854, p. 5.

35. Hart quoted in Williams, "Widening the World," 565–86; *Philadelphia North American* review reprinted in Mason Brothers advertisement, *NYTr*, 22 December 1854, p. 1. Although it is hardly an impartial source, the *Olive Branch* reported that one-half of *Ruth Hall*'s reviews were positive, but it sneered that her partisans included "women writers," "boarding school girls," and "injured women." Among this readership it was reported that "she is regarded as a *victim*—an innocent, blessed, lamb-like sufferer—an angel." *Olive Branch*, 3 February 1855, p. 2. See also William Gilmore Simms to William Elliot, Woodlands, 8 January [1855], in Simms, *Letters of William Gilmore Simms*, 3:358, in which he remarks, "*Ruth Hall* I have not read. I have long known Willis to be a contemptible skunk, & I think I once told you so. I knew that he lied, & I could believe all the rest of him."

36. "To My Aged Father" appeared in the *Youth's Companion, Olive Branch, True Flag, Boston Transcript*, and the *Musical World*, and in the last accompanied by a poem, "A Winter Visit to Idlewild." For evidence of N. P. Willis's close relationship with the literary coterie at the *Boston Transcript*, whose aid he often requested, see particularly Tryon, *Parnassus Corner*, 178–204; NPW to James T. Fields, Idlewild, 20 January 1855, Henry E.

Huntington Library, San Marino, CA. Dating Richard Willis's return to his brother's camp is difficult. With Oliver Dyer at his side, Richard certainly sustained his sister's cause in the summer during which both *Fern Leaves* and "Apollo Hyacinth" took American readers by storm. And if N. P.'s complaint of late June 1853 registered with his brother, we have no evidence of it; until the following summer, the *Musical World* featured extensive advertisements for Fern's books (as did the *Home Journal,* for that matter). But none appeared for *Ruth Hall;* by December 1854, Richard clearly felt that his sister had gone too far.

His discomfort may have been building for some time. In November 1853 Oliver Dyer gave up his interest in the *Musical World* just as Fern moved to the *Saturday Evening Post.* Although no evidence documents the cause of this split, perhaps Richard no longer felt comfortable with either his sister's reckless familial polemics or her loudest cheerleader, even if, loving brother that he was, he remained unwilling to make a public issue of their disagreements. Significantly, Richard does not appear in *Ruth Hall.* Nonetheless, Fern never seems to have regarded her younger brother as she did other male relations; after the novel's publication, the two maintained ties, and Richard often spoke of Fern fondly. See Warren, *Fanny Fern,* 128–29.

37. "He was like a brother to me," says Zippa in the play, "the kindest brother sister ever had." *HJ,* 13 January 1855, pp. 1 and 2.

38. Richmond to Maria Clemm, [Westover, Massachusetts], "Thursday noon" [ca. January 1855], reprinted in Poe, *Edgar Allan Poe* 56–58.

39. "Domestic misunderstandings" appears in the *NYTr,* 16 December 1854, p. 3. Nathaniel Hawthorne alone among the nation's literary authorities confessed to relishing the book's venom: "The woman writes as if the devil was in her; and that is the only condition under which a woman ever writes anything worth reading." But this was written only for private consumption. Hawthorne to William D. Ticknor, Liverpool, 2 February 1855, reprinted in Hawthorne, *Century Edition of the Letters of Nathaniel Hawthorne,* 17:307–8.

40. *NYTi,* 20 December 1854, p. 2.

41. For this line of criticism, see the review of "Ruth Hall," *Harper's New Monthly Magazine* 10 (March 1855): 550–53.

42. Elizabeth Cady Stanton, "Ruth Hall," *Una* 3 (February 1855): 29–30. Interestingly, the *Una's* initial notice of the book (which predates Stanton and Dall's interchange) suggests just how successfully Fern's sentimental polemics were playing with at least some readers. The book "chained us to our room all bright New Year's day, when others were out making calls," the reviewer noted appreciatively. Fern "exposes hypocrisy fearlessly, and in sympathy with the poor victim, the bosom swells with indignation and just scorn; it melts the heart with its touching pathos, and the eyes overflow with tears; smiles follow these like April sunshine." "Ruth Hall," *Una* 3 (January 1855): 13.

43. Caroline Healey Dall, "Ruth Hall," *Una* 3 (March 1855): 42–43.

44. For Moulton's salacious charges, see the *True Flag,* 30 December 1854, p. 3; 6 January 1855, p. 3; and 13 January 1855, p. 3.

45. [Moulton], *Life and Beauties of Fanny Fern; Boston Post,* 20 February 1855, p. 1. Not surprisingly, Willis was rumored to have been mixed up in Moulton's counterbiography, a possibility that led his friend Bayard Taylor to complain, "Somebody is spreading the report that Willis wrote (or got up) *The Life and Beauties of F. F.* which is an atrocious falsehood. What are we coming to?" For Willis's part, he has been quoted as writing to G. P. Morris, "Fanny Fern matters will hurt nothing, only shame and grieve our family. The public opinion will soon be correct enough." Bayard Taylor to Orville J. Victor, Milwaukee, 28 February 1855, reprinted in Taylor, *Unpublished Letters of Bayard Taylor in the Huntington Library,* 40; NPW to GPW, Idlewild, 10 January 1855, quoted in *NYTi,* 9 November 1894, Saturday supplement, p. 819.

46. For Bonner's pursuit and capture of Fern, see Derby, *Fifty Years*, 202–7; Warren, "Uncommon Discourse," 51–68. See also the *New York Atlas*'s "Fanny Ahead!" which reported that *Ruth Hall* sold 30,000 copies, while her brother's *Out-doors at Idlewild* (issued only weeks earlier) had yet to sell out its first edition of 3,000 copies. This report is quoted in Desmond, "The Widow's Trials," 246.

47. For "Ruth-less Hall," see Greenwood, "Fanny Fern—Mrs. Parton," 74. For Fern's riposte, see FF to editor, *New Bedford Mercury*, 31 January 1855, quoted in *Boston Post*, 11 February 1855, p. 4. This letter was also reprinted in the *Weekly New York Tribune*, 17 February 1855. The original is now held in the Alderman Library at the University of Virginia.

48. For the Bulwers' marriage troubles, see Blain, "Rosina Bulwer Lytton and the Rage of the Unheard," 211–36. For allusion to Lady Bulwer during the *Ruth Hall* episode, see *NYA*, 17 December 1854, newspaper clipping, MNS-SFF.

49. This biographical innovation did not escape contemporary notice. In reviewing James Parton's *Life of Greeley*, the *Southern Quarterly Review* observed that "biographies used to be written upon a tombstone. They are now issued as a continuous periodical posted up to the last paragraph of the distinguished subject. . . . Men ambitious of fame might at least postpone the narrative of their life till it is over. But they discount their posthumous fame for a present pittance of notoriety." Review of "Life of Horace Greeley, Editor of the New York Tribune," *Southern Quarterly Review*, n.s., 11 (January 1855): 272.

50. [Marguerittes], *Match-Girl*. With its transparent portraits of famous characters including, in addition to Willis and the Forrests, "Mr. And Mrs. Field Close" (the Godwins), "Zephalinda Bayes" (Cornelia Willis), "Sylvius Dysart" (Charles O'Conor), and "Jessie Finch" (Anne Lynch), the novel's scandal was crystal clear. As one observer crowed salaciously, "the startling portion of the book is a secret and hitherto unrevealed history of the most wonderful divorce case that ever appeared in our courts." Once the "springs of action" and "secret motives" were revealed, he predicted that "violent partisanship will be again aroused." *(Philadelphia) Evening Bulletin*, 21 September 1855, p. 2.

51. Sarah Preston Everett Hale to Edward Everett Hale, Boston, 26 September 1855, Hale Family Papers, Ms group #71, Sophia Smith Collection, Smith College, Northampton, MA. For a glimpse at the sensationalist advertising techniques playing up the exposure of celebrity, see the *(Philadelphia) Sunday Dispatch*, 7 October 1855, p. 3, and Cumming's *(Philadelphia) Evening Bulletin*, 21 September to 14 December 1855.

The *Evening Mirror*'s identification of *The Match-Girl*'s author as Madame Julie de Marguerittes, the daughter of an Anglo-Italian Jewish doctor, is probably correct. Accompanied by her first husband, the ardent Bonapartist Count de Marguerittes, this aspiring author, playwright, and songstress had once been an intimate of Catherine Forrest's circle; at the height of the divorce troubles the two even shared lodgings. But the trial's immediate aftermath brought a falling out. When financial reverses connected to a failed operatic debut threatened to impound her property, Madame de Marguerittes's promoter, sometime literary compatriot, and future husband George "Gaslight" Foster (a nativist journalist best known for his sensational urban sketches) approached John Van Buren with the proposal that his client turn evidence against Catherine Forrest in return for a "loan" to cover debts. Whatever the reason, nothing immediately came of this scheme, though there is evidence that Foster did receive some financial assistance. Four years later, Julie de Marguerittes again needed money. In the meantime, her husband had returned to France to support Napoleon III and she, claiming desertion, had married Foster. But by 1855, he was languishing in Moyamensing Prison on a forgery conviction.

Faced with the prospect of supporting herself and freeing her incarcerated husband, there is every reason to believe the new Mrs. Foster was ready to capitalize on her inside knowledge of the Forrest affair. She had already relinquished rights to her *Ins and Outs of Paris* to cover one of the four bank notes Foster had been convicted of forging. In March 1855 her imprisoned husband was searching for the final $200 for his bail. If we are to believe *The Match-Girl*, there might have been further motives for Marguerittes's authorship: in the novel, George Foster's character is seduced and abandoned by Caroline St. Maur. Information on Marguerittes and Foster is sketchy. For Foster, see Foster, *New York by Gas-light and Other Urban Sketches*, 27–45; Griswold, *Passages from the Correspondence and Other Papers of Rufus Wilmot Griswold*, 292, 294, 298; *NYTi*, 17 April 1856, p. 4. For Marguerittes, see *NYT:* 24 June 1866, p. 1; Odell, *Annals of the New York Stage*, 153; A. Wilson, *History of the Philadelphia Stage, 1835 to 1855*, 23; "A Titled Actress: Julie Granville, the Countess Marguerittes," newspaper clipping, M-HTC; *C&E*, 2 June 1851, p. 2. For specific details related to the couple's connection to the cast of characters in the Forrest affair, see "Mrs. Forrest's Suite," *Gleason's Pictorial Drawing-Room Companion* 2 (20 March 1852): 191; *NYH*, 22 February 1852, p. 2, and 2 May 1852, p. 2; *NYTi*, 2 October 1851, p. 2; NPW to BM, [New York], 29 January 1851, MiD(BM). See also Foster to Van Buren, 850 Broadway, [24 April] 1852; Foster to Van Buren, *n.p.*, [ca. late April 1852]; and N. D. French to unknown, New York, 29 April 1852; Foster, cashier's checks; E. de Marguerittes to Edwin Forrest, Clinton Hotel, New York, 14 March 1853, all in PU(EF).

52. Simms to Evert Augustus Duyckinck, Charleston, 13 October [1855], Simms, *Letters of William Gilmore Simms*, 3: 405–6. Forrest's modern biographer, Richard Moody, suggests that *The Match-Girl* was merely one more burden for the famous actor to bear. But this conclusion underestimates both the psychological and legal rewards such a fantasy of redress might have had for one so tormented. Only weeks after the novel's issue, John Van Buren once again took Edwin Forrest's case before the New York courts, arguing that public opinion had effectively reversed the original court's decision against his client so that all back alimony ought to be waived. This conjunction of events alone should at least raise questions regarding the hand behind *The Match-Girl*. Moody, *Edwin Forrest*, 324, 331–34.

53. *Paul Fane* was announced in late October 1855, ran in the *Home Journal* from January to August 1856, and was published by Charles Scribner in November of the same year.

54. For advertisements and calls for a novel, see *Boston Evening Transcript*, 17 November 1856, p. 3; *NYTr*, 5 December 1856, p. 1; and "N. P. Willis," *Arthur's Home Magazine* 4 (September 1854): 239. "Death-narrative" in NPW to GPM, Idlewild, [ca. January 1856], NN-B. For "rubbish," see NPW to Joseph Broughton, Glenmary, 7 June 1842, #12230, New York State Library, Albany, NY.

55. NPW, *Paul Fane*, 11, 17, 401.

56. Ibid., 24, 51–2, 201–2, 398.

57. For quotations describing the spiritualist aesthetic and Samuel Laurence (whose name Willis spells, probably wrongly, as "Lawrence"), see *HJ*, 15 July 1854, p. 2, and 5 May 1855, p. 2. Somewhat confusingly, Willis had once also made a similar case about the genius of painters (in a tale entitled "Mabel Wynne") using the example of Sir *Thomas* Lawrence, whom, Willis said, painted the "magnetic atmosphere" of a sitter. But this famous English portrait painter was long dead by the 1850s; Samuel Laurence was still very much alive and probably painted Willis's portrait in these years, as he had most certainly produced a crayon drawing of the American author in the 1830s.

58. NPW, *Paul Fane*, 23, 207–9, 267–70, 399.

59. Ibid., 394–98.

60. NPW to [Edmund Quincy], Idlewild, 24 December 1856, CtY(NPW). Willis's letter on how to read *Paul Fane* appeared in *HJ*, 10 January 1857, p. 2. "Snob" appeared in *NYTi*, 2 December 1856, p. 2.

61. Unidentified newspaper clipping, N. P. Willis folder, M-HTC.

CHAPTER NINE

1. Holmes, "The New Portfolio," 108. See also Pennell, *Charles Godfrey Leland, a Biography*, 1:292–93, which quotes Holmes's remark: "We put poor Willis to bed in Mount Auburn on Thursday and tucked him up in as fleecy a white blanket as the careful old mother would weave for him with her loom of cloud and wind. It was on his sixty-first birthday that he died, and it is as it were this morning that I read those lines of his, just out:—I'm twenty-two, I'm 22, / They idly give me joy, / As if I should be glad to know, / That I was but a boy. Whether I first read them this morning, or almost forty years ago, they have been always in my memory since the time."

2. *NYTi*, 22 January 1867, p. 4.

3. Richmond to "Muddie" [Mrs. Maria Clemm], 14 July 1867, reproduced in Poe, *Edgar Allan Poe*, 167; Hayward, "Nathaniel Parker Willis," 212; Beers, 66; newspaper clipping [ca. late 1870s] appended to NPW to——, 6 January 1858, Autograph File, MH. The trajectory of Willis's posthumous British literary reputation mirrored that of his American reputation. See Gohdes, "British Interest in American Literature," 356–62.

4. NPW, *Out-doors at Idlewild*, vii.

5. Beers, 352, quoting William Makepeace Thackeray.

6. Parton to J. T. Fields, 13 February 1867, quoted in Warren, *Fanny Fern*, 12; Richards and Elliott, *Julia Ward Howe, 1819–1910*, 136. When William Gilmore Simms heard of Willis's death, he was moved to similar sentiments. "So Willis has made his mortal exit," he wrote a friend. "In the flush of his career, conceding him large merits as a man of talents, I yet held him in contempt as a man. In his latter days I pitied him. Let him rest in peace!" Simms to Evert A. Longfellow, Charleston, 25 January [1867], reproduced in Simms, *Letters of William Gilmore Simms*, 5:9.

7. For Willis's journalistic precedent, see Hayward, "Nathaniel Parker Willis," 216–17; and R. Stoddard, *Recollections, Personal and Literary*, 83–85. Edgeworth quoted in Hart, *Lockhart as Romantic Biographer*, 36. Holmes, "An After-Breakfast Talk," 71–75.

8. Ernst and Schwartz, *Privacy*, 44–70, 74–77; and Mensel, " 'Kodakers Lying in Wait,' " 24–45.

SOURCES AND
BIBLIOGRAPHY

ABBREVIATIONS

AMM	*American Monthly Magazine*
Beers	Beers, Henry Augustin. *Nathaniel Parker Willis.* Cambridge: Riverside Press, 1885.
BM	Brantz Mayer
BR	*Boston Recorder*
BR&T	*Boston Recorder and Telegraph*
C&E	*Morning Courier and New York Enquirer*
CtY	Beinecke Rare Book and Manuscript Library, Yale University, New Haven, CT
CtY(KP)	Ker Porter Collection, Beinecke Rare Book and Manuscript Library, Yale University, New Haven, CT
CtY(NPW)	Nathaniel Parker Willis Letter Collection, Beinecke Rare Book and Manuscript Library, Yale University, New Haven, CT
DLC	Manuscripts Division, Library of Congress, Washington, DC
EM	*(New York) Evening Mirror*
FDC	Herald edition of the *Forest Divorce Case.* New York: Dewitt and Davenport, 1852.
FF	Fanny Fern [Sara Payson Willis Parton]
GJP	George James Pumpelly
GPM	George Pope Morris
HJ	*(New York) Home Journal*
IaU	University of Iowa Libraries, Special Collections, Iowa City, IA
JBVS	John Bleecker Van Schaick
JP	Jane Porter
MB	Boston Public Library, Rare Books and Manuscripts Division, Boston, MA

MBC	Congregational Library, Boston, MA
MeWC	Colby College Library, Colby College, Watertown, ME
MH	Houghton Library, Harvard University, Cambridge, MA
MHi	Massachusetts Historical Society, Boston, MA
M-HTC	Harvard Theatre Collection, Houghton Library, Harvard University, Cambridge, MA
MiD(BM)	Brantz Mayer Papers, Burton Historical Collection, Detroit Public Library, Detroit, MI
MNS-SFF	Fanny Fern Papers, Sophia Smith Collection, Smith College, Northampton, MA
MW&T	*Musical World and Times*
NAR	*North American Review*
NHi	New-York Historical Society, New York City, NY
NjM(NPW)	Nathaniel Parker Willis Collection, Joint Free Public Library of Morristown and Morris Township, Morristown, NJ
NjP	Manuscripts Divisions, Department of Rare Books and Special Collections, Princeton University Libraries, Princeton, NJ
NjP(CS)	Charles Scribner's Sons Archives, Author Files I, Box 170, Manuscripts Division, Department of Rare Books and Special Collections, Princeton University Library, Princeton, NJ
NM	*New Mirror*
NN	Manuscripts and Archives Division, New York Public Library, Astor, Lenox, and Tilden Foundations, New York City, NY
NN-B	Berg Collection of English and American Literature, New York Public Library, Astor, Lenox, and Tilden Foundations, New York City, NY
NNC	Rare Book and Manuscript Library, Butler Library, Columbia University, New York City, NY
NNC(NPW)	Letters of Nathaniel Parker Willis, Rare Book and Manuscript Library, Butler Library, Columbia University, New York City, NY
NOwHi	Tioga County Historical Society, Owego, NY
NPW	Nathaniel Parker Willis
NYA	*(New York) Atlas*
NYH	*(New York) Daily Herald*
NYM	*New York Mirror*
NYTi	*New York Daily Times*
NYTr	*(New York) Daily Tribune*
PHi(D)	Dreer Collection, Historical Society of Pennsylvania, Philadelphia, PA
PHi(G)	Simon Gratz Collection, Historical Society of Pennsylvania, Philadelphia, PA
PP	*(Philadelphia) Pennsylvanian*
PU(EF)	Edwin Forrest Collection, Special Collections, Van Pelt Library, University of Pennsylvania, Philadelphia, PA
RSW	Richard Storrs Willis
Ruth Hall	Parton, Sara Willis. *Ruth Hall, and Other Writings.* Edited by Joyce W. Warren. New Brunswick: Rutgers University Press, 1986 [orig. 1855]
ViU	Special Collections Department, University of Virginia Library, Charlottesville, VA
WM	*(New York) Weekly Mirror*
WSL	Walter Savage Landor

ARCHIVES CONSULTED

American Antiquarian Society

Archives of American Art, Smithsonian Institution

Boston Athenaeum

Boston Public Library, Rare Books and Manuscripts Division

Brown University Library, Special Collections

Chicago Historical Society

Cincinnati Historical Society

Colby College Library, Special Collections

Columbia University, Rare Book and Manuscript Library, Butler Library

Congregational Library

Connecticut Historical Society

Cornell University Library, Department of Manuscripts and University Archives

Cornwall (New York) Public Library

Detroit Public Library, Burton Historical Collection

Duke University, Special Collections

Folger Shakespeare Library

Harvard University, Houghton Library (including Harvard Theater Collection)

Haverford College Library

Henry E. Huntington Library, Department of Manuscripts

Historical Society of Pennsylvania

Johns Hopkins University, Milton S. Eisenhower Library

Joint Free Public Library of Morristown and Morris Township

Knox College Archives

Library of Congress, Manuscript Division

Longfellow National Historical Site, National Park Service

Maryland Historical Society

Massachusetts Historical Society

Morristown National Historical Park

Newberry Library

New Hampshire Historical Society

New-York Historical Society

New York Public Library, Henry W. and Albert A. Berg Collection

New York Public Library, Rare Books and Manuscripts Collection

New York State Library, Manuscripts and Special Collections

New York University, Fales Library

Pennsylvania State University, Fred Pattee Library

Phillips Academy Library

Pierpont Morgan Library

Princeton University Library, Rare Books and Manuscripts Division

Smith College, Sophia Smith Collection

Stanford University Library, Department of Special Collections

State Historical Society of Wisconsin

Tioga County (New York) Historical Society

University of California, Los Angeles, Department of Special Collections

University of Chicago, Joseph Regenstein Library

University of Illinois, Rare Book Room

University of Indiana, Lilly Library

University of Iowa Library, Special Collections

University of Kansas, Special Collections, Kenneth Spencer Research Library

University of Michigan, William L. Clements Library, Special Collections

University of Minnesota Library, Manuscript Division

University of North Carolina at Chapel Hill, Southern Historical Collection

University of Pennsylvania, Charles Patterson Van Pelt Library, Special Collections

University of South Carolina, South Caroliniana Library

University of Virginia, Alderman Library, Special Collections Department

Vermont Historical Society

Victoria and Albert Museum

Wellesley College Library, Special Collections

Williams College, Chapin Library

Yale University, Beinecke Rare Book and Manuscript Library

SELECTED PERIODICALS

Age (London) (1835–36)

American Monthly Magazine (1829–31)

American Monthly Magazine (New York and Boston) (1833–36)

American Traveller (1828–31)

Arthur's Home Magazine (1854)

Baltimore American and Commercial Daily Advertiser (1836)

Boston Courier (1827–31)

Boston Daily Advertiser (1854–55)

Boston Daily Bee (1851)

Boston Daily Mail (1850)

Boston Daily Times (1852)

(Boston) Evening Transcript (1854–56)

Boston Post (1854–55)

Boston Recorder (also Recorder and Telegraph) (1816–31)

Boston Statesman (1828–31)

Boston Watchman-Examiner (1827–31)

Bower of Taste (1828–30)

Broadway Journal (1845–46)

Christian Examiner (1827–36)

Cumming's (Philadelphia) Evening Bulletin (1849–55)

Democratic Review (1854–55)

Dollar Magazine (1841–42)

Edinburgh Review (1834–36)

Fraser's Magazine (1831–36)

Gleason's (later Ballou's) Pictorial Drawing Room Companion (1851–57)

Graham's Magazine (1843–45)

Harper's New Monthly Magazine (1854)

(Harrisburg) Pennsylvania Telegraph (1850)

Home Journal (1846–67)

Knickerbocker (1833–55)

Literary Gazette and Journal of Belles Lettres (London) (1835–36)

Literary World (1847–52)

Louisville Daily Courier (1851–52)

(Macon) Georgia Citizen (1850–51)

Metropolitan Magazine (1834–36)

Morning Courier and New York Enquirer (1829–55)

Musical World and Times (1852–55)

National Press (1846)

New-Englander (1843–44)

New England Galaxy (and Boston Mercury) (1827–36)

New England Weekly Review (1828–31)

New Mirror (1843–44)

(New York) Atlas (1849–52)

New York Daily Herald (1830–52)

New York Daily Times (1851–70, 1897, 1901)

New York Daily Tribune (1842–55)

New-Yorker (1836–41)

(New York) Evening Mirror (1844–47)

New York Evening Post (1835–52)

(New York) Evening Star (1833–40)

New York Mirror (1828–1839)

New York Morning Express (1850–51)

(New York) Morning Star (1851)

New York Review (1825)

(New York) Spirit of the Times (1831–38)

(New York) Sunday Times and Noah's Weekly Messenger (1850–51)

(New York) Weekly Mirror (1844–45)

(New York) Weekly Universe (1850)

North American Review (1828–55)

Olive Branch (1851–55)

(Philadelphia) American Banner (1850–52)

Evening Bulletin (1852)

Philadelphia) Pennsylvanian (1849–52)

(Philadelphia) Public Ledger (1849–50)

(Philadelphia) Saturday Evening Post (1853–54)

(Philadelphia) Sunday Dispatch (1850–56)

Pittsburgh Saturday Visitor (1851)

Police Gazette (1850–52)

Punch (London) (1845)

Putnam's Magazine (1853–57)

Quarterly Review (1835)

Rhode Island American and Providence Gazette (1828–29)

Salem (Massachusetts) Gazette (1828–30)

Southern Quarterly Review (1855)

Spectator (London) (1835)

Times (London) (1834–36)

True Flag (1853–55)

Una (1854–55)

Wilmington (North Carolina) Daily Journal (1852)

PRINCIPAL PUBLICATIONS OF NATHANIEL PARKER WILLIS

1827   Sketches. Boston: S. G. Goodrich.

1828   The Legendary, Consisting of Original Pieces, Principally Illustrative of American History, Scenery, and Manners. Edited by N. P. Willis. 2 vols. Boston: S. G. Goodrich.

1829   *Fugitive Poetry.* Boston: Pierce and Williams.
        The Token, A Christmas and New Year's Present. Edited by N. P. Willis. Boston: S. G. Goodrich.

1831   *Poem Delivered before the Society of United Brothers, at Brown University, on the Day Preceding Commencement, September 6, 1831. With Other Poems.* New York: J & J. Harper.

1835   *Melanie and Other Poems.* Edited by Barry Cornwall. London: Saunders and Otley. [An expanded American edition, published by Saunders and Otley in New York, followed in 1837.]
        Pencillings by the Way. 3 vols. London: John Macrone. [Revised and expanded London editions appeared in 1836, 1839, and 1842; several additional editions followed in the 1850s and 1860s. The last British printing was in 1942. A first American edition (reprinting the London edition of 1835) was issued by the Philadelphia publishers Carey, Lea, and Blanchard in 1836. An expanded second American edition came out as part of Morris's and Willis's "Mirror Library" series in 1844. In 1853 an abbreviated reprinting of this 1844 edition appeared as part of Charles Scribner's uniform series of Willis's works. Other American publishers seem to have negotiated reprint rights to this last edition. There was also a Belgian edition (a reprint of the second London edition) issued in Brussels by the Belgian Printing and Publishing Society, Hauman, Cattoir in 1836.]

1836   *Inklings of Adventure by the Author of "Pencillings by the Way."* 3 vols. London: Saunders and Otley. [In New York, Saunders and Otley issued three American editions (each of two volumes) the same year.]

1838   *American Scenery; or, Land, Lake, and River. Illustrations of Transatlantic Nature. From Drawings by W. H. Bartlett, Engraved in the First Style of the Art . . . The Literary Department by N. P. Willis.* 2 vols. London: George Virtue. [Originally issued serially in thirty parts bound in paper. London, Boston, and Philadelphia editions followed in 1840. Another London edition appeared in 1858.]

1839   *A l'Abri, or The Tent Pitch'd.* New York: Samuel Colman.
        Bianca Visconti; or, The Heart Overtasked. New York: Samuel Colman.
        Tortesa the Usurer. A Play. New York: Samuel Colman.
        Two Ways of Dying for a Husband. I. Dying to Keep Him, or Tortesa the Usurer. II. Dying to Lose Him, or Bianca Visconti. London: Hugh Cunningham. [Except for two short prefaces, this was a reprint. It eventually appeared in the United States as part of the *Mirror Library.*]

1840   *Letters from under a Bridge. And Poems.* London: George Virtue. [This is a slightly amended edition of the 1839 edition of *A l'Abri*, to which is added several poems not in the original.]
        Loiterings of Travel. 3 vols. London: Longman, Orme, Brown, Green, & Longmans.
        Romance of Travel, Comprising Tales of Five Lands, by the Author of Pencilings [sic] by the Way. New York: Samuel Colman. [Eight of these tales appeared in *Loiterings of Travel.*]

1842   *Canadian Scenery Illustrated. From Drawings by W. H. Bartlett. The Literary Department by N. P. Willis.* 2 vols. London: George Virtue. [Another London edition appeared in 1858.]
        The Scenery and Antiquities of Ireland, Illustrated from Drawings by W. H. Bartlett; The Literary Portions of the Work by N. P. Willis and J. Stirling Coyne. 2 vols. London: George Virtue.

1843   *Poems of Passion.* New York: Morris, Willis.

The Sacred Poems of Nathaniel Parker Willis. New York: Morris, Willis. [Volumes with this title were reprinted in 1844, 1847, 1848, 1851, 1853, 1858, 1860, 1862, 1863, and 1868.]

1844 *The Lady Jane, and Other Humourous* [sic] *Poems.* New York: Morris, Willis.

The Mirror Library. New York: Morris, Willis, 1843–44. [This inexpensive series, edited by Morris and Willis, included reprints of several of Willis's books.]

Lecture on Fashion, Delivered before the New York Lyceum, June 1844. New York: Morris and Willis.

Letters from under a Bridge . . . The Only Complete Edition. New York: Morris, Willis. [A slightly revised and expanded edition of *A l'Abri.*]

The Poems, Sacred, Passionate, and Humorous. New York: Clark & Austin. [Six editions of this volume were issued between 1844 and 1846. Revised and enlarged editions with this title appeared in 1849, 1852, 1854, 1856, 1859, 1861, 1862, 1863, 1864, 1865, 1866, 1867, 1868, 1869, 1870, 1872, 1873, 1875, 1878, and 1889.]

1845 *Dashes at Life with a Free Pencil.* Five paper-covered parts. New York: Burgess, Stringer. [A London edition of this compendium of previously published tales and ephemera appeared in three volumes issued by Longman, Brown, Green, & Longmans in 1845.]

1846 *The Complete Works of Nathaniel Parker Willis.* New York: J. S. Redfield. [A reprint of the *Mirror Library* and *Dashes at Life.* Redfield issued *The Miscellaneous Works of Nathaniel Parker Willis* (New York, 1847) from these sheets. In 1849, the Philadelphia publisher Carey and Hart issued a volume entitled *The Prose Works of Nathaniel Parker Willis* that was printed from Redfield's plates. Other editions appeared in 1850, 1852, and 1855.]

1850 *Life, Here and There: or Sketches of Society and Adventure at Far-Apart Times and Places.* New York: Baker and Scribner. [The sketches in this volume appeared earlier in *Inklings,* 1836 and *Dashes at Life,* 1845, part 1. Several publishers reissued this volume in 1853, 1854, and 1856.]

People I Have Met; or Pictures of Society and People of Mark, Drawn under a Thin Veil of Fiction. New York: Baker and Scribner. [A reprint, predominantly from *Dashes at Life,* which was issued in London in 1850 and 1866 as *Pictures of Society and People of Mark.* Other American publishers reissued the volume in 1853.]

The Poetical Works of Nathaniel Parker Willis. London: George Routledge. [Other editions appeared in 1853, 1867, 1868, 1878, 1883, and 1888.]

Rural Letters and Other Records of Thought at Leisure, Written in the Intervals of More Hurried Literary Labor. New York: Baker and Scribner. [Contains "Letters from under a Bridge" and other published newspaper columns. This volume was reprinted in 1853, 1854, and 1856 by other publishers.]

1851 *Hurry-Graphs; or, Sketches of Scenery, Celebrities and Society, Taken from Life.* New York: Charles Scribner. [Editions by several other publishers appeared in 1853, 1854, and 1856.]

Memoranda of the Life of Jenny Lind. Philadelphia: Robert E. Peterson.

Trenton Falls, Picturesque and Descriptive. New York: Published for the Proprietor by George P. Putnam. [Other editions appeared in 1862, 1865, and 1868.]

1853 *Fun-Jottings; or, Laughs I Have Taken a Pen To.* New York: Charles Scribner. [Predominantly reprints from *Dashes at Life.* Other publishers reissued this volume in 1854 and 1855.]

A Health Trip to the Tropics. New York: Charles Scribner. [A London edition was issued by Sampson Low, Son in 1854.]

Summer Cruise in the Mediterranean, on Board an American Frigate. New York: Charles Scribner. [A reprint extracted from the 1844 edition of *Pencillings by the Way.* Other publishers reissued the volume in 1854 and 1856.]

1854 *Famous Persons and Places.* New York: Charles Scribner. [Another American imprint of this volume appeared in 1855.]

1855 *Out-doors at Idlewild: or, The Shaping of a Home on the Banks of the Hudson.* New York: Charles Scribner.

The Rag-Bag, a Collection of Ephemera. New York: Charles Scribner. [Material from *Dashes at Life,* along with additional editorial columns.]

1857 *Paul Fane; or, Parts of a Life Else Untold.* New York: Charles Scribner. [Sampson Low, Son issued a London edition the same year.]

1859 *The Convalescent.* New York: Charles Scribner. [Sampson Low, Son also issued a London edition in 1859.]

SELECTED BIBLIOGRAPHY

Abbott, John S. C. *The Mother at Home.* New York: Arno Press, 1972 [orig. London, 1834].

Adams, Charles Francis. *Diary of Charles Francis Adams.* Edited by Richard Alan Ryerson. 8 vols. Cambridge: Belknap Press, 1968.

Adams, Florence Bannard. *Fanny Fern, or, a Pair of Flaming Shoes.* West Trenton, NJ: Hermitage Press, 1966.

Adburgham, Alison. *Silver Fork Society: Fashionable Life and Literature from 1814 to 1840.* London: Constable, 1983.

Allen, Michael. *Poe and the British Magazine Tradition.* New York: Oxford University Press, 1969.

Allibone, Samuel Austin. *A Critical Dictionary of English Literature and British and American Authors.* 3 vols. Philadelphia: J. B. Lippincott, 1871.

Allmendinger, David F., Jr. *Paupers and Scholars: The Transformation of Student Life in Nineteenth-Century New England.* New York: St. Martin's Press, 1975.

Altick, Richard D. *Life and Letters: A History of Literary Biography in England and America.* New York: Alfred A. Knopf, 1965.

Amavasinghe, Upali. *Dryden and Pope in the Early Nineteenth Century: A Study of Changing Literary Taste.* Cambridge: Cambridge University Press, 1962.

"An Old Lawyer." *Review of the Forrest Divorce: Containing Some Remarkable Disclosures of the Secret Doings of the Jury.* New York: Stringer and Townsend, 1852.

Auser, Courtland. *Nathaniel P. Willis.* New York: Twayne Publishers, 1969.

Baker, Thomas N. "Robert Shelton Mackenzie." *American National Biography.* New York: Oxford University Press, forthcoming.

Bartlett, John. *Dictionary of Americanisms: A Glossary of Words and Phrases Usually Regarded as Peculiar to the United States.* 2d edition. New York: Johnson Reprints Corporation, 1968 [orig. 1859].

Baym, Nina. *American Women Writers and the Work of History, 1790–1860.* New Brunswick, NJ: Rutgers University Press, 1995.

Beck, Charles H. "John Van Buren: A Study in By-Gone Politics." *Magazine of American History* 17 (January–April 1887): 58–70, 202–13, 318–29.

Beers, Henry A. *Nathaniel Parker Willis.* Boston: Houghton, Mifflin, 1885.

Benton, Richard P. "*The Masque of the Red Death*—The Primary Source." *American Transcendental Quarterly* 1 (1969): 12–13.

———. "Poe's *Lionizing*: A Quiz on Willis and Lady Blessington." *Studies in Short Fiction* 5 (Spring 1968): 239–44.

Berlant, Lauren. "The Female Woman: Fanny Fern and the Form of Sentiment." *American Literary History* 3 (Fall 1991): 429–54.

Bigelow, John. *Retrospections of an Active Life.* 2 vols. New York: Baker and Taylor, 1909.

———. "Some Recollections of Charles O'Conor." *Century Magazine* 29 (March 1885): 725–36.

Blain, Virginia. "Rosina Bulwer Lytton and the Rage of the Unheard." *Huntington Library Quarterly* 53 (Summer 1990): 211–36.

Blair, Hugh. *Lectures on Rhetoric and Belles Lettres.* Philadelphia: James Kay, 1829.

Blanchard, Laman. *Life and Literary Remains of L. E. L.* London: Henry Colburn, 1841.

Blumin, Stuart. *The Emergence of the Middle Class: Social Experience in the American City, 1760–1900.* Cambridge: Cambridge University Press, 1989.

Boswell, James. *Life of Johnson.* Edited by George Birkbeck Hill. 6 vols. Oxford: Clarendon Press, 1934–50.

Branch, Edward Douglas. *The Sentimental Years.* New York: Hill and Wang, 1965.

Braudy, Leo. *The Frenzy of Renown: Fame and Its History.* New York: Oxford University Press, 1986.

Brevoort, Henry. *Letters of Henry Brevoort to Washington Irving.* Edited by George S. Hellman. New York: G. P. Putnam's Sons, Knickerbocker Press, 1918.

Briggs, Peter M. "Laurence Sterne and Literary Celebrity in 1760." *The Age of Johnson: A Scholarly Annual* 4 (1991): 251–73.

Brumberg, Joan Jacobs. *Mission for Life: The Story of the Family of Adoniram Judson, the Dramatic Events of the First American Mission, and the Course of Evangelical Religion in the Nineteenth Century.* New York: Free Press, 1988.

Bryant, William Cullen. *Letters of William Cullen Bryant.* Edited by William Cullen Bryant II and Thomas G. Voss. 6 vols. New York: Fordham University Press, 1975–1992.

Buckingham, Joseph T. *Personal Memoirs and Recollections of Editorial Life.* 2 vols. Boston: Ticknor, Reed, and Fields, 1852.

Buckley, Peter. "To the Opera House: Culture and Society in New York City, 1820–60." Ph.D. diss., State University of New York at Stony Brook, 1984.

Buell, Lawrence. *New England Literary Culture from Revolution to Renaissance.* Cambridge: Cambridge University Press, 1986.

———. "Literature and Scripture in New England between the Revolution and the Civil War." *Notre Dame English Journal* 15 (Spring 1983): 1–18.

———. *Literary Transcendentalism: Style and Vision in the American Renaissance.* Ithaca: Cornell University Press, 1973.

Bulwer, Edward George. *Pelham, or, the Adventures of a Gentleman.* Edited by Jerome McGann. Lincoln: University of Nebraska Press, 1972 [orig. 1828].

Buntline, Ned [pseud. E. C. Z. Judson]. *The Mysteries and Miseries of New York: A Story of Real Life.* New York: Berford, 1848.

Bushman, Richard, L. *The Refinement of America: Persons, Houses, Cities.* New York: Alfred A. Knopf, 1992.

Camfield, Greg. "The Moral Aesthetics of Sentimentality: A Missing Key to *Uncle Tom's Cabin.*" *Nineteenth-Century Literature* 43 (December 1988): 319–45.

Cayton, Mary Kupiec. *Emerson's Emergence: Self and Society in the Transformation of New England, 1800–1845.* Chapel Hill: University of North Carolina Press, 1989.

Cecil, David. *A Portrait of Charles Lamb.* London: Constable, 1983.

Clark, Willis Gaylord, and Lewis Gaylord Clark. *The Letters of Willis Gaylord Clark and Lewis Gaylord Clark.* New York: New York Public Library, 1940.

Cohen, Patricia Cline. "Ministerial Misdeeds: The Onderdonk Trial and Sexual Harassment in the 1840s." *Journal of Women's History* 7 (Fall 1995): 34–57.

Collins, A. S. *The Profession of Letters: A Study of the Relation of Author to Patron, Publisher, and Public, 1780–1832.* London: George Routledge and Sons, 1928.

Conforti, Joseph A. "Edwardsians, Unitarians, and the Memory of the Great Awakening, 1800–1840." In Conrad Wright, *American Unitarianism, 1805–1865.* Boston: Massachusetts Historical Society and Northeastern University Press, 1984.

Cooke, George Willis. *John Sullivan Dwight, Brook Farmer, Editor, and Critic of Music: A Biography.* Boston: Small, Maynard, 1898.

Cooper, James Fenimore. *The Letters and Journals of James Fenimore Cooper.* Edited by James Franklin Beard. 6 vols. Cambridge: Belknap Press, 1960–68.

Cott, Nancy F. "Passionlessness: An Interpretation of Victorian Sexual Ideology, 1790–1850." *Signs* 4 (Winter 1978): 219–36.

Coultrap-McQuin, Susan. *Doing Literary Business: American Women Writers in the Nineteenth Century.* Chapel Hill: University of North Carolina Press, 1990.

Crawford, Mary Caroline. *Famous Families of Massachusetts.* 2 vols. Boston: Little, Brown, 1930.

Cross, Barbara M. *Horace Bushnell: Minister to a Changing America.* Chicago: University of Chicago Press, 1958.

Cummings, Asa. *A Memoir of the Reverend Edward Payson, D. D.* New York: American Tract Society, 1830.

Curtis, Benjamin Robbins. *A Memoir of Benjamin Robbins Curtis; with Some of His Professional and Miscellaneous Writings.* New York: Da Capo Press, 1970 [orig. 1879].

Curtis, George Ticknor. "Reminiscences of N. P. Willis and Lydia Maria Child." *Harper's New Monthly Magazine* 81 (October 1890): 717–20.

Curtis, George William. "Some Early Letters of George William Curtis." Edited by Caroline Ticknor. *Atlantic Monthly* 114 (September 1914): 363–76.

Daughrity, Kenneth L. "Poe's 'Quiz on Willis.'" *American Literature* 5 (March 1933): 57–62.

———. "The Life and Works of Nathaniel Parker Willis." Ph.D. diss., University of Virginia, 1935.

Derby, J. C. *Fifty Years among Authors, Books, and Publishers.* New York: G. W. Carleton, 1884.

Desmond, Stewart E. "The Widow's Trials: The Life of Fanny Fern." Ph.D. diss., New York University, 1988.

Dorson, Richard M. "Mose the Far-famed and World Renowned." *American Literature* 15 (November 1943): 288–300.

Douglas, Ann. *The Feminization of American Culture.* New York: Alfred A. Knopf, 1977.

Elfenbein, Andrew. *Byron and the Victorians.* Cambridge: Cambridge University Press, 1995.

Emerson, Ralph Waldo. *The Collected Works of Ralph Waldo Emerson.* Historical introduction and notes by Joe Slater. Text by Alfred R. Ferguson and Jean Ferguson Carr. Vol. 2, *Essays: Second Series.* Cambridge: Belknap Press, 1983.

———. *Journals and Miscellaneous Notebooks.* Edited by William H. Gilman et al. 16 vols. Cambridge: Belknap Press, 1960–82.

———. *The Journals of Ralph Waldo Emerson, with Annotations.* Edited by Edward Waldo Emerson and Waldo Emerson Forbes. 10 vols. Cambridge: Riverside Press, 1909.

Endicott, William Crowninshield. "Reminiscences of Seventy-Five Years." *Proceedings of the Massachusetts Historical Society* 46 (November 1912): 208–33.

Englizian, H. Crosby. *Brimstone Corner: Park Street Church, Boston.* Chicago: Moody Press, 1968.

Ernst, Morris L., and Alan U. Schwartz. *Privacy: The Right to Be Left Alone.* New York: MacMillan, 1962.

Fassett, Frederick Gardiner, Jr. *A History of Newspapers in the District of Maine, 1785–1820.* Orono, ME: University Press, 1932.

Fatout, Paul. "Amelia Bloomer and Bloomerism." *New York Historical Society Quarterly* 34 (October 1952): 361–72.

Fay, Susan Barrera. "A Modest Celebrity: Literary Reputation and the Marketplace in Antebellum America." Ph.D. diss., George Washington University, 1992.

Fisher, Sidney George. *A Philadelphia Perspective: Diary of Sidney George Fisher, 1834–1871.* Edited by N. B. Wainwright. Philadelphia: Historical Society of Pennsylvania, 1967.

Flower, Milton E. *James Parton: The Father of Modern Biography.* Durham: Duke University Press, 1951.

Forrest Divorce Case: New York Herald Edition. New York: Dewitt & Davenport, 1852.

Forrest Divorce Case: Police Gazette Edition. New York: Stringer & Townsend, 1852.

Forster, John. *Walter Savage Landor: A Biography.* 2 vols. London: Chapman and Hall, 1879.

Foster, George. *New York by Gas-light and Other Urban Sketches.* Edited by Stuart Blumin. Berkeley: University of California Press, 1990.

Fuess, Claude M. *The Old New England School: A History of Phillips Academy Andover.* Boston: Houghton Mifflin, Riverside Press, 1917.

Fuller, Margaret. *The Letters of Margaret Fuller.* Edited by Robert N. Hudspeth. 6 vols. Ithaca: Cornell University Press, 1994.

Gabler, Neal. *Winchell: Gossip, Power, and the Culture of Celebrity.* New York: Knopf, 1994.

Gabler-Hover, Janet. *Truth in American Fiction: The Legacy of Rhetorical Idealism.* Athens: University of Georgia Press, 1990.

Garfield, James A. *A Diary of James A. Garfield, 1848–1871.* Edited by Harry James Brown and Frederick D. Williams. 4 vols. East Lansing: Michigan State University Press, 1967.

Gilfoyle, Timothy Y. *City of Eros: New York City, Prostitution, and the Commercialization of Sex, 1790–1920.* New York: W. W. Norton, 1992.

Gilman, Daniel C. *The Life of James Dwight Dana.* New York: Harper and Brothers, 1899.

Goffe, Lewis Center. "The Fiction of Nathaniel Parker Willis." Ph.D. diss., Boston University, 1961.

Gohdes, Clarence. *American Literature in Nineteenth-Century England.* New York: Columbia University Press, 1944.

———. "British Interest in American Literature During the Latter Part of the Nineteenth Century as Reflected by Mudies Select Library." *American Literature* 13 (January 1942): 356–62.

Goodrich, Samuel G. *Recollections of a Lifetime.* 2 vols. New York: Miller, Orton, and Mulligan, 1857.

Grant, Anne. *Memoir and Correspondence of Mrs. Grant of Laggan.* Edited by J. P. Grant. 3 vols. London: Longman, Brown, Green, and Longmans, 1845.

Greenough, Frances Boott. *Letters of Horatio Greenough to His Brother, Henry Greenough.* Boston: Ticknor, 1887.

Greenough, Horatio. *Letters of Horatio Greenough, American Sculptor.* Edited by Nathalia Wright. Madison: University of Wisconsin Press, 1972.

Greenspan, Ezra. *Walt Whitman and the American Reader.* Cambridge: Cambridge University Press, 1990.

Greenwood, Grace. "Fanny Fern—Mrs. Parton." In *Eminent Women of the Age.* Edited by James Parton. Hartford: S. M. Betts, 1868.

Grimsley, Elizabeth Todd. "Six Months in the White House." *Journal of the Illinois State Historical Society* 19 (October 1926–January 1927): 42–73.

Griswold, Rufus Wilmot. *Passages from the Correspondence and Other Papers of Rufus Wilmot Griswold.* Cambridge, MA: W. M. Griswold, 1898.

Guarneri, Carl. *The Utopian Alternative: Fourierism in Nineteenth-Century America.* Ithaca: Cornell University Press, 1991.

Hale, Edward Everett, Jr. *The Life and Letters of Edward Everett Hale.* 2 vols. Boston: Little, Brown, 1917.

Hall, Basil. *Travels in America.* Graz, Austria: Akademische Druck-u. Verlagsanstalt, 1965 [orig. 1829].

Halttunen, Karen. *Confidence Men and Painted Women: A Study of Middle-Class Culture in America, 1830–1870.* New Haven: Yale University Press, 1982.

Hansen-Taylor, Marie, and Horace E. Scudder, eds. *Life and Letters of Bayard Taylor.* 2 vols. Boston: Houghton, Mifflin, 1884.

Harris, Susan K. *Nineteenth-Century American Women's Novels: Interpretive Strategies.* Cambridge: Cambridge University Press, 1990.

Hart, Francis R. *Lockhart as Romantic Biographer.* Edinburgh: Edinburgh University Press, 1971.

Hartog, Hendrik. "Lawyering, Husbands' Rights, and 'the Unwritten Law' in Nineteenth-Century America." *Journal of American History* 84 (June 1997): 67–96.

Harvey, John. *Men in Black.* Chicago: University of Chicago Press, 1995.

Hawthorne, Nathaniel. *The Century Edition of the Letters of Nathaniel Hawthorne.* Edited by Thomas Woodson, James A. Rubino, L. Neal Smith, and Norman Holmes Pearson. Vol. 7, *The Letters, 1853–1856.* Columbus: Ohio State University Press, 1987.

Hayward, Edward F. "Nathaniel Parker Willis." *Atlantic Monthly* 54 (August 1884): 212–22.

Holmes, Oliver Wendell. "A Mortal Antipathy." In Vol. 7, *The Works of Oliver Wendell Holmes.* Boston: Houghton Mifflin, Riverside Press, 1892.

———. "The New Portfolio." *Atlantic Monthly* 55 (January 1885): 105–11.

Holt, Anna C. "A Medical Student in Boston." *Harvard Library Bulletin* 6 (Autumn 1952): 372–80.

———. "An After-Breakfast Talk." *Atlantic Monthly* 51 (January 1883): 65–75.

———. *John Lothrop Motley: A Memoir.* Boston: Houghton, Osgood, Riverside Press, 1879.

Howe, Daniel Walker. *The Unitarian Conscience: Harvard Moral Philosophy, 1805–1861, with a New Introduction.* Middletown, CT: Wesleyan University Press, 1988 [orig. 1970].

Hudson, Frederic. *Journalism in the United States from 1690 to 1872.* New York: Harper and Brothers, 1873.

Ireland, Robert M. "The Libertine Must Die: Sexual Dishonor and the Unwritten Law in the Nineteenth-Century United States." *Journal of Social History* 23 (Fall 1989): 27–44.

Jack, Ian. *English Literature, 1815–1832.* Oxford: Clarendon University Press, 1963.

Jacobs, Harriet. *Incidents in the Life of a Slave Girl.* Edited by Jean Fagan Yellin. Cambridge: Harvard University Press, 1987.

Jones, Howard Mumford. *America and French Culture, 1750–1848.* Chapel Hill: University of North Carolina Press, 1927.

Karcher, Carolyn L. *The First Woman in the Republic: A Cultural Biography of Lydia Maria Child.* Durham: Duke University Press, 1994.

Kasson, John. *Rudeness and Civility: Manners in Nineteenth-Century Urban America.* New York: Hill and Wang, 1990.

Kelley, Mary. *Private Woman, Public Stage: Literary Domesticity in Nineteenth-Century America.* New York: Oxford University Press, 1984.

Kendrick, A. C. *The Life and Letters of Mrs. Emily C. Judson.* New York: Sheldon, 1860.

Kett, Joseph F. *Rites of Passage: Adolescence in America, 1790 to the Present.* New York: Basic Books, 1977.

Kirkland, Leigh. " 'A Human Life': Being an Autobiography of Elizabeth Oakes Smith: A Critical Edition and Introduction." Ph.D. diss., Georgia State University, 1994.

Korobkin, Laura Hanft. "The Maintenance of Mutual Confidence: Sentimental Strategies at the Adultery Trial of Henry Ward Beecher." *Yale Journal of Law and the Humanities* 7 (Winter 1995): 1–48.

Lang, Andrew. *The Life and Letters of John Gibson Lockhart.* London: J. C. Nimmo, 1897.

Lawrence, Vera Brodsky. *Strong on Music: The New York Music Scene in the Days of George Templeton Strong, 1836–1875.* Vol. 1, *Resonances, 1836–1850.* New York: Oxford University Press, 1988; and Vol. 2, *Reverberations, 1850–1856.* Chicago: University of Chicago Press, 1995.

Lockhart, John. *Memoirs of the Life of Sir Walter Scott, Bart.* 7 vols. Edinburgh: Robert Cadell, 1837.

Longfellow, Henry Wadsworth. *The Letters of Henry Wadsworth Longfellow.* Edited by Andrew Hilen. 6 vols. Cambridge: Belknap Press, 1966.

Lowell, James Russell. *New Letters of James Russell Lowell.* Edited by M. A. DeWolfe Howe. New York: Harper and Brothers, 1932.

Lystra, Karen. *Searching the Heart: Women, Men, and Romantic Love in Nineteenth-Century America.* New York: Oxford University Press, 1989.

Madden, Richard R. *Literary Life and Correspondence of the Countess of Blessington.* 3 vols. London: T. C. Newby, 1855.

Mallett, Mark E. " 'The Game of Politics': Edwin Forrest and the Jacksonian Democrats." *Journal of American Drama and Theatre* 5 (Spring 1993): 31–46.

[Marguerittes, Julie de]. *The Match-Girl; or, Life Scenes as They Are.* Philadelphia: William White Smith, 1855.

Mayo, Lawrence Shaw. "The America That Used to Be from the Diary of John Davis Long." *Atlantic Monthly* 130 (December 1922): 721–30.

McConachie, Bruce A. *Melodramatic Formations: American Theatre and Society, 1820–1870.* Iowa City: University of Iowa Press, 1992.

McGinnis, Patricia I. "Fanny Fern, American Novelist." *Biblion, University Library Journal of the State University of New York at Albany* 2 (Spring 1969): 1–37.

Mensel, Robert E. " 'Kodakers Lying in Wait': Amateur Photography and the Right of Privacy in New York, 1885–1915." *American Quarterly* 43 (March 1991): 24–45.

Merideth, Robert. *The Politics of the Universe: Edward Beecher, Abolition, and Orthodoxy.* Nashville: Vanderbilt University Press, 1968.

Mitford, Mary Russell. *The Friendships of Mary Russell Mitford.* Edited by the Reverend A. G. L'Estrange. New York: Harper and Brothers, 1882.

Moody, Richard. *Edwin Forrest: First Star of the American Stage.* New York: Knopf, 1960.

———. *The Astor Place Riot.* Bloomington: Indiana University Press, 1958.

Moore, Thomas. *The Journal of Thomas Moore.* Edited by Wilfred S. Dowden. 6 vols. Newark: University of Delaware Press, 1983.

Moragné, Mary E. *The Neglected Thread: A Journal from the Calhoun Community, 1836–1842.* Edited, with Preface and Backgrounds, by Delle Mullen Craven. Columbia: University of South Carolina Press, 1951.

Morgan, Lady Sydney. *Passages from My Autobiography.* New York: D. Appleton, 1859.

Morrison, Alfred. *The Blessington Papers.* [London]: Printed for private circulation, 1895.

Mott, Frank Luther. *A History of American Magazines.* 5 vols. Cambridge: Belknap Press, 1938 [orig. 1930].

[Moulton, William]. *Life and Beauties of Fanny Fern*. New York: H. Long and Brother, 1855.

Munby, Alan Noel Latimer. *The Cult of the Autograph Letter in England*. London: University of London, Athlone Press, 1962.

Nash, Cristopher. *Narrative in Culture: The Uses of Storytelling in the Sciences, Philosophy, and Literature*. London: Routledge, 1990.

Odell, George C. D. *Annals of the New York Stage*. New York: Columbia University Press, 1931.

Oxford English Dictionary. 2d edition. 20 vols. Oxford: Clarendon Press, 1989.

Parton, Ethel Thomson. "Fanny Fern at the Hartford Female Seminary." *New England Magazine*, n.s., 24 (March/August 1901): 94–98.

———. "Fanny Fern: An Informal Biography." Unpublished typescript.

Parton, James. *Fanny Fern: A Memorial Volume*. New York: G. W. Carleton, 1873.

Parton, Sara Willis. *Ruth Hall and Other Writings*. Edited by Joyce Warren. New Brunswick: Rutgers University Press, 1986 [orig. 1855].

———. *Rose Clark*. New York: Mason Brothers, 1856.

———. *Fern Leaves from Fanny's Port-Folio, Second Series*. Auburn: Miller, Orton, & Mulligan, 1854 [orig. Auburn: Derby and Miller, 1853].

———. *Little Ferns for Fanny's Little Friends*. Auburn: Derby and Miller, 1854.

———. *Fern Leaves from Fanny's Port-Folio*. Auburn: Derby and Miller, 1853.

Paulding, James Kirke. *The Letters of James Kirke Paulding*. Edited by Ralph M. Alderman. Madison: University of Wisconsin Press, 1962.

Peeples, Lawrence Scott. "Tales from the Magazine Prison House: Democracy and Authorship in American Periodical Fiction, 1825–1850." Ph.D. diss., Louisiana State University, 1994.

Pennell, Elizabeth Robins. *Charles Godfrey Leland, a Biography*. 2 vols. Boston: Houghton, Mifflin, Riverside Press, 1906.

Pennsylvania State House Journal (Harrisburg, 1850).

Pennsylvania State Senate Journal (Harrisburg, 1850).

Poe, Edgar Allan. *The Letters of Edgar Allan Poe*. Edited by John Ward Ostrom. 2 vols. Cambridge: Harvard University Press, 1948.

———. *Edgar Allan Poe: Letters and Documents in the Enoch Pratt Free Library*. Edited by Arthur H. Quinn and Richard S. Hart. New York: Scholars' Facsimiles & Reprints, 1941.

Postlewait, Thomas. "Autobiography and Theatre History." In *Interpreting the Theatrical Past: Essays on the History of Performance*. Edited by Thomas Postlewait and Bruce A. McConachie. Iowa City: University of Iowa Press, 1989.

Pray, Frances Mary. "A Study of Whittier's Apprenticeship as a Poet." Ph.D. diss., Pennsylvania State University, 1930.

Prentiss, George L. *The Life and Letters of Elizabeth Prentiss*. New York: Anson D. F. Randolph, 1882.

Rabinowitz, Richard. *The Spiritual Self in Everyday Life: The Transformation of Personal Experience in Nineteenth-Century New England*. Boston: Northeastern University Press, 1989.

Read, Elizabeth T. *Memoir of Miss Elizabeth T. Read, of New Bedford, Massachusetts*. Edited by John S. C. Abbott. New York: Edward O. Jenkins, 1847.

Revelations of Asmodeus, or Mysteries of Upper Ten-Dom; Being a Spirit Stirring, A Powerful and Felicitous Exposé of the Desolating Mystery, Blighting Miseries, Atrocious Vices, and Paralyzing Tragedies, Perpetrated in the Fashionable Pandemoniums of the Great Empire City. New York: G. G. Graham, 1849.

Richards, Addison T. "Idlewild: The Home of N. P. Willis," *Harper's Monthly Magazine* 16 (January 1858): 145–66.

Richards, Irving T. "Longfellow in England: Unpublished Extracts from his Journals." *PMLA* 51 (December 1936): 1123–34.

Richards, Laura E., and Elliott, Maud Howe. *Julia Ward Howe, 1819–1910.* Boston: Houghton Mifflin, 1916.

Robinson, Elwyn B. "The Public Ledger: An Independent Newspaper." *Pennsylvania Magazine of History and Biography* 64 (January 1940): 43–55.

———. "The *Pennsylvanian*: Organ of the Democracy." *Pennsylvania Magazine of History and Biography* 62 (July 1938): 350–60.

Robinson, Henry Crabb. *The Correspondence of Henry Crabb Robinson with the Wordsworth Circle.* Edited by Edith J. Morley. 2 vols. Oxford: Clarendon Press, 1927.

Rosa, Matthew. *Silver Fork School: Novels of Fashion Preceeding Vanity Fair.* New York: Columbia University Press, 1936.

Sadleir, Michael. *The Strange Life of Blessington.* Boston: Little, Brown, 1933.

———. *Bulwer: A Panorama. Part One: Edward and Rosina, 1803–1836.* Boston: Little, Brown, 1931.

Schlesinger, Elizabeth Bancroft. "Fanny Fern: Our Grandmother's Mentor." *New-York Historical Society Quarterly* 38 (October 1954): 501–19.

Shields, David S. *Civil Tongues and Polite Letters in British America.* Williamsburg, VA: University of North Carolina Press for the Institute of Early American History and Culture, 1997.

Shulman, David. "N. P. Willis and the American Language." *American Speech* 23 (1948): 39–47.

Silverman, Kenneth A. *Edgar A. Poe: Mournful and Never-Ending Remembrance.* New York: HarperCollins, 1991.

———. *A Cultural History of the American Revolution.* New York: Thomas Y. Crowell Company, 1976.

Simms, William Gilmore. *The Letters of William Gilmore Simms.* Edited by Mary Oliphaunt and D. C. Duncan Eaves. 6 vols. Columbia: University of South Carolina Press, 1952.

Simond, Louis. *Journal of a Residence in Great Britain, During the Years 1810 and 1811.* New York: Eastburn, Kirk, 1815.

Simpson, Lewis P. *The Federalist Literary Mind: Selections from the Monthly Anthology and Boston Review, Including Documents Relating to the Boston Athenaeum.* Baton Rouge: Louisiana State University Press, 1962.

Sklar, Kathryn Kish. *Catharine Beecher: A Study in American Domesticity.* New Haven: Yale University Press, 1973.

Smith, Mortimer. *The Life of Ole Bull.* Princeton: Princeton University Press for the American-Scandinavian Foundation, 1947.

Snelling, William Joseph. *Truth: A Gift for Scribblers.* 2d edition. Boston: Stephen Foster, 1831.

Snyder, Stephen H. *Lyman Beecher and His Children: The Transformation of a Religious Tradition.* Brooklyn: Carlson, 1991.

Spacks, Patricia Meyer. *Gossip.* Chicago: Chicago University Press, 1986.

Spiller, Robert E. *Fenimore Cooper: Critic of His Times.* New York: Russell and Russell, 1963 [orig. 1931].

———. *The American in England During the First Half-Century of Independence.* New York: Holt, 1926.

Sprague, William B. *Annals of the American Pulpit.* 9 vols. New York: Robert Carter and Brothers, 1857.

Stevenson, Lionel. *The Wild Irish Girl: The Life of Sydney Owenson, Lady Morgan (1776–1859)*. London: Chapman and Hall, 1936.

Stoddard, Eve Walsh. "The Genealogy of Ruth: From Harvester to Fallen Woman in Nineteenth-Century England." In *Old Testament Women in Western Literature*. Edited by Raymond-Jean Frontain and Jan Wojcik. Conway, AK: UCA Press, 1991.

Stoddard, Richard Henry. *Recollections, Personal and Literary*. New York: A & S Barnes, 1903.

Stokes, Anson Phelps. *Memorials of Eminent Yale Men*. 2 vols. New Haven: Yale University Press, 1914.

Strong, George Templeton. *Diary of George Templeton Strong*. Edited by Allan Werms and Milton Halsey Thomas. 4 vols. New York: Macmillan, 1952.

Strong, L. G. A. *The Minstrel Boy: A Portrait of Tom Moore*. New York: Alfred Knopf, 1937.

Sullivan, Alvin. *British Literary Magazines*. Westport, CT: Greenwood Press, 1983–86.

Sumner, Charles. *The Selected Letters of Charles Sumner*. Edited by Beverly Wilson Palmer. 2 vols. Boston: Northeastern University Press, 1990.

———. *Memoir and Letters of Charles Sumner*. Edited by Edward M. Pierce. New York: Arno Press and New York Times Press, 1969.

Super, R. H. *The Publication of Landor's Works: Supplement to the Bibliographical Society's Transactions, No. 18*. London: Bibliographical Society, 1954.

Sutherland, John. "Henry Colburn, Publisher." *Publishing History* 19 (1986): 59–84.

Tasistro, Louis Fitzgerald. *Random Shots and Southern Breezes*. 2 vols. New York: Harper and Brothers, 1842.

Taylor, Bayard. *The Echo Club, and Other Literary Diversions*. Boston: J. R. Osgood, 1876.

Taylor, William R., and Christopher Lasch. "Two 'Kindred Spirits': Sorority and Family in New England, 1839–1846." *New England Quarterly* 36 (March 1963): 23–41.

———. *The Unpublished Letters of Bayard Taylor in the Huntington Library*. Edited by John Richie Schultz. San Marino: Henry Huntington Library, 1937.

Thomas, Dwight, and Jackson, David K. *The Poe Log: A Documentary Life of Edgar Allan Poe, 1809–1849*. Boston: G. K. Hall, 1987.

Thomas, Ella Gertrude Clanton. *The Secret Eye: The Journal of Ella Gertrude Clanton Thomas, 1848–1889*. Edited by Virginia Ingraham Burr. Chapel Hill: University of North Carolina Press, 1990.

Thornton, Tamara Plakins. *Handwriting in America: A Cultural History*. New Haven: Yale University Press, 1996.

Tomc, Sandra. "An Idle Industry: Nathaniel Parker Willis and the Workings of Literary Leisure." *American Quarterly* 49 (December 1997): 780–805.

Tompkins, Jane P. *Sensational Designs: The Cultural Work of American Fiction, 1790–1860*. New York: Oxford University Press, 1985.

Toole, Robert M. " 'Illustrated and Set to Music': The Picturesque Crescendo of Idlewild." *Journal of the New England Garden History Society* 4 (Spring 1996): 1–12.

Tryon, W. S. *Parnassus Corner: A Life of James T. Fields, Publisher to the Victorians*. Cambridge: Houghton Mifflin Riverside Press, 1963.

Tuckerman, Charles. "Some Old New Yorkers." *Magazine of American History* 23 (June 1890): 433–49.

Underhill, A. Leah. *The Missing Link in Modern Spiritualism*. New York: Arno Press, 1976 [orig. 1885].

Vaux, Calvert. *Villas and Cottages*. New York: Harper and Brothers, 1857.

Walker, Keith. *Byron's Readers: A Study of Attitudes toward Byron, 1812–1832*. Salzburg: Institut für Anglisisk und Amerikanistik, 1979.

Ward, Julius H. *The Life and Letters of James Gates Percival.* Boston: Ticknor and Fields, 1866.

Ward, Nathaniel. *The Simple Cobler of Aggawam in America.* Edited by P. M. Zall. Lincoln: University of Nebraska Press, 1969 [orig. 1647].

Warren, Joyce W. "Uncommon Discourse: Fanny Fern and the *New York Ledger.*" In *Periodical Literature in Nineteenth-Century America.* Edited by Kenneth M. Price and Susan Belasco Smith. Charlottesville: University Press of Virginia, 1995.

———. *Fanny Fern: An Independent Woman.* New Brunswick: Rutgers University Press, 1992.

Watts, Stephen A. "Masks, Morals, and the Market: American Literature and Early Capitalist Culture, 1790–1820." *Journal of the Early Republic* 6 (Summer 1986): 127–49.

Whitman, Walt. *The Uncollected Poetry and Prose of Walt Whitman.* Edited by Emory Holloway. 2 vols. Garden City: Doubleday, Page, 1921.

Wickwar, William. *The Struggle for the Freedom of the Press, 1819–1832.* London: George Allen and Unwin, 1928.

Williams, Susan S. "Widening the World: Susan Warner, Her Readers, and the Assumption of Authorship." *American Quarterly* 42 (December 1990): 565–86.

Williamson, Jefferson. *The American Hotel.* New York: Arno Press, 1975 [orig. 1930].

Wilson, Arthur Herman. *A History of the Philadelphia Stage, 1835 to 1855.* Philadelphia: University of Pennsylvania Press, 1935.

Wilson, James Harrison. *The Life of Charles Anderson Dana.* New York: Harper and Brothers, 1907.

Wolf, Edwin, II. *The Book Culture of a Colonial American City: Philadelphia Books, Bookmen, and Booksellers. Lyell Lectures in Bibliography, 1985–6.* Oxford: Clarendon Press, 1988.

Wood, Ann Douglas. "The 'Scribbling Women' and Fanny Fern: Why Women Wrote." *American Quarterly* 22 (Spring 1971): 3–24.

Wood, Gordon S. *The Radicalism of the American Revolution.* New York: Knopf, 1992.

Woolsey, Theodore S. "Theodore Dwight Woolsey: A Biographical Sketch." *Yale Review,* n.s., 1 (January 1912): 239–60.

Yannella, Donald, and Kathleen Malone, Yannella, eds. "Evert A. Duyckinck's *Diary: May 29–November 8, 1847.*" In *Studies in the American Renaissance.* Boston: Twayne, 1978.

INDEX

Abbott, John S. C., 95–96
Aberdeen, Lord, 62, 79, 81, 205n43
Adams, Charles Francis, 84
Adams, John (headmaster of Phillips Academy), 19
Age, 80
Alexander, Francis, 33
Allen, "Dummy," 145
Allston, Washington, 31, 124
Almack's, 54, 91
American Art-Union, 124, 212n20
American Monthly Magazine, 40–51, 58–60, 84. *See also* Willis, Nathaniel Parker
Andover Theological Seminary, 19, 95
Anglo-American antipathy, 74–77, 80–85, 111, 130
annuals. *See* gift-books
Anthology Society, 40
anti-sentimentalism, 121, 126–28, 142
Anti-Slavery Standard, 178
"Apollo Hyacinth" (Fern), 166–68, 173, 219n21
Appleton, T. G., 46
"Are There Any Men among Us?" (Fern), 168
aristocracy, American sentiment against, 103–04, 108–11, 130
Arthur's Home Magazine, 11
Associationism. *See* Fourierism
Astor Place Opera House, 108–10

Astor Place Riot, 111–12, 117, 130, 136, 156
Athenaeum (London), 173
Athenaeum, or Spirit of the English Magazines, 40
Atlantic, 188
autobiographical fiction, 18, 35–36, 91–92, 183–86
Autobiography (Barnum), 181

Barnum, Phineas T., 7, 104, 106, 181
beauty, 15, 17–18, 26, 41–42, 95, 124
Bedford, Christiana. *See* Underwood, Christiana
Beecher, Catharine, 21, 161
Beecher, Edward, 35, 37
Beecher, Lyman, 17, 21, 24, 32, 35
Benjamin, Mary, 59–60, 64, 76, 185
Benjamin, Park, 59, 200n48
Bennett, James Gordon, 9, 11, 110–11, 126–29, 133, 136, 139, 145, 153, 155–56, 212n29
biography and autobiography, 4, 6–7, 50–51, 77–78, 180–81, 223n49. *See also* autobiographical fiction
Blackwood's Edinburgh Magazine, 42–43
Blair, Hugh, 51
Blessington, Countess Marguerite, 61–62, 67, 72–74, 79, 81, 84–85, 104, 133, 137–38, 203n26

bloomerism, 144–45
Blue Belles of England, The (Trollope), 85
Bonner, Robert, 180
Book of the Boudoir (Morgan), 44
Book of Martyrs (Foxe), 17
Boston, social and economic conditions, 53
Boston Courier, 52–53
Boston Daily Mail, 126
Boston Latin School, 19
Boston Post, 179
Boston Recorder, 21–23, 31, 38, 52
Boston Statesman, 30, 32, 34, 49, 52
Boston Times, 146
Boston Transcript, 173
Boswell, James, 6–7, 77
Bower of Taste, 45, 57
Bowery B'hoys, 110, 130, 154, 156
Bowring, John, 65–67
Briggs, Charles, 100, 123
British literary culture, 14, 40–43, 46, 53–
    56, 61–62, 67–68, 70–71, 81
Broadway Tabernacle, 98
Broadway Theatre, 140, 154
Brook Farm utopian community, 120, 145
Brother Jonathan, 87. *See also* Willis,
    Nathaniel Parker
Brougham's Lyceum, 154, 156
"Brown's Day at the Mimpson's" (Willis),
    91
Brummel, Beau, 54
Bryant, William Cullen, 23, 71, 117
Buckham, George, 138
Bull, Ole, 7, 10
Bulwer, Edward, 54, 61, 73–75, 79, 81, 189
Bulwer, Rosina, 181
Bumstead, Lucy Willis (sister of N. P.
    Willis), 167–68, 219n21
Buntline, Ned, 156
Bushnell, Horace, 11, 27, 38, 103
Byron, Lord George, 14, 56–57, 77, 189,
    207n21

Calcraft, Captain Granby, 121, 136, 142–43,
    149, 151, 155
Calvinism. *See* Congregationalism, orthodox
Carlyle, Thomas, 75
Carr, Mr., 66, 201n9
celebrity, culture of, 3–14, 34–35, 44–45, 61–
    62, 64, 70–79, 82–85, 87–96, 115–16,

118, 134, 138–40, 151–56, 158, 165,
    168, 172–80, 185, 188–91
Chanfrau, Francis, 110
Channing, William Ellery, 32, 71
Chatham Theatre, 109–10
Chevely; or, The Man of Honour (Bulwer, R.),
    181
Child, Lydia Maria, 50
Childe Harold (Byron), 14
Christian Examiner, 56–57, 78–79
Chubbuck, Emily, 92–94
*Citation and Examination of William
    Shakespeare* (Landor), 67
Clark, William Gaylord, 46
Clifton, Josephine, 135, 145–46, 151–52
Coddington, Mary Inman, 138–39
"Codfish Aristocracy," 111. *See also* Upper
    Ten Thousand
Colburn, Henry, 54, 63
Coleridge, Samuel Taylor, 31
Columbian Magazine, 93
companionate marriage ideals, 119, 144. *See
    also* sentimental persuasion
Complete Works (Willis), 92
Congregationalism, orthodox, 15–24, 35, 37–
    38, 195n20
Consuelo (Sand), 120–21, 211n14
Conversations with Lord Byron (Blessington),
    61, 72
Cooper, James Fenimore, 7, 65, 201n10
Cornwall, Barry. *See* Proctor, Bryan Waller
Corsair, The (Byron), 14, 54
Corsair, The (magazine), 87. *See also* Willis,
    Nathaniel Parker
Courier and New York Enquirer, 72, 123, 137
Courier and Etats-Unis (New York), 127
cultural hegemony, 98–100. *See also* natural
    aristocracy

Dalhousie, Earl and Lady of, 62, 80
Dall, Caroline Healey, 178
Dana, Richard Henry, Sr., 24, 46
dandyism, 43–44, 54–58, 62, 89–90, 96–97,
    103. *See also Pelham;* Willis, Nathaniel
    Parker
Dawes, Rufus, 31
Day Book, 137
Democratic Review, 173
Derby and Miller (publishing firm), 164–65
Deveraux (Bulwer, E.), 54

Dewey, the Reverend Orville, 22
Dickens, Charles, 7, 54, 104
Disraeli, Benjamin, 73, 81
Disowned, The (Bulwer, E.), 54
divorce, American attitudes toward, 118–19, 128–29
domestic ideology. *See* femininity, popular attitudes about; sentimental persuasion
Domestic Manners of the Americans (Trollope), 74
D'Orsay, Count Alfred, 61, 73, 186
Doty, William, 145, 215n24
Drum, Augustus, 126
Dudevant, Aurore. *See* Sand, George
duels and dueling. *See* honor
Duke of Gordon. *See* Aberdeen, Lord
Durham, "Radical Jack," 61
Duyckinck, Evert, 43, 130
Dwight, Louis, 19
Dwight, Timothy, 15, 20
Dyer, Oliver, 164, 167–68, 218n20, 219n23. *See also* Walter, John

Eclectic Review, 71
Edgeworth, Maria, 189
Edinburgh Literary Review, 71
Edinburgh Review, 62, 80
Eldredge, Charles (first husband of Fanny Fern), 161, 171, 216n6
Eldredge, Ellen (daughter of Fanny Fern), 165
Eldredge, Grace (daughter of Fanny Fern), 165
Eldredge, Mary (mother-in-law of Fanny Fern), 165
Eldredge, Sara Willis. *See* Fern, Fanny
"Elia." *See* Lamb, Charles
Ellsler, Fanny, 7, 121
Emerson, Ralph Waldo, 24, 37, 96, 100
English, Thomas Dunn, 181
etiquette. *See* gentility
Eugene Aram (Bulwer, E.), 54
evangelical religion, 3, 9, 16. *See also* Congregationalism, orthodox
Evening Star (New York), 71
Everett, Edward, 46
Examiner, 73

"Fairy Land" (Poe), 46
fancy balls. *See* masquerade balls

Fanny Hill (Cleland), 32
Farrington, Samuel P. (second husband of Fanny Fern), 161–62, 171, 179–80, 216n8
Farrington, Sara Eldredge. *See* Fern, Fanny
fashion and fashionable culture, 11, 40, 43–44, 47, 73, 90, 96–100, 103–05, 116, 126–28, 134. *See also* over-refinement
"Fashion" (Mowatt), 97
fashionable novels. *See* "Silver Fork" novels
"fashionable socialism." *See* Forrest affair
Federalists and Federalism, 15–16, 40, 45, 47
Female Prose Writers of America (Hart), 174
feminism, 11, 91, 178. *See also* companionate marriage ideals
femininity, popular attitudes about, 9–10, 47–48, 119, 121, 148–49, 177–78
The Feminization of American Culture (Douglas), 4
Fern, Fanny (sister of N. P.), 18, 173, 182, 218n17
    early life, 160–65
    feminist impulses, 169, 220n24, 220n31
    identity concealed and revealed, 165–66, 172, 221n33
    literary impulses, 165–72
Fern Leaves from Fanny's Port-Folio (Fern), 164–67, 171–73
Fields, James T., 101, 187, 221n36
Flowers, Anna, 140, 143, 146–51, 156
"Floy" (penname of Ruth Hall), 171–72, 220n29
Fonblanque, Albany, 73–74, 79
Fonthill, 118, 125. *See also* Forrest, Edwin
Forester, Fanny. *See* Chubbuck, Emily
Forney, John Wien, 132, 146, 156, 214n39
Forrest Affair, 115–57
    "Consuelo" note, 116–17, 119–20, 129, 144, 149, 151
    "fashionable socialism," 120–21, 126–28, 133
    "Forney" letter, 146, 149
    "Fourier" letter, 144–45
    "Mercer Street plot," 147, 149, 151
    publicity, 117–21, 123–24, 126–28, 134–35, 137–39, 141, 151–52
    servant testimony, 116, 121, 125, 148–49, 152
    Washington Square incident, 115–16, 128–33

Forrest, Catherine Sinclair (wife of Edwin), 116–22, 125–26, 135–37, 142–45, 147–51, 152–55, 181

Forrest, Edwin, 7, 111–12, 115–21, 124–26, 128–33, 135–37, 140, 145–49, 152–54, 181–82

Forrest, Eleanora (sister of Edwin), 118

Fourierism, 116, 120, 127–28, 144–45, 151, 155–56

Fraser's Magazine, 71, 80

free love. *See* Fourierism

Frémont, John C., 96, 208n23

French culture, 65–66, 124, 127–28

friendship, ideals of, 10–11, 28–30, 185. *See also* sentimental persuasion

Fry, Edward, 108, 110, 210n54

Fry, William Henry, 110

Fuller, Hiram, 182

Fuller, Margaret, 46, 55

Garfield, James, 158

Garrick, David, 6

Garvin, Robert, 121, 143, 148, 151

Gates, Horace (character in *Ruth Hall*), 171–72. *See also* Parton, James

gender relations, 4, 9–12, 47–48, 123–24, 133, 160, 166–67, 184–85

gentility, 9–12, 21–24, 31, 51, 72, 87–89, 97, 105, 121, 124–25, 131, 139–40, 150–51, 154–55. *See also* over-refinement, fears of

gentlemanliness. *See* gentility

Georgia Journal and Messenger, 134

gift-books, 28–30

Glenmary (home of N. P. Willis), 86, 88, 159

Godey's Ladies' Book, 87, 177

Godwin, Fanny, 117

Godwin, Park, 117–18, 128, 144, 149, 213n39

Goodrich, Samuel, 28–29, 39, 46

Goupil, Vibert, and Company, 124

Graham's Magazine, 87, 90, 93, 95

Granby (Lister), 54

Grant, Anne, 81

Grant, Zilpah, 21

Greeley, Horace, 46, 101, 128–29, 133, 137, 155, 181

Greene, Nathaniel, 30

Greenough, Henry, 65

Greenough, Horatio, 65–67, 201n11

Hackley, the Reverend Dr., 121, 147

Hadad (Hillhouse), 23

Hale, Edward Everett, 55

Hale, Nathan, Sr., 40

Hale, Sarah Josepha, 40, 48

Hall, Captain Basil, 74

Halleck, Fitz-Greene, 27

Harding, Chester, 31

Harper's Monthly Magazine, 87

Hartford Female Seminary, 21, 161

Hartford Review, 48

Harvard College, 15, 19, 20

Hawes, Joel, 21

Hawkes, Dr., 145

Hawthorne, Nathaniel, 30, 222n39

Hazlitt, William, 41

Health Trip to the Tropics, A (Willis), 159

Hill, Frederic, 48–49

Hillhouse, James, 23, 28, 31

Holmes, Dr. Oliver Wendell, 17, 187, 190

Home Journal, 92–93, 96–97, 124–27, 137–38, 158–59, 163, 167, 173, 175, 180, 183, 186, 188. *See also* Morris, George Pope; Willis, Nathaniel Parker

honor, 11, 82–84, 102, 115–116, 122–23, 134, 139–40, 157

Hosack, Dr. David, 27

hospitality, 69–70, 72, 74–76, 78–79, 142–44. *See also* journalistic ethics

Hôtel Dieu, 69

Howard, Captain William A., 143, 148–49, 151–52

Howe, Julia Ward, 189

Howe, Samuel Gridley, 65, 187, 201n8

Hunt, Henry, 129

Hunt, Leigh, 75

Hurry-Graphs (Willis), 158

Hutin, Madame, 52

Idle Man (Dana), 24

Idlewild (home of N. P. Willis), 159–60, 188

Imaginary Conversations (Landor), 67

Incidents in the Life of a Slave Girl (Jacobs), 4

Independent, 139

Ingersoll, Caroline, 145–46, 151
Inklings of Adventure (Willis), 84
Inman, Henry, 138
International Art-Union, 124
Irving, Washington, 7, 62, 111, 159
Italian opera, 105–11

Jacobs, Harriet, 4, 217n10
Jamieson, George, 117, 119–20, 129, 131, 144, 146, 149, 151–54. *See also* Forrest affair
Jefferson, Thomas, 100
Jeffrey, Lord Francis, 62
"Jepthah's Daughter" (Willis), 22
Jerdan, William, 49
Journal of a Residence during Several Months in London (Wheaton), 78
journalistic ethics, 44–45, 69–79
Judson, Adoniram (husband of Chubbuck, Emily), 93–94
Judson, E. C. Z. *See* Buntline, Ned
Judson, Mrs. Emily Chubbuck. *See* Chubbuck, Emily

Kemble, Fanny, 129
Kent, John, 143, 148, 150–51
Kettell, Samuel, 46–47
Knickerbocker, 46
Kock, Paul de, 127
Kossuth, Louis, 141

Ladies' Magazine, 40, 43
Lafayette, Marquis de, 65
Lamb, Charles, 42–43, 62, 68, 159
Landon, Letitia. *See* L. E. L.
Landor, Walter Savage, 67, 202n13
Laurence, Samuel, 184
Lawless, Ellen, 147
Lawson, James, 117–18, 144, 146, 148, 182
Lay of the Last Minstrel (Scott), 14
"Leaves from a Colleger's Album" (Willis), 30
"Leaves from the Heart-Book of Ernest Clay" (Willis), 92
"Lecture on Fashion" (Willis), 98–101, 103, 109
Legendary, The, 30, 41, 91. *See also* Willis, Nathaniel Parker

L. E. L., 43, 49
"Leper, The," (Willis), 38
"Letter to the Unknown Purchaser and Next Occupant of Glenmary" (Willis), 159
"Letters from under a Bridge" (Willis), 86, 159
letters of introduction, 64–68, 78
liberal Christianity. *See* Unitarians and Unitarianism
Life and Beauties of Fanny Fern (Moulton), 179–80, 222n45
Life of Johnson (Boswell), 6–7, 77
Lincoln, Mary Todd, 95, 188
Lind, Jenny, 7
"Lionizing" (Poe), 73
Lippard, George, 9
literary culture. *See* print culture
Literary Gazette, 49, 71
Literary Remains of the Late Henry Neele, reviewed by Willis, 50
"literary scripturism," 14, 16, 22–24, 26
Literary World, 90
Liverpool Journal, 71, 73–74
Lockhart, John, 74–75, 77–79, 82, 100
London Literary Souvenir, 71
London Magazine, 43
Longfellow, Henry Wadsworth, 74–75, 88, 187
Louisville Daily Courier, 131–32
Lowell, James Russell, 100, 187
"Lunatic's Skate, The," (Willis), 26
Lynch, Anne, 10, 88, 117
Lyrical Ballads (Wordsworth), 24

Mackenzie, Robert Shelton, 71, 73–74, 203n21, 204n31
Macready, William Charles, 111–12, 122, 130, 156
Macrone, William, 76
Maginn, William, 80
"Man of the World's View of the Onderdonk Case" (Willis), 123–24
Mann, Horace, 31–32, 46
Marguerittes, Julie de, 182, 223n51
Marmion (Scott), 78
Marryat, Frederick, 81–83
Mason Brothers (publishing firm), 168, 173–74
"Masque of the Red Death" (Poe), 69

masquerade balls, 52–53
Match-Girl, The; or Life Scenes as They Are (Marguerittes), 181–83, 224n52
Mathews, Cornelius, 43
Mayer, Brantz, 122
McCabe, Barney, 148–49, 156
Melanie and Other Poems (Willis), 63
Memoirs of Johann Wolfgang Goethe, 37
Metropolitan Magazine, 81–83
middle-class culture. *See* gentility
Mitchell, William, 107
Mitford, Mary Russell, 62, 70–71
"Misanthropic Hours" (Willis), 21–22, 24
Monthly Anthology and Boston Review, 40
Moore, Thomas, 42, 56, 72, 75, 77, 80, 203n25
Morgan, Lady Sydney, 8, 44
Morning Herald (London), 71
Morris, George Pope, 60, 63, 68, 71, 73, 81, 88, 101, 110, 139, 183, 188
Morse, Samuel F. B., 65
"Mose," 110. *See also* Bowery B'hoys; Chanfrau, Francis
Mother at Home, The (Abbott), 95
Moulton, William, 162, 165, 171, 179
Mount Auburn Cemetery, 187
"Muddie" (Maria Clemm, E. A. Poe's mother-in-law), 176–77
Musical World and Times, 160, 164, 166–67, 175
My Courtship and Its Consequences (Wikoff), 181
Mystéres de Paris (Sue), 104
Mysteries and Miseries of New York (Buntline), 104

nativism, 110–12, 130, 136. *See also* populism; social conservatism
natural aristocracy, 99–101, 112, 114
Neal, John, 46
neo-Edwardseanism. *See* Congregationalism, orthodox
New Bedford Mercury, 180
New England Galaxy, 48
New England Weekly Review, 47–48
New-Englander, 103
New Mirror, 88. *See also* Morris, George Pope; Willis, Nathaniel Parker
New Monthly Magazine (London), 40–41, 63
New Orleans Picayune, 146

New York City, social and economic conditions, 27–28, 60, 86–87, 89, 97–98, 103–04, 109–10, 127
New York Daily Herald, 87, 110–12, 119, 121, 124–27, 129, 132–33, 136, 141–42, 145, 147–48, 150, 152–53, 155–56. *See also* Bennett, James Gordon
New York Daily Times, 124, 141, 154, 177–78, 186, 187. *See also* Raymond, Henry
New York Daily Tribune, 87, 101, 124–25, 128–29, 131–32, 137, 156, 173, 177. *See also* Greeley, Horace
New York *Enquirer*, 34
New York *Evening Mirror*, 102–03, 182. *See also* Fuller, Hiram; Willis, Nathaniel Parker
New York Evening Post, 112, 129, 131
New York Hotel, 102
New York Ledger, 180
New York Mirror, 45, 60, 87, 93, 138, 180. *See also* Morris, George Pope; Willis, Nathaniel Parker
Niblo's Garden, 106
"Noctes Ambrosianae," 42–43
North American Review, 24, 40–41, 43, 83, 127
"North, Christopher." *See* Wilson, John
Norton, the Reverend Thomas, 162, 171

Oakley, Judge, 141, 149, 151–52, 155
O'Connell, Daniel, 72, 75, 80
O'Conor, Charles, 118–19, 135, 137, 145–52, 154, 214n6, 216n43
Oeuvres (Sand), 127
Olive Branch, 162, 164–65, 171
Olympic Theatre, 107, 109
Onderdonk affair, 123, 138, 158
opera, Italian, 105–14
orthodoxy. *See* Congregationalism, orthodox
Otis, Mrs. Harrison Gray, 31, 59, 100
Our Village (Mitford), 62
Outdoors at Idlewild (Willis), 90, 188
over-refinement, fears of, 11–12, 22–23, 51–58. *See also* refinement

Palmo's Opera House, 106–07
Panton, Henry, 117
Park Street Congregational Church (Boston), 15, 35, 37
Park Theatre, 106

Panic of 1837, social effects of, 98
Parton, James (third husband of Fanny Fern), 168, 171–72, 181, 189, 219n22. *See also* Gates, Horace
Parton, Sara Willis. *See* Fern, Fanny
passionalism. *See* Fourierism
patriarchalism. *See* social conservatism
Paul Clifford (Bulwer, E.), 54
Paul Fane; or, Parts of a Life Else Untold (Willis), 183–86
Paulding, James Kirke, 73
Payson, the Reverend Edward, 16, 18, 91
Pelham (Bulwer, E.), 54–58, 85, 199n36
Pencillings by the Way (Willis), 80, 84–8, 92, 100, 178, 188, 191
Pennsylvanian, 132. *See also* Forney, John Wien
penny press, 9, 99, 110, 116, 126–28, 133
Percival, James Gates, 13, 202n15
personality and "personalities," 12, 76–84, 177. *See also* celebrity
Peter's Letters to His Kinsfolk (Lockhart), 80
Philadelphia North American, 174
Phillips Academy (Andover, Massachusetts), 19
Peregrine Pickle (Smollett), 6
Pierce and Williams (publishers), 58
Pierpont, John, 46
Poe, Edgar Allan, 4, 46, 69, 73, 90, 176, 181–82
Poetical Works (Wordsworth), 24
poetry, 10–11, 13–15, 18, 20–26, 28, 30–31, 34, 50–51, 88, 95–96
Police Gazette, 121, 141
popular letters. *See* print culture
populism, 121, 126–28, 132. *See also* nativism; social conservatism
Porter, Jane, 63, 79, 81, 83
Portland Tribune, 90
Prentice, George, 47
print culture, 3–12, 14, 17, 34–35, 39–40, 44–51, 72, 87–88, 117–18
privacy, 12, 44–45, 189–90
Proctor, Bryan Waller, 62–63
Providence Daily Journal, 53
public characters. *See* celebrity, culture of
Pumpelly, George James, 27–28, 30, 32–34, 36–37, 58
Punch, 85

Quarterly Review, 74–75, 79, 83

Ramble among Musicians in Germany, A (Holmes), 69, 202n15
Randall, Josiah, 118
Raymond, Henry, 123–24, 138, 212n19
Raymond, Samuel Marsden, 121, 136, 142–43, 148, 151, 156, 213n32
Read, Elizabeth, 95–96
Red Bank (New Jersey) Phalanstery, 120, 145
refinement. *See* gentility; over-refinement, fears of
"Returned Love Letters" (Willis), 138
Revelations of Asmodeus (anon.), 104
revivals and revivalism, 19–20, 25
revolutions of 1848, 128, 130
Revue Encyclopédique, 65
Rice, Thomas D. ("Jim Crow"), 7
"Right to Privacy, The" (Warren and Brandeis), 190
Rich, Dr, John B., 121, 142
Richmond, "Annie," 90, 176–77, 188
"right naming," 165, 170
Rives, William Cabell, 66
Rivington and Brown (booksellers), 6
Roberts, George, 146
Robinson, Henry Crabb, 68
roman à clef, 54, 166–67, 169–72, 180–86. *See also* autobiographical fiction
Romanticism, 10, 13–15, 24, 26, 30, 36–37, 40–42, 69, 77, 91, 95, 195n20
Rose Clark (Fern), 180
Rousseau, Jean-Jacques, 6
Royall, Anne, 9
Ruth Hall (Fern), 4, 165, 168–80
Rynders, Captain Isaiah, 136, 154

"Sacrifice of Abraham" (Willis), 22
Salem Gazette, 48, 77
Sand, George, 120, 127–28, 143
Saunders and Otley (publishing firm), 63
Savage, James, 59
Scott, Sir Walter, 14, 54, 78
Seamore Place, 68, 73
Sedgwick, Catherine, 7, 71
Sedgwick, Theodore, 118, 136, 146
sensationalism. *See* penny press
sensibility, cult of. *See* sentimental persuasion

sentimental persuasion, 4, 9–12, 15, 28–30, 90–96, 113, 116, 119, 121, 125–26, 139–40, 142, 154, 160, 169–77, 193n11. *See also* anti-sentimentalism

"servant problem." *See* Forrest affair, servant testimony

Shelley, Percy Bysshe, 43

Sigourney, Lydia, 46

"Silver Fork" novels, 54–58

Simms, William Gilmore, 182

Simond, Louis, 78

Sinclair, Catherine. *See* Forrest, Catherine

Sinclair, Margaret. *See* Voorhies, Margaret

Sinclair, Virginia (sister of Catherine Forrest), 122

Sketches (Willis), 13, 29

Sketches of Public Characters, 78

social conservatism, 121, 126–28, 133. *See also* nativism; populism

Southern Literary Messenger, 73

Southern Quarterly Review, 177

Southey, Robert, 43, 62

Spanish Dance. *See* waltz

Specimens of American Poetry (Kettell), 46–47

Spirit of the Times (New York), 69

Sprague, William, 46

Spurzheim, Dr. Johann, 69

Stanton, Elizabeth Cady, 11, 178

Sterne, Laurence, 56

Stevens, Andrew, 125–26, 129, 132, 147–48, 213n39, 215n30

Stories of American Life by American Authors (Mitford), 71

Stowe, Calvin, 23, 38

Stowe, Harriet Beecher, 10, 48

St. Paul's Church (Boston), 37, 187

Strong, George Templeton, 107, 154

style. *See* fashion

Sue, Eugene, 104, 127

Sumner, Charles, 31, 100

Sunday Age, 108

"Sunnyside" (home of Washington Irving), 159

Swisshelm, Jane, 139

taste. *See* gentility

Taylor, Bayard, 84, 222n45

Taylor, Jeremy, 43

Thackeray, William Makepeace, 55, 85

theatrical culture, 5–7, 52

Tibbetts, Mr. (character in *Ruth Hall*). *See* Moulton, William

Times, The (London), 82–83, 137

"Tinturn Abbey" (Wordsworth), 36

The Token, 30. *See also* Willis, Nathaniel Parker

"To My Aged Father" (Willis), 175

"Tortesa, the Usurer" (Willis), 175

Toryism. *See* Anglo-American antipathy

Travellers' Club, 62

Tremont Hotel, 51–52, 122

Tremont Theatre, 52

Trinitarianism. *See* Congregationalism, orthodox

Trippings in Author-Land, (Chubbuck), 93

Trollope, Frances,

True Flag, 162, 164–65, 171, 179

true womanhood. *See* sentimental persuasion

Truth; a New Year's Gift for Scribblers (Snelling), 49–50, 78, 82

Una, 178, 222n42

Uncle Tom's Cabin (Stowe), 10

Underwood, Christiana, 121, 143, 148, 211n15

Unitarians and Unitarianism, 13, 15–16, 19, 22, 25, 31, 35, 46, 52

United States (American frigate), 67

"Unwritten Music" (Willis), 41–42

"Unwritten Poetry" (Willis), 35–36

Upper Ten Thousand, 101–04, 108, 114, 155, 208n40

Van Buren, John, 136, 142–45, 147, 149–50, 152–53, 215n39

Van Buren, Martin, 65

Van Schaick, John Bleecker, 27–28, 31, 32, 36–37, 58–59, 63

Vivian Grey (Disraeli), 54

Voorhies, Frank (husband of Margaret), 116

Voorhies, Margaret Sinclair (sister of Catherine Forrest), 116–17, 122, 136, 143, 149, 156, 211n3

Walsh, Mike, 110

Walter, John (character in *Ruth Hall*), 172. *See also* Dyer, Oliver

waltz, 31, 53

Ward, Nathaniel, *The Simple Cobler of Aggawam*, 97

Ware, Henry, Jr., 13

Warner, Susan, 48, 162

Warren, Joyce, 4, 217n12, 218n20, 219n21, 220n24, 220n25, 221n33

Watts, Alaric A., 71

Webb, James Watson, 72, 110, 137–39, 150

Webster, Daniel, 31, 46, 84

Westminster Review, 65

Whigs and Whiggishness, 100–01, 112, 121, 131, 135

Whitman, Walt, 110

Whittier, John Greenleaf, 24, 56

The Wide, Wide World (Warner), 162

Wikoff, "Chevalier," 121, 181

Willis, Cornelia Grinnell (second wife of N. P.), 122, 137, 143, 150, 188

Willis, Edward Payson (brother of N. P.), 123, 126, 211n18

Willis, Hannah Parker (mother of N. P.), 16–18, 44, 63, 95

Willis, Imogen (daughter of N. P. and Mary Stace), 86, 217n10

Willis, Julia (sister of N. P.), 26, 160

Willis, Louisa (sister of N. P.), 19

Willis, Lucy (sister of N. P.). *See* Bumstead, Lucy Willis

Willis, Mary Leighton Stace (first wife of N. P.), 76, 86, 122, 162, 185

Willis, Nathaniel (father of N. P.), 3, 15–17, 19–20, 42, 62

Willis, Nathaniel Parker, 3–5, 8–12, 173
  arcadianism, 86, 159–160
  and Astor Place riot, 112–14
  autobiographical writing, 30, 35–36, 91–92, 183–86
  as Bazaleel Wagstaff Bayes in *The Match-Girl*, 181
  and Blessington, Margueritte, 61–64, 67–68, 73–74, 79–80, 84, 104, 137–38, 204n30
  and "The Blidgimses," 102, 208n35
  British literary success, 63–64, 88
  as "Cassius" (pseudonym), 30–32, 34, 47
  and celebrity, 8–9, 10–12, 44–45, 69–74, 87–88, 139–40, 157–58, 171, 177, 188–91
  and Chubbuck, Emily, 92–94
  college life, 20, 25–28
  dandyism, literary and sartorial, 43–44, 62, 89–90, 96–97, 103
  as "Epicurus" (pseudonym), 35
  excommunication, 35, 37–38, 150
  and fashion, 11, 40, 43–44, 90, 96–100, 103–05
  and father, 16–17, 19–21, 25–26, 175
  and Fern, Fanny, 160–64, 166–75, 179–80
  financial situation, 28, 39–40, 58–59, 68, 84, 88, 90, 163
  and Forrest, Catherine, 122–25, 135
  and Forrest, Edwin, 115–16, 128–33, 137, 153
  and friendship, ideals of, 90–94, 184–85
  and gift-books, 28–30
  and Glenmary, 86, 88
  health, 130, 159, 183, 188
  and honor, 11, 82–84, 102, 115–16, 122–23
  as "Hyacinth Ellet" in *Ruth Hall*, 170–72, 174
  and Idlewild, 159–60, 188
  as "John Paul Jefferson Jones" in *Vanity Fair*, 85
  journalistic style, 40–45, 55, 69–70, 89–92, 138, 207n13
  manhood, style of, 11, 49, 130–31, 135–36, 139, 153
  and mother, 17–21, 44, 95, 174, 187
  and Morris, George Pope, 60, 68–69, 71, 73, 81, 87–88
  and natural aristocracy, 88–89, 99–101, 112, 114
  and opera, 105, 107–09, 112–14
  Pelhamite propensities, 43–45, 55–56, 58, 60
  and "Pencillings by the Way" imbroglio, 72–76, 79–85, 100–01, 204n29
  as poet, 13–14, 20–24, 88, 94–96
  poetic exemplars, 23–24
  and portraiture, 90, 184, 206n6, 224n57
  psychological insecurities, 50–51, 64, 100–01
  and Pumpelly, George, 27–28, 30, 32–34, 36–37, 58
  religious sentiments, 10–11, 13–15, 18–20, 25, 38, 41–42, 94–96, 207n18

Willis, Nathaniel Parker (*cont.*)
republican sensibilities, 100–03, 108–09, 112–13, 122, 209n52
Romantic sensibilities, 10–11, 24, 26, 30, 36–38, 41–44, 69
as "Roy" (pseudonym), 13, 21–22, 30–31, 34, 38, 171
and "Scriptural Sketches," 13–14, 21–24, 26, 38, 95–96, 103
and sentimental persuasion, 9–11, 90–96, 113, 116, 126
sexual impropriety, reputation for, 32–35, 47–50, 59–60, 62–63, 123–24, 137–39, 184–85
social talents, 27–28, 31–32, 61–68, 100
and spiritualism, 186
as tastemaker, 9, 88–89, 96–105, 112, 124–25, 127–28
testimony in Forrest trial, 142–43, 148, 150–53
travels, 39–40, 61–71, 124
and Upper Ten Thousand, 101–04, 112–14
and Van Schaick, John Bleecker, 27–28, 31, 32, 36–37, 58–59, 63
and Willis, Cornelia Grinnell, 122, 137, 150–51
and Willis, Mary Stace, 76, 83, 86, 122, 162
and Willis, Richard, 124, 167–68, 175, 219n21, 222n36
and women, 10–11, 32–36, 47–50, 59–60, 62–63, 76, 90–96, 113–14, 122–25, 138–39, 160–64, 168, 174, 176–77, 184–85, 210n59
Willis, Richard Storrs (brother of N. P.), 121, 142–43, 149, 151, 160, 164, 167–68, 173, 175, 219n21, 222n36
Willis, Sara (sister of N. P.). *See* Fern, Fanny
Wilson, John, 62, 100
Woolsey, Miss, 33–34, 36, 59, 197n43
Wordsworth, William, 24, 30, 42, 62

Yale College, 15, 20, 25–28